SOUTHERN BAPTISTS
IN THE INTERMOUNTAIN WEST (1940–1989)

SOUTHERN BAPTISTS
IN THE INTERMOUNTAIN WEST (1940–1989)

A Fifty-Year History of Utah, Idaho, and Nevada Southern Baptists

E. W. Hunke Jr.

PROVIDENCE HOUSE PUBLISHERS
Franklin, Tennessee

BX
6245
.H86
S68
1998

Copyright 1998 by E. W. Hunke Jr.

All rights reserved. Written permission must be secured from the publisher to use or reproduce any part of this book, except for brief quotations in critical reviews or articles.

Printed in the United States of America

02   01   00   99   98   1   2   3   4   5

Library of Congress Catalog Card Number: 97-76348

ISBN: 1-57736-086-9

Scripture verses taken from the HOLY BIBLE, NEW INTERNATIONAL VERSION. Copyright © 1973, 1978, 1984 International Bible Society. Used by permission of Zondervan Bible Publishers.

Cover by Bozeman Design; cover paintings by Edna Maxson

Photographs provided courtesy of Home Mission Board, SBC; Arizona Historical Archives; and E. W. Hunke Jr.

PROVIDENCE HOUSE PUBLISHERS
238 Seaboard Lane • Franklin, Tennessee 37067
800-321-5692

DEDICATION

The Southern Baptist witness in Idaho, Nevada, and Utah owes its existence to laypersons who initiated the work, to God-called ministers who laid their lives on an altar of sacrifice to serve these pioneers, and to the families who suffered the privations and misunderstandings of the call to missions in the Intermountain West.

The financial support from Southern Baptists nationwide helped stabilize small churches, and the work teams from associations and churches advanced the cause of Christ. Aggressive leaders from the Home Mission Board, SBC, and the sponsoring state conventions and partnerships pressed the claims of Christ on new and growing communities.

The faithful corps of district missionaries (general, pioneer, western, associational, pastoral, and mountain) traversed deserts and mountains and searched the valleys and towns and cities to win lost people to Jesus Christ. They started new missions, organized new churches, and constituted new associations; they spent meager personal incomes to subsidize inadequate travel funds; they slept in their automobiles or the homes of people willing to help; they ate meat offered them when they could see in the children's faces that such treats came only on special occasions; they endured many long separations from their own families—for their Lord.

To these pioneers of the faith, many of whose faces are pictured in the following pages of this history, this book is lovingly and joyfully dedicated.

Words from Isaiah the Prophet

Isaiah 51:1–3
Listen to me, you who pursue righteousness
and who seek the Lord:
Look to the rock from which you were cut
and to the quarry from which you were hewn;

Look to Abraham, your father,
and to Sarah, who gave you birth.
When I called him he was but one,
and I blessed him and made him many.

The Lord will surely comfort Zion
and will look with compassion on all her ruins;
He will make her deserts like Eden,
her wastelands like the garden of the Lord.
Joy and gladness will be found in her,
thanksgiving and the sound of singing.

Isaiah 40:3–5
A voice of one calling:
"In the desert prepare the way for the Lord;
make straight in the wilderness a highway for our God.

Every valley shall be raised up,
every mountain and hill made low;
the rough ground shall become level,
the rugged places plain.

And the glory of the Lord will be revealed,
and all mankind together will see it.
For the mouth of the Lord has spoken."

Isaiah 52:7–8
How beautiful on the mountains
are the feet of those who bring good news,
who proclaim peace,
who bring good tidings,
who proclaim salvation,
who say to Zion, "Your God reigns!"

Listen! Your watchmen lift up their voices;
together they shout for joy.
When the Lord returns to Zion,
they will see it with their own eyes.

Isaiah says to "look to the quarry" (our forefathers), to remember the loneliness of Abraham and John the Baptist (early pioneers), to cherish their message of "comfort to Zion" (God's promises), and to honor those whose "beautiful feet" carried God's "good tidings."

CONTENTS

Acknowledgments   11
Abbreviations   13
Introduction   15

1. MOMENTOUS BEGINNINGS
   DECADES THROUGH THE 1940S   23

2. REMARKABLE ADVANCES
   THE DECADE OF THE 1950S   73

3. SIGNIFICANT CHANGES
   THE DECADE OF THE 1960S   139

4. IMPORTANT DIRECTIONS
   THE DECADE OF THE 1970S   197

5. MEANINGFUL DEVELOPMENTS
   THE DECADE OF THE 1980S   265

Appendices   337
   A. CHRONOLOGICAL LIST OF ASSOCIATIONS   339
   B. ALPHABETICAL LIST OF CHURCHES (BY STATE/CITY)   341
   C. CHRONOLOGICAL LIST OF MISSIONARIES   355
   D. COMBINED LIST OF ASSOCIATIONS AND MISSIONARIES   357

Selected Bibliography   363
About the Author   365
About the Artist   368

ACKNOWLEDGMENTS

Many hundreds of people, letters, documents, and books contributed to this research project, far too many to name in acknowledgments here. I extend grateful thanks to each one:

To bibliographical resources listed in *Southern Baptist Jubilee in the West (1940–1989)*, a four-volume study I completed in 1996, which was published by the Home Mission Board and placed in sixty colleges, state offices, and historical societies;

To the forty-six pioneer, general, associational, and pastoral missionaries who gave me materials, photographs, and biographical resumes with their spiritual journeys;

To the writers of western history and historical backgrounds, especially Roy Johnson, Don Ledbetter, Anita Welsh, Earl Jackson, Richard Ashworth, Lewis Demster, and James Myers;

To state and national mission board associates who helped me gather and research materials; to Nelda Kent, the ASBC archivist; Michael McCullough of Nevada; and Bea Conrad of Utah;

To my office secretaries: Janet Haman (deceased), Saralee Debley, Wanda English, Dixie Hunke, Milidene McConnell (deceased), Dixie Foster (deceased), Dorothy Stuart, Sandra Killebrew, Marjorie Selman, Mary Cannon, Marguerite Priest, and Martha McDowell;

To former Baptist Home Mission Board leaders Larry Lewis, Bob Banks, and Leonard Irwin who encouraged me to gather and write history, and those who sent many photographs;

To former Southern Baptist leaders Charles Ashcraft and Darwin Welsh of Utah-Idaho, and Ernest Myers of Nevada, who gave me the time, counsel, information, and materials requested;

To my friend Edna Maxson who painted four beautiful scenes especially for the cover of this book;

To my wife who wrote the fiftieth anniversary history of Grand Canyon Baptist Association entitled *Remember the Wonders*, who researched early beginnings in the Intermountain West, who gave time to proofread, and who encouraged me to complete this book;

To my brother Robert W. Hunke who made many trips from New Mexico to Arizona to encourage me, configure my computer, recover lost data, and show personal interest in my hobby to record history for the coming generations. Bob, the first person I led to Christ, died at Albuquerque, New Mexico, on April 1, 1995.

My grateful thanks to each of you,
Edmund William (Bill) Hunke Jr.

ABBREVIATIONS

ABC	American Baptist Convention (Northern)
AOBU	Arkansas, Ouachita Baptist University
ASBC	Arizona Southern Baptist Convention
BCNM	Baptist Convention of New Mexico
BGCA	Baptist General Convention of Arizona (name changed to Arizona Southern Baptist Convention)
BGCOW	Baptist General Convention of Oregon-Washington (name changed to Northwest Baptist Convention)
BJC	Baptist Joint Committee on Public Affairs
BSSB	Baptist Sunday School Board
BSU	Baptist Student Union
BYBC	Backyard Bible Club
CBC	California Baptist College
CBGC	Colorado Baptist General Convention
DMB	Domestic Mission Board (name changed to Home Mission Board, SBC in 1874)
FBC	First Baptist Church
FMB	Foreign Mission Board, SBC (name changed to the International Mission Board in 1997)
FSBC	First Southern Baptist Church
GCC	Grand Canyon College (University)
GGBTS	Golden Gate Baptist Theological Seminary
GCU	Grand Canyon University
HMB	Home Mission Board, SBC (name changed to the North American Mission Board in 1997)
HMS	Home Mission Society (Northern)
HSU	Hardin-Simmons University
HPC	Howard Payne College

LBC	Louisiana Baptist Convention
MSC	Mission Service Corps
NABC	Nevada Area Baptist Convention (name changed to Nevada Baptist Convention in 1979)
NOBTS	New Orleans Baptist Theological Seminary
NPBC	Northern Plains Baptist Convention
NVBC	Nevada Baptist Convention
NVBF	Nevada Baptist Fellowship
NWBC	Northwest Baptist Convention (Oregon-Washington)
OBU	Oklahoma Baptist University
SBC	Southern Baptist Convention
SBTS	Southern Baptist Theological Seminary
SBGCC	Southern Baptist General Convention of California (name changed to the California Southern Baptist Convention in 1990)
SLC	Salt Lake City
SS	Sunday School
SWBTS	Southwestern Baptist Theological Seminary
TXBC	Texas Baptist Convention
UINRMC	Utah-Idaho-Nevada Regional Mission Committee
UINRMF	Utah-Idaho-Nevada Regional Mission Fellowship
UIRMC	Utah-Idaho Regional Mission Committee
UISBC	Utah-Idaho Southern Baptist Convention
UISBF	Utah-Idaho Southern Baptist Fellowship
VBS	Vacation Bible School
WBC	Wayland Baptist College (University)
WMU	Woman's Missionary Union

INTRODUCTION

The Intermountain West, also known as the Great Basin of the West, challenges all who witness its majesty. As readers behold the beauty of this land and its great spiritual need, they should ask God to give blessing and victory to His people where:

Fantastic formations like Arches, Bryce, Valley of Fire, Zion, Hell's Canyon, Craters of the Moon, and the Hoover Dam stagger the imagination;

Lovely lakes like Mead, Tahoe, Pyramid, Great Salt, Pend Oreille, Coeur d'Alene, Bear, Flaming Gorge, and Powell soothe the soul;

Rampaging rivers like the Clearwater, Salmon, Snake, Virgin, Green, Colorado, Truckee, and Carson shatter the stillness; and

Magnificent mountain ranges like the Bitterroot, Sawtooth, Wind River, Uintah, Wasatch, Sierra Nevada, and Cascade stretch across the horizon.

In the midst of this majesty dwell the people fettered by the religion which teaches: "As God once was, we are; and as God now is, we shall become." The Mormons teach that each person is a Son of God like Jesus is a Son of God. They need to behold His majesty—to know Jesus as the *only begotten* (one of a kind) Son of the Living God who shed God's blood at the cross of Calvary for our sin.

On November 15, 1958, I took Solomon F. Dowis from Tucson to Nogales, Mexico, to bargain shop. "Sol," as his friends knew him, said he had never traveled that road, and he was slated to retire from the Home Mission Board in just six weeks. The great mission strategist did not make this extended trip just to see Mexico. He wanted to get me away from the crowd and lay his burden for the Intermountain West (Nevada, Utah, Idaho) on me. He related his vision and dream and asked me to implement them as best I could. I accepted his mantle aware that I was only one of many on whom Dowis would lay his burden. No single person could ever shoulder the whole task of this Southern Baptist "giant with the gravelly voice." His voice to the masses still rings in my ears, "I have now told you what I wanted to tell you and now I am going to tell you what I told you."

Dowis saw Idaho, Nevada, and Utah as a unit. He sought to develop a tri-state convention to be named Intermountain Baptist Convention. Clyde Barrow, a Kentuckian with great parliamentary skill who pastored Idaho Falls, Calvary Baptist Church, had drafted the Intermountain Baptist Convention constitution and bylaws. Idaho, Nevada, and Utah were linked together for many years. Willis J. Ray, a Texan with Kansas roots, became Dowis's point man for the development of SBC work in the West. Dowis said, "If you will go to Arizona, the Home Mission Board will go with you." Dowis handpicked his associates under the leadership and direction of the Holy Spirit.

When California state mission director, A. C. Turner, asked me to serve as a California missionary, Dowis said, "Let Hunke season for a while; he has a long life to live." After I served as pastor of Vernal, Utah, First Baptist Church, in the Intermountain West, Dowis approved me to serve as a missionary and later as the state mission director for Baptist General Convention of Arizona with the responsibility for the work in Idaho, Nevada, Utah.

Our love for the Intermountain West grew. Jim, our younger son, was born at Vernal. While at Vernal I helped the pastorless Artesia, Colorado, First Baptist Church through preaching, leading summer Vacation Bible School, and broadcasting their radio program on our Vernal station. When Darwin Welsh, a former Artesia pastor and UISBC executive director, heard about my struggle with leaving the Intermountain West to serve in Arizona, he opened opportunities for me to return to the Intermountain West for conferences, Bible teaching, and revivals every year until he retired in 1989. I am grateful for his friendship.

This history book pays tribute to the Home Mission Board of the Southern Baptist Convention and its leaders, to associational (general, western, pioneer) missionaries, and to leaders of the state conventions who worked in missions and evangelism. The work of leaders related to the Baptist Sunday School Board, Woman's Missionary Union, and the Brotherhood will be written by others.

Chapter one provides the reader with a brief review of major historical themes in the growth of the West in order to position the work of Southern Baptists in a time frame. J. B. York of Georgia established Independence Flat, Idaho, Baptist Church on November 14, 1887, but comity agreements prevented this Southern Baptist pastor from affiliating with his own convention. In later history SBC work began with planting the Roosevelt, Utah, Baptist Church on July 2, 1944; the Hawthorne (Babbitt), Nevada, Calvary Baptist Church on October 25, 1947; and the Kimberly, Idaho, First Baptist Church in August 1950.

Dowis believed that home mission work must be related to the state convention and that all home mission money must be channeled through the state convention. A casual reader may feel that undue emphasis is placed on the Arizona, California, and Northwest state conventions, but work in Idaho, Nevada, and Utah remained in a vital relationship with the three state conventions until after the constitution of their own conventions: Utah-Idaho on October 26, 1964, and Nevada on October 16, 1978. In 1997 SBC churches in the panhandle of Idaho continued to relate to either the Northwest or the Utah-Idaho Southern Baptist Conventions. Some churches on the eastern border of California affiliated with the Nevada Baptist Convention when it organized in 1978.

Western State Executive Directors

Arizona

Willis Jackson and Ida Ray, BGCA executive director (1944–1956).

Charles Lloyd McKay, ASBC executive director (1956–1970).

Roy Fortson Sutton, ASBC executive director (1970–1978).

California

Sheldon Gambrell Posey, SBGCC executive director (1951–1961).

Grady C. Cothen, SBGCC executive director (1961–1966).

Robert D. and Ruth Hughes, SBGCC executive director (1966–1984).

Western State Executive Directors

Northwest

Fred B. Moseley, NWBC executive director (1962–1965).

Dan C. and Harriet Stringer, NWBC executive director (1971–1979).

Cecil C. and Jeannine Sims, NWBC executive director (1980–1994).

Utah-Idaho, Nevada

Charles H. and Sara Ashcraft, UISBC executive director (1965–1970).

Darwin E. Welsh, UISBC executive director (1971–1989).

Ernest B. and June Myers, NVBC executive director (1978–1992).

Western State Mission Directors

Arizona

Frank W. and Lois Sutton, BGCA state mission director (1952–1956).

E. W. (Bill) and Naomi Hunke, ASBC state mission director (1958–1966).

Jess L. and Joyce Canafax, ASBC state mission director (1971–1982).

California

A. C. Turner, SBGCC state mission director (1951–1956).

Edmond R. and Lurie Walker, SBGCC state mission director (1956–1963).

Ralph E. Longshore, CSBC state mission director (1963–1988).

Western State Mission Directors

Northwest

Roland Parks Hood, BGCOW state mission director (1952–1965).

W. C. and Fanny B. Carpenter, NWBC state mission director (1965–1978).

William K. and Alice Peters, NWBC state mission director (1978–1986).

Utah-Idaho, Nevada

Clyde C. Billingsley, UISBC state mission director (1971–1978).

Bruce and Berniece Gardner, UISBC state mission director (1978–1992).

Donald W. and Anne Mulkey, NVBC state mission director (1980–1990).

Momentous Beginnings

Decades through the 1940s

The Intermountain West embraces the states of Idaho, Nevada, and Utah. Because the great mountain ranges are so inaccessible and harsh, the explorers, priests, fur trappers, gold seekers, military leaders, cattle men, miners, railroaders, and immigrants explored its treasures later than other regions. The father of our country, George Washington, died December 14, 1799, unaware of the opportunities of the great American West.

Priests Investigate the Intermountain West

Roman Catholic priests traveled with Spanish conquistadors to bring the Indians to God. The historical trail marker at Fillmore, Utah, records:

> The written history of the Intermountain Region begins with the remarkably accurate diary of Father Escalante, a Spanish Franciscan priest. He and Father Dominquez, together with eight companions, were the first white men to have been here. On a futile journey, trying to locate a direct route between Santa Fe, New Mexico, the center of Catholic missionary activity, and Monterey, California, recently established as a port of entry for goods from Spain and southern New Mexico, they traveled most of Utah east and south of the Salt Lake

Valley. On the return journey to Santa Fe, they crossed this divide [Fillmore, Utah] in October 1776. A list of wanderings over strange trails, and their missionary work among Indian tribes, furnishes one of the most impressive accounts of exploration and heroism in the history of the West. Their travels extended more than 600 miles, over the mountains and deserts, without competent guides or any knowledge of the country before them. Depending only on the information and assistance from Indians, they endured hardship and privation and finally reached their Santa Fe destination on January 2, 1777.

Military Forts Protect Occupied Territory

The Spanish, aware of British, French, and Russian advances in the West, explored the North American coast as they searched for a great river of the West. Spain built military forts (*presidios*) at San Diego, Monterey, San Francisco, and Santa Barbara, and frontier towns (*pueblos*) at San Jose with settlers (*pobladores*). The Russians did not have a military presence in the West until 1812 when they established Bodega Bay, California, and built Fort Ross north of the Russian River to protect their territories.

Vancouver explored the North American coast for Great Britain. On September 28, 1790, seventeen years after the Boston Tea Party, U.S. captain Robert Gray sailed his small ship, *Columbia Redeviva*, out of Boston Harbor. After he and his men exchanged greetings with Vancouver off the Washington coast, he sailed into the mouth of a great river on May 11, 1792. He named the new river *Columbia* after his ship and claimed the "Great River of the West" and all the land it drained for the U.S.A.

Alexander MacKenzie left his post on Peace River above Lake Athabaska on May 9, 1793, in a canoe with nine people, a dog, and supplies. They traveled through Peace River Canyon, crossed the Continental Divide, floated down Fraser River, and climbed steep mountains. After securing a canoe from Bella Coola Indians, they reached the Pacific Ocean twelve years before Lewis and Clark made their historic journey.

Thomas Jefferson Connects the Atlantic and Pacific

On March 4, 1801, the U.S.A. inaugurated fifty-seven-year-old Thomas Jefferson as its third President. Jefferson, former U.S.A. ambassador to France, sent special envoy James Monroe to Robert Livingston in France with instructions to buy New Orleans and the Louisiana territory from Napoleon Bonaparte. He doubled the land area of the U.S.A. by signing the treaty on May 2, 1803. Jefferson reasoned that the amount of water in the Mississippi and Columbia rivers came from melting snow on a mountain range in the middle of the continent. He sent Meriwether Lewis, his private secretary, and William Clark on their journey on May 14, 1904. Clark's vast knowledge of the West, the Army, and the special relationships made him valuable. Aided by Bird Woman Sacajawea, the trio completed a successful venture, built Fort Clatsop at the mouth of the Columbia River, and arrived back home in St. Louis on September 23, 1806.

Fur Trappers Explore the Intermountain West

After hearing of Lewis and Clark's successful expedition, the fur traders and trappers entered the Intermountain West and reached Idaho in 1809. William Ashley founded Rocky Mountain Fur Company and led expeditions up the Missouri. Hudson Bay Company trappers explored Nevada in 1825. Bridger discovered Great Salt Lake and fur trader Peter Ogden explored it. Jedediah Smith and Thomas Fitzpatrick found South Pass in the Wind River Mountains for use on the Oregon Trail. Nathaniel Wyeth established a fur-trading post near Pocatello at Fort Hall. The fiery adventures of Bible-toting Smith inspired Boston school teacher Hall Kelly to travel to Oregon and return to Boston to encourage missions.

After Northwest Baptist Convention (NWBC) executive director, Cecil Sims, read Dale L. Morgan's biography titled *Jedediah Smith and the Opening of the West*, he summarized the book this way:

> Had Jedediah Smith any idea of what life held for him, he probably would have tried to reenter his mother's womb. The

first 28 years of his life gave no hint of events the next decade would bring. Prodded by poverty and encouraged by the lure of the West, he signed on with a beaver trapping brigade leaving St. Louis in April 1822. Jedediah Smith became the epitome of the mountain men of the West—tough, resourceful, inquisitive, persistent, wise, perceptive, and above all else, a survivor. While Smith was all of these, he possessed one characteristic for which mountain men were not famous—Smith was a Christian—a Bible believing, godly man of great personal dignity. His biographer notes, "He made the wilderness his place of meditation, the mountain top his altar, and religion an active, practical principle from the duties of which nothing could seduce him."

When Jedediah Smith left St. Louis in 1822, he knew a little about the journey of Lewis and Clark. He knew there was a Pacific Ocean, Columbia River, and Rocky Mountain Range. His travels over the next ten years gave a message to an emerging nation known as the United States. There is a great land out there in the West—the prairies are vast—the mountains are rugged—the valleys are rich—the trees are tall—the rivers are full of fish and beaver—the Indians are treacherous—but it is available to the man with the courage to go after it.

Between April 1822 and May 1831, Jedediah Smith experienced enough of life to last for a century. He survived three Indian massacres, a life scarring attack by a grizzly bear, and imprisonment at the hand of Mexicans. Nature induced calamities of thirst, hunger, freezing cold, burning heat, drenching rain, and blinding snow were normal for Smith. His pursuit of beaver pelts became almost incidental to his discovery of trails through the mountains and paths across the desert. Smith died at the hands of Comanche Indians in May 1831.

As much as any one man, Jedediah Smith is responsible for the Northwest becoming a part of the United States. His discovery of a pass through the Rocky Mountains for wagons eventually led to the establishment of the Oregon Trail. Then came a flood of Americans to the Great Northwest. Had it not been for Smith and his persistent search for new beaver territory, this great section of our nation would have remained a part of the British empire. . . . Let us not forget, long before Jedediah Smith left the comforts of St. Louis, our Lord laid aside robes of heaven and entered this world, knowing the price he must pay so we could embark on heaven's trail (*Northwest Baptist Witness*, 12/7/83).

Three developmental stages marked the frontier: the pioneers who trapped, the settlers who cleared land and planted crops, and the tradesmen or skilled workers who created communities. Lawyers, preachers, doctors, storekeepers, teachers, and bankers followed to work in the established communities.

Missionaries Arrive in the Intermountain West

Lyman Beecher's "Plea for the West" stimulated home missions work in the West. Christians feared that pioneers would fall into barbarianism if removed from churches. Protestants feared Roman Catholics would build a strong empire. The first missionaries to Idaho arrived in 1830. Parker and Whitman looked for opportunities with the American Fur Company in 1835.

After four Nez Perce Indian braves walked two thousand miles to St. Louis to ask about Jesus the Savior that fur traders talked about, Marcus and Narcissa Whitman, William Gray, and the Henry Spaldings traveled west to build Presbyterian Indian missions. When measles killed many Cayuse Indians in 1847, Cayuse chiefs Tilaukait and Tamsuky killed Whitman, burned the mission building, took forty-six hostages, and demanded a ransom. Hudson Bay Company trapper, Peter Ogden, gave sixty-two blankets, sixty-three shirts, six hundred rounds of ammunition, thirty-seven pounds of tobacco, and twelve flints as a ransom to deliver the missionaries.

Henry and Eliza Spalding established their mission on the Clearwater River in Idaho in 1836. They built the first printing press, first sawmill, first gristmill, first church, first school, and first irrigation project in Idaho. Indian unrest forced them to Oregon, but years later he resumed his work at Lapwai near Lewiston. Spalding died among people he loved on August 3, 1874. Following a simple funeral service by Nez Perce Indians, they buried him in a cemetery near the mission.

Americans Emigrate West on Wagon Trains

In 1841 the Bidwell-Bartleson overland emigration route to California opened, and wagon trains followed the California Trail through South Pass into the Humbolt region of Nevada. The first wagon train left Independence, Missouri, on May 1 with forty-seven persons and arrived in California on November 4, 1841. The Oregon Trail, which carried a thousand Americans to Oregon country through the future state of Idaho in 1843, carried three thousand in 1845 and inspired Salisbury to write:

> The Oregon Territory was conquered by ox team and covered wagon; the farmer and his plow; the missionary and his grist and saw mills. Never in history has so great a land been won so quickly with peaceful means (Salisbury, *Here Rolled the Covered Wagons*, 58).

The Donner Party met with many disasters. They lost their way in the Wasatch Mountains of Utah; spent too much time crossing the Salt Flats; dealt with Indians, party strife, and misfortune; and encountered heavy snow in the Sierra Mountains. Eighty-seven began the trip and only forty-seven survived to reach their destination. Baptist layman David Lenox, captain of an 1843 wagon train, his wife Louisa, and family left Platte City, Missouri, for Oregon in 1843. They observed the Lord's Day with rest, prayer, and reading the Word of God. Lenox did not leave his wagons and pack trains at Ft. Hall as was the custom, but continued to the Columbia River Dalles and rafted them to Willamette Valley. The Lenox family organized the West Union Baptist Church, first Baptist church in the West, in their home fourteen miles west of Portland.

The Southern Baptist Convention (SBC) was constituted on May 8, 1845, at the Augusta, Georgia, First Baptist Church (FBC) by 236 delegates representing 165 churches and nine associations. At the second annual SBC meeting in 1846, the SBC committee on new fields of labor for domestic missions called attention to the movement of people through the Intermountain West to California and a need for missionaries.

The Home Mission Society (HMS) sent Osgood Church Wheeler to San Francisco and Hiram Walter Read to Los Angeles to start Baptist work. At the urging of military and civil leaders, Read stopped at Santa Fe, New Mexico, to preach Christ in New Mexico and Arizona.

U.S.A. Military Forces Conquer the West

In 1834 the U.S. Army established military posts at Fort Boise and Fort Hall in Idaho. In 1842 John C. Fremont explored the Wind River, Missouri River, Pyramid Lake area of Nevada, and the Sierra Nevada Mountains. He returned home by way of Nevada and Utah. In 1846 the United States declared war on Mexico. Gen. Zachary Taylor moved into northern Mexico, Gen. Winfield Scott into Mexico City and Vera Cruz, and Col. Stephen Kearny into California and Santa Fe. Every battle ended in a U.S. victory. Kearny took possession of the land which the United States bought from Mexico after the Treaty of Guadalupe Hidalgo. Nevada and Utah were established in this territory along with California, parts of Texas, Arizona, Colorado, Oklahoma, and Kansas.

Mormons Arrive in the Intermountain West

Joseph Smith organized the Mormons, Church of Jesus Christ of Latter Day Saints, at Fayette, New York, April 6, 1830. Practices of polygamy brought Mormons into violent clashes with authorities in New York and Illinois. After the death of Joseph Smith, Brigham Young led Mormons westward on a trail to the Great Salt Lake Valley of Utah where they established Salt Lake City (SLC). The Mormons established the provisional State of Deseret with headquarters at SLC and adopted their first constitution in 1849. They established Mormon Station (Genoa), the first settlement in

Nevada in 1849, and built irrigation canals in Idaho in 1855.

Mining Becomes a Major Industry

After Marshall discovered gold while erecting a sawmill for Johann Augustus Sutter in 1849, an estimated eighty thousand prospectors emigrated to California. Forty-six Baptist preachers passed through San Francisco on the way to gold country by August 1850. Ray Allen Billington described the early West as:

> Ramshackle mining camps appropriately labeled Poker Flat, Hangtown, Whiskey Bar, Placerville, Hell's Delight, Git-Up-and-Git, Skunk Gulch, Dry Diggings, Grub Gulch, Red Dog, and the like. Rooms rented for $1,000 a month and eggs cost $10 a dozen . . . (Bragdon, McCutchen, *History of a Free People*, 307).

Miners discovered more silver than gold in the Comstock Lode of Nevada. When prospectors discovered gold at Orofino Creek in Idaho, the Mormons built Franklin, Idaho, as their first permanent settlement in Idaho. Many new travelers headed West to the gold and silver mines in Idaho, Nevada, Colorado, and British Columbia.

American Indians Challenge U.S.A. Authority

When the miners invaded the mountains, crews built railroads, and cattlemen moved cattle onto the grasslands, threatened Indians in the West went on the war path. Sioux, Crow, Blackfeet, Arapaho, and Cheyenne attacked in the North; and Comanche, Kiowa, Southern Cheyenne, Ute, Apache, and Southern Arapaho attacked in the South. War parties from the estimated 225,000 Indians massacred more than a thousand white men, women, and children. Retribution fell on the innocent and guilty alike. Indians submitted to U.S. authority in 1865 at the close of the Apache and Navajo wars. Congress passed an act to establish reservations for the Indians in 1866–1867. The 1871 Indian Appropriation Act ruled that Indian tribes were a part of the United States and no longer separate, independent nations.

The Nez Perce Indian uprising (1877–1878) in eastern Oregon became so hostile that Grande Ronde Baptist Association said that adverse circumstances kept people from attending church meetings. After the defeat of the Nez Perce in October 1877, Bannocks and other southern Idaho tribes began to pillage and murder. When the Indians surrendered to the U.S. Army, the government vowed to permit Ute Indians to keep a large section of southwest Colorado, but in 1882 Congress opened the same area to homesteading.

Land Grants Increase Traffic to the Mountain West

The Homestead Act of 1862 gave 160 acres of land to a person over twenty-one years of age who lived on the land and improved it. Public lands, given to states by the Morrill and Land Grant acts of 1862, provided funds to educate the citizens and to establish state universities. As Americans entered the West, Congress divided the territory into states. Oregon attained U.S.A. statehood February 14, 1859. Washington, Idaho, parts of Montana, and Wyoming were later formed on the remaining land.

On March 2, 1861, Congress recognized Nevada and the Dakotas as territories. President James Buchanan approved and signed the action. Idaho and Montana were established in 1863.

Congress granted statehood to Nevada on October 31, 1864. The state located its capitol at Carson City and declared "all for our country" as its motto. Nevada adopted the mountain blue bird as state bird, the bristlecone pine and single leaf pinion as state trees, and "Home Means Nevada" as the state song.

Pioneer homesteaders knew little about luxury. Mail service ended during the Civil War. Weeks and months passed between chance meetings of pioneers. Isolation and loneliness took a toll. The Pony Express carried mail west for a brief time. The Butterfield Overland Mail inaugurated service from Memphis and St. Louis to California in 1858. The Pacific Telegraph Act led to construction of telegraph lines, and on June 16, 1861, the first message was transmitted from San Francisco to Washington, D.C.

Civil War Divides the Nation

Soon after the U.S.A. elected Abraham Lincoln as President, the slavery issue plunged the nation into Civil War. Seven states in the South sent delegates to Montgomery, Alabama, to form a new confederacy. Lincoln died an untimely death on April 14, 1865, when actor John Wilkes Booth assassinated him. The war ended in 1865, but it left the South financially and spiritually destitute. Domestic Mission Board (DMB) assets in confederate money had become worthless.

Baptist work in the New Mexico Territory declined during the Civil War. The HMS withdrew all Baptist missionaries by 1866 and Baptist work ceased. Income of the DMB dropped to fifteen thousand dollars. Southern Baptists terminated California as a mission field. Missionaries dropped from 159 in 1860 to 36 in 1863. The *Home and Foreign Journal* ceased.

Southern families whose homes had been devastated by the war looked for a new place to live. Southern California land could be bought for a few cents an acre. The prospect of cheap land and a better life led families to load possessions onto wagons and head west. Los Angeles erected thousands of new houses.

Idaho City, Idaho, First Baptist Church

Hiram Hamilton, a Stockton, California, beekeeper, organized Idaho City, Idaho, FBC in 1864. He used a Methodist building for Baptist services. In a few months Methodists gave the building to Baptists, but on May 20, 1865, the church building and entire town of Idaho City burned to the ground. Hamilton preached to Bannock and Shoshone Indians after the disaster.

Railroads Link the Atlantic and Pacific Oceans

When Asa Whitney first suggested that a railroad be built to span the American continent from the Atlantic to the Pacific, Congress considered the idea wild. Four great western surveys were undertaken by the government from 1867–1877: (1) a survey of the fortieth parallel by Clarence King; (2) a geological survey of Nebraska and Wyoming by Ferdinand V. Hayden; (3) a survey of the one-hundredth meridian by Lt. George Wheeler; and (4) a survey of Utah, Arizona, and Nevada by Maj. John Wesley Powell. Powell gained national attention in 1869 for his ride through the Grand Canyon on the Colorado River.

Hiram Walter Read, New Mexico HMS missionary, traveled with the Texas Western Railway survey crew in May 1854 seeking to find the best possible rail route from Texas to California. While working near Fort Yuma, Read preached the first Baptist sermon in what is now the state of Arizona to settlers and military people. When railroads from Chicago and San Francisco were completed, two trains met at Promontory Point, Utah. Union Pacific and Central Pacific Railroad representatives connected the rails by driving a golden spike into the ground with a silver hammer. Rail travel accelerated the westward movement as families traveled to the new opportunities under the 1863 Homestead Act.

Boise, Idaho, Boise City Baptist Church

Boise, Idaho, Boise City Baptist Church was organized in 1867 by Hiram Hamilton. Destruction of his Idaho City, Idaho, church by fire on May 20, 1865, did not discourage the Baptist pastor. After he moved to Boise City to start a new church, he opened Boise Valley Seminary to train believers. He supplemented his income by serving as Idaho state legislature chaplain.

During 1870–1871 Baptists planted the first church in Montana at Helena, in Wyoming at Laramie, and in Washington at Puyallup. Idaho governors G. C. Smith and Preston Leslie were church members.

Reno, Nevada, First Baptist Church

Reno, Nevada, FBC (Northern) organized in 1875. When the Nevada-Sierra Baptist Convention constituted as the first Nevada convention on April 14, 1911, it met in the church building.

Congress Creates Seven New Western States

The largest movement of population in American history came in the years following the Civil War. Settled areas in the West grew one hundred fold. As primitive living conditions improved, hostile Indians disappeared, mineral empires and cattle kingdoms fell, and economic well-being emerged, westerners developed an agriculture that was indigenous to the geography. A magnificent Intermountain West climate drew many to the West. Railroads provided economical transportation for Americans to emigrate.

From 1880 to 1900 the population of Idaho grew from 32,610 to 161,772, Nevada dropped from 62,266 to 42,335, and Utah grew from 143,963 to 276,749. Congress granted statehood to seven western states (1876–1896): Colorado, North Dakota, South Dakota, Montana, Washington, Idaho (July 3, 1890), and Utah (January 4, 1896).

Ogden, Utah, First Baptist Church

Ogden, Utah, FBC (Northern) was organized in 1881 by Dwight Spencer. The charter members pledged their own personal property in 1882 to secure funds to build their church building. Ogden FBC started missions at Mound Fort and Wilson Lane.

Salt Lake City, Utah, First Baptist Church

The SLC, Utah, FBC (Northern) organized in 1883 in the home of an Ohio Baptist mining company superintendent. Mormons expressed opposition by denying use of facilities. Non-Mormon churches had no option but to meet in the homes of members. In 1844, after a fund-raising campaign in the East, the FBC received gifts from John D. Rockefeller to build a worship center and school. Byron Morse, a Philadelphia missionary and physician, opened a free dispensary for the poor in SLC church facilities.

Independence Flat, Idaho, Baptist Church

The Independence Flat, Idaho, Baptist Church was organized on November 14, 1887, by J. B. York of Georgia. Short Mountain Baptist Church of Cowlington (Indian Territory), ordained York to preach at age eighteen. Baptist General Association of Western Arkansas and Indian Territory voted to send a missionary to Idaho Territory to minister to Nez Perce Indians and raised $235. York, his wife, and five small children traveled by emigrant train from Oklahoma Indian Territory to Riparia and on to Lewiston, Idaho, by steamer. Lewiston, Idaho, had two grocery stores and twelve saloons and gambling dens. After one night in a Lewiston hotel, the Yorks made a four-day trip to the Camas Prairie by freight wagon. They stayed in barns at Sweetwater and Mason Creek when heavy snow made travel difficult. They spent one night at a Cottonwood hotel and a fourth night in a rancher's home. York preached the first sermon by a Baptist minister north of Moscow, Idaho, in a log school building. Eight persons organized the Independence Flat Baptist Church on Christmas Day in 1887: J. B. and Martha York, Benjamin and Jane Cowling, William and Amanda Manes, and Steven and Minnie McPherson. York located sixteen Baptists at Cottonwood, preached a revival, and baptized twenty-two converts in below zero temperature. J. B. York, the son of a Baptist preacher and devoted Christian mother, organized sixteen churches and missions and organized a Baptist association. He returned to his pulpit on his eighty-first birthday in 1936 to preach again to the people he loved. Initially the church affiliated with Southern Baptists, but after York's resignation and retirement, the church related to Northern Baptists until 1981 when SBC missionary Larry Maxwell was called as pastor.

Home Mission Society Moves Emphasis West

Toward the end of the century, Northern Baptists shifted their major emphasis westward. In 1882 the HMS spent as much money in the West as in the rest of the nation. The HMS reported 799 of its 1,180 missionaries in the West in 1900. The SBC would not recover from the Civil War for another forty years. Although the SBC in annual sessions continued to approve motions for its DMB to send workers west, resources were not there to fund them. In 1874 the DMB changed its name to the Home Mission Board (HMB).

In 1881 Dwight Spencer, pioneer Idaho HMS missionary, wrote a stirring report of the spiritual needs in Idaho. Rebecca Mitchell of Illinois read the article and determined to help meet the needs by herself. She traveled to the remote mining town of Eagle Rock,

Idaho, purchased a shanty, and organized a school. In 1884 Eagle Rock, Idaho, FBC (Northern) built a church building with funds raised by Rebecca Mitchell. Idaho Baptist Convention later met in the new facility.

Western HMB Pioneer S. F. Dowis Is Born in Georgia

Solomon Franklin Dowis was born in Fulton County, Georgia, on May 19, 1891, to William and Hanna Dowis. He had eighteen brothers and sisters—seven died. He attended the Norman Institute, Mercer University, and Southern Baptist Theological Seminary (SBTS). He married Frances Mae Freeman November 5, 1915, and they had four children. He pastored Baptist churches in Kentucky and Georgia, and served as the Atlanta, Georgia, city missions director and HMB cooperative missions department director (1946–1958). In 1947 he wrote the HMB correspondence Bible courses. After the death of his first wife, he married Frances Flury in December 1955. After retiring in 1958, he served eight churches as interim pastor. Dowis died on November 5, 1967, and was buried in Westview Cemetery, Atlanta, Georgia. Wendell Belew, an associate, said, "In my opinion, no one meant more to the enlargement of our convention or was more responsible for golden (SBC) years than Dowis." Courts B. Redford, successor to J. B. Lawrence, said, "No person in HMB history established more new phases of SBC mission work or reached so many people with the gospel as did Dowis."

Baptists Begin New Churches in Railroad Cars

The American Baptist Publication Society bought *The Evangel*, a railroad chapel car, with gifts from some business men, including John D. Rockefeller and James B. Colgate. By 1915 the society had seven railroad cars in service. The eighty-by-eleven-foot chapel cars were longer than coaches but looked the same. A car contained living quarters for an evangelist, a chapel seating one hundred people on oak pews, an organ, pulpit, and blackboard. The railroad company pulled the cars over lines without charge and put them on sidings in towns needing a church. Nevada Baptists used *The Goodwill*, a railroad chapel car, to organize Elko

(NBC) FBC November 12, 1911, with Wilbur Howell, pastor; and Winnemucca (NBC) FBC in 1912 with F. T. Barkman, pastor. On April 14, 1911, Nevada Baptists constituted the Nevada-Sierra Baptist Convention, the first Baptist convention in Nevada.

THE TWENTIETH CENTURY

The 1900 census reported that 161,772 citizens lived in Idaho, 42,335 in Nevada, and 276,749 in Utah. The first auto crossed the continent from San Francisco to New York in 1903. The 1906 fire and earthquake in San Francisco focused attention on the West when 503 people died and losses were set at $350,000,000. An influenza epidemic in 1918 killed twenty million people worldwide, including 548,000 in the U.S.A. New Mexico Baptists canceled their annual convention because of the plague. Congress passed an enabling act on June 10, 1910, to permit Arizona and New Mexico to attain state status.

Baptist Convention of New Mexico Constitutes

Texas, whose history challenged Southern Baptists to attempt the impossible, launched Southwestern Baptist Theological Seminary (SWBTS) on March 14, 1908. The following year the SBC approved a report saying that Arizona and southern California would some day belong to Southern Baptists. When Texas farmers and oil companies moved in large numbers to New Mexico, a sudden shift in Baptist loyalties occurred. After a stormy Baptist convention session at Tucumcari, New Mexico, FBC in 1910, fifty-three messengers walked to the First Presbyterian Church and organized the SBC-related Baptist General Convention of New Mexico. The two conventions met at the Clovis FBC to constitute the Baptist Convention of New Mexico (BCNM) on June 19, 1912. The BCNM voted to affiliate with the SBC.

When Phoenix, Arizona, First Southern Baptist Church (FSBC) organized on March 27, 1921, it affiliated with the BCNM. Harry P. Stagg, BCNM executive secretary (1938–1968), married Phoenix pastor C. V. Rock's daughter. During the decade of the 1940s, New Mexico Baptists started SBC churches in southern Colorado and Utah as the BGCA began to evangelize Nevada, Idaho, and Utah.

Fallon, Nevada, Piute Indian Baptist Mission

The Fallon, Nevada, Piute Indian Baptist Mission (Northern) was started in 1908 by Lillian Corwin of Woman's Society to reach the Piute Indians. Fallon, Nevada, FBC assisted the mission with educational help for Piutes and Shoshones at Reno and Fallon, and to Washoes at Garderville. In 1920, J. G. Brendel, an Oklahoma missionary, preached there and baptized thirty-four Piutes.

Opal (Beaird) Dillman Moves to Vernal, Utah

Opal Beaird moved from Lamesa, Texas, to Colorado at the age of eight with her family. When her father saw that the land was too alkaline for farming, he moved his wife and six children to a four-room log cabin at Vernal, Utah. Opal met Harold Dillman in eighth grade, dated him four years, and became engaged. In 1928 the Beairds sold their farm and moved back to Texas. After Dillman completed mortician training, he moved to Texas, trusted Christ as Savior, and married Opal Beaird. Dillman wrote, "On July 7, 1930, I was converted and joined the Hamlin, Texas, FBC. God spoke to me forcefully in 1939 when he called us to Utah as missionaries."

The Contemporary Scene Is Shattered by Depression

C. P. Rodgers completed the first transcontinental airplane flight across the United States in eighteen days. Alexander Graham Bell and Thomas Watson completed the first telephone call from New York to San Francisco in 1915. The 1920 U.S.A. census reported 431,866 citizens in Idaho, 77,407 in Nevada, and 449,396 in Utah. When the stock market crashed on October 29, 1929, stock losses reached an estimated fifty billion dollars in our nation's worst depression. The crash devastated the West and prosperity ended.

Citizens elected Franklin Delano Roosevelt, Democrat and thirty-second U.S.A. President, to four consecutive terms (1933–1945). He closed the banks on March 6, 1933, and called a special one-hundred-day session of Congress to pass "The New Deal." The gold standard ceased on June 5, 1933. Prohibition ended when the thirty-sixth state formally adopted the twenty-first amendment. The Social Security Act was approved on August 14, 1935. The San Francisco Exposition focused new attention on the West.

Baptist General Convention of Arizona Constitutes

Southern Baptists had not constituted a state convention west of Texas and Oklahoma until 1912 when BCNM organized at Clovis, New Mexico, FBC. Arizona Southern Baptists organized Gambrell Memorial Baptist Association on October 29, 1925, at Globe, Arizona, FSBC and affiliated with the BCNM. A committee, which met in the summer of 1928 at Groom Creek Assembly to consider organization of a convention, recommended that it be formed. Messengers from ten churches traveled to Globe, Arizona, FSBC on September 20, 1928, to form the Baptist General Convention of Arizona (BGCA). W. S. Wiley, a Baptist Sunday School Board (BSSB) staff member, told of his dream that the SBC would extend to the Pacific Ocean. The BCNM executive secretary, C. W. Stumph, encouraged constitution of the new Arizona state convention.

When Bonnie Ball O'Brien wrote the HMB executive director in 1981 to gather background material for her Colorado book, Tanner asked Bill Hunke to respond. He wrote:

> The BGCA was constituted in 1928 at Globe, Arizona, by the messengers from ten Gambrell Memorial Baptist Association churches affiliated with BCNM. Because of comity agreements, the HMB did not initially work with the new Arizona convention. The BSSB provided Arizona with financial help in the form of salary assistance for S. S. Bussell, a BSSB field worker, and permitted Bussell to serve as a part-time BGCA executive secretary.
>
> HMB participation in areas outside the traditional South came in response to SBC action at San Antonio in 1942. The SBC interpreted the HMB's field of service as the U.S.A. and all its

territories. The SBC nationwide thrust came after the 1942 SBC position statement. Two Baptist deacons moved from Texas to Roosevelt, Utah, and started Roosevelt Baptist Church in 1944. Both deacons, Harold Dillman and Robert Johnson, died in SLC, Utah, this past year. The deacons knew Willis J. Ray in Texas, so they looked to Phoenix for help. Grand Canyon Baptist Association, nearest to Roosevelt, Utah, invited the Roosevelt and Artesia, Colorado, churches to send messengers as charter churches of the association. O. R. Delmar left his Arizona church to begin the church at Casper, Wyoming. Rapid development of state conventions in Arizona, California, Alaska, Oregon-Washington, and Kansas-Nebraska with so few churches led the BSSB and HMB to establish a "Minimum Guideline for SBC Denominational Assistance." The Colorado convention was the first constituted with these new guidelines.

On the denominational scene, the battle of comity agreements with the Northern Baptist Convention seemed to cease with the 1942 SBC action in San Antonio. Many of the states and communities have had to come to grips with this issue in later years. The NBC (American) became so involved in putting out fires emerging from their split and formation of the Conservative Baptist Convention that comity battles with the SBC ceased.

The SBC Begins the Western Mission Movement

The Great Depression and dust bowl uprooted millions of people from Oklahoma, Texas, and Arkansas. John Steinbeck, in *The Grapes of Wrath*, compared the move of Okies and Arkies west on the ribbons of asphalt to the Indians' "trail of tears." Model A Fords moved masses of people to the western lands of promise. In World War II after Japan bombed Pearl Harbor in 1941, the military moved thousands of Southern Baptists to western states. High wages lured the Southerners to work in the vegetable fields of Arizona and the citrus orchards and vineyards of California. Oil exploration moved people into the Mountain West in the 1940s. Population losses staggered southern states: Oklahoma lost 604,900, North Carolina 63,000, and Arkansas 250,000 in just thirteen years. The SBC moved from a traditional base in eighteen states to reach into all fifty states by 1972. The pioneers had a strong SBC denominational consciousness; it led them to seek affiliation back home. This rapid SBC expansion has no parallel in American Christianity.

Southern Baptists Begin Working in the West

Leonard B. Sigle, Klamath Falls, Oregon, FBC pastor, reached Oregon in 1931. Since Southern Baptists had not yet arrived, he worked with Landmark Baptists. He became a Southern Baptist missionary on March 1, 1949, and began working in Nevada. The SBC organized eighteen new western churches (1930–1934): Arizona (3), California (1), Washington (2), Hawaii (1), New Mexico (10), and Colorado (1). The SBC reported no churches in Idaho, Nevada, and Utah. The U.S. census reported that the combined population of Idaho, Nevada, and Utah, reached 1,185,430 persons in January 1940. War in the Orient led the SBC Foreign Mission Board (FMB) to loan missionaries from Southeast Asia to Hawaii. The Chinese and Japanese living in Hawaii held promise for both the FMB and Hawaii. By 1952 the FMB had forty-seven Hawaii missionaries. In 1937 Dud Poyner rented a tent to hold revivals in the San Joaquin Valley of California. After preaching a revival, Poyner would organize an SBC church. He organized new churches at Delano, Oildale, Porterville, Lamont, and Arvin. He baptized 65 in the Lamont revival and left the church with 101 members. R. W. Lackey of Oklahoma reported that 123 of the 125 people who attended a revival in California in 1938 were from Oklahoma. On April 13, 1939, messengers from four churches organized the San Joaquin Valley Missionary Baptist Association of California. They employed Dud Poyner (1939–1940) as missionary and designated the whole state as their territory.

Early Home Mission Board Leaders

Solomon Franklin Dowis, HMB cooperative missions (1946–1958).

Fred A. McCaulley, HMB western field-worker (1946–1960).

Early HMB leaders meet for constitution of the UISBC at Salt Lake City, Utah, October 29, 1964. Pictured L-R: A. B. Rutledge, HMB missions; C. E. Autrey, HMB evangelism; Charles Lloyd McKay, ASBC executive director; and Courts Redford, HMB executive director.

Wiley Henton, HMB building/loan director (1947–1960).

B. Frank Belvin, HMB Indian missions director (1951–1955).

First Intermountain West Church and Association

Harold and Opal Dillman organized the Roosevelt (UT) Baptist Church on July 2, 1944, with eight charter members. They gave the church a lot on which they erected this building in October 1946.

On October 18, 1950, messengers from the Roosevelt, Vernal, Provo, and Clearfield, Utah, and Artesia, Colorado, FBCs organized the Utah Baptist Association in the Roosevelt sanctuary. The churches had affiliated with Grand Canyon association of Arizona.

The seventy-five people who organized Utah association (bottom two pictures) drove through snow to attend. The first SBC churches at Casper, Wyoming, and Denver, Colorado, also affiliated with Utah.

Writers of this period attribute the rapid SBC growth from 1940 to 1989 to five factors: (1) the emigration of Southerners to find work; (2) the unhappiness with practices and beliefs of Northern Baptists; (3) the unchurched cities and towns without a Baptist church because of comity agreements; (4) the SBC actions showing the West as a great pioneer mission field; and (5) the HMB support of state conventions, lifting visions, and giving guidelines to get the job done. Dowis described the period as one of great expansion. Editor James L. Watters wrote:

> In His final quest to encounter mankind at the cross roads of his culture, a continuing encounter symbolized by a Cross, God brought forth in the American West the great populist tribe of the new Israel known as Southern Baptists: those people with little cracker box cathedrals strewn haphazardly across the grandeur of God's best creative work; those people with the audacity to believe in their calling to tell the good news to all the world (Watters, *Northwest Baptist Witness*, 9/16/85, 5).

Nicy Murphy, the Northern Plains Baptist Convention (NPBC) Woman's Missionary Union (WMU) secretary, wrote that God tapped the resources of U.S.A. military to plant defense and training installations in strategic cities, and he used major oil companies and construction firms to build bases where he could place SBC men and women in the West. The Baptists came with a "warm, Bible-based evangelistic zeal and an organizational know-how" to gather people of like faith and order into the Bible study fellowships, new missions, and churches (Murphy, *The 30th Child of Southern Baptists*, 2).

World War II Plants Southern Baptists in the West

When war threatened the United States, the military began building air fields at Boise and Mt. Home, Idaho, at Las Vegas, Nevada, and at Clearfield, Utah. Germany invaded Russia. The military movements by Japan created great concern in the West. The Navy completed its new naval air station at Kodiak, Alaska.

The base increased the city's population from 500 to 2,500 residents.

Charles Madry, FMB executive secretary, arrived at Honolulu, Oahu, Hawaii, on December 3, 1941, to discuss reinforcements for the Hawaiian Baptist Mission. He endured the Japanese bombing of Pearl Harbor when planes struck on December 7, 1941. The death toll reached 2,300, and nineteen U.S. ships were sunk or damaged. Congress declared war on Japan the next day, and then on Germany and Italy after they declared war on the U.S.A.

Southern Baptists had little understanding of religious needs in the West in the early 1940s. Their first awareness came when Robert W. Lackey, Southern Baptist General Convention of California (SBGCC) executive secretary, spoke to the 1941 SBC at Birmingham, Alabama. He reported that sixteen SBGCC churches gave seventy-six dollars to the SBC Cooperative Program, and asked that messengers from the SBGCC churches be seated. Lackey asked that California be recognized as a cooperating constituency.

In response, the president appointed a special committee to consider the request and to report back at San Antonio in 1942. Committee members A. J. Barton, J. B. Rounds, John Jeter Hurt, and M. E. Dodd did not take the request seriously. Northern Baptists had severely criticized the SBC in 1928 when BGCA constituted. Dodd had pastored Los Angeles, California, Temple (Northern) Baptist Church. He quickly told the committee he was a bitter SBGCC opponent. Dodd made a trip to California in 1942 to preach for Northern Baptists, but denied a request of SBGCC leaders to meet them at the Greenhorn Mountain summer assembly. Only J. B. Rounds visited California to investigate the thirty small SBC churches with three thousand members.

Rounds Challenges Southern Baptists to Go West

W. W. Hamilton of Louisiana, SBC president, gaveled the 4,774 messengers at the 1942 SBC at San Antonio to order hoping that debates over California messengers might not reach the floor. San Antonio's Municipal Auditorium had no air-conditioning to cool the messengers' sweat-wet shirts and dresses. They listened, nodded, amened, and dozed in response to business as usual. On day three, a hot cloudless Monday, J. B. Rounds of Oklahoma rose to his feet and said, "After a careful study of the situation and . . . the provisions of Constitution and By-Laws . . . , we recommend that the SBGCC be admitted to membership in the SBC." The debate erupted, and fifteen speakers raged for more than two hours. Oklahoma, Texas, and Arkansas messengers, about one-half of the messengers, carried the motion. SBGCC messengers were seated. The SBC action may have been the most meaningful decision in SBC life since 1845. The inevitable decision came because history was forged by fierce, desperate depression, dust bowl, and war. Okies, Arkies, and Texans had moved west by the tens of thousands. The messengers expressed concern about loved ones in the West. Everett Hullum wrote that the decision required the SBC to develop a whole new philosophy of growth and institute structures, plans, and finances to meet the western challenge and opportunity. He said that attitudes of outreach would be redefined, ideas about themselves would be reexamined, and SBC faith would be clarified. They stumbled into a new consciousness of direction and future (Hullum, *1979 HMB Teaching Guide for Adults*, 18).

The HMB Lays Foundations for Advance

The HMB reported to the Birmingham, Alabama, SBC that their national mission program included nineteen missionaries at work in New Mexico and Arizona among Spanish and Indian people. The HMB vision for the West involved only language missions. Arizona SBC churches had been sending messengers to the SBC since 1928. After the SBC seated the California messengers in 1942, the HMB reported that requests from Arizona and California led the HMB to discuss the placement of general missionaries in both the cities and rural areas of the West. The HMB sent its first eleven student summer missionaries to work with French-speaking people of south Louisiana in June 1942. The use of the college and university students during summer months provided for significant advance in the West.

After Baptist Student Unions began participation in the HMB student program, the HMB reported as many as 3,400 students at work on mission fields by 1955. Because of the Great Depression, a massive debt by the HMB, the SBC's inability to collect pledges amounting to seventy-five million dollars, and the default of an HMB treasurer who embezzled more than one million dollars, the HMB could not project a plan for western missions. When the HMB paid off the debt on May 12, 1943, J. B. Lawrence wrote:

> We rejoice to report that the debt which has hampered the Board in its work for the past 15 years has been paid. Relieved of this burden the Board is now ready and is making its plans to enlarge its work in the various fields. I can now speak of the tragic years through which we have passed with assurance because they have become an asset. We rejoice in the fact that we have handled our debt problem without disturbing the denomination with special appeals and without asking special consideration of any sort. . . . Crushed with debt and besmirched with the odium of the defalcation of a trusted officer, the HMB struggled under tremendous difficulties. In that tragic hour there was but one thing we could do and that was to travel with Christ towards tomorrow. This we did. We put the promises of God to the test. . . . He gave the pillar of cloud by day and fire by night to lead us across the Red Sea of discouragement and through the wilderness of financial disaster and across the Jordan of debt payment into the Promised Land of credit integrity and financial security. He put our feet on a solid rock of pay-as-you-go (Lawrence, 1944 SBC Annual, 280).

HMB Employs Solomon Dowis to Lead Western Missions

The HMB employed Solomon F. Dowis, Atlanta, Georgia, city missionary, as its national missions director on January 1, 1943. Dowis led eight HMB programs: western, mountain, pioneer, rural church, western, surveys, military, and juvenile delinquent work. L. O. Griffith later presented a paper on the life and ministry of Dowis to the Georgia Baptist Historical Society to preserve his personal information for the archives.

BGCA Employs Willis J. Ray as Executive Director

Because S. F. Dowis, the HMB cooperative missions secretary, preached at Texas district associational meetings, Dowis and Willis J. Ray became close friends. One day Dowis said to Ray, "The HMB cannot now do work in Arizona, but if you will go, then I'll get the HMB to go with you." After a year on the Texas staff, Ray accepted the offer to serve as the BGCA executive secretary (1944–1956).

The BGCA employed Willis Jackson Ray as executive secretary on June 2, 1944. Ray, a magnificent pioneer, led an army of Southern Baptists from Arizona into the Intermountain West, Rocky Mountains, and Great Plains. In 1993 the Arizona Southern Baptist Convention (ASBC), named its state mission offering after the pioneer. Ray, the tenth of twelve children, was born March 31, 1896, saved at age ten, and baptized through thin ice on Mule Creek. He grew up in Comanche County, Kansas, married Ida Margaret Shearer, and they had two children. Ray attended Wayland Baptist College (WBC) and graduated from Hardin-Simmons University (HSU).

While editor of the Texas *White Deer Review,* he received his call to ministry. He pastored churches at Lockney, Petersburg, and Littlefield. He served as Texas district eight missionary at Big Spring, and district six missionary at San Antonio. His volunteer student mission program led 257 people to Christ in seven weeks of Vacation Bible School (VBS). The HMB studied his soul-winning approach. Ray served as the executive assistant and superintendent of rural evangelism for W. W. Melton, the Texas Baptist Convention (TXBC) executive secretary. Ray started SBC state evangelism conferences. From his place of leadership in Arizona, he launched the BGCA on its northern mission to reach nine and a half states with the gospel. After the death of his wife, Ida Margaret, Ray married Aurelia Lois Bennett. The Colorado Baptist General Convention (CBGC) executive board employed him as executive secretary in 1956. He died at age ninety-six on December 6, 1992, at Payson, Arizona.

God Prepares His Ministers for the West

God in his timing placed Lackey in California, Rounds in the West, the Dillmans in Utah, Sigle in Nevada, Dowis at the HMB, and paid the HMB debt. God also prepared pastoral leadership for Idaho and the Intermountain West. Lavoid Robertson wrote this story:

> I am the youngest of eleven children with five brothers and five sisters. My dad was a share cropper who worked cotton fields in large Texas Johnson grass farms. We had Christian parents. . . . I was fifteen years old when World War II started. In 1944, at the age of eighteen, I joined the Army and received training at Ft. Hood, Texas. On my furlough and way overseas to the Pacific, while eleven of us were in the living room of our small farm house, . . . the oil stove exploded. I tried to open a door and pulled a glass door knob off in my hand. All were seriously burned. In the next few day we lost Mother, Dad, a sister, a sister-in-law, and a nephew. I spent sixteen months in Army hospitals and was released from the Army on June 12, 1946, after eleven plastic surgeries.
>
> I praise God that those who died were Christians. Those left who were not Christians at that time have since become Christians. One thing I could never get away from—the dying testimony of my mother. I carried my mother out of that burning house. When we got out, I realized that she was burned all over her body. I pulled my Army coat off and put it over her and began to weep. She reached out and touched me and smiled and said, "Lavoid, I always prayed that God would allow me to live until all of you children were grown. He has and now I am ready to go be with Him!" Dying grace! How wonderful! (Robertson, letter to Hunke, 10/3/77).

Robertson gave his life to the Lord. He married a beautiful girl, pastored the Twin Falls, Idaho, and Clearfield, Utah, Baptist churches, and served as the Utah-Idaho Southern Baptist Convention (UISBC) state evangelism director until retirement.

Golden Gate Baptist Seminarians Serve Nevada

Nevada became a training center for the students enrolled at Golden Gate Baptist Theological Seminary (GGBTS) in Marin

County. Proximity provided opportunities for hundreds of students. The 233-mile trip across the Sierra Nevada Mountains on Interstate 80, or along U.S. Highway 50 by Lake Tahoe, provided travelers with a spectacular, historic adventure. California chartered GGBTS on July 12, 1944, after Pastor Isam Hodges led Golden Gate Baptist Church to start a school with sixty-two students (twenty ministerial) on September 4, 1944. The school initially met on Grove and Addison Streets in Berkeley, California, near the University of California. The SBC purchased 148 acres of land turned down by the United Nations for $386,105. The value of the acreage and sixty-five buildings in 1977 was $9,373,000. The seminary trained 3,300 students in twenty-five years (1952–1977).

Dillmans Organize First Intermountain SBC Church

On July 2, 1944, one month after U.S.A. and allied military forces invaded Europe at Normandy Beach, Harold and Opal Dillman and Robert and Cora Johnson organized the Roosevelt, Utah, Baptist Church with eight charter members. Roosevelt Baptist Church is the oldest SBC church in the Intermountain West.

After Harold and Opal Dillman married in Texas, they arranged to move back to northeastern Utah in October 1942 and reestablish a Roosevelt, Utah, mortuary business. They returned to Utah to win family and friends to Christ. Both wished to start an SBC church. Dillman drove a refrigerated truck to Colorado in the fall of 1942 with friends to hunt deer. He agreed to drive the truck provided they let him take his furniture to Roosevelt on the way north. He said the move cost him $2.47. Robert and Cora Johnson joined the Dillmans at Roosevelt in 1944. W. C. Bennett, a Carrizo Springs, Texas, FBC pastor, accepted an invitation from the Dillmans and Johnsons to preach a revival at the Episcopal church building in Roosevelt. Following the revival, the Roosevelt Baptist Church organized. Harold and Opal gave a lot to the church on which to build their first cinder-block building. The new church affiliated with Central association and BGCA. Early pastors were Robert Cure, Charles Ray, Bill Trow, David Pate, Lee Roebuck, Ferris Winn, James Minnis, Lyle Kreuger, William Gamblin, Andy Underhill, Jack Maddox, Jackie Thomason, Troy Richardson, David Carver, and Bill Roberts.

The SBC Speaks Clearly on Comity

The 4,301 messengers attending the 1944 SBC annual meeting at Atlanta, Georgia, listened to HMB leaders report on expanding work and voted for agencies to become fully and appropriately involved in California Southern Baptist missions. The SBC spoke clearly on matters of comity by declaring themselves free of all territorial limitations in the U.S.A. A new interest in the West germinated.

The Lord Prepares Leaders for Utah and Nevada

Robert Lowe, early SBC pioneer pastor to Utah, wrote in 1997 that he had reached the age of eighty and wished to recall early Utah experiences. He wrote:

> Mayo and Celia Brown attended the same schools my wife Dot and I attended in Jackson, Mississippi. After Mayo returned from Europe while in military service, he was stationed at Kearns, Utah. One day in 1945 after his return to Mississippi Mayo said, "Someone must go to Utah and preach to Mormon people." Seven years later my wife Dot and I loaded up and moved to Utah to start an SBC church. We had no support, but I got a job. We started in a school and after three years we averaged nineteen per week in SS and church services (Lowe, letter to Hunke, 8/12/97).

God also showed his concern for Nevada when he began preparing Leonard Sigle, the Interstate Baptist Mission director, who was at work in Alaska, California, Oregon, and Washington from 1941 to 1944. When Sigle left Oregon to move to Modesto, California, he organized Modesto Temple Baptist Church in the home of boyhood friend Ernest Roberson. After he pastored the Modesto church five years, the HMB and SBGCC employed him to work in Nevada.

BGCA Employs Allen Barnes as Missionary (Utah)

Soon after the Roosevelt, Utah, Baptist Church affiliated with the BGCA, Willis J. Ray sent the first BGCA missionary to work in Utah revivals and summer VBSs. The HMB and BGCA employed Allen B.

Barnes on February 1, 1945, as the missionary to Gila Valley association in Arizona. Barnes served for six months as the Phoenix, Arizona, FSBC associate pastor. He had come to Phoenix in 1943 looking for a climate to ease family illness. He began serving as the summer missionary to Utah in 1945 because of the Arizona heat. Barnes, a New Orleans Baptist Theological Seminary (NOBTS) graduate, pastored New Orleans Metaire Baptist Church for eight years. During his ministry in Arizona and Utah from 1945 to 1949, Barnes organized nine churches and led hundreds of people to Christ.

BGCA Employs Herbert Spraker as Missionary (Utah)
Willis J. Ray met Herbert Ross Spraker in Texas and asked him to move to Arizona and serve as a missionary. The HMB and BGCA employed him as missionary to northern Arizona (1945–1948) August 23, 1945, and he lived at Flagstaff, Kingman, and Prescott. In the summer of 1946 Willis Ray sent missionary Spraker to serve as a second summer missionary for Utah revivals and summer VBSs.

Spraker was born June 3, 1891, in Liberty County, Texas. He was saved, baptized in Cobles Creek, licensed to preach September 15, 1915, and ordained on May 7, 1916, at Midway, Texas, Cobles Creek Baptist Church. He graduated from Sam Houston Normal School, worked as a store clerk, and taught school (1922–1923) in Walker County, Texas. He married Fannie Morgan on October 19, 1913. Following her death in September 1915, he married Hattie Lawlis on February 20, 1920. He pastored Texas Baptist churches in Walker County, and at Riverside, Dodge, Oakhurst, Cook Springs, Elmina, West Columbia, Sugarland, Houston, Sweeny, and Velasco. He served as chaplain for Texas prisons in Brazoria and Ft. Bend counties. Spraker died on May 30, 1953, and was buried at Huntsville, Texas.

BGCA Employs T. T. Reynolds as Missionary (Nevada, Utah)
T. T. Reynolds, the third SBC missionary assigned to summer missions in Utah, lived at Kingman, Arizona. After the HMB and the BGCA employed him on December 1, 1945, he served in southern Nevada and northwestern Arizona. He later pastored

Artesia, Colorado, FBC in the Intermountain West.

T. T. Reynolds was born September 8, 1897, at Franklin, Texas. When he was three years of age, his father died, and he helped his mother and sister with farm work. He was saved at age fourteen and surrendered to preach at age twenty-seven. The Houston, Texas, Calvary Baptist Church pastor, W. M. Harrell, encouraged him in his work and ministry for the Lord. He graduated from high school in Franklin, Texas, and spent two years in college at Houston and two years in seminary at SWBTS. He worked for six years as a Houston electric company clerk before entering full-time ministry. He married, had two children, and pastored Texas churches for eighteen years before entering western missions. Reynolds succeeded Milton Cunningham as Kingman, Arizona, FBC pastor in December 1944 but had to return to Houston, Texas, for one year to hospitalize his wife who was very ill. Friends described him as a gentle, unassuming, consecrated man of God.

Sacramento Valley Baptist Association Constitutes

The SBGCC first became involved in Nevada when the Babbitt (Hawthorne), Nevada, Calvary Baptist Church affiliated with the Sacramento Valley (Missionary) Baptist Association in 1947. Ed Moon was the first California SBC missionary to work in Nevada. Messengers from eight churches organized the Sacramento Valley association of California on October 10, 1945. The Hawthorne church was the first Nevada church to affiliate with Sacramento Valley association and the SBGCC.

HMB Evangelism Targets Revivals and Crusades

In 1866 the SBC authorized the HMB to "direct future labors chiefly upon the basis of evangelism and promote a comprehensive system of evangelism including appointment of evangelists." W. W. Hamilton, Weston Bruner, Oscar E. Bryan, and Ellis Fuller served as HMB nationwide evangelism superintendents from 1906 to 1928. In 1923 the HMB employed forty-six preachers and singers to lead the revival crusades. After the heavy debt crushed the HMB in the 1930s, the position remained vacant until the HMB employed Roland Q. Leavell in 1937 to direct its program of evangelism. As the West developed in the 1940s, each state convention employed a state evangelist: B. N. Lummus in California, Milton Cunningham in Arizona, and Paul McCasland in Oregon-Washington (1951).

Artesia (Dinosaur), Colorado, First Baptist Church

After A. C. Maxwell preached a revival at Artesia, Colorado, Mrs. Tom Elliott called a meeting of interested people to discuss the need for a Baptist church. Maxwell led in organizing Artesia FBC on March 27, 1946. On May 29 the church voted to affiliate with Central association of Arizona and the BGCA. Artesia FBC became a founding church of Grand Canyon association of Arizona on August 29, 1946. The church called on neighboring Roosevelt and Vernal churches to permit their pastors to serve Artesia on an interim basis. The early pastors were John Alexander, R. M. Miller, T. T. Reynolds, A. K. Peveto, Noland Beaird, R. L. Harper, Harold Dillman, Marvin Elam, E. W. Hunke Jr. (int.), and Darwin Welsh. Contractor Charlie Tague moved a building to Artesia.

BGCA Votes to Extend Work into the Intermountain West

Willis J. Ray, a friend of Harold and Opal Dillman, knew that the Roosevelt, Utah, Baptist Church had been organized on July 2, 1944. After Ray sent BGCA missionary Allen Barnes to Utah in the summer of 1945, the Dillmans began discussing the possibility of Roosevelt affiliating with BGCA. On December 11, 1945, the BGCA executive board discussed the possibility of accepting SBC churches from neighboring states into BGCA fellowship. Willis Ray reported that if any congregation in any western state sought HMB help, the HMB would refer it to the BGCA. After board discussion, John Davis moved that "the BGCA look with favor on receiving churches of like faith and order from the neighboring states." The motion was adopted.

Roosevelt, Utah, Baptist Church asked that its messengers be seated by the Central association of Arizona on April 27, 1946. The positive vote made the Roosevelt church the first SBC church outside the Arizona borders to affiliate with BGCA. Hilton Crow noted that in the decade that followed, SBC churches from nine western states affiliated with the BGCA. Lay preacher Harold

Dillman and pastor R. E. Cure of Roosevelt, Utah, Baptist Church attended the BGCA eighteenth annual session at Glendale, Arizona, on October 29–31, 1946. The two were seated as the first out-of-state messengers to BGCA. Cure gave the report on SBC work in Utah. Artesia, Colorado, FBC sent messengers to the Central association annual meeting in October 1946 but sent no messengers to BGCA.

HMB Leaders Advance Work in the West
After Fred Eastham led HMB evangelism for two years (1944–1945), the HMB employed Charles E. Matthews (1946–1955) to develop a "Southern Baptist program of evangelism." Matthews asked the HMB to employ a state evangelism secretary for each state convention. The HMB and SBGCC employed C. E. Wilbanks (1948–1950), and the HMB and BGCA employed Leroy Smith (1948–1955).

S. F. Dowis fell in love with the West. He attended the annual meetings of western state conventions every year. While preaching at the SBGCC tenth annual convention on November 2, 1949, he said, "I have attended every convention in California since 1943. I have become so attached to the work in the West that I sometimes think I should call my wife, tell her to dispose of what goods we have in Atlanta, and come out to California." More than one thousand SBC messengers and visitors at Long Beach heard Dowis preach at this largest gathering in California SBC history.

HMB Employs Fred McCaulley as Western Field Representative
The remarkable growth of SBC work in the West pointed to the need for a western field representative. The HMB employed Fred A. McCaulley as the first western field-worker on February 11, 1946. After his discharge as U.S. Army chaplain at Camp Fannin, Texas, he moved to California to help develop SBC work.

McCaulley was born on June 16, 1893, at Lake City, Iowa. He graduated from Central State Normal School of Norman, Oklahoma, Oklahoma Baptist University (OBU), and SWBTS. He was awarded a D.D. degree by California Baptist College (CBC) in 1966. McCaulley married Ona Violet Harris, and they had three children. He served as Oklahoma Baptist state SS secretary

(1920–1933); OBU public relations director and principal of OBU academy (1933–1935); SWBTS public relations director (1935–1940); Waco, Texas, Bellmead Baptist Church pastor (1936–1943); a U.S. Army chaplain (1943–1946); and HMB fieldworker (1946–1960). After retirement in 1960, he served as a speaker for world mission conferences, colleges, seminaries, assemblies, and churches. He preached in eight foreign countries and the fifty states. The November 25, 1993, *Christian Index* reported, "Former field-worker Fred McCaulley, who instituted the HMB Tentmakers Program in 1951, died November 15 following an illness. He was one hundred years old."

During his first year, McCaulley visited 131 California SBC churches, 46 Arizona SBC churches, and 20 New Mexico SBC churches. He visited the SBC seminaries at New Orleans, Ft. Worth, and Berkeley to recruit workers. His first report listed twenty additions by letter, twelve by baptism, 168 rededications, and thirty-six other professions of faith. The field assigned to McCaulley included California, Arizona, and New Mexico. He spoke to Baylor University ministerial students in early 1946. E. W. Hunke Jr., a ministerial student, met the pioneer missionary at Baylor. Naomi Savage (Hunke) met him at Camp Sierra, California, BSU retreat in August 1946. The McCaulleys and the Hunkes became friends who corresponded until his death.

Grand Canyon Baptist Association Constitutes

When the Grand Canyon association organized at Prescott, Arizona, FBC on August 29, 1946, its territory covered northern Arizona, Utah, and western Colorado. Messengers from the SBC churches at Wickenburg, Kingman, Prescott, and Flagstaff met at Prescott FSBC to organize Grand Canyon association, and invited the Artesia, Colorado, FBC and Roosevelt, Utah, Baptist Church to affiliate as founding churches. The associational area reached from Wickenburg, Arizona, to Idaho and western Colorado. After five years' affiliation with Grand Canyon association, the Utah and Colorado churches organized Utah Baptist Association in 1950. Arizonans developed close personal relationships to the north and attended the Utah camps and associational meetings. Ira Marks, the first missionary to live in Utah, worked with the Grand Canyon association until the Utah association organized.

Vernal, Utah, First Baptist Church

After the Beaird family moved into Vernal from Craig, Colorado, in 1918, they began praying for a Baptist church in Vernal. A son, Nolan, surrendered to preach and pastored Provo, Utah, FBC (1948–1950), and Vernal, Utah, FBC (1950–1953). After organizing, the Vernal FBC affiliated with Grand Canyon association and the BGCA. Early pastors were Bob Cure, Harold Dillman, B. H. McAlister, Nolan Beaird, E. W. Hunke, James Akin, Norman Bethany, Andy Underhill, Raymond McDonald, Bill Patton, Don Kimbrough, Howard Porter, and Herb Stoneman. Naomi Ruth Hunke described the beginnings of the Vernal FBC, the second SBC church formed in Utah, as follows:

> In 1946 Roosevelt Baptist Church bought a lot in Vernal, Utah, for a church. On November 10, 1946, they began a revival on the lot under a large army mess tent which had been purchased for this purpose. Bob Cure preached with Harold Dillman leading the singing. "Robert Johnson loaned us his oil burner for heat in the tent," Harold reported. "It snowed four inches one night while we were having services. The revival led to the organization of Vernal FBC under the tent on November 22, 1946, with seventeen charter members." Vernal organized a month too late to be a founding church of Grand Canyon association, but joined the association's activities from the beginning. Charlie Tague completed construction of the building, and it was dedicated in May 1954 (Hunke, *Remember the Wonders*, 34).

SBGCC Employs Edward Moon as Missionary (Nevada)

The HMB and SBGCC employed Edward Walter Moon as missionary to Sacramento Valley association in 1947. Moon became the fourth HMB missionary to work in the Intermountain West, the first sent by the SBGCC. His involvement began when Babbitt (Hawthorne) Calvary Baptist Church contacted the HMB for help.

Pioneer Missionaries in the 1940s

Allen B. Barnes Sr., HMB/BGCA general missionary (1945–1949).

T. T. Reynolds, HMB/BGCA general missionary (1945–1946).

Herbert Ross Spraker, HMB/BGCA general missionary (1946–1948).

Edward Walter Moon, HMB/SBGCC general missionary (1947–1950).

Fred M. DeBerry Sr., HMB/BGCA general missionary (1948–1949).

Troy E. Brooks, HMB/BGCA general missionary (1948–1958).

The HMB Western Mission Program

Annual HMB Western Mission Conference Leaders (circa 1950). Seated L-R: J. P. Edmonds, BSSB; S. F. Dowis, HMB; and Mrs. George Martin, WMU. Standing L-R: Willis J. Ray, BGCA; and Merrill D. Moore, SBC Executive Committee. The HMB held the annual Western Mission Conferences until Glorieta Baptist Assembly completed the New Mexico facilities and the conferences were held there.

HMB/BGCA Western Pioneer Missionaries (1954). Back row L-R: J. W. Hardin, southern Arizona; Troy Brooks, southern Nevada and northern Arizona; L. A. Watson, Colorado and Dakotas; and Bennie Delmar, Wyoming and Montana. Front row L-R: Frank W. Sutton, BGCA state mission director; T. M. Gillham, greater Phoenix; Ira Marks, Idaho and Utah and eastern Nevada; E. W. Hunke Jr., central Arizona; and Willis J. Ray, BGCA state executive director.

The HMB sent Fred McCaulley and Wiley Henton, who suggested that they contact Edward Moon. Moon was born in Edmonson County, Kentucky; graduated from William Jewel College and SBTS; and pastored Baptist churches at Louisville, Kentucky, and Richmond, Virginia. The HMB and SBGCC employed him as the missionary to Sacramento Valley, Sacramento-Sierra, Calvary, Orange County, Arrowhead, and Trinity Southern Baptist associations during his years of service.

SBC Growth in the West Creates Problems

Ten separate events or actions taken by state conventions in the West put the states on a collision course and created a whole set of new problems for the HMB. S. F. Dowis listed problem areas needing study by the SBC leaders in Arizona, California, and New Mexico. He believed a new understanding was needed.

1. BGCA approved a unilateral decision to seat messengers from neighboring states on December 11, 1945. BGCA sent workers to Utah in the summer when Arizona was hot.

2. Roosevelt, Utah, Baptist Church affiliated with Central association of Arizona on April 27, 1946, Grand Canyon association on August 29, 1946, and the BGCA on October 29, 1946.

3. The Artesia, Colorado, FBC affiliated with the BGCA and Central association of Arizona on May 29, 1946, and became a Grand Canyon association founding church on August 29, 1946. The church was located eight hundred miles from the state office.

4. Sweet Home, Oregon, FBC affiliated with SBGCC on June 30, 1946, rather than affiliating with Northwest Baptist Association of Oregon-Washington.

5. Five Oregon Baptist churches and two Washington Baptist churches voted to disband Interstate Baptist Mission, form the new Northwest association, and relate to the SBGCC.

6. Felton Griffin and Alaska Baptist work were set adrift when the Interstate Baptist Mission disbanded. The HMB expressed concern about the future of Baptist work in Alaska.

7. J. B. Lawrence, the HMB executive secretary, had written Felton Griffin in Alaska to ask for his presence at the SBC annual meeting at St. Louis, Missouri, in May 1947.

8. The SBGCC employed H. A. Zimmerman on April 25, 1947, as its missionary to Oregon-Washington. Zimmerman had formerly served as the BGCA executive secretary.

9. The BCNM organized several new SBC churches in southern Colorado and planned to start more missions.

10. The SBGCC had a special concern for Nevada. Hawthorne, Nevada, Calvary Baptist Church had affiliated with the Sacramento Valley association and the SBGCC in 1947.

S. F. Dowis Tours the West to Resolve Problems
S. F. Dowis dealt with problem areas immediately, with care, and only after he had facts in hand. Willis J. Ray, BGCA executive secretary, drove HMB leaders Dowis, McCaulley, and Henton on a two-thousand-mile tour of Arizona in February 1947. Other Arizona SBC leaders on the tour were R. H. Tharp, H. R. Spraker, Barry Garrett, Roy Sutton, Milton Cunningham, and Billy Barclay. After the tour, Dowis and McCaulley took an evening train to San Diego where a similar tour of California was planned. While in California, Dowis and McCaulley met with state executive secretaries and preached at a GGBTS Bible conference. Roy Sutton wrote:

> In early 1947 I met S. F. Dowis in Tucson. As I remember, I drove a car as the Baptist leaders toured Arizona mission fields. Later I drove a car for Dowis, Judge McCall and his

wife, and Duke McCall in Oregon and California. Other than Willis Ray, Dowis was the single most influential man in the history of western missions. He had a tremendous grasp of missions and especially associational missions. He was a marvelous advocate for western states at the HMB offices (Sutton, letter to Hunke, 4/30/91).

S. F. Dowis Leads Historic Prescott Planning Meeting

One hundred twenty-five California, New Mexico, and Arizona pastors, missionaries, and denominational workers assembled with HMB leaders at Prescott, Arizona, Church Conference Center on May 26–30, 1947. The group hammered out a partnership concept of SBC missions. Dowis, who was committed to the concept that HMB funds could not be spent to support work in any state unless the work was affiliated with an SBC state convention, led the meeting. The meeting resolved problems related to overlapping mission fields; secured support for Willis J. Ray and BGCA to reach out to nine states to the north; established a way for the HMB, state conventions, and associations to work together in reaching goals; and created a fellowship among western workers. The SBGCC agreed to work in western Nevada and the BGCA in eastern Nevada, Utah, and southern Idaho. The BCNM agreed to continue working in Colorado. Leaders from Washington and Oregon, though not yet constituted, agreed to focus on the Idaho panhandle. With the tensions resolved, Southern Baptist leaders prayed that God would give them the West. The Prescott conference pointed to the need for a western assembly ground similar to Ridgecrest.

HMB Employs Wiley Henton as Western Field Representative

After the Prescott planning meeting with resulting agreements between the HMB and the New Mexico, Arizona, Oregon-Washington, and California state conventions, the HMB employed Wiley Logan Henton as its second western field representative. Henton's positions of leadership in the BGCA gave him close contact with the early SBC work in Idaho, Nevada, and Utah.

Henton was born September 18, 1893, at Dallas in Polk County, Oregon, to Merit Francis Sigel and Annie Bell (White) Henton. His father served as a minister and his mother as a school teacher. He had two brothers and four sisters. He trusted Christ as his Savior at age twenty-two in January 1916, was baptized in August 1916 by the Colmor, New Mexico, FBC, and ordained on July 23, 1924, by the Montezuma Baptist Church of Las Vegas, New Mexico. He attended grade schools at Dallas, Grass Valley, and Demoss Springs, Oregon, and Phoenix, Arizona. He graduated from Montezuma High School at Las Vegas, New Mexico, and New Mexico State Teachers College at Silver City, New Mexico. He married Joan (Jo) Vivian Marlow at Deming, New Mexico, on November 29, 1929, and they had two children. He worked as a farmer, carpenter, steam engineer, minister, and school teacher. He pastored churches at Silver City and Melrose, New Mexico, and at Casa Grande and Globe, Arizona.

The HMB employed him as the western field representative with church loans and buildings (1947–1960). After retirement in 1960, he continued to live at Globe, Arizona. His health deteriorated until he was confined to the hospital for months prior to his death on August 7, 1983. Truman Webb, Frank Jackson, and Jimmie Woods led the funeral service. Jo Henton died on February 28, 1994.

First Utah Associational Meeting Convenes at Roosevelt

Grand Canyon association pastors and laypersons met for the first Intermountain West associational meeting at the Roosevelt, Utah, Baptist Church on August 22, 1947. The two-day conference required that Arizonans drive twelve hundred miles round-trip to the meeting. Five of the seven Grand Canyon association churches were represented. In addition to pastors and laypeople, the BGCA sent state workers and officers: Willis Ray, S. S. Bussell, the Lester Probsts of Prescott, Mrs. Bill Roberson, and Mrs. Homer Roberts, the WMU president.

Babbitt (Hawthorne), Nevada, Calvary Baptist Church

SBC deacons Ben Felts and Lester Hampton from Hawthorne Naval base organized Babbitt, Nevada, Calvary Baptist Church on October 25, 1947, with seventeen charter members. The church wrote the HMB for help. In response, the HMB sent Fred McCaulley and Wiley L. Henton to meet with the church. The HMB leaders, aware of the recently approved relationships made at Prescott, Arizona, suggested that Calvary Baptist Church leaders affiliate with SBGCC. Edward Moon, the Sacramento Valley associational missionary, served as interim pastor of the church.

On August 14, 1948, the Calvary Baptist Church voted to affiliate with SBGCC. In September 1948 the Felts and Mrs. Abrams drove 270 miles across the Sierra Nevada Mountains to attend the Sacramento Valley association meeting at Auburn. Tehachapi, California, FSBC pastor Homer D. Wilkes and missionary Moon led the church in a 1948 revival which resulted in ten added by baptism and five by letter. The Calvary Baptist Church changed its name to Hawthorne FSBC to become Nevada's first SBC church. Early pastors were E. E. Smedley, L. E. Chism, Homer Davenport, J. C. Anderson, W. P. Brian, Charles Day, James Minnis, Bernard Ford, Tom Bacon, J. R. Sammons, Paul Chambliss, Ernest Hewett, and Bob McDuffie.

BGCA Employs Fred DeBerry as Missionary (Utah and Nevada)

After J. N. Phillips, the Phoenix area missionary, resigned to return to the pastorate in 1947, the HMB and BGCA employed Fred M. DeBerry Sr. as Central associational missionary on March 2, 1948. DeBerry worked summers in Utah camps and VBSs.

DeBerry was born March 25, 1913, at Martha, Oklahoma. He was saved at age ten through the influence of his parents and baptized in August 1923 by the Martha Baptist Church pastor, A. F. Agee. He graduated from the Martha High School, OBU, and attended SWBTS. He married Leona White on May 29, 1932, and they had two children. The associational missionary was called to pastor the Phoenix Mission Drive Baptist Church. The HMB and SBGCC employed him as missionary to San Joaquin Valley and Mojave Desert associations (1951–1953). He also served the Sequoia, Fresno Southern, Fresno-Madera, Tri-County, Midway, Shasta, and Sierra Butte associations. While serving as the Mojave Desert missionary, DeBerry helped organize the Boulder City, Nevada, FSBC, on May 13, 1951, the first SBC church in southern Nevada. After his retirement he worked as a funeral director and associate pastor of SBC churches in California.

Baptist General Convention of Oregon Constitutes

Twelve Oregon and seven Washington SBC churches constituted Northwest Baptist Association on April 25, 1947, and affiliated with the SBGCC. Robert E. Milam of Portland served as the first moderator. The HMB and SBGCC executive board elected Roland Hood, a Texas City, Texas, pastor, as the first SBC missionary to Oregon and Washington. After eleven months' association with the SBGCC, the Northwest association churches constituted the Baptist General Convention of Oregon March 31, 1948. BGCO later added Washington to its name (BGCOW).

BGCOW Employs Robert Milam as Executive Secretary

The BGCOW elected Robert E. Milam as the executive secretary on April 13, 1948. During his tenure of service, the Idaho panhandle became a mission field of the BGCOW. Milam, a native of Florence, Texas, emigrated to the Pacific Northwest with his parents. He returned to Texas to graduate from Howard Payne College (HPC) and SWBTS. He pastored Texas Baptist churches until Portland, Oregon, Antioch Baptist Church called him as pastor in 1944. Milam served as a member of the Interstate Baptist Mission and as the first BGCOW executive secretary. After his retirement in 1961, he served as the BGCOW capital needs secretary and coordinator of Canadian Southern Baptist work. Milam's contact with students at SWBTS provided him resources needed to call ministers to the Northwest.

BGCA Employs Troy Brooks as Missionary (Nevada)

Troy E. Brooks deserves recognition as one of the West's greatest missionaries. He served as the first BGCA missionary to southern Nevada. He and his wife Katherine were loved by student summer missionaries who helped them conduct VBSs. When E. W. Hunke Jr. served as Brooks's supervisor, he reported that Brooks stopped his car in Las Vegas one day, leaned on the steering wheel, and shook the car as he wept over the city. The HMB and BGCA employed Brooks as the missionary to southern Nevada and northern Arizona on June 1, 1948. He was born on March 19, 1892, at Bangs, Texas, to Francis Marian and Margaret Amanda Brooks. He was saved at the age of eight in 1900, baptized in a pond by the Bangs Baptist Church, and ordained as minister in 1923. Brooks graduated from Mulewater, Texas, High School, University of Arkansas, HPC, and Baptist Bible Institute (NOBTS). He married Katherine Stapp September 1, 1920, and they had one son. Brooks pastored twelve churches and missions. He served as a missionary in Texas and a U.S. Army chaplain. Fred McCaulley and Willis Ray were instrumental in his decision to move west. Katherine Brooks, a native of Burnet, Texas, planned to go with her husband to Brazil as SBC foreign missionaries, but health problems after the birth of her child and the SBC financial crises stopped them.

Brooks served Grand Canyon, Mohave, Little Colorado, Estrella, Yuma, and Hassayampa associations. He served southern Nevada and led in organizing the Lake Mead Baptist Association. An automobile accident terminated the ten-year Nevada and Arizona ministry of the veteran missionary (1948–1958) when his car left the road ten miles south of Kingman on June 16, 1958, and plowed into a huge boulder. His two summer missionaries were not injured. He remained in the Kingman hospital several weeks and was later confined to the Ft. Whipple Veterans' Hospital at Prescott for four months. Brooks decided to retire at the age of sixty-six. He moved to Tucson to pastor Corona de Tucson Baptist Church for eight years. In 1970 they moved to El Paso, Texas. Katherine Brooks wrote:

I am glad to have lived long enough to see what God has wrought from 1948 till now. I am eighty-five, live alone, attend my own affairs, a very quiet life now. In 1972 we moved to Canutillo, Texas, to be near our son. Troy was overcome with Parkinson's disease and was an invalid for the last five years of life. On April 5, 1982, God called him home. While age eighty-five, Troy preached a sermon to men as he sat in his wheel chair. He died at the age ninety (K. Brooks, letter to Hunke, 3/9/86).

First Uintah Baptist Encampment Meets at Big Park, Utah

The first Uintah Baptist Assembly met at Big Park in Uintah Canyon, Utah, on July 13–17, 1948. Fred McCaulley, HMB western field-worker of Fresno, California, led morning worship, and S. F. Dowis, HMB cooperative missions secretary of Atlanta, Georgia, led evening worship. Californians George Burnett, Bonnie Beaird, and Royal Beaird assisted in the camp. A large number of SBC people began moving into eastern Utah in 1948 because of rich oil deposits in the Red Wash area. Geologists searched for oil and drillers sunk new wells. Because so many of the oil workers came from the strong SBC states like Oklahoma, Texas, and Louisiana, the small Utah SBC churches began to grow. Offices for oil industry located first at Vernal, but later moved to SLC.

McCaulley Reports to the SBC at Memphis

Fred A. McCaulley reported to the 8,843 SBC messengers at the annual meeting at Memphis that he preached in nineteen states and Alaska in 1947. He reported seventy-nine baptisms, 107 additions to the churches, and forty-one professions of faith. He said he wrote 3,774 letters, more than ten each day. He attended 2,125 meetings with 54,791 people in attendance. The western SBC states were organizing a new church every six days.

Provo, Utah, First Baptist Church

Harold Dillman led some Roosevelt Baptist Church surveyors to Provo to take a religious census in early 1948. Three people came to services after reading a newspaper ad. BGCA missionary Allen B. Barnes Sr. and two student missionaries led a VBS. Provo, Utah, FBC organized August 23, 1948, at the Provo Odd Fellows Hall with the Roosevelt pastor, Charles Ray, preaching. The new church affiliated with Grand Canyon association and the BGCA. The church purchased a former Mormon Ward building. Four men surrendered to the gospel ministry: John Hughes, Claude Summers, Cecil Morgan, and James Barrett. Early pastors were Nolan Beaird, George Williams, Mayo Brown, T. L. Collins, James McFatridge, Roy Worthley, Sid Baskin, Ray Chasteen, Don Plott, Phillip McKown, and John Meador.

Sierra Butte Baptist Association Constitutes

Sacramento Valley association of California disbanded at its fourth annual meeting in 1948 to form the Sacramento-Sierra and Sierra Butte Baptist associations. Hawthorne, Nevada, Calvary Baptist Church, which had affiliated with Sacramento Valley association in 1947, helped form the Sierra Butte association.

SBGCC Employs Leonard Sigle as Missionary (Nevada)

The HMB and SBGCC employed Leonard Bonnie Sigle as the missionary to the Sierra Butte association on March 1, 1949. Northern Nevada churches affiliated with the association (1949–1954). After Sigle transferred to Feather River association of California (1954–1958), he continued working with Nevada.

Sigle was born on February 24, 1905, at Hobart, Oklahoma, to Christopher and Mary Ann (Liebmann) Sigle. His engineer father owned the Clinton, Oklahoma, Coca-Cola bottling plant and an ice cream factory. Sigle was saved at the age of fourteen, baptized by Clinton FBC pastor Harry Morgan, and ordained in 1924. He began preaching at age sixteen and never worked at a secular job. He attended HPC and graduated from OBU and SWBTS. Sigle married Edrie Ernestine Wilson on September 2, 1931, and they had three sons. He pastored Baptist churches at Deer Creek, Midway, Randlett, and Mt. Pleasant. After graduation in 1930, he moved to Klamath Falls, Oregon, FBC as a pastor.

Initially, he worked with the Landmark Baptists because SBC work had not started in the Pacific Northwest, and he served as Interstate Baptist Mission director. Sigle pastored churches at Longview, Washington, and Modesto, California. The HMB and SBGCC employed Sigle as the missionary, on March 1, 1949, to serve Sierra Butte (1949–1954), Feather River (1954–1958), and Nevada (1959–1969) associations. Sigle retired December 31, 1970, and continued to start new churches. He started fifty-eight new missions and churches before he died on August 15, 1976. Sigle was buried at Kennewick, Washington. His wife died on November 20, 1994, in Washington.

When Nevada Baptist Fellowship held its first meeting at the Sparks, Nevada, Temple Baptist Church on April 27–28, 1964, E. W. Hunke Jr. stayed with the Sigles in their home and developed a close friendship which continued to Sigle's death. Don Ledbetter, an early Nevada SBC pastor who later served as the Nevada Baptist Convention (NVBC) evangelism director, regarded L. B. Sigle as one of God's greatest servants. Ledbetter wrote his thesis on SBC work entitled *History of Nevada Southern Baptists*.

Utah Southern Baptists Continue to Prosper

Utahns held a second annual Utah Southern Baptist Encampment on July 11–19, 1949, at Little Park in Uintah Canyon, Utah. The camp director reported seventy-one registered, nineteen saved, and forty-five rededications. The staff reported that the 1948 attendance was doubled. Churches participating were Vernal FBC; Artesia, Colorado, FBC; Roosevelt Baptist Church; and Provo FBC. Three days of heavy rain nearly forced camp closure, but rains let up after the people prayed. The featured speakers were Courts Redford, Fred McCaulley, and Wiley Henton from the HMB staff, and Fred DeBerry, Phoenix Central association missionary.

Sixty people from the Roosevelt, Vernal, and Provo churches met at the Roosevelt Baptist Church for simultaneous revival fellowship in 1949. The speakers were Leroy Smith, evangelism secretary for the BGCA and H. A. Zimmerman, pastor at Richland, Washington. The Roosevelt church provided dinner, and Provo FBC baptized three converts.

HMB Leaders Renew Commitments to the Intermountain West

As the 1940s decade neared an end, HMB leaders Lawrence, Dowis, and McCaulley assured Southern Baptists in Idaho, Utah, and Nevada that the HMB intended to provide resources needed to finish the task. J. B. Lawrence produced a series of radio broadcasts known as the *Good News Hour* for release in 1949. The BGCA paid one thousand dollars toward the cost of these programs. The *Baptist Hour* featured pastor R. G. Lee, pastor of the Memphis, Tennessee, Bellevue Baptist Church, as its preacher in 1949. Three weekly radio programs sponsored by Vernal, Artesia, and Roosevelt provided a way to send the gospel from Vernal's only radio station. Utah churches paid for the programs and often aired the HMB recordings by J. B. Lawrence, HMB executive secretary. He believed that the SBC must develop "a denominational consciousness, not bigotry or denominational strut and brag; but a common life growing out of common faith." He wrote, "Denominations must have religious basis for existence. There must be a central, unifying motive. . . . Denominational consciousness is therefore another word for religious patriotism." Lawrence wanted the people to know they were Baptists and why they were Baptists (Owen, *Church Planting at the End of the Twentieth Century*, 9). S. F. Dowis wrote:

> The western mission program in Arizona, California, and New Mexico, is jointly promoted by state mission boards and the HMB. The needs of these fields are so much greater than other fields, we approach problems as pioneer mission work. Missionaries are general missionaries assigned by the state boards to specific fields of work. (Dowis, 1949 SBC Annual, 191).

Fred McCaulley wrote:

> SBC work in the West is new, thrilling, and productive. Ten years ago the first SBC church of California came into being; seventeen years earlier Arizona had her first; and before that, New Mexico voted single alignment with the SBC. . . . The HMB now supports twenty-eight field-workers who reported 2,235 professions of faith and 1,323 additions to the churches by letter. Please come over into the Macedonia of the West and help us—with your prayers, your preachers, and your purses! (McCaulley, 1949 SBC Annual, 191).

The 1940s Decade Ends on a High Note

Grand Canyon association held its fourth annual meeting at Provo, Utah, FBC on October 4–5, 1949, under the direction of John Johnston of Kingman, Arizona. Grand Canyon association reported nine churches: five in Arizona, three in Utah, and one in Colorado. Willis Ray said that in driving to the meeting, he passed through twenty-six communities with five to ten thousand people which had no Baptist church. Roosevelt, Utah, pastor, Charles Ray, preached the annual sermon on "Ministering to the Misguided." Allen B. Barnes, the first HMB/BGCA missionary to enter the Intermountain West to work in Utah, resigned and returned to a Phoenix pastorate.

The HMB and BGCOW employed Clifford Ervin Boyle as missionary to Washington State (1949–1950). He served as associate executive, and *Pacific Coast Baptist* editor, and made attempts to start SBC churches in Spokane and Idaho's panhandle. Lucille, his wife, worked alongside him at the Portland Baptist building, and as GGBTS Northwest Center librarian. She helped preserve Northwest history.

Phil Jones, HMB researcher, reported that from 1945 to 1949 the Southern Baptists in Nevada organized two churches and in Utah organized three churches. No SBC churches were located in Idaho. The other western states organized 238 new churches. SBC work in the Intermountain West had just begun in the 1940s.

Charter Members of the New SBC Churches

Rupert (ID) FSBC organized on June 14, 1953, with fifteen charter members. The Worthley home served as the first meeting place with Roy Worthley as the first pastor. The Worthley family spent their lives starting new SBC churches in the West.

Ely (NV) FBC organized on April 4, 1955. The mission began with an HMB student summer missionary survey and revivals led by George Stevens and Fred Barnes. Provo (UT) FBC sponsored the new mission and Roy C. Leverett served as the first pastor.

Twin Falls (ID) FSBC organized on September 24, 1955, with thirty-three charter members. The Pocatello FSBC sponsored the mission. Harold Dillman served as the first pastor. More than one hundred people joined FSBC during Dillman's ministry from 1955 to 1957.

REMARKABLE ADVANCES

THE DECADE OF THE 1950S

As the decade of the 1950s dawned, the U.S. census reported 588,637 people in Idaho, 160,637 in Nevada, and 688,862 in Utah. The combined population of the three states grew from 1,185,430 in 1940 to 1,438,136 in 1950, a 21 percent gain in one decade. Many non-Mormon people moved into the Intermountain West. Congress gave the American Indians full citizenship in the three-state area.

The HMB began promotion of the new "Southern Baptist Program of Evangelism" in the 1950s. Simultaneous revivals were held east of the Mississippi River in 1949 and west of the river in 1950. Three evangelism secretaries served the Intermountain West: Leroy Smith (BGCA) worked in Idaho, eastern Nevada, and Utah; Paul McCasland (BGCOW) worked the Idaho panhandle; and Hershell Stagg (SBGCC) worked western Nevada until he died in August 1957. Lewis Steed (1958–1970) succeeded McCasland.

BGCOW Employs Gilbert Skaar as Pastor-Missionary (Idaho)

On January 1, 1950, Gilbert Orville Skaar began serving as pastor of the only SBC church at Spokane, Washington. He wrote, "Dr. R. E. Milam heard we finished seminary and were at my folks' home at Newport, Washington. He arranged for us to visit Spokane FSBC. The ten members present extended a call. The

BGCOW provided $100 per month, so we moved to the field with $300 per month income." His assignment was to establish an SBC church and association. Skaar made initial contacts with the Idaho panhandle.

Skaar was born on August 26, 1924, at Sandpoint, Idaho, to Christian and Sigrid H. Skaar. He had three brothers and three sisters. Skaar was saved November 1, 1945, at age twenty-one, baptized in December 1945 by Preston, Lancashire, England, Carey Baptist Church, and ordained January 25, 1948, by Abilene, Texas, Calvary Baptist Church. Skaar served with the U.S. Army Infantry (1943–1946). He wrote, "I was reared in a Lutheran home. I could have been saved since the Lutherans preach some gospel, but I had not committed my life to His full Lordship. At the end of World War II, I gave my life to the Lord in Belgium and was baptized by an English church." Skaar graduated from Newport, Washington, High School, HSU, and SWBTS. He married Greta Rozelle on July 12, 1946, at Dallas, Texas, and they had five children. He pastored SBC churches at Ely, Texas; Norris Bend, Oklahoma; Spokane, Washington; Vancouver, British Columbia; and Medford, Oregon. He wrote, "In five years our church at Spokane led out in establishing three associations, building one building, starting two missions, and reached out to Idaho. Our growing SS exceeded two hundred in attendance." The HMB and BGCOW employed him as the missionary to Spokane (1950–1952). He served Mt. Baker, Olympic, Southwest Washington, Coast, and Myrtlewood associations. After retirement in 1990, he served four months as a volunteer in Inland Empire association, the place where he began his ministry.

1950 SBC Annual Session Meets at Chicago

S. F. Dowis reported to the 1950 SBC annual meeting at Chicago, Illinois, that HMB western missions cooperated with the Arizona, California, Kansas, New Mexico, and Oregon state conventions. SBC work had extended into the Intermountain and Rocky Mountain West. The HMB launched the five-year crusade to double the number of the churches and missions in its outposts.

BGCA Employs Ira Marks as Missionary (Utah-Idaho-Nevada)

The distance from Phoenix BGCA offices to the churches in northern Utah required that the HMB and BGCA place a missionary in Utah. When the Marks family arrived at SLC, Utah, on February 15, 1950, SBC churches were located at Roosevelt, Vernal, and Provo, Utah, and Artesia, Colorado. His 1950 report showed that four churches had 202 members. Marks helped organize SBC churches at Casper, Wyoming; Denver, Colorado; Ely, Nevada; and Idaho Falls, Idaho. Churches from each of these four states affiliated with Utah association when it was constituted on November 18, 1950.

Ira I. Marks, a native of Carnegie, Oklahoma, was educated at Tyler, Texas, Commercial Business College, Oklahoma State Teachers College, OBU, and NOBTS. He and his wife, Gracie, had two daughters. Marks worked as a Western Bell Telephone Company accountant for eight years. When God called him, he gave his life to mission work in Louisiana and Utah. He pastored New Orleans West Tenth Street Baptist Church and Louisiana First Baptist churches at Jeanerette, Plaquemine, and Krotz Springs. His Louisiana Atchafalaya work attracted nationwide attention after he built the "Little Brown Church" on a ferry to go to the isolated French-speaking villages. He built a hospital and schools at Myette Point, Grand River Flats, Bayou Boutte, Little Pass, and Hog Island. Marks employed twenty-four missionaries to work alongside him in Louisiana. He started sixty-two SBC churches during his ministry: nineteen in Louisiana, eleven in Idaho, one in Nevada, twenty-five in Utah, one in South Dakota, one in Wyoming, four in Colorado, one in California, and one in Oklahoma. The HMB and BGCA employed Marks as missionary to Twin Buttes, Salt Lake, Gideon, and Golden Spike associations. He left Utah to serve as a pastoral missionary in North Dakota, and lead a California children's home. When Gracie died on August 18, 1977, after forty-two years of marriage, Marks wrote, "Her home going was a sudden shock, a lot of heartache and loneliness to me, but to her it was the better day of tomorrow for which she had been living and dreaming." After retirement and remarriage, Marks returned to Louisiana. He later moved to Missouri to pioneer SBC work in Iowa.

SBC Ministers Follow Their Members West

Ministers followed Southern Baptists to the Intermountain West. People brought their church letters and raised up churches where they could worship God. They talked about the local church, evangelism, missions, Bible study, and the ordinances. The early Southern Baptists, misunderstood and mistaken for sheep stealers, had actually refused to take Northern Baptist members into an SBC church without rebaptism to prevent criticism. Southern Baptists worshiped God in remodeled chicken coops, store buildings, parks, and abandoned church buildings.

Third Utah Encampment Meets in Uintah Mountains

The third annual Utah Southern Baptist Encampment met July 31–August 5, 1950, in an Uintah Mountains' recreation area thirty miles northwest of Roosevelt. The camp reported 132 registered, twenty-four saved, four for special service, and twenty rededications. The study course books were taught by Mrs. Ruth Ely, Mrs. W. Barry Garrett, Miss Eunice Louise May, and Miss Regina Sliger. May and Sliger led morning watch; Wiley Henton, HMB staff member of Globe, Arizona, led morning worship and campfire services; W. Barry Garrett, editor of the Arizona *Baptist Beacon*, led evening worship services.

Kimberly, Idaho, First Baptist Church

Following a revival led by Alvin Bennett in August 1950 at the local Grange Hall, the Kimberly FBC organized with eighteen charter members. The church affiliated with the Columbia Basin association of Oregon and the BGCOW until October 3, 1953, when it affiliated with the Twin Buttes association of Idaho and the BGCA. The early pastors were Loren Esley, Milo Davis, James Wright, Morgan Berry, William Gamblin, Frank Holt, Larry Roberts, Riley McCall, Sam Overacre, Glenn Munkres, Larry Angel, Dan Smith, and Terry Brown.

Dragerton, Utah, Carbon Missionary Baptist Church

Dragerton, Utah, Carbon Missionary Baptist Church organized on September 1, 1950, with ten charter members. The church affiliated with Utah association and the BGCA. Baptist deacons, Joe Carroll and Tom Middleton, who knew nothing about each other or SBC work in Utah, started the Dragerton mission in 1950. After they rented a school room, they invited pastor Robert Clements of Greenville, Texas, to preach a revival and start the new mission. Layman J. D. Weiss led the singing. Missionary Ira Marks reported forty-four in SS and that the work was doing well. Early pastors were Charles Ray, John Watson, Milton Simmons, S. E. Cearley, S. W. Badgett, and Lloyd Hicks.

Salt Lake City, Utah, Rose Park Baptist Church

Rose Park Baptist Church organized on November 12, 1950, with seventeen charter members. Ira and Gracie Marks opened their SLC, Utah, home to start the mission in 1950. The work affiliated with Utah association and the BGCA. The church bought a site to erect one of the "little brown chapels of the West." William and Bessie Fleming gave fifty thousand dollars to build the brick veneer building across the street from the Rose Park Shopping Center. Early pastors were Ira Marks (int.), J. O. Perkinson, Charles Ray, James McFatridge, Darwin Welsh, and Guy Ward. The church started new missions at Kearns, Glendale, Clearfield, Bountiful, and SLC.

Utah Baptist Association Constitutes

Messengers from five churches made plans to constitute Utah association while attending Grand Canyon association's fifth annual session at Flagstaff, Arizona, October 3, 1950. Utah association constituted at Roosevelt on November 18, 1950, with messengers from six Baptist churches: Roosevelt Baptist Church; Artesia, Colorado, FBC; Vernal FBC; Provo FBC; Dragerton, Carbon Missionary; and SLC Rose Park. Thirteen messengers traveling from Provo to the meeting turned back in heavy snow and missed the session. SLC, Dragerton, and Clearfield messengers also missed the meeting. The Saturday meeting attracted seventy-five people. Roosevelt pastor Charles Ray served as first moderator. SBC churches located at Casper, Wyoming; Denver, Colorado; and Pocatello and Idaho Falls, Idaho, later affiliated with Utah association.

SBGCC Employs S. G. Posey as Executive Secretary

The mission needs of California so overwhelmed SBGCC leaders that they made no serious attempt to reach Nevada. Robert W. Lackey and A. F. Crittendon, SBGCC executive secretaries, laid the foundations for California. Sheldon Gambrell Posey, the SBGCC's third executive secretary employed on January 1, 1951, included the Intermountain West in his strategy to reach Nevada. Posey, the son of a Baptist preacher, was born in 1893 near Brookhaven, Mississippi. He graduated from SWBTS in 1918 and pastored SBC churches in Oklahoma, Mississippi, Louisiana, and Texas. Posey and his wife, Katiebel, left San Antonio, Texas, Temple Baptist Church to serve as the GGBTS religious education department head. He commanded respect from his fellow workers because of his integrity, principles, confidence, encouragement, communication skills, and administrative ability.

Idaho Falls, Idaho, Calvary Baptist Church

Fred Buckendorf opened his home to constitute the Idaho Falls, Idaho, Calvary Baptist Church on March 26, 1951, with forty-eight charter members. Ira Marks led the organizational service. Pastor C. Lee Bullard, arrived on October 7, 1951. The church affiliated with Utah association and the BGCA, the first in Idaho to work with Utah Southern Baptists. Arco Atomic Research Center, located near Idaho Falls, opened the way for many experienced SBC workers to move into Idaho. Arco generated electricity from atomic energy. Early pastors were Ira Marks (int.), Lee Bullard, J. B. Rounds (int.), Clyde Barrow, Roland Smith (int.), George Eichler, Bruce Gardner, William Warren, and Herb Stoneman. Calvary sponsored missions at Rupert, Soda Springs, Preston, Glen's Ferry, Mt. Home, Blackfoot, St. Anthony, and Salmon.

HMB Employs State Mission Leaders

S. F. Dowis, "the father of cooperation," wanted to help the state conventions employ state mission secretaries rather than add to his Atlanta HMB staff. The increasing numbers of churches and pastors in Idaho, Nevada, Utah, and in the Rocky Mountains required additional workers. The HMB and state conventions employed A. C. Turner (SBGCC) February 1, 1951; Roland P. Hood (BGCOW) October 1, 1952; and Frank W. Sutton (BGCA) December 15, 1952.

SBGCC Employs A. C. Turner as State Mission Secretary

A. C. Turner, the first state missions secretary employed to work in the West, demonstrated a keen interest in the Intermountain West. After preaching a revival at Vernal, Utah, he participated in the first Utah, Idaho, Nevada mission fellowship in 1954.

A. C. Turner was born at Martinsville, Texas, on February 25, 1893, to John T. and Sarah Jane (Fuller) Turner. He had three brothers and two sisters. After he trusted Christ at age nineteen in 1912, the Martinsville, Texas, Baptist Church baptized him. He married Parrot Eason on May 9, 1917, in Rotan, Texas, and they had five children. Turner taught public school for ten years. Turner wrote, "We didn't graduate from grade school, we finished; I taught before I graduated from Blum, Texas, High School." He attended the East Texas Normal School, HSU, and SWBTS. Turner pastored Texas Baptist churches for twenty-seven years. The HMB and SBGCC employed him as missionary to Golden Gate, Contra Costa, and San Francisco associations (1950–1951). He served the Orange County association (1956–1958), and retired on December 31, 1958. He died August 30, 1974, and his wife died April 29, 1982.

Clearfield, Utah, First Baptist Church

Two mission SSs, one in the Lawrence Cure home and the other in the Ben Graham home, started without the knowledge of the other. Consolidation of the two SSs led to organization of the Clearfield, Utah, FBC on April 1, 1951, with twenty-nine charter members. The new church affiliated with Utah association and the BGCA. FBC met in the North Davis Junior High School until a building was erected on a lot owned by Ben Graham. Early pastors were John L. Smith, Walter W. Fordham, W. E. Greene, Richard Mobley, John Upchurch, and Lavoid Robertson.

In 1952 Clearfield, Utah, FBC reported that it sponsored a weekly radio program, four missions, and a bulletin mailed to the three hundred people on the mailing list. Each mission pastor provided his own support: Ray McKinney, Roy; Fred Higginbotham, Ogden; John Watson, Sahara Village; and L. R. Brooks, Layton. Neither the sponsoring Clearfield church nor the missions owned property. When Clearfield bought land, Ira Marks placed one of the "little brown chapels of the West" on the lot for services.

Boulder City, Nevada, First Southern Baptist Church

Wesley and Hattie Nickelson and their daughter, Louise, began praying for an SBC church in Boulder City. The first service on April 29, 1951, at the Camp Williston Fire Hall attracted nineteen people. The Boulder City, Nevada, FSBC organized on May 13, 1951. Organizational council members were J. L. Eddings of Phoenix; Fred DeBerry, SBGCC missionary (1951–1953); Ben Goddard of Dallas; Troy Young of Bullhead City; John Masterson; and James McCaleb of Ft. Worth, Texas, an SWBTS student. The new church initially affiliated with Mojave Desert association of California and the SBGCC. When Mohave association of Arizona was constituted on October 28, 1951, the church affiliated with the BGCA. Missionary Troy Brooks (1948–1958) worked with the southern Nevada church. Charlie Tague helped the church with building plans. Early pastors were J. L. Eddings, Maurice Wicker, M. K. Wilder, Louis Nimmo, Matthew Doyel, Walter Oman, Stephen Neesley, and Timothy Walsh.

Young People Contribute to Western Missions

Young people continued to make SBC advance possible by giving their summers to the Lord as student summer missionaries. In 1951 the HMB sent fifteen young men to northern California to work in missions and lumber industry jobs. Fred McCaulley, the HMB western field man, directed the program named "Tentmakers" until he retired in 1960. The work expanded to include adults who moved to mission fields, secured employment, and opened new ministries in the areas.

Casper, Wyoming, First Southern Baptist Church

L. W. Barbee of Seminole, Oklahoma, moved his family to Casper, Wyoming, in 1951. They met with other oil-related workers on June 24, 1951, for Bible study and fellowship at a Mountain States Power Company building. Ira Marks, the Utah HMB/BGCA general missionary, and the Rex Ray family, South China foreign missionaries, helped organize the Casper FSBC on July 15, 1951, at the Casper City Hall. On Monday, July 16, 1951, O. R. Delmar wrote:

> When the people here at Casper asked me to come over to this great state of Wyoming and help them establish a Southern Baptist church, I and the church at Tolleson, Arizona, felt honored to have that privilege. Although I had been absent from the pulpit two Sundays to attend the SBC, the Tolleson FBC graciously voted to permit me three more Sundays absence in order that they and I might have a small part in this great missionary enterprise. Several of the members at Tolleson would have come with me if they could have possibly come. They are as much concerned about the starting of this work as I am. We need more churches with that same missionary spirit. This church organized yesterday morning and has twenty charter members so far. . . . The newly organized church has called me as pastor. I have not given an answer yet and I don't know what it will be. If I come to the definite conclusion that it is God's call also, you know what I'll do. Your friend, Bennie

Because of time constraints, FSBC delayed a vote to affiliate with the Utah association and BGCA until Wednesday, July 18, 1951. Casper FSBC, the oldest church in Wyoming, affiliated with the Utah association for fifteen months and with the BGCA until the Colorado convention began operation in 1956. The church helped constitute Southern Baptist Association of Colorado-Wyoming October 14, 1952, and organized other churches in Wyoming and in Montana.

Utah Baptist Encampment Meets at Uintah Canyon

The fourth annual Utah Southern Baptist Encampment, which met in Uintah Canyon from July 30–August 4, 1951, reported 173 campers and twenty-eight visitors registered, forty-two saved, five for special service, and seventeen rededications. The program leaders were Lucy Lan, morning watch; Ft. Worth, Texas, Broadway Baptist Church pastor, Guy Moore, morning worship; WMU director, Mrs. Charles Griffin, missions hour; BGCA executive director, Willis Ray, evening worship services; HMB staff member, Lewis Martin, campfire services; and visiting workers Ruth Ely of Phoenix, Horace Crowder of Dallas, Bob King of Ft. Knox, Kentucky, and Glenn Blaisdell of Corpus Christi, Texas.

Mohave Baptist Association Constitutes (Nevada-Arizona)

On October 28, 1951, four BGCA churches from southern Nevada and northwestern Arizona constituted the Mohave association. The distance Boulder City, Nevada, FBC had to travel to get to meetings at Barstow, California, led the church to help form the new Mohave association of Arizona and affiliate with the BGCA. The Kingman, Arizona, FBC experienced similar problems traveling to Grand Canyon association meetings at Prescott or Flagstaff. Churches dissolved Mohave association after thirteen years of service to form the Lake Mead association of Nevada and River Valley association of Arizona.

Denver, Colorado, Temple Baptist Church

Denver, Colorado, Temple Baptist Church organized August 19, 1951, in the Hank Taylor home with sixty charter members. When the charter membership roll closed on October 28, 1951, the church reported 153 members. D. A. Bryant served as the first pastor. Mrs. Matt Hunter wrote T. C. Gardner, *Texas Baptist*

Standard editor, for help in organizing the SBC church. The three planning meetings to prepare for organization were at the Hunter and Taylor homes. Ira Marks, HMB/BGCA general missionary, attended the August organizational service. The church, which met in a funeral home and later in the Central Business College, affiliated with Utah association and the BGCA. The Denver church sent messengers to constitute the Southern Baptist Association of Colorado-Wyoming on October 14, 1952. The church affiliated with Utah association for fourteen months.

SBC Foundations Laid at Ogden

In 1952 Robert and Dot Lowe arrived at Clearfield, Utah, where he took a secular job to support his family, rented the house next door to John L. Smith, and started a new mission with Louise May and six members of the Lowe family. After three years of work the mission averaged nineteen in SS. Lowe wrote:

> My wife was never discouraged, but on one day she asked, "Did the Lord really call you out here or did you just want to take a trip out west?" I responded, "Yes the Lord moved me to Ogden; you will see that confirmed soon." The next Sunday two cars of new people drove up in front of our home where the church met. One of the men, Howard Yochum, rolled up his sleeves, and helped me double attendance and secure an empty building to enlarge our church facilities. In two years Ogden Calvary Baptist Church was averaging 123 in services.

BGCOW Employs Lewis S. Steed as Missionary (Idaho)

Roy L. Johnson, BGCOW historian, reported Idaho SBC churches at Kimberly and Gooding when Steed began his ministry at Spokane in 1952. The two churches affiliated with the BGCA October 3, 1953, when the Twin Buttes association of Idaho constituted.

Lewis Steed was born December 19, 1912, at Smyrna (Atlanta), Texas, saved at age seventeen, and baptized in Warker Pond by the Texas church. He wrote, "My Grandfather told me about accepting Christ. I was plowing in the field, stopped, went out to a wooded area, prayed, and gave my life to Christ. I went forward in the revival service that night." He married Lucille Whatley, and they had four children. After graduating from Atlanta High School; East Texas Baptist College; Arkansas, Ouachita Baptist University (AOBU); and SWBTS, he pastored Texas Baptist churches at Nacogdoches and DeKalb. While he served as Renton, Washington, FBC (American) pastor in January 1950, they started a mission. When he learned that the Renton church had many SBC members who wished to have SBC affiliation, Steed resigned the sponsoring church to pastor the new mission, the first SBC work in the Seattle area (1950).

Steed served as military chaplain in World War II and in the Korean Conflict. The HMB and BGCOW employed him as missionary on March 1, 1952, to serve Columbia Basin (1952–1953), Inland Empire (1952–1958), and Coulee (1955–1958) associations. During his five years in Spokane he started thirteen churches and built five church buildings. Steed initiated the SBC work at Kellogg, Lewiston, and Bonner's Ferry, Idaho. The HMB and BGCOW employed him as the BGCOW evangelism secretary on February 1, 1958.

White Rocks, Utah, Ute Indian Baptist Mission

On November 19, 1951, thirty-five people met for the first SBC Indian service in Utah at White Rocks with Roosevelt Baptist Church as sponsor. When the church organized November 26, 1953, seventy-five people attended. Indians from across the U.S.A. sent two thousand dollars to help establish the work. Harold Dillman, the first pastor, led the church to affiliate with Utah association and the BGCA. Early pastors were Lee Roebuck, H. T. York, Harmon Popham, Calvin Sandlin, and John Blake. Charlie Tague constructed a new building for the Indian congregation with HMB funds.

Ely, Nevada, First Baptist Church

On July 11, 1952, Ely, Nevada, sent a Macedonian call to Ira Marks, BGCA missionary in Utah, asking for help in starting a new church at Ely. Provo, Utah, FBC agreed to sponsor the mission. HMB summer missionary Milt Hughes found thirty-five Baptists when he took a religious census. Pastor George D. Stevens of Vinton, Virginia, expressed concern for Nevada on August 16, 1952, when he wrote BGCA editor W. Barry Garrett:

> On our way home from the convention in San Francisco we stopped for worship at Wells, Nevada. At the close of the service the local people spoke of the great need for religious work in Nevada, and they definitely pled for Southern Baptists to undertake this work. The appeal so deeply impressed me that I wrote our Home Board about it. Some eight months later I was delighted to have a letter to the effect that Brother Ira I. Marks would supervise this work. Brother Marks has proven himself a zealous missionary in exploring the possibilities, laying the foundations and getting the work started. He has ability, consecration, and initiative. I was overwhelmed when he wrote and asked me to hold a revival in Ely and when my church so eagerly underwrote the expense of this venture. My family and I have been here a week. We have been cordially received and had wonderful cooperation. We have discovered very cultured and prominent people who seem anxious to help in establishing a Baptist church. People in general seem hungry for the gospel. There are more than 5,000 people here and only 100 of them actively attend the protestant churches. The need is thus evident. We thank God for our Home Mission Board, for Brother Marks and his consecrated leadership, and for the privilege of preaching and working here.

Fred Barnes, HMB missionary to ranchers, preached a revival at Ely, Nevada, on April 19–26, 1953, and reported five saved. Sunday afternoon, April 26, Southern Baptists gathered at McGill, Nevada, to baptize several new believers in a swimming pool.

Missionary Ira I. Marks commanded great respect from the pastors because of his tireless work. He led pastors to preach and to practice missions. Idaho, Nevada, and Utah pastors met once each quarter to help their missionary knock on doors and start the new missions, or to strengthen one needing help. The quarterly associational workers conference for Idaho, Utah, and Nevada gathered at Ely in June 1954. The missionary and pastors spent the afternoon visiting prospects.

Provo FBC organized the Ely FBC in 1955 with missionary Ira I. Marks moderating the service. The new church affiliated with Utah association and the BGCA. Missionary Marks secured Roy Leverett, a mine worker from Morenci, Arizona, who completed his college work at WBC, to serve as the first pastor. Marks wrote, "Brother Leverett has a wife and a daughter nine. He worked in a garage while his wife worked in the WBC nursery to defray their expenses. He is thirty-nine years of age and is willing to pay the price that is necessary to lay the foundation for a church at Ely." The early pastors were Leverett, John H. Stout, W. R. Ward, Foy King, Herbert Hughes, Horace Kennedy, Earl Hosea, James Hux, and John Babb. The church building was constructed by Charlie Tague.

Utah Baptist Encampment Meets at Little Park

The annual Utah Baptist Encampment met from July 28 to August 2, 1952, in the Uintah Mountains near Little Park. Utah laymen and pastors erected two large associational tents for the three hundred people expected to attend. Leon Woods of Midland, Texas, and the Leroy Smiths of Phoenix, Arizona, who concluded a summer of travel, led the camp which recorded fifty-two decisions. Nine HMB summer missionaries helped: John Odom, Dwight Dudley, Gerald Buckley, Elsa and Joan Gish, and the Milt Hughes and Travis Ellis families.

Tooele, Utah, First Baptist Church

The SLC, Utah, Rose Park Baptist Church organized the Tooele FBC on July 11, 1952, with twelve charter members and Odell Whitten as the first pastor. Program personalities at the organizational meeting were James McFatridge, Charles Ray, John Smith, and Nolan Beaird. The church affiliated with Utah association and the BGCA. Whitten, an Odessa, Texas, Baptist pastor, started the Tooele work in his home February 17, 1952. One month later the mission rented a hall for three dollars per month to help accommodate an overflow crowd of fifty people. Early pastors were Odell Whitten, Arvel Miller, Ira I. Marks (int.), George Williams (int.), Varion Stogner, C. Lee Bullard, John Shugart (2), Floyd Baker, Tom Underwood, and Verrell Leeper. Charlie Tague constructed the building.

Price, Utah, First Baptist Church

The Dragerton, Utah, FBC organized Price FBC August 7, 1952, with twenty-four charter members and Jimmie Flynn as pastor. Flynn worked in the nearby mines to provide a living for his family. The organizational meeting featured Harold Dillman, Charles Ray, Lester Rose, Mrs. Jimmie Flynn, John Odom (HMB summer missionary), John L. Smith, M. M. Crawford, Ira Marks, Nolan Beaird, and William Trow. The new church affiliated with Utah association and the BGCA. This eighth Utah SBC church met in a Seventh Day Adventist church until they completed a block building in fifty-two days. Missionary Ira Marks wrote a letter on May 14, 1953, to *Baptist Beacon* editor W. Barry Garrett, saying:

> Brother Myron M. Crawford came to us last summer after several weeks of correspondence back and forth as he considered coming to Utah to build the Little Brown Church in the West project, but it became evident we could not get financial help on the project. Price FBC organized and extended a call to Crawford about six months ago. He first worked in the mine to make a living for his wife and two small boys. They called him full time as pastor and began building immediately. . . . When they could not seat revival crowds in the Adventist building, they began their services on the last Sunday of the simultaneous revivals.

When Graham, Texas, pastor Harry Holmes preached a revival at Price, the members visited 1,140 people, recorded eighty decisions, and had forty-two people unite with FBC. The early pastors were Charles Ray (int.), Jimmie Flynn, Myron Crawford, N. T. James, M. M. Berry, James Sollie, Paul Boothe, James Guy (int.), S. E. Cearley, Riley McCall, Dick Burns, and Ronald Fullerton.

Western Mission Conference Moves to Glorieta

S. F. Dowis, HMB cooperative missions secretary, announced that he moved the annual western mission conference from March 1953 at Fresno, California, to June 22–28, 1953, at the New Mexico Glorieta assembly grounds. He said, "This change is being made to cooperate with the BSSB in building a great summer program."

BGCOW Employs Roland Hood as State Mission Superintendent

The HMB and BGCOW employed Roland Parks Hood as BGCOW state missions superintendent on October 1, 1952. Hood worked in the Idaho panhandle, Oregon, Washington, and western Canada. Hood was born March 5, 1902, at Thornton, Texas, to Luther Henderson and Daisy (Parks) Hood. He had two sisters. Hood was saved at the age of eight, and baptized by Houston, Texas, Baptist Temple Church. He graduated from the Houston Heights High School, Baylor, and SWBTS. He married Rhoda Davidson on January 26, 1927, and they had two children. He pastored Texas Baptist churches at Angleton, Alta Loma, Galena Park, Elmira, New Waverly, and Texas City where he served eighteen and one-half years. On October 9, 1948, the HMB and SBGCC employed him as the northwestern missionary (1948–1949) to follow H. A. Zimmerman. When Canadians began attending BGCOW meetings on August 13, 1951, he gave attention to SBC work in Canada. The BGCOW employed him as associate executive/mission director on October 1, 1952. He served as BGCOW interim executive secretary (1965–1966) and executive secretary (1966–1968). His wife Rhoda served as the BGCOW WMU executive director (1949–1962). After his retirement December 1, 1968, Hood directed overseas tours, opened new missions, helped churches secure pastors, and visited nursing homes. His wife died June 1, 1987. Hood died on May 3, 1989.

Utah Association Holds Second Annual Session

Utah Baptist Association held its second annual meeting at Clearfield, Utah, FSBC on October 2–3, 1952. Messengers from ten churches and representatives from ten missions registered. Charles Ray directed the sessions. The association elected William Trow as moderator, Harold Dillman as clerk, Nolan Beaird as treasurer, Ben Graham as SS superintendent, and Mrs. George Williams as WMU president. George Williams agreed to serve as the Utah Baptist Encampment president. Ira Marks reported on the chapels.

The October 16, 1952, *Baptist Beacon* featured an article about the "little brown chapels of the West." Missionary Ira I. Marks, well known for his floating brown chapels built atop ferry boats in Louisiana's Atchafalaya River to reach remote families, initiated the concept in Utah and Idaho. Marks constructed the portable chapels (some painted white) for two thousand dollars each for use in new mission work. The units were made in four-by-eight-foot panels, so they could be assembled, disassembled, and moved by flatbed truck.

Gooding, Idaho, First Southern Baptist Church

The Idaho Falls, Idaho, Calvary Baptist Church organized the Gooding FSBC on November 20, 1952, under the leadership of pastor C. Lee Bullard of Idaho Falls. The new church affiliated with the Columbia Basin association of Oregon and the BGCOW. When the Twin Buttes association of Idaho organized October 3, 1953, the Gooding FSBC affiliated with the new association and the BGCA. The early pastors were Ken Conners and Clay Coursey.

Ray Pays Tribute to Utah SBC Pioneers

BGCA executive secretary Willis J. Ray, a former newspaper reporter and editor, captured Southern Baptist attention with his article "Rays" in the *Baptist Beacon*. On November 27, 1952, he paid tribute to Utah SBC pioneers:

> Some of us do not realize the sacrifices some of our trained young ministers, with their families, are making in order to open and develop new fields here in the West. When these men feel it is God's will for them to make the sacrifice, they do it gladly. The work in Utah has been opened and developed to the place of nine churches by the sacrifices of Charles Ray, Nolan Beaird, George Williams, John Smith, William G. Trow, and our field-worker, Ira I. Marks. These men have come and stayed. George Williams and his lovely family came to First

Baptist Church of Provo in 1950. They came at sacrifice of salary and convenience. The car and clothing must last like that of the children of Israel when they moved to the promised land. Many of these ministers must drop their insurance and annuity to live within their small incomes.

Roy, Utah, First Baptist Church

The Clearfield, Utah, FBC organized the Roy FBC on December 11, 1952, in the community administration building with fifty-six charter members. Ray McKinney, who later served as a New Mexico associational missionary, led in starting the Roy mission in his home. FBC affiliated with Utah association and the BGCA. Members of the organizational council were John L. Smith, Bill Trow, Fred Higginbotham, Charles Ray, Walter White, R. L. Harper, Ira Marks, Nolan Beaird, J. B. Rounds, Bob Lowe, James Gish, and L. R. McKinney. The church, which later met in a fire station, purchased nine lots and built a red split-brick building in 1959. Early pastors were Ray McKinney, Jessie Willsie, James McFatridge, John L. Smith, Dick Turner, Richard Lunsford, Dennis Daniel, and Logan Thomas.

BGCA Employs Frank Sutton as State Missions Secretary

When BGCA work expanded north to the nine states in the Rocky and Intermountain West, the HMB and BGCA employed Phoenix Eastside Baptist Church pastor, Frank Wesley Sutton, as BGCA state mission secretary on December 15, 1952. Eastside was giving 32 percent to missions through the Cooperative Program.

Sutton was born October 4, 1903, at Nolanville, Texas, to Andy Madison and Nora V. (Davis) Sutton. He had three sisters. After trusting Christ at age thirteen, he was baptized by the Nolanville church in South Nolan Creek. He wrote, "I was deeply convicted of my sins during the ten day camp meeting which our church held each summer. Two weeks later I surrendered my heart to Christ in a Methodist camp meeting." The Ardmore, Oklahoma, Immanuel Baptist Church ordained him in October 1928. Sutton graduated from the Gene Autrey, Oklahoma, High School and OBU and attended SWBTS. He married Lois Fay Southerland on July 3, 1932, and they had two children. He pastored Oklahoma Baptist churches at Zanise, Wirt, Graham, County Line, and Duncan, and at Nocona, Texas, and Phoenix, Arizona. While at Nocona, Sutton and his wife felt called to serve in pioneer missions and were praying individually and unknown to each other for God to open the door. Before they opened a letter which arrived, Lois Fay said, "We are going to Phoenix." They knew the call was from God. The HMB and BGCA employed him as the first BGCA state mission director (1952–1956). After retirement, he pastored the Phoenix Elsinore Baptist Church for ten years. His wife died on January 13, 1993. Sutton, age ninety-four, continued attending meetings in Phoenix in 1997.

J. B. Rounds Serves as Vernal Interim Pastor

Retired pioneer missionary J. B. Rounds pastored Vernal FBC on an interim basis when Nolan Beaird resigned. After visiting with Rounds at Vernal on April 29, 1953, missionary Ira Marks struck a deer on his way home. He was seriously hurt in the collision and suffered a broken knee and injury to his hip. Pastor Earl Bigelow of Lakeside, California, preached the April revival for Vernal FBC when his sister and her husband lived there. On his return to California, Bigelow visited the San Diego Midway Baptist Church revival where E. W. Hunke Jr. was preaching. After Bigelow shared his concern about Vernal, the Hunkes agreed to preach at Vernal in May 1953. Hunke wrote:

> When Rounds' minority report challenged the 1942 SBC at San Antonio, Texas, few realized just how bold the new mission venture would become. SBC messengers broke loose from the chains of regionalism that bound them to the Bible belt for a century and reached out to all of the U.S.A. J. B. Rounds was in retirement when I met him a decade after this minority report. I looked into the face of this spiritual giant while I waited to preach in view of a call at Vernal FBC. The church sang "ready to go, ready to stay, ready my place to fill, ready for service lowly or great, ready to do His will." I knew Rounds planned the service and selected the music. I cannot forget the mighty storm at Wolf Creek Pass at Utah Baptist

Assembly the night a tent fell on Rounds. Not wanting to trouble anyone, he lay all night under the wet and cold canvas. The next morning Rounds said, "I missed daily Bible reading last night for the first time in forty-two years." He could not find his flashlight.

J. B. Rounds, a former HMB Indian mission director and Oklahoma Baptist Convention executive director, wrote that he would marry Miss Gracia Tarmon at the Oklahoma City Trinity Baptist Church on January 19, 1955. Rounds returned to Oklahoma City to live at 1307 Linwood. Utah Southern Baptists greatly admired Rounds for his tireless work and his absolute confidence in the success of Southern Baptists in the Intermountain West.

Gusher, Utah, Baptist Church

The Roosevelt, Utah, Baptist Church organized Gusher Baptist Church on May 28, 1953, with fifteen charter members. Members of the organizational council were William Trow, J. B. Rounds, Charles Ray, John L. Smith, Ira Marks, Myron Crawford, John Watson, Herbert Johnson, and Harold Dillman. Dillman, the first pastor, presented the need for a church; Rounds preached a doctrinal sermon; Smith discussed the church covenant; Ray talked about Baptist articles of faith; Agnes Denver and Adelche White sang a special song accompanied by Dorothy Dillman; Marks presented the charge to the church; and Crawford preached an evangelistic sermon. Mary Denver came forward as a candidate for baptism. The new church affiliated with Utah association and the BGCA. The early pastors were Harold Dillman, Nolan Beaird, Harmon Popham, and Raymond McDonald.

The Gusher, Utah, Baptist Church ordained Harold Dillman to the gospel ministry on July 7, 1953, the first SBC ordination in Utah. The ordination council members were Ira Marks, moderator; E. W. Hunke Jr., charge to church and candidate; and Frank Belvin, HMB Indian missions director, sermon. Special music was provided by pastor and Mrs. William Trow accompanied by Naomi Ruth Hunke.

Rupert, Idaho, First Baptist Church

The Rupert, Idaho, FBC organized June 14, 1953, with fifteen charter members and affiliated with Twin Buttes association and the BGCA. The Worthley family started the mission in their home. The father earned his living as a sheet metal worker, but his main business was starting SBC missions. He said, "I find the places without SBC work in Baptist minutes. I compare that with available sheet metal job offerings in the union paper. When I find a job in a town with no SBC church, I accept it as a call from God. I take the job and go start a new mission." The early pastors were Roy Worthley, Fred Higginbotham, and Charles Aday.

Pocatello, Idaho, First Southern (Gate City) Baptist Church

The Idaho Falls, Idaho, Calvary Baptist Church organized the Pocatello FSBC (Gate City) on June 14, 1953, with thirty-seven charter members under the direction of pastor C. Lee Bullard. The church, which affiliated with Twin Buttes association and the BGCA, ordained Morris Wall as their first pastor, the first recorded SBC ordination in Idaho. Early pastors were Morris Wall, Arthur Nunn, Gary Christopherson, Jack Galligher, Charles Fowler, and Lu Gilman.

Lewiston, Idaho, Clearwater (Orchards) Baptist Church

Missionary Lewis Steed of Spokane, Washington, led initial planning meetings for a new Lewiston, Idaho, SBC church in the Carey Philley home two weeks before the organization. Lewiston, Idaho, Clearwater (Orchards) Baptist Church was organized August 2, 1953, and affiliated with the Columbia Basin association and the BGCOW. W. C. Carpenter arrived from Portales, New Mexico, in 1955 to serve as the HMB/BGCOW pastoral missionary. He organized other churches and constituted the Lewis-Clark association of Idaho. The early pastors were Ray Worley, Jack Stanfield, Truitt Rogers, Gene Medaris, Holt Sodeman, Don Clark, Ronald Seibert, W. C. Carpenter, Vernon Holliday, Carlton Flowers, and Monte Holloway.

Twin Buttes Baptist Association Constitutes (Idaho)

Messengers from four churches affiliated with the Utah association and BGCA constituted Twin Buttes association of Idaho on

October 3, 1953, at Pocatello FSBC. The founding churches were Kimberly FBC, Pocatello FSBC, Gooding FBC, and Rupert FBC. Idaho Falls, Idaho, Calvary Baptist Church pastor, C. Lee Bullard, served as moderator; Roy Worthley as vice-moderator; Ward Roberts as treasurer; and Mrs. Jack Dodson as clerk.

Feather River Baptist Association Constitutes (Nevada-California)

The messengers from ten northwestern Nevada and northeastern California churches constituted the Feather River association on October 7, 1953. Five churches constituting the association came from Sierra-Butte and one from Sacramento Sierra association. An earlier Feather River association had been constituted in 1944 but disbanded October 2, 1945, to constitute Sacramento Valley association. The SBGCC reported allocation of travel monies to L. E. Chism, Babbitt (Hawthorne), Nevada, pastor, to assist in starting new SBC churches and missions in Nevada.

Western Mission Growth Exhausts HMB Resources

On October 12, 1953, when Utah association held its third annual meeting, missionary Ira I. Marks reported that Utah association had sixteen organized churches and twenty-four preaching stations in Idaho, Nevada, and Utah. The churches conducted twenty-three VBSs in the summer of 1953.

S. F. Dowis asked westerners to be "patient, understanding, and sympathetic." The rapid growth in the western and pioneer states had exhausted HMB financial resources. When the SBGCC board met November 2, 1953, the eve of the Santa Barbara convention, they voted to raise the 1954 Cooperative Program goal to twenty-five thousand dollars.

HMB researcher, Phil Jones, reported that from 1950 to 1954 seventeen SBC churches were organized in the Intermountain West: five in Idaho, five in Nevada, and seven in Utah. Jones noted that each of these churches returned church letters in 1975.

Carson City, Nevada, First Baptist Church

The Dallas, Texas, Ross Avenue Baptist Church sponsored the Carson City FBC in 1954. The new church affiliated with Feather

River association and the SBGCC. L. D. Fisher served as the first pastor. In 1965 the Carson City church building was destroyed by an explosion from a gas leak. Early pastors were Elmer Herron, T. L. Collins, C. R. Gibson, Walter Pegg, Alfred Engleman, Paul Lewis, Ernest B. Myers (int.), Terry Arnold, and Ken DeLyser.

Reno, Nevada, Highland Terrace (FSBC) Baptist Church

Carson City, Nevada, FBC organized the Reno, Nevada, Highland Terrace (FSBC) in early 1954. The church affiliated with Feather River association and the SBGCC. The Reno church organized six churches, which in turn established five new churches that were sponsoring eight missions in 1989. The early pastors were J. L. Dugger, B. G. Bouchillion, W. R. Ward, Bob Rochelle, Jarrell Griffin, Claude Simmons, Jay Orr, Bob Wells (int.), David Kanton, Rudy Duett, Ernest Myers Jr., Bob McDuffie, Walker Campbell (int.), Ernest Myers Sr. (int.), Murray Day, and Tony Smith.

HMB Employs Courts Redford as Executive Secretary

When J. B. Lawrence retired from HMB leadership in 1953, Samuel Courts Redford had served twenty years as his associate. He knew all the details of the work and the fields served by the HMB and had a keen interest in SBC work in the Intermountain West. He assumed leadership of the HMB at age fifty-five, served for eleven years, and retired on December 31, 1964.

Redford was born September 4, 1898, at Calhoun, Missouri, to Eugene and Alice (Berry) Redford, a descendant of President Zachary Taylor. He grew up on farms and said he attended schoolhouse churches until he went to college. Redford graduated from Lone Wolf, Oklahoma, High School, OBU, University of Missouri, and SWBTS. He married Helen Ruth Ford of Henrietta, Texas, on May 24, 1921, and they had ten children. He served as Shawnee, Oklahoma, FBC associate pastor, OBU and SWBTS religious education and Bible professor, Southwest Baptist College president, Missouri Baptist Convention state staff member, HMB associate executive (1943–1954), and HMB executive director (1954–1964).

General Missionaries in the 1950s

Leonard Bonnie Sigle, HMB/SBGCC missionary to Nevada (1949–1969).

Ira and Gracie Marks, HMB/BGCA missionary to tri-states (1950–1961).

W. C. and Fanny Carpenter, HMB/BGCOW missionary to Idaho (1955–1959).

W. P. Brian, HMB/SBGCC pastoral missionary to Nevada (1955–1959).

J. Kelly Simmons, HMB/BGCA missionary to Idaho (1956–1957).

Joe and Elli Howard, HMB/BGCOW missionary to Idaho (1958–1967).

Charlie Tague, The Master's Builder

Charles and Virginia Tague gave their lives as church builders in the West (1952–1996).

Tague built thirty-eight buildings in Utah, Nevada, Colorado, Montana, California, and Mexico.

Vernal (UT) FBC organized in this tent during a snowstorm on November 26, 1946.

Tague finished the Vernal FBC building, his first, in May of 1954 and helped to dedicate it.

Tague pilots a tram. He hauled many volunteers around during a long church building career.

Tague and Pastor Gordon Elenbaas lay a cornerstone for Pleasant Grove (UT) FBC in 1960.

Courts Rayford made this first report to the SBC at the annual meeting in St. Louis, Missouri, in 1954:

> It is with gratitude to our Heavenly Father for His abounding love and marvelous blessing that I bring this my first report of the HMB of the SBC. The "Five Year Crusade" has entered its fifth year. In four years the HMB reports that the number of missionaries increased from 754 to 937 and student missionaries from 271 to 466. The HMB reports 1,081 new churches and 2,573 missions. In four years our SBC churches have baptized 1,467,820 converts, an increase of twenty-four percent over the previous four years.

Redford directed a HMB "Four Year Crusade, 1955–1958," helped start 1,598 new churches, expanded SBC work to all fifty states, increased income from $1.97 million to $5.86 million, and helped constitute the state conventions in Colorado, Indiana, Michigan, Ohio, and Utah-Idaho. He developed a jointly employed missionaries concept with state conventions, established the Canadian Baptists relationships, increased home missionaries from 936 to 2,353, enlarged chaplaincy so that it reached civilians, and improved the HMB church loan fund from $2.8 million to $16.6 million. Redford died April 11, 1977, and was buried at Boliver, Missouri. His wife died in 1979.

Ogden, Utah, Calvary Baptist Church

Clearfield, Utah, FBC organized the Ogden Calvary Baptist Church on January 8, 1954, with thirteen charter members. The new church affiliated with Utah association and the BGCA. Robert Lowe, the founding pastor, served the church for nine and a half years. In 1997 at the age of eighty Lowe wrote:

> I still look back to Utah as the greatest experience of my life. I served as a pioneer in an almost foreign culture supporting myself with help from my wonderful family of five girls and with never a complaint from any of them nor their wonderful

mother. We also left one baby there in the sandy soil of the cemetery in South Ogden. Anything that followed has been easy compared to Utah, but it was worth it.

The church bought property in 1957 and started construction in November 1958. High winds blew the building down, but construction started again and the new building was dedicated in February 1963. The early pastors were Robert Lowe, John Green, Robert Compere, Cliff Howery, and John Hamrick.

Henderson, Nevada, Temple (FSBC) Baptist Church
Matt Hale of Phoenix, Arizona, became burdened for Henderson and surveyed the city. The Boulder City FBC sent seven members to help establish Henderson, Nevada, Temple Baptist Church. When the church organized on January 10, 1954, with forty-eight charter members, it affiliated with Mohave association and the BGCA.

Mark Daniel of Waco, Texas, served as the first pastor (1955–1957). In three years Daniel led the Henderson church to establish five new churches: Las Vegas FSBC; Las Vegas Nellis; North Las Vegas Calvary; Las Vegas Redrock; and Henderson Faith. Daniel and E. W. Hunke Jr. graduated from the Waco, Texas, High School in the same 1942 graduating class. Hunke wrote:

> For three years Troy Brooks drove around Las Vegas praying, weeping, and looking for a foothold. Then God answered his prayer and sent Mark Daniel and Charles Ashcraft into the heart of Las Vegas. When the Sunrise Baptist Church organized as the fifth SBC church in Las Vegas, none had buildings. The devil tried to make us believe that we could not build a church unless we had a lot and money to build the first unit building. If Las Vegas had waited, we would have no churches there today.

After Charlie Tague completed the Parker, Arizona, pastorium, Daniel called Tague and asked him to build a 120-foot-long church building. During construction tornado-like winds blew all the roof trusses off. Insurance companies paid restoration costs. While at Henderson, Tague assisted the pastors, Charles Ashcraft, Wayne White, Robert Smith, and M. K. Wilder, with building plans for the Las Vegas FSBC, Nellis, Redrock, and Boulder City churches. Early pastors were Coker, Virgil Clubb, A. R. Coleman, Bernard Ford, Jim Sartain, Marvin Elam, Louis Gerdes, and Robert Holmes.

Kellogg, Idaho, First Baptist Church

The Dishman, Washington, FBC organized Kellogg, Idaho, FBC on April 4, 1954, with thirty charter members. The Kellogg mission began on November 1, 1953, when thirty-eight people gathered in one room at an Elk Creek, Idaho, church building. Gilbert Skaar, R. E. Milam, and Roland Hood participated in the constitutional service. The new church affiliated with Columbia Basin association and the BGCOW. The early pastors were Vernon Beggs, C. J. Mallett, Bruce Shrum (2), Frank Barnes, Tom Baird, James Fuller, Carl Estes, J. B. Greer, Jim McGuire, and Robert Cure. Polaris, Idaho, FBC merged with the Kellogg FBC in 1959.

Utah-Idaho-Nevada Regional Baptist Fellowship Forms

Representatives from fifteen Idaho, Nevada, and Utah SBC churches met at the SLC, Utah, Bethesda Bible Chapel on May 5–6, 1954, to create the Utah-Idaho-Nevada Regional Baptist Fellowship (UINRBF). Before arriving at SLC, the SBC leaders attended a Denver regional meeting. They spent a night at Vernal, Utah, to lead a dedication service for the new Vernal FBC building. The SBC leaders included: Porter Routh, SBC Executive Committee; Courts Redford, HMB; Jack Maben, BGCA president; Barry Garrett, *Baptist Beacon* editor; and A. C. Turner, SBGCC mission director who had just closed the revival he preached for Vernal FBC.

Utah Advances in the Summer of 1954

Naomi Hunke's brother, Kenneth Dean Savage, served as student intern at Vernal, Utah, FBC in the summer of 1954 after completing his first year at Fuller Theological Seminary in

California. He preached at the Roosevelt, Artesia, Vernal, and Gusher churches and on the Vernal radio station. He led VBS at Artesia and Vernal, and served on staff of the Utah Baptist Encampment in 1954. He said, "During my 1954 summer in Utah I determined that pastoral ministry was God's plan for my life." Savage later pastored the American Baptist churches at North Hollywood and Palm Desert, California.

During the summer of 1954 a retired Texas Baptist minister and his wife, previously unknown to the Hunkes, took them to lunch in Vernal, Utah. They said, "William and Bessie Fleming sent us on this journey west to find all the SBC preachers we could, take them to eat, and assure them of the Flemings' concern and prayer for the work in the West."

The HMB added a third western field-worker August 1, 1954, by employing George Cummins as the western missions superintendent at SLC, Utah. The HMB bought property on U.S. Highway 40 in SLC with plans to build the J. B. Lawrence Memorial building to serve as a western mission center. Cummins argued that the HMB western office should be located in Denver rather than SLC. When agreement could not be reached, the HMB canceled the project and sold the property to SLC Highland Baptist Church.

The Great Basin Zone of Utah association met at Ogden Calvary Baptist Church in June 1954 with thirty-eight in attendance. The six churches and three missions reported that the SS increased from 332 to 501. SLC Rose Park Baptist Church announced that plans for a groundbreaking service were set for July 11, 1954.

Idaho SBC Youth Meet for the First Statewide Retreat

BGCA missionary Ira Marks enlisted E. W. Hunke Jr., Vernal, Utah, FBC pastor, to go to Twin Falls, Idaho, in June 1954 to lead the first one-day youth retreat. Forty-six Idaho young people met at a camping area south of Twin Falls. Marks also asked the Vernal pastor to meet with three families wanting to start a Twin Falls SBC church. The Keysers and Masseys of Twin Falls asked Hunke to consider becoming their pastor, but he asked not to be considered because of a tenure of only one year at Vernal FBC. Hunke, who had helped ordain Harold Dillman at Gusher, Utah, told the group that Dillman planned to graduate from GGBTS in about one year and wished to return to Utah-Idaho. Harold and Opal Dillman arrived at Twin Falls, Idaho, July 1, 1955, after they had completed their studies. Others soon joined with the church in the basement rented for services at 333 Highland Avenue. Hunke also visited with the Roy L. Worthley family at Rupert, Idaho, FSBC, while he was in south central Idaho. Worthley served with Naomi Hunke at the Calwa Baptist Mission in California.

Utah Baptist Encampment Meets at Wolf Creek Pass

Utah Baptist Encampment met on August 2–7, 1954, at Wolf Creek Pass in the Uintah Mountains. E. W. Hunke Jr., camp program director, reported 232 registered, fifty-two saved, twenty-five rededications, and eight for special service. Eual Lawson of New Mexico, who baptized Naomi (Savage) Hunke at age seven at Wilson, Oklahoma, FBC, served as pastor. Victor Kaneubbe served as missionary, and J. B. Rounds of Oklahoma led campfire services.

BGCA Employs Utah Pastor as Missionary

Willis J. Ray, BGCA executive director, wrote to the Vernal FBC pastor, E. W. Hunke Jr., on October 5, 1954, saying, "You were unanimously elected as general missionary. We feel that you are God's man for the place; we pray that you will accept and start work soon. We had hoped that you could go to work by October 1 but did not want to disturb you while you were in your revival." The Hunkes moved to Casa Grande, Arizona, on November 1, 1954, to serve as the BGCA missionary to four associations across central Arizona that reached from California to New Mexico.

Yerington, Nevada, First Baptist Church

The Hawthorne, Nevada, Calvary Baptist Church started a new mission at Yerington in April 1953 with Charles Day as pastor. The Yerington FBC organized in September 1954 and affiliated with the Feather River association and the SBGCC. The early pastors were R. Morris, Irvin Derry, Coleman Burke, and L. E. Chism.

Inland Empire Baptist Association Constitutes (Idaho-Washington)
On October 11, 1954, messengers from SBC churches in the Idaho panhandle, northeast Washington, British Columbia, and Alberta met at Spokane, Washington, to organize the Inland Empire association. Gilbert Skaar served as the first moderator.

Charlie Tague Surrenders Life to Church Building Ministry
The Vernal, Utah, FBC church Training Union director, Charlie Tague, gave his life to constructing church buildings for the Lord in October 1954. Tague spent many hours together with his pastor building the Vernal church facility and talking about God's work. When his pastor, E. W. Hunke Jr., moved to Arizona in October 1954, Tague told him he wanted to spend the rest of his life constructing houses for the worship of God.

Charles Tague, the third of twelve children, was born to Joe and Angie Tague, on a farm in Butler County, Kansas. The family moved to town to find a school for the children. He was saved at age nine in a Methodist church. At age sixteen Tague worked as a carpenter in oil fields. On December 17, 1941, he joined the U.S. Navy and served aboard the *Selfridge* searching for U-boats in the Pacific. Soon after V-J Day, the Navy discharged Tague, and he spent 1945–1946 at San Pedro designing and building cabinets. In 1946 he received a contract to build a Vernal, Utah, motel, and he bought out the local lumberyard. His contact with Southern Baptists came when Nolan Beaird, Vernal FBC pastor, asked him for credit and help in building a new facility. After Wilcy Henton approved the loan application, Tague agreed to serve as contractor. He saw the building through to completion and dedication. Tague moved a building to add to the Artesia, Colorado, FBC after an oil corporation gave the facility to the church for paying off eighty-one dollars in back taxes. The day a jack slipped off a big moving timber and hit him in the head, he surrendered his life to God. Within two months Tague moved to Arizona to assist his former pastor and Stanfield FBC with a stalled building project. During Tague's ministry he constructed thirty-eight church buildings in Utah, Nevada, Colorado, Montana, California, and Mexico. Twenty-eight of these were in Utah.

Moab, Utah, First Baptist Church

Dragerton, Utah, Carbon Missionary Baptist Church organized the Moab FBC on Friday January 28, 1955, in the Mozark Machine Shop with thirty-two charter members. The new church voted to affiliate with Utah association and the BGCA. Eighty-five people, including fourteen ordained ministers, gathered to witness the birth of a new SBC church. H. M. Neff of Grand Junction, Colorado, who served as the first pastor, commuted to services each week. The discovery of uranium in southeastern Utah led to the emigration of people from the South in 1955. Members of the organizational council were Dalton Keith, Cal Gore, Anthon Wade, Bob McLeroy, Eddie Scroggins, J. W. Stone, Frank Sutton, N. T. James, W. W. Fordham, John Watson, John L. Smith, Ira Marks, Charles Ray, and James Akin. Ray read articles of faith; Fordham read the church covenant; and Frank W. Sutton, the BGCA state mission director, preached the sermon. The hand of Christian fellowship was extended to members of the new congregation. Early pastors were Leland Goodman (2) and Homer Wickes.

BGCOW Employs W. C. Carpenter as Missionary (Idaho)

Missionary Lewis Steed of Spokane, Washington, had organized Lewiston, Idaho, Clearwater (Orchards) Baptist Church on August 2, 1953, but the church had not grown. Because Idaho communities in the panhandle were growing, Lewiston needed a strong pastor who could establish a Baptist association. The HMB and BGCOW employed W. C. Carpenter of New Mexico as a pastoral missionary, the first SBC missionary to reside in Idaho.

William Carl Carpenter Jr. was born on June 23, 1914, at McLean, Texas, to William Sr. and Claudia (Kinard) Carpenter. He had three brothers and two sisters. Carpenter was saved at age ten through his parents' influence, baptized in July 1924 by the McLean, Texas, FBC, and ordained in 1939 by Tulia, Texas, Kaffir

Baptist Church. He wrote, "Mother expressed her concern as did a song leader in a revival. God showed me my need, and I responded." After graduation from McLean, Texas, High School, Baylor University, and SWBTS, he attended WBC. He married Fannie Bratcher on March 16, 1940, and they had five daughters. He pastored Texas Baptist churches at Tulia, Gainesville, and Kennedale; and New Mexico churches at Hobbs (associate pastor), Jal, Raton, and Portales before moving to Lewiston, Idaho. He wrote, "C. W. Bradford, a Raton, New Mexico, FBC deacon, moved to Lewiston, Idaho, and wrote me about coming north. I knew when I read the letter that God was leading me to Lewiston. God's Holy Spirit provided." The HMB and BGCOW employed him as pastoral missionary at Lewiston (1955–1959) and as the NWBC mission director (1965–1978) for northern Idaho, Oregon, Washington, and Canada. When Carpenter retired in 1978, the HMB and NWBC asked him to return to Lewiston as the missionary for the Lewis-Clark association of Idaho (1978–1980). After Fannie B. died of cancer on February 21, 1989, he married Norma Kathryn Nebling on November 23, 1990. He and his wife continued serving churches in retirement.

Sparks, Nevada, Temple Baptist Church
Reno, Nevada, FSBC organized the Sparks Temple Baptist Church in 1955. The church affiliated with Feather River association and the SBGCC. The early pastors were J. L. Dugger, Glenn Gurley, T. L. Collins, Crile Dean, Walter Guillaume, Ronald Coons, J. R. Sammons, Eugene Edwards, and Tim Gregory.

South Lake Tahoe, California, Lakeshore Baptist Church
Sponsoring Carson City, Nevada, FBC organized the South Lake Tahoe, California, Lakeshore (FSBC) Baptist Church in 1955. The church affiliated with Feather River association and the SBGCC. Charles Redmond served as the first pastor. The early pastors were Frank Reaves, Gene Hambin, Dwight Myers, D. M. Gentry, Andy Jackson, Gordon Siler, James Rigler, Arlie L. McDaniel, Sam B. Worley, Mike Proctor, Mark Johns, Dick Sanders, Adrian Hall (int.), Michael Hogue, and Gene Lee.

Winnemucca, Nevada, First Baptist Church

Don Ledbetter wrote, "A Swede from Oklahoma named Gustafson, who installed radar bubbles on top of Winnemucca Mountain, advertized [sic] that evangelical services would meet in his home." Reno, Nevada, FSBC agreed to sponsor the mission. The Winnemucca, Nevada, FBC organized in 1955 and affiliated with Feather River association and the SBGCC. George Roskan served as the first pastor. Early pastors were W. E. Dittmer, LaVern Inzer, Lennox Medford, Rex Thompson, and Charles Grisham (Ledbetter, *The History of Nevada Baptists*, 8/22/92).

Boise, Idaho, Mountain View Baptist Church

Denton, Texas, Highland Baptist Church organized the Boise, Idaho, Mountain View Baptist Church February 6, 1955, with thirty-seven charter members and Bob Wayman as the first pastor. GGBTS classmates, Robert E. Wayman and E. W. Hunke Jr. spent lunch time together each day while in seminary. One day in 1952 Hunke asked Wayman what he planned to do after graduation. Without hesitation, he replied, "I am going back to Boise, Idaho, where I was stationed as a serviceman, and start an SBC church." The church affiliated with Twin Buttes association and the BGCA. Initially the church met in a G.A.R. Hall at 714 State Street. J. S. Amyx Jr., a charter member and local contractor, used volunteer labor to construct the first building in 1956. Amyx died in his SS class on May 12, 1974. Early pastors were Bob Wayman, Clyde Godfrey, Bill Thornton, Oval Walker, Royce Shumate, and Gene Crewse. Highland church started new missions at Caldwell, Mountain Home, and Boise.

Western Preachers See Churches Grow

Eight Arizona SBC preachers led simultaneous revivals in Utah and Idaho on April 17–24, 1955, under the direction of Leroy Smith, the BGCA state evangelism director. The preachers, who rode in two cars up Highway 89, stopped to see the Grand Canyon and found it obscured by snowfall.

Fred McCaulley, HMB western field-worker, reported in 1955 that he preached sixty-two sermons, taught forty-eight classes, led fifty-seven prayer meetings, and had eighty-four saved, twenty-five additions by letter, and thirty-five by baptism. The new Tentmaker program had grown from fifteen in 1951 to sixty in 1952 and to seventy-six in 1954.

Logan, Utah, First Baptist Church

Farmersville, Louisiana, FBC organized the Logan, Utah, FBC on May 2, 1955, with twenty-four charter members and Leon Maxwell of Farmersville as the first pastor. The church affiliated with Utah association and the BGCA. Early pastors were John Strom, Jimmy Floyd, Al Norris, Riley McCall, and Jon Engstrom.

Las Vegas, Nevada, First Southern Baptist Church

The Las Vegas, Nevada, FSBC organized on June 26, 1955, with thirty-three charter members. The church affiliated with Mohave association and the BGCA. After pastor Charles Ashcraft of the Los Alamos, New Mexico, FBC visited Las Vegas in 1954 and found no SBC church, he left his New Mexico pastorate and moved his wife, Sarah, and three sons to Las Vegas. In January 1955 he used equity from sale of his Los Alamos home for living expenses. He visited and witnessed for four months before starting the Las Vegas mission on May 8, 1955. The Ashcrafts, who had a son with polio needing surgery, refused HMB pastoral aid saying that, "God will supply our needs. Others need denominational support more than we do." He resigned to serve as the first UISBC executive secretary on January 1, 1965. Charlie Tague helped the church with its building plans. FSBC started missions at Twin Lakes (1964), Paradise Valley (1980), and Foothills Southern (1989) in Las Vegas. Other early pastors were Dan C. Stringer Jr., George Wilson, Darrell Evenson, Douglas Wooderson, Jim McLeroy, and Bill Underwood.

Nevada Baptist Association Constitutes (Nevada)

Messengers from Nevada SBC churches affiliated with Feather River association of California constituted Nevada association on July 19–20, 1955, at the Tahoe Village, Lake Tahoe, California, Lakeshore Baptist Church. The association affiliated with the SBGCC. These churches were Carson City FBC; Hawthorne Calvary Baptist Church; Reno FSBC; Sparks Temple Baptist Church; Winnemucca FBC; and Yerington FBC. Tahoe Village, California, Lakeshore Baptist Church affiliated later. At the request of the Nevadans, the HMB and SBGCC permitted Feather River associational missionary, L. B. Sigle, to move to Sparks, Nevada, to serve as the Nevada association missionary. Sigle had related to Nevada churches as SBGCC missionary to Sierra Butte association (1949–1954) and Feather River association (1954–1958).

Bonners Ferry, Idaho, First Baptist Church

The Bonners Ferry, Idaho, FBC organized on July 22, 1955, with fourteen charter members. The church affiliated with Inland Empire association and the BGCOW. When five families from Texas moved to Bonners Ferry and found no SBC church, they contacted missionary Lewis Steed of Spokane for help. He helped them start the mission. The early pastors were Arnold Ashburn (int.), Jack Kehler, Bobby Vann, Fred Opper, Leo Mangum, Joe Howard (int.), Lee Brock, Don Pemp, Robert Kerby, Robert Kock, and Charles Stockett.

Caldwell, Idaho, First Southern (Jordan Valley) Baptist Church

The Boise, Idaho, Mountain View Baptist Church organized the Caldwell FSBC September 6, 1955, with twenty-seven charter members. The Caldwell mission started on March 6, 1955, in the Odd Fellows Hall with Pastor Bob Wayman preaching. Eight people united with the church in the first service. Organizational council members were Bob Wayman, Harold Dillman, Ira Marks, Clyde Barrows, J. Amyx Sr., and Mr. Zink. When J. O. Camp led the simultaneous revival on April 17–24, 1955, thirty-two joined by letter and one by baptism. Keith Hamm served as first pastor. The new church affiliated with Twin Buttes association and BGCA. Early pastors were Bob Floyd (int.), J. E. Bradford, J. B. Greer (2),

Frank Boydston, Dick Ashworth, Wayne Naylor, Lewis Demster, Donald Douglass, and Gail Graves.

Salt Lake Baptist Association Constitutes (Utah)

Messengers from eight Utah and Nevada churches constituted the Salt Lake association on September 12–13, 1955: Ely, Nevada, FBC; Tooele FBC; Clearfield FBC; SLC Rose Park Baptist Church; Logan FBC; Ogden Calvary Baptist Church; Provo FBC; and Roy FSBC. The association elected Charles Ray moderator and Orville Miller clerk.

SBGCC Employs W. P. Brian as Pastoral Missionary (Nevada)

After the constitution of Nevada association July 19, 1955, the HMB and SBGCC employed W. P. Brian as pastoral missionary of the Hawthorne church. He served as missionary in Nevada and the Mojave Desert area of California. His mailing address was P.O. Box 1364, Hawthorne, Nevada. Brian, a native of Desdemona, Texas, attended WBC and graduated from HSU. He served as the missionary for four SBGCC associations: Shasta Southern and Sierra Butte Southern (1955–1956) and Mojave Desert Southern and Nevada (1955–1959). Long distances, difficult mountain travel, and the time changes in Nevada and California made missionary work difficult for both Brian in Nevada and Sigle in California.

Twin Falls, Idaho, First Southern (Magic Valley) Baptist Church

The Pocatello, Idaho, FSBC organized the Twin Falls FSBC on September 24, 1955, with thirty-three charter members. The church affiliated with Twin Buttes association and the BGCA. After the church bought property on the corner of Washington and Filer Streets, it completed its first unit in July 1956. During Harold Dillman's ministry more than one hundred joined the fellowship, twenty-five by baptism. The Dillmans moved to Cedar City, Utah, in 1957 to serve as pastoral missionary for southwestern Utah. Early pastors were Dillman, D. E. Acker, Lavoid Robertson, Bennie Wright, Howard Wheeler, Cleve Milling, and Aster Williams. When the church ceased to meet after losing its military pastor, missionary Lewis Demster reorganized the church and changed the name to Magic Valley Baptist Church.

Changes Provide for New Growth

Twin Buttes association of Idaho voted in annual session in October 1955 to continue its quarterly statewide meetings and to divide southern Idaho into three zones: Boise, Twin Falls, and Pocatello. Each zone later formed into an association.

The BGCA seated messengers from seven new Intermountain West churches at the November 8–10, 1955, BGCA annual meeting which was held at Phoenix Central Baptist Church. There were three from Idaho, two from Nevada, and two from Utah. S. F. Dowis, who represented the HMB, preached to the messengers from the Intermountain West.

When Charlie Tague and Robert and Cora Johnson completed a new building for Shelby, Montana, FBC in December 1955, Tague moved to Phoenix to help Grand Canyon College (GCC) build their student center. Willis Ray then sent Tague to Tacna, Arizona, to construct a portable unit. While attending Bible study at the Darlin home in Tacna, and worshiping at Wellton FBC, he met and married Virginia Seale.

When Leroy Smith resigned as BGCA state evangelism secretary on December 31, 1955, to serve on the CBGC staff, the HMB and BGCA employed W. D. Lawes to succeed him. Lawes served southern Nevada, Utah, Idaho, and Arizona. Wade Armstrong succeeded H. H. Stagg as the SBGCC evangelism secretary to serve western Nevada in 1956 when Stagg accepted a missionary position. Lewis Steed continued to serve the BGCOW in northern Idaho. Charles Matthews, the HMB evangelism leader, retired in 1955 and was replaced by Leonard Sanderson of Louisiana in 1956.

Lake Mead Baptist Association Constitutes (Nevada)

Following the annual Mohave Baptist Association annual meeting at Henderson, Nevada, FSBC October 3, 1955, messengers from three Nevada SBC churches constituted Lake Mead association: Henderson FSBC, Boulder City FSBC, and Las Vegas

FSBC. Charles Ashcraft, Las Vegas FSBC pastor, served as the first moderator. A one hour time difference between Arizona and Nevada created problems which led to the constitution of the new association.

Burley, Idaho, First Baptist Church

The Burley, Idaho, FBC organized on December 15, 1955, with twenty-four charter members. Fred Higginbotham had started the Burley mission at a four-unit apartment house located at Albion and Sixteenth Streets in 1955. The new church affiliated with Twin Buttes association and the BGCA. Organization council members were Clyde Barrow, Morris Wall, Ira Marks, and Clinton Ridgeway. The early pastors were Fred Higginbotham, Oval Walker, Ben Pate, Richard Horn, Willis Blair, Donald Douglass, Kyle Robertson, Mark Haumschilt, and B. G. Stumberg.

Lovelock, Nevada, First Baptist Church

Winnemucca, Nevada, FBC organized the Lovelock FBC in 1956. The new church affiliated with Nevada association and the SBGCC. Early pastors were Frank Sisson, L. D. Fisher, LaVern Inzer (int.), Lewis Bridges, Bob Kock (supply), Clem McGregor, Silas Lash, Wayne Maynard (int.), Don Lewis, Roger Fraye, Charles Anderson, and Ted Kern.

BGCA Employs Kelly Simmons as Missionary (Idaho)

After Willis Ray preached at Shreveport, Louisiana, FBC on February 27, 1955, and told of Idaho mission needs, the church sent funds to the HMB for a new missionary. The HMB and BGCA employed North Waco (Texas) Baptist Church pastor, J. Kelly Simmons, to serve as the general missionary to Idaho on January 1, 1956. Simmons was born at Westminster, Texas, in 1905. He was saved at Sherman, Texas, in 1916, and ordained to the ministry in 1927. He graduated from Baylor University with a journalism major, and attended SWBTS. Simmons taught high school, served as chaplain in World War II, and pastored six Texas churches. He was awarded the Bronze Medal for service on the Normandy beaches on D-Day, and was given the rank of lieutenant-colonel in the chaplaincy reserves. After his first wife died and left him with four small children, Simmons married Edna, the widow of a medical doctor, who traveled west with him in mission work. He served in Idaho for one year before moving to Arizona to serve Gila Valley, Estrella, and Yuma associations. His experience as a newspaper reporter in Sherman, Texas, equipped him to serve as editor for three Baptist papers: *Baptist Beacon* of Arizona (1958–1960); *Rocky Mountain Baptist* of Colorado (1960–1961); and *California Southern Baptist* (1961–1963). Before Simmons died of cancer on February 1, 1963, at the age of fifty-eight, his editorials about his struggle with cancer received nationwide attention. He was buried at Waco, Texas, after memorial services were held at both Fresno, California, and Waco.

Las Vegas, Nevada, Nellis Baptist Church

Chaplain Aubrey Halsell, who had initiated Alaska SBC work on September 19, 1943, was stationed at Las Vegas, Nevada, Nellis Air Force Base in 1956. Halsell announced that a Baptist service would be held at the Air Force Base chapel. After he introduced Charles Ashcraft, Las Vegas FSBC pastor, Ashcraft preached, gave an invitation, and organized the Nellis Baptist Church on January 22, 1956, with thirteen charter members. The church affiliated with Lake Mead association and the BGCA. Services were held at the Mayfair Shopping Center until the church erected its own building. Charlie Tague assisted the church with building plans. Early pastors were Robert Smith, Jack Walker, Robert Norvell, Bill Duncan, Karel Sylvanus (2), Quinton Montgomery, Vancil Gibson, Oran Brown (int.), and Loyd Nelson.

Las Vegas, Nevada, Charleston Heights (Redrock) Baptist Church

Henderson, Nevada, FSBC organized the Las Vegas Charleston Heights (Redrock) Baptist Church on May 6, 1956, with six charter members. Wayne White served as the first pastor. Members of the council were Charles Ashcraft, Marion K. Wilder, Virgil Reeves, and Joe Singleton. The church affiliated with Lake Mead association and the BGCA. The FMB employed Wayne and Winnie White as missionaries to Mexico in 1963. Charlie Tague helped the church with building plans. Early pastors were Wayne White, Don Loving, Vern Baker, Roy Worthley, Carey Smith, and Larry Worley.

HMB Leaders Report Continuing Growth in the West

C. C. Warren of North Carolina, SBC president, challenged the 12,254 messengers at the Kansas City SBC in 1956 to start 30,000 churches and missions. The "30,000 Movement" (1956–1964) provided Southern Baptists with momentum for nine years. George W. Cummins, the HMB western missions superintendent at SLC, reported that the HMB now worked in fifteen western states.

The HMB western church loan-building worker, Wiley Henton, reported the HMB spent $213,985 constructing mission buildings in 1955. He led 141 conferences, visited 350 churches, held four revivals, and preached 237 sermons.

Fred McCaulley, HMB field-worker for western U.S.A., reported that Tentmakers included two categories of workers: regulars (full time) and reserves (summer only). A Tentmaker earned his own living and volunteered in Christian service under direction of a missionary or pastor. In 1955, forty-one reserves visited 2,243 homes and had eighty-nine professions of faith. McCaulley visited 245 churches, ninety-seven campuses, preached 388 sermons, and held fourteen revivals resulting in seventy-four added to the churches.

Charles Ray reported that Utah Baptists held the Utah Baptist Encampment on July 16–21 at Soapstone. W. W. Fordham and Charles Ray worked as camp directors and Ira Marks as camp manager. Pastor H. W. Bartlett of Big Springs, Texas, preached, and HMB missionary Vena Aguillard told missionary stories.

Roy Ferguson reported that Twin Buttes association sponsored the Idaho summer camp at Sun Valley, Idaho, on August 6–10, 1956. Pastor Guy Moore of Ft. Worth, Texas, Keith Hamm, Carroll Peaden, Sid Davis, J. Kelly Simmons, Edna Simmons, Charles Ray, Ila Westerman, Jerry Cook, Virginia Berg, and Mrs. Virgil Swenson served as the program leaders.

In 1956 Wiley Henton reported that he visited 359 churches, led five revivals, and preached 198 sermons which resulted in 130 saved, 193 additions to churches, and seventy-five commitments for special service. He valued the HMB mission buildings built in 1956 at $105,480. Fred McCaulley reported that 194 Tentmakers served in 1956. McCaulley preached 242 sermons, had thirty-two saved, and thirty-one surrender for special service.

Monticello, Utah, First Southern Baptist Church

Cortez, Colorado, FSBC organized the Monticello, Utah, FSBC in September 1956. Bob McLeroy, a carpenter by trade, served as the first pastor. The church affiliated with Colorado's San Juan association and the BCNM. After FSBC purchased a lot, the city refused to grant the church the building permit because the city wanted the right-of-way for a road through the property. After the building was completed, the city refused to let the church hook up to the water supply. Wings for Christ flew many supply pastors to Monticello to keep the work alive. Early pastors were James Stone, Jack Hanna, Chris Woodard (2), Byron Moore, T. J. Gamble, and Vernon Schafter.

Kearns, Utah, First Baptist Church

The SLC, Utah, Rose Park (FSBC) Baptist Church organized the Kearns FBC September 30, 1956, with thirty-eight charter members. Council members were Charles Ray, James McFatridge, John Smith, George Williams, Ira Marks, Roger Baxter, Louis Warren, L. C. Woods, Walter White, and Ralph Hall. Roy Ferguson served as the first pastor. The church affiliated with Salt Lake association and the BGCA. After meeting for many years in the pastor's home, an Army barracks building, and a community hall, the church bought land and entered a new building constructed by Charlie Tague in September 1958. The early pastors were Roy Ferguson, Bill Thornton, Earl Keating (int.), Russell Whetstone, Ron Chamberlain, David Henshaw, Randy Gunter, and Talmage Crawford. The church started missions at Granger and West Jordan.

BGCA Employs Charles McKay as Executive Secretary

On October 1, 1956, the BGCA employed Charles Lloyd McKay, the BSSB enlistment/evangelism director, as BGCA executive secretary, and approved the new staff plan he recommended. McKay was born on May 27, 1908, the third of six children of Charley C. and Sally Williams McKay at Pelahatchie, Mississippi. He was saved and baptized at age twelve. He taught school for seven years. After graduation from Mississippi College and NOBTS (Th.D.), he pastored Mississippi and Louisiana Baptist churches. At age nineteen, he married Fana Measells, and they had two daughters. Because McKay increased Pascagoula, Mississippi, FBC's SS enrollment from 865 to 1665 in two years, the BSSB employed him to promote "A Million More in 54" and the "30,000 Movement."

Blanding, Utah, First Baptist Church

The Monticello, Utah, FBC organized the Blanding FBC in 1957 with Eugene Edge as the first pastor. The church affiliated with San Juan association of Colorado and the BCNM. The early pastors were Otis Edwards, Eugene Ege, I. C. McBride, John Casement, Charles Zehnder, Carroll Redwine, Roger Stacy, Wayne Fults, Ken Prewett, and R. M. Torres.

Rangely, Colorado, First Baptist Church

The Artesia, Colorado, FBC organized Rangely, Colorado, FBC in 1957 with thirty-eight charter members. FBC affiliated with Utah association and the BGCA. Darwin E. Welsh pastored both churches until September 1957 when he moved his family to SLC to pastor Rose Park (FSBC) Baptist Church.

Twin Falls, Idaho, Eastside Baptist Church

The Twin Falls, Idaho, Eastside Baptist Church organized on October 24, 1957, and affiliated with Magic Valley association and the BGCA. After Robert Schreckenburg started the Jackpot, Nevada, mission in 1975, he provided child care and Bible study for casino workers. Magic Valley association withdrew from the church and it affiliated with Nevada association and the SBGCC.

Richie Weers and Doug Arendsee served as early pastors. After Eastside gave up the Jackpot mission in 1985, the church again affiliated with Magic Valley association and the UISBC.

HMB Formalizes the Pastoral Missionary Program

The HMB formally launched the pastoral missionary program on January 1, 1957, with nine requirements: (1) the area must have a city with thirty thousand residents; (2) the pastor must start new missions; (3) the church and pastor must agree on a program; (4) the church would select a pastor with HMB approval; (5) the HMB would provide two hundred dollars as salary and the state one hundred dollars; (6) the state board would supervise the missionary; (7) twelve months would be allowed before starting a new mission; (8) the subsidy would be decreased each year; and (9) the sponsoring church would supervise the mission work.

SBGCC Employs Edmond Walker as State Mission Director

After the resignation of A. C. Turner as SBGCC state mission director, the HMB and SBGCC employed Edmond Richmond Walker as the associate executive/missions secretary on January 1, 1957. Walker, who led the El Monte, California, Calvary Baptist Church for seven years, added 1,100 members to the church, 523 of them by baptism. He was deeply interested in Nevada Baptist work, and made frequent visits to train leadership there.

Walker was born on September 12, 1918, at Elizabeth, Arkansas. He was saved at age fourteen and baptized in Viola, Arkansas. He said, "I was bringing cows home on a farm when I remembered someone saying this might be our last day. I knelt in the field and prayed for Christ to save me." He graduated from high school, AOBU, SBTS, and GGBTS (Th.D.). Walker married Lurie Brown, and they had two sons. He wrote:

> At the age of nineteen while I was in AOBU, God and summer missionaries, Ottis Denney and Lavern Davis, influenced me to look west for my ministry. Lurie and I came to California on our honeymoon. Clel Collier asked me to speak at

E. W. Hunke Jr. 117

> Sacramento, Gardenland Baptist Church. When I returned to seminary for the final year, I felt a definite call to California. I corresponded with A. F. Crittendon and John Farmer. When I graduated, we packed the car and drove west to take secular work and start a new mission. A telegram from a Modesto, church arrived at my brother's home in San Diego, asking us to come for Wednesday prayer service. They called me that evening.

Walker pastored churches in Arkansas, Kentucky, and Indiana. He pastored at Modesto four years and at El Monte for seven years. After he served as SBGCC assistant and the interim executive director (1957–1963), the Hawaii Baptist Convention employed him as executive director (1963–1982). On retirement, the HMB employed him as a national consultant on senior adult ministries. He suffered with Parkinson's disease. A July 16, 1992, stroke paralyzed his right leg, and he entered a Sacramento convalescent home where he died on January 19, 1994.

Salt Lake City, Utah, Highland Baptist Church

The SLC, Utah, Rose Park (FSBC) Baptist Church organized the SLC Highland Baptist Church February 12, 1957, with ten charter members. The new church affiliated with Salt Lake association and the BGCA. The church secured the property which the HMB purchased to build a J. B. Lawrence Memorial building for its western office. Charlie Tague constructed the building in 1959. The early pastors were Roland Smith and W. C. "Bill" Rounds, son of Utah pioneer J. B. Rounds.

BGCA Employs Barron Honeycutt as Missionary (Idaho)

After Barron E. Honeycutt served as the BGCOW missionary to Columbia Basin association in Oregon (1954–1957), the HMB and BGCA employed him as the missionary to Twin Buttes association on March 1, 1957. Honeycutt led Twin Buttes to disband and form three new associations: Boise Valley, Eastern Idaho, and Magic Valley. When he resigned in 1958, he returned to North Carolina.

A Tribute to Some Pioneer Pastors

Gilbert O. and Greta Skaar, first Idaho-born SBC pastor (1951–1956).

Jim and Beverly McLeroy, both NVBC presidents (1981–1983; 1986–1987).

Morris Thomas Wall, first pastor ordained in Idaho (1953–1956).

Arthur Leonard Nunn Jr., first U-I Fellowship president (1960–1961).

Charles H. Ashcraft, Las Vegas, NV/FSBC founder (1955–1965).

Lavoid Robertson and Bill Thornton pastored in both Utah and Idaho.

Historic Meetings in the Intermountain West

First Idaho-Nevada-Utah Regional Fellowship Meeting. *Representatives from fifteen Idaho, Nevada, and Utah SBC churches met at the SLC, Utah, Bethesda Bible Chapel on May 5–6, 1954, to create a three-state regional fellowship. SBC leaders who helped form the regional fellowship were Courts Redford and Solomon F. Dowis, HMB; Porter Routh, SBC Executive Committee; A. C. Turner, SBGCC; and Jack Maben, Barry Garrett, and Willis J. Ray, BGCA.*

Utah-Idaho Southern Baptist Convention Organized. *Fifty-two Utah and Idaho churches sent 363 messengers and visitors to organize the UISBC at the SLC, Utah, FSBC on October 29, 1964, with operations to begin on January 1, 1965. The fifty-two churches affiliated with seven associations: Boise Valley, Magic Valley, and Eastern Idaho in Idaho; and Golden Spike, Salt Lake, Utah, and Gideon in Utah. A. B. Cash, HMB pioneer missions secretary, helped organize the board.*

Mountain Home, Idaho, First Southern Baptist Church

The Boise, Idaho, Mountain View Baptist Church organized the Mountain Home, Idaho, FSBC on March 15, 1957, with thirty-eight charter members. Organizational council members were Ray T. Hart, Robert Wayman, Harold Dillman, Bradley Sloan, J. S. Amyx, and B. E. Honeycutt. Earlier attempts by J. B. Rounds to start the Mountain Home work ended when an airman died in a plane crash. The church affiliated with Boise Valley association and the BGCA. After the purchase of land in 1956, the church completed its first unit in 1959. Early pastors were Bob Floyd, J. S. Amyx. Ray T. Hart, Gale Walters, Alton Thomas, Mayo Brown, E. J. Chafin, Raymond Cearley, Dale Freeman, C. A. Thomas, and George Slaughter.

Glenns Ferry, Idaho, Laird Memorial (FBC) Baptist Church

The Idaho Falls, Idaho, Calvary Baptist Church organized the Glenns Ferry, Idaho, Laird Memorial (FBC) Baptist Church in June 1957 with seven charter members. Organizational council members were B. E. Honeycutt, Ray T. Hart, Robert Wayman, Les Gentry, C. R. Barrow, Harold Dillman, Fred Higginbotham, W. B. Chandler, and Ed Fast. The church affiliated with Twin Buttes association and the BGCA. In June 1953 Larry Maxwell rented a V.F.W. Hall at Glenns Ferry, Idaho, to preach his first sermon to two high school friends from Gooding. The mission met later in a one-room school building purchased as a memorial to airman Laird who died in a plane crash. The early pastors were Milton Hass, Harold Ernce, Larry Maxwell (2), Norman Bellury, Leonard Vose, A. L. Davis, Bill Cline, Harry Johnson, and Jim Burton. Glenns Ferry started new missions at Stanley and Clayton, Idaho; worked with migrants in labor camps; reached out to Indians; and ordained Donald Forbes and James Myers to the ministry.

North Las Vegas, Nevada, Calvary Baptist Church

The Henderson, Nevada, FSBC organized the North Las Vegas Calvary Baptist Church September 29, 1957, with sixteen charter members. Virgil Reeves served as the first pastor. The church affiliated with Lake Mead association and the BGCA. Council members were Charles Ashcraft, Troy Brooks, M. K. Wilder, and Jack Coker. The church purchased property March 25, 1957, and entered their first permanent building in 1958. The early pastors were Virgil Reeves, James G. Jamieson (2), Hugh Hamilton, Sherman Lawson, Bob Warren, Earl Hosea, and Jaffus Haley.

Idaho Southern Baptists Constitute Three Associations

Twin Buttes association dissolved in 1957 to form three new Idaho associations. Messengers from three churches constituted Boise Valley (Treasure Valley) association at Caldwell. Members of the constitutional council were Bob Wayman, Ray T. Hart, Keith Hamm, Ben Slack, Edward Kanady, Jesse Bradford, and Mary Brennan. Messengers constituted Magic Valley association. In 1969 these churches reported thirty-six baptisms, 626 members, $41,686 total gifts, and $7,174 in mission gifts. The messengers constituted Eastern Idaho association. In 1969 these churches reported sixty baptisms, 909 members, $53,459 total gifts, and $5,703 in mission gifts. All three associations affiliated with the BGCA.

Wilder Views Nevada SBC Future as Impossible

M. K. Wilder, a former Boulder City, Nevada, FSBC pastor, felt that work in the Silver State would be long and hard. In a taped interview in 1957, he said:

> Notice that the towns and population in the state of Nevada are strung along its borders. Las Vegas, Boulder City, and Henderson churches, and those in the southern section are with the Arizona convention. Then come up a ways. This area will never amount to much because of the sparseness of its population. Go up to the area around Reno, and you have another situation, but look how far you have to travel for any kind of fellowship . . . I think that Reno and that northern area should stay with the California convention.

Las Vegas should stay with the Arizona convention. Ely and Wendover should go with Utah, and those up around Battle Mountain should go in with Idaho. I don't see any other way to work it; it's pathetic when you look at the map where you see the whole heart of Nevada like a desolate desert with firing ranges and atomic energy test fields. I do not see how Nevada could ever organize. Utah and Idaho are hard; Nevada is impossible.

Pleasant Grove, Utah, First Baptist Church

Provo, Utah, FBC organized the Pleasant Grove, Utah, FBC in a private home with twenty-three charter members on October 6, 1957, with Gordon Elenbaas serving as the first pastor. Members of the organizational council came from nine SBC churches. The new church affiliated with Salt Lake association and the BGCA. After meeting in the library for two years, the church bought land, built the first unit, and laid the cornerstone on December 6, 1959, with Mayo Brown, Provo FBC pastor, preaching. Charlie Tague built the new church facility. Early pastors were Gordon Elenbaas, Claude Hill, James Minnis, and James Akin.

Mayo and Celia Brown accepted the call of Provo, Utah, FBC on December 1, 1957, and moved to Utah. The U.S. Air Force stationed Brown at SLC on his return from Europe. After his discharge in 1945, he returned home with the conviction that some must go to Utah to preach to the Mormons. Brown's testimony led Robert and Dot Lowe to go to Ogden in 1952. Lowe wrote:

> On a four week trip to North Carolina in 1957 to celebrate my parents' fiftieth anniversary, I visited Mayo and Celia at Ethel, Mississippi, where Mayo served as pastor. As they looked at my slides, Celia said that she saw the church where Mayo was to pastor (Lowe, letter to Hunke, 8/12/97).

Brown led a revival at the pastorless Provo FBC in September on Lowe's recommendation, and in October 1957 the church extended a call to the Browns to come to Utah.

BGCA Employs E. W. Hunke Jr. as State Mission Secretary

The BGCA employed Edmund William Hunke Jr. as the state stewardship secretary in December 1956, and later joined the HMB in employing him as associate executive/state mission secretary on December 3, 1957. He served as superintendent of the HMB/BGCA cooperative mission work in Utah, Idaho, Nevada, and Arizona (1956–1966).

Nampa, Idaho, First Southern Baptist Church

Caldwell, Idaho, FSBC organized the Nampa FSBC on December 17, 1957, with twenty-eight charter members. Caldwell FSBC pastor Keith Hamm led the service. The new church affiliated with Boise Valley association and the BGCA. Council members were B. E. Honeycutt, Ray T. Hart, Robert Wayman, and Grover Eppely. Early pastors were E. J. Jenkins, Roy Myers (int.), Larry Rothchild, Leo Sullivan, Herbert Johnson, Gordon Ball, Ralph Bowen, and Harry Johnson. Nampa FSBC started missions at Meridian, Emmett, Nyssa (OR), and Faith.

Sun Valley, Nevada, First (Green Valley) Baptist Church

J. L. Dugger organized the Sun Valley, Nevada, First (Green Valley) Baptist Church in 1958. The church affiliated with Nevada association and the SBGCC. Early pastors were Ray Canary, E. T. Wimberly, Jonathan Jackson, J. C. Scarbrough, Adrian Spencer, Jim Haggard, Bob Wells (int.), Charles Grisham, Steven Junke, William Hines, William Parker, Walt Alexander, John Hopkins, Jess DeBoard, Don Ledbetter (int.), and J. R. Sammons.

BGCA Reports Personnel Changes in the Intermountain West

The HMB transferred Irvin Dawson, missionary to the Spanish-speaking people of Sacramento, California, to the BGCA on May 1, 1957. Dawson served as language missions director for Utah, Idaho, Nevada, and Arizona (1957–1966).

The fourth annual Utah-Idaho-Nevada Regional Mission Fellowship (UINRMF) met at the Twin Falls, Idaho, FSBC on May 14, 1957. The speakers were Charles McKay of Phoenix, Courts

Redford of Atlanta, and Charles Leonard of the FMB. Sid Davis led the singing; BGCA general missionaries B. E. Honeycutt of Idaho and Ira Marks of Utah reported on missionary work; and Herman Sollie of Utah and Clyde R. Barrow of Idaho preached.

After completing the Winslow, Arizona, FBC facility in 1958, Charlie Tague and his family returned to Utah where they lived for the next eight years. They purchased a home at 4730 Delsa Drive in SLC for $12,850 and wondered how to make the seventy-eight-dollar-per-month payments on their small income. Tague built new church buildings at Kearns, Highland, Pleasant Grove, Holladay, Granger, Glendale, Bountiful, Tooele, Layton, White Rocks, and Logan, in Utah; Evanston in Wyoming; and Beatty and Ely in Nevada.

On January 1, 1958, the HMB and BGCA employed four pastoral missionaries: M. K. Wilder at Page, Arizona; E. J. Jenkins at Nampa, Idaho; Bob Wayman at Richfield, Utah; and Harold Dillman at Cedar City, Utah. On January 13, 1958, HMB/BGCA pastoral missionary Bob Wayman of Richfield, Utah, wrote:

> It is too early to say how the work will shape up. However, the prospects look good, and we have found some real interest. We have not yet decided on a place to hold our services, but we intend to start public services on the first Sunday in February. We had a private service yesterday for the first time with nine present and an eight dollar offering.

Harold Dillman wrote:

> I began my official duties as the pastor missionary at Cedar City on January 1, 1958. Since arriving here, we have received definite promises from four families to support a regular church program here soon. In a neighboring community there is a SS with Baptist leadership that teaches the shed blood of Christ as the plan of salvation, and some attending are being saved.

Pocatello, Idaho, Central Baptist Church

Pocatello, Idaho, FSBC organized the Pocatello Central Baptist Church on January 5, 1958, with thirty-seven charter members. The Idaho Falls Calvary Baptist Church pastor, Clyde Barrow, preached the sermon. Organizational council members were Ray Mills, C. R. Barrow, Mike Marko, and Gale Walters. The church affiliated with Eastern Idaho association and the BGCA. Raymond Glass served as the first pastor.

Brigham City, Utah, First Baptist Church

The Brigham City FBC met at the War Memorial building March 23, 1958, and organized with eleven charter members. The church affiliated with Salt Lake association and the BGCA. After they purchased property in June 1959, they completed a new building in 1961. The early pastors were William Harris Jr., James Morgan, Horace Fisher (int.), John Embery, Cecil Morgan, Tom Vance, Robert Copeland, Charles Greene, and James Herod.

Las Vegas, Nevada, Sunrise Baptist Church

The Las Vegas, Nevada, Nellis Baptist Church organized the Las Vegas Sunrise Baptist Church on April 13, 1958, in an auto garage with thirty-seven charter members. Organizational council members were Troy Brooks, Robert Smith, Wayne White, H. Merritt, Virgil Reeves, and E. W. Hunke Jr. Other program participants were Virgil Clubb, R. Loden, and Eugene Mockerman, the first pastor. The new church affiliated with Lake Mead association and the BGCA. Sunrise purchased and remodeled the auto garage for church use. The church purchased property, broke ground for its first building on August 30, 1959, and completed the first unit in 1962. The early pastors were Mockerman, E. L. Pennington, Everett Moore, Stanley Unruh, Don Oliver, and Michael Rodrigues.

BGCOW Employs Joe Howard as Missionary (Idaho)

The HMB and BGCOW employed Joe Theo Howard as missionary to Inland Empire association on May 1, 1958. The SBC churches located in the Idaho panhandle affiliated with Inland Empire association. Howard was born January 10, 1902, at Devine, Texas, to Steven M. and Clara (Essary) Howard. He had three brothers and five sisters. Howard trusted Christ at age ten on June 15, 1912, and was baptized five days later in J. R. Howard's pond across the street from Devine, Texas, Black Creek Baptist Church. The church ordained Howard on September 10, 1923. He married Elli Bryson on June 14, 1925, at Devine, Texas, and they had two children. After he graduated from San Marcos Baptist Academy, Baylor University, and SWBTS, he pastored churches at Corpus Christi, Floresville, Timpson, and Houston, Texas. He moved to the Northwest to pastor the Roseburg, Oregon, Vine Street Baptist Church. The HMB and BGCOW employed him as missionary to Coulee and Inland Empire (1958–1967) associations. He established a site fund in 1965 and bought three future church sites. Howard retired on December 31, 1967, and moved to Kerrville, Texas. After his wife, Elli, died in September 1972, he married Rita Pope on May 1, 1973. In 1990 Howard wrote, "I am eighty-eight years of age and very sick and disabled. I spent my life in Baptist work. I worked in retirement until I became disabled at age eighty-two."

Ketchum, Idaho, First Baptist Church

Twin Falls, Idaho, FSBC organized the Ketchum, Idaho, FBC in May 1958 with eighteen charter members. Harold Dillman led VBS in the mornings and a revival in the evenings to start the new mission. Nine who made decisions during the revival formed the mission on Sunday afternoon at Odd Fellows Hall. The new church affiliated with Magic Valley association and the BGCA. Council members were B. E. Honeycutt, James Wright, Fred Higginbotham, and Robert Schreckenburg. Honeycutt preached the organizational sermon. Early pastors were J. C. Farrington, D. E. Acker, Ronald Seibert, and Pete Owen.

UINRMF Fifth Annual Session Meets at SLC

The UINRMF met at the SLC, Utah, Rose Park Baptist Church on May 12–13, 1958, for its fifth annual session. The thirty-six churches located in Idaho, Nevada, and Utah sent ninety-two representatives to conduct official business. James Staples led the first session which featured an historical presentation by E. W. Hunke Jr. and messages by Charles McKay of Phoenix, B. E. Honeycutt of Pocatello, Clyde Barrow of Idaho Falls, Mrs. Robert Fling of WMU Birmingham, and James Stertz of the FMB Richmond. Darwin Welsh of SLC welcomed the messengers, and E. J. Jenkins of Nampa responded. Las Vegas, Nevada, FSBC pastor Charles Ashcraft presided at the second session which featured messages by Leonard B. Sigle, Quincey, California; Bill Bouchellon of Reno; Edmond Walker, SBGCC; L. E. Coleman, SBC Brotherhood; and S. F. Dowis, HMB. Fred Higginbotham read the scripture and led in prayer. SLC, Utah, Highland Baptist Church pastor Roland Smith led the third session which featured messages by Ira Marks, SLC; Harold Dillman, Cedar City; Charles Ray, SLC; Taylor Daniel, Relief and Annuity Board; and Raymond Rigdon, BSSB. Cecil Archer led the music and S. F. Dowis led a panel discussion. After discussion, messengers voted to organize the tri-state Utah-Idaho-Nevada SBC with plans to begin operations on January 1, 1960. Messengers asked the BGCA and SBGCC to retain a percentage of Utah-Idaho-Nevada Cooperative Program funds to start the convention.

Ogden, Utah, Ben Lomond Baptist Church

Ogden, Utah, Ben Lomond (Emmanuel) Baptist Church organized on June 12, 1958, with twenty-four charter members in room 208 at the Lincoln School. The new church affiliated with Salt Lake association and the BGCA. Early pastors were James Sollie, W. E. Greene, Newell Willis, Thomas Parks, Kenneth Wood, Dick Erwin, Larry Mack, Bill Johnson, James Hubbard (int.), Randolph Gunter (int.), Deral Dockins, and Herman Sollie.

Utah Southern Baptists Constitute Two New Associations

Messengers from six churches affiliated with the Salt Lake association constituted Golden Spike association in October 1958. The founding churches were Brigham City FBC, Logan FBC, Roy FBC, Ogden Calvary Baptist Church, Clearfield FBC, and Ogden

Ben Lomond Baptist Church. The association affiliated with the BGCA. James McFatridge, the Roy FBC pastor, served as the first moderator.

Messengers from three SBC churches affiliated with the Utah association constituted the Gideon association of Utah in October 1958. The founding churches were Moab FSBC, Dragerton FBC, and Price FBC. The new association affiliated with the BGCA. Price FBC pastor, Paul Booth, served as the first moderator.

Clarkston, Washington, Trinity Baptist Church

The Lewiston, Idaho, Orchards Baptist Church organized the Clarkston, Washington, Trinity Baptist Church in November 1958 with twenty-six charter members. The mission started on March 2, 1958. The church affiliated with the Inland Empire association and the BGCOW. The early pastors were Don Gurney and Bob Civil.

Waitsburg, Washington, First Baptist Church

The Lewiston, Idaho, Orchards Baptist Church organized the Waitsburg, Washington, FBC in November 1958. Travis Lawton served as the first pastor. The church affiliated with Inland Empire association and the BGCOW. The church met in a residence until April 1962 when they entered their new building.

BGCA Employs Jack Maben as Missionary (Nevada-Arizona)

After a serious automobile accident forced the retirement of Troy Brooks (1948–1958), the HMB and BGCA employed Jackson Knox Maben as missionary to southern Nevada and northwestern Arizona. He served seven months and resigned to pastor Prescott, Arizona, FSBC. Maben was born on August 2, 1910, at Rotan, Texas, to William Jackson and Clara Owen Maben. He had one brother and two sisters. He was saved at age nineteen through the influence of his parents, baptized in 1929, and ordained by Phoenix, Arizona, FSBC in 1934. He wrote, "God's Holy Spirit used the concern and prayer of my mother and sister, the preaching of my pastor, C. M. Rock, and the witness of friends to strike conviction into my heart, reveal the love of Jesus, and bring me to submission." He graduated from Ray, Arizona, High School, Arizona State University, and SWBTS. He married Margaret Ruth Roden at Phoenix in 1933, and they had two children. He wrote, "I had a deepening conviction that the Lord Jesus wanted me in the ministry. Communities with no Baptist witness concerned me greatly. At the summer assembly in 1933, I surrendered to God's call." He pastored SBC churches at Tolleson, Phoenix, Glendale, and Prescott and served as U.S. Army chaplain in the South Pacific in World War II. He served four associations: Lake Mead, Grand Canyon, Mohave, and Troy Brooks (1958–1959). After their retirement, the Mabens moved to Sun City, California.

S. F. Dowis Preaches His Final Sermon to the BGCA

The BGCA met for its thirtieth annual session at the Tucson, Arizona, FSBC on November 12–14, 1958, with messengers from Utah, Idaho, and Nevada churches present. The BGCA reported twenty new churches organized and thirty missions started during the year. A dramatic pageant, *Triumph of Thirty Years*, written by editor J. Kelly Simmons was presented to fifteen hundred people at the University of Arizona auditorium at the Thursday evening session. S. F. Dowis, HMB cooperative missions secretary, preached on the theme "Pioneers of Progress," his last sermon to the BGCA before his retirement on December 31, 1958. After the convention, Dowis said that he had never traveled south of Tucson to the Mexico border and wished to make the trip before his retirement. E. W. Hunke Jr., BGCA associate executive/mission director, agreed to take the pioneer. Dowis crossed the border into Nogales, spent a half day haggling with Mexican shopkeepers about prices, and enjoyed the day off. On the trip Dowis described his strategy for the tri-state convention. Retirement prevented Dowis from completing his dream for the West.

The HMB reorganized in 1959 and replaced S. F. Dowis with M. Wendell Belew (1959–1964) who directed associational missions for developed areas, and A. B. Cash who directed pioneer mission work. Cash related to Nevada, Utah, and Idaho because the HMB continued to view the three states as a pioneer mission area.

Camps and HMB Leaders Foster Evangelism

The annual Utah Baptist Encampment met at the Soapstone Basin tent city near Kamas, Utah, on July 21–26, 1958. The director reported that 278 registered and seventy-seven made decisions. The program personalities were George Wilson, Charles L. McKay, Bertha Wallis, Ruth Ely, Lillie Blaisdell, and C. E. Archer. The husband and wife teams who assisted at camp were the Deene Campbells, Lyle Blaisdells, and E. T. Hutsons.

Utah Baptist Encampment at Soapstone in 1959 registered 246 campers and reported thirty-nine others attending. Albert McClellan, SBC Executive Committee program director, led the sessions. The camp director, Darwin Welsh, reported thirty saved, six for special service, and thirty-seven rededications. Mayo Brown agreed to serve as the 1960 camp director.

Leonard Sanderson resigned as HMB national evangelism director in 1959 and was succeeded by evangelism professor C. E. Autrey from SWBTS. Autrey quickly employed seven associates to assist him in an aggressive nationwide program. The BGCA, SBGCC, and BGCOW continued to promote evangelism efforts in the Intermountain West: W. D. Lawes (BGCA) served Idaho, southern Nevada, and Utah; D. Wade Armstrong (SBGCC) served northern Nevada; and Lewis Steed (BGCOW) served the panhandle of Idaho.

BGCA Employs Roy Ferguson as Missionary (Idaho)

After Barron Honeycutt resigned as the missionary to Idaho, the HMB and BGCA employed Kearns, Utah, FBC pastor, Roy Johnson Ferguson, as the missionary to southern Idaho. Ferguson was born on February 19, 1922, at Paris, Texas, to Roy Ester and Mary Louise (Johnson) Ferguson. He had one sister. He was saved at age nine in a revival through his parents' influence, baptized in a ranch tank by the Odessa, Texas, FBC, and ordained on December 26, 1946, by Odessa Belmont Baptist Church. He wrote, "During a revival I went to Mother and Father and told them I wanted to be baptized. After talking with them and the pastor and evangelist, I made a public profession of faith." He married Dorothy Jean Cody September 25, 1943, at Sherman, Texas, and they had two children. He graduated from the Odessa, Texas, High School, Baylor University, and SWBTS. He pastored churches at Rye and Moody, Texas; Grand Junction, Tennessee; Oil City, Louisiana; and Kearns, Utah. The HMB and BGCA employed him as the missionary to Eastern Idaho association (1959–1975), and Boise Valley and Magic Valley associations (1959–1984). After they retired in 1984 they continued to live at Boise.

BGCOW Employs Ed Byers as Missionary (Idaho)
Baptist churches from Texas and Oklahoma provided funds for the BGCOW to employ James Edwin Byers as missionary to Idaho on January 1, 1959. W. C. Carpenter, the Lewiston, Idaho, Orchards Baptist Church pastor-missionary, had established SBC churches in the area and planned to organize Lewis-Clark association. Byers was born May 28, 1913, at Hobbs, New Mexico, to Ernest and Minnie Byers. He was saved at age six through his parents' influence and baptized at age thirteen by the Hobbs, New Mexico, FBC. He wrote, "Mother and Dad explained what Jesus came to earth to do, that He gave eternal life to those who trusted Him. Their whole devotion nurtured me in the faith." Byers married Mattie Noble Brownd, and they had two daughters. He graduated from Lovington High School, New Mexico A & M, University of New Mexico, and SWBTS. He worked as an accountant, a geologist, and as pastor of Texas Baptist churches at Clarendon and Shamrock. He wrote:

> In a missions emphasis led by J. Ed Taylor of the HMB, my wife and I, unknown to each other, made our decisions to serve in pioneer missions. After W. C. Carpenter invited us to

a Lewiston, Idaho, revival, we moved to the Northwest. Carpenter was involved in ambitious new work with three missions and a new church. I left moved by the challenge, and we accepted the call extended to go.

Byers served as the Lewis-Clark associational missionary (1959–1972). The churches supported his thirteen-year ministry in the Northwest. After his retirement, Byers served four years as mission service corps volunteer in Texas and as National Prayer Corps coordinator at the BSSB at Nashville, Tennessee.

Glendale, Utah, First Baptist Church

The SLC, Utah, Rose Park (FSBC) Baptist Church organized the Glendale FBC September 13, 1959, with nineteen charter members. Council members were Charles Ray, Darwin Welsh, Bill Rounds, Roland Smith, James McFatridge, Bill Thornton, Joe Eubanks, W. E. Greene, Roger Baxter, J. H. Sollie, G. L. Elenbaas, and Robert F. Lowe. The church affiliated with Salt Lake association and the ASBC. Charlie Tague completed the first building in 1960. Early pastors were Roger Baxter and Randolph Gunter.

Craigmont, Idaho, Prairie Baptist (Highland) Church

The Craigmont, Idaho, Prairie (Highland) Baptist Church organized in July 1959. The name of the new church came from its location on the Camas Prairie. The church met in the American Legion cabin and Knights of Pythias Hall. It affiliated at first with Inland Empire association and the BGCOW. The church helped constitute Lewis-Clark association of Idaho on September 9, 1959. Gene Garrett served as the first pastor. Early pastors were Rick Ricci, Charles Didato, Carl Dittemore, James Arndt, Clyde Barnes, W. C. Carpenter, Rande Rash, and John Fowler.

Moscow, Idaho, Trinity Baptist Church

Moscow, Idaho, Trinity Baptist Church organized on September 1, 1959, with Richard Turner as the first pastor. The church met initially in the American Legion cabin and Seventh Day Adventist church, but in January 1963 the church occupied its own building. The new church affiliated with Lewis-Clark association and the BGCOW. Early pastors were Don Gurney, Bendon Ginn, Terry Posey, Bobby Parker, and Michael Burcyznski.

Layton, Utah, First Southern (Layton Hills) Baptist Church

Clearfield, Utah, FBC organized the Layton FSBC on September 6, 1959, with forty-one charter members. The church affiliated with Golden Spike association and the BGCA. Layton FSBC added 162 new members during Harold Dillman's tenure. After the church bought its property in 1960, Charlie Tague built the building; the first services were held there on April 8, 1962. The early pastors were L. R. Brooks, Marion Riley, Harold Dillman, Michael Donahoo, and Jim Harding. Harding, whose father served as Missouri Baptists' executive director, pastored Layton five years. UISBC employed him as the state SS director in 1990 and executive director in 1995.

Lewis-Clark Baptist Association Constitutes (Idaho)

Messengers from four SBC churches organized the Lewis-Clark association on September 9, 1959: Lewiston Orchards, Waitsburg FBC, Craigmont Prairie, and Clarkston Trinity. The organization of the association, planned at Camp O'Hara in July 1959, provided for better fellowship and less travel. The association, located in the area visited by the Lewis and Clark Expedition (1804–1807) at the junction of the Clearwater and Snake rivers, chose to affiliate with the BGCOW. E. W. Hunke Jr., BGCA associate executive/state mission director, had contacted W. C. Carpenter at Lewiston and the BGCOW state leaders about the possibility of the Idaho panhandle churches helping form the new Idaho-Nevada-Utah state convention. Idaho churches would have provided the numbers needed to constitute the three-state convention, but the Idaho panhandle churches chose not to relate.

The 30,000 Movement Creates New Mission Work

The Baptist Jubilee Advance was launched in 1959 by the SBC and seven North American Baptist bodies. The SBC promoted the five-year program (1959–1964) along with the 30,000 Movement. A number of new missions started in 1959.

Tooele, Utah, FBC started the Grantsville Baptist Mission on March 19, 1959. It affiliated with Salt Lake association and the BGCA. Varion Stogner served as the first pastor. Charlie Tague constructed the first building in 1960.

Ketchum, Idaho, FBC started the Richfield Baptist Mission on May 13, 1959. It affiliated with Magic Valley association and the BGCA. A. L. Webster served as the first pastor.

Cedar City, Utah, FBC started the Beaver Baptist Mission in 1959. Harold Dillman served the mission until school teacher Eugene Henderson of Texas arrived to serve as first pastor. It affiliated with Salt Lake association and the BGCA. Wings for Christ ministers from GCC served as supply pastors.

Logan, Utah, FBC started Preston, Idaho, Baptist Mission, according to a May 21, 1959, news release by Ira Marks. The mission affiliated with the Golden Spike association and the BGCA. John A. Strom served as the first pastor. Charlie Tague constructed the building when Jimmy Floyd served as pastor.

Edmond Walker (SBGCC) and E. W. Hunke Jr. (BGCA) traveled to Idaho, Utah, and Nevada in August and September 1959 to conduct stewardship conferences. S. F. Dowis had initially divided Nevada east (BGCA) and west (SBGCC), but the two state mission directors felt that a better mission strategy could emerge with the SBGCC working northern Nevada and the BGCA working southern Nevada. They agreed to shift the areas of work while visiting at Ely, Nevada. The Ely FBC moved its affiliation from Salt Lake association (BGCA) on October 13, 1959, to Nevada association and the SBGCC.

Idaho-Nevada-Utah Fail to Qualify as a State Convention

After the rapid proliferation of new SBC state conventions in the 1940s, the HMB and BSSB agreed on a policy regarding minimum requirements that a new state convention must meet to qualify for SBC support. In the spring of 1959, messengers from Idaho, Nevada, and Utah churches meeting at the UINRMF agreed to constitute Intermountain Baptist Convention. Operations were to begin on January 1, 1960. When SBC churches from the Idaho panhandle chose not to send messengers to help constitute the new convention, the HMB and BSSB felt that the three states did not have the strength to meet qualifications. They could not operate financially.

Courts Redford, the HMB executive secretary, called leaders to attend an "Intermountain Conference" at the Fresno Hotel in Fresno, California, on June 23, 1959. SBC leaders attending the meeting were Courts Redford, Charles McKay, S. G. Posey, A. B. Cash, Ira I. Marks, L. B. Sigle, Roy Ferguson, Walter Ward, J. C. Anderson, Clyde Godfrey, Edmond Walker, Darwin Welsh, Charles Ray, Raymond Glass, A. B. Rutledge, E. W. Hunke Jr., Robert Lowe, and Eleanor Cossley. Floyd Looney and Jo Turk joined in the afternoon session. Redford reported that the churches did not meet minimum HMB/BSSB requirements for a state convention. After discussion, a committee composed of Sigle, Hunke, Ward, Rutledge, and Walker developed a summary statement. Redford suggested that the UINRMC deal with this issue at its regularly scheduled meeting in SLC on September 17, 1959.

The HMB and BGCA drafted a cooperative agreement document on September 8, 1959, at Phoenix, Arizona. The new agreement called for a decision among board directors rather than administrators. It dealt with planning missions and evangelism, and funding agreed upon plans, implementation, and administration by a jointly funded state mission director. Since the HMB considered that the BGCA and SBGCC were no longer pioneer mission fields, the states moved from area superintendents to associational missionaries.

Nevada SBC Churches Withdraw from Utah-Idaho Relationship

The UINRMF met at the SLC, Utah, Rose Park Baptist Church on September 17, 1959. A. B. Rutledge, HMB mission director, and E. W. Hunke Jr., BGCA associate executive/state mission director, met with Idaho, Nevada, and Utah church representatives to report on the BSSB/HMB decisions reached at Fresno. The messengers discussed options. The UINRMF constitution and bylaws committee had finished their work for an "Intermountain Baptist Convention." A suggested budget was ready. The date had been set to constitute a new state convention. When the UINRMF voted to rescind its action and voted to continue affiliation with the BGCA and SBGCC, Nevada churches discontinued sending messengers to the regional conferences and severed their relationship with Idaho and Utah.

Arizona governor Paul Fannin welcomed the 971 messengers and guests to the BGCA annual meeting at the Phoenix Eastside Baptist Church on November 11–13, 1959. The BGCA executive associate/state mission director, E. W. Hunke Jr., presented a document on the mission work in Idaho, Nevada, and Utah, and reported that the UINRMF voted not to constitute the new convention, and to retain relationships with the BGCA and the SBGCC. Messengers voted to approve the new cooperative agreement with the HMB.

Following the disappointing announcement by HMB leaders that Utah-Idaho-Nevada did not qualify for state convention status, and that Nevada churches were withdrawing from the fellowship, E. W. Hunke Jr. flew to SLC to meet with Utah-Idaho leaders on December 24, 1959. They formed the Utah-Idaho Regional Mission Committee (UIRMC) and adopted a new goal to have 107 churches and missions and nine thousand members by 1964. Hunke announced that the HMB planned to give $54,410, and the BGCA $11,650, for Utah-Idaho work in 1960. The UIRMC established three 1960 meetings to check progress toward meeting the goals.

As the decade of the 1950s closed, the future of Nevada SBC work remained unclear. How could one small state like Nevada ever qualify for state convention status when the three states could not qualify together? Phil Jones, an HMB researcher, reported that 447 new SBC churches were organized in the West from 1955 to 1959. Idaho reported nine new churches, Nevada ten, and Utah eleven.

Mission Buildings in Utah and Idaho

The Little Brown Chapels of the West. *Missionary Ira I. Marks became famous for floating "Little Brown Chapels" built on barges for use in Louisiana's Atchafalaya River before moving west. Marks built the movable little brown chapels to start new missions in Idaho, Nevada, and Utah. The Salt Lake City Rose Park Baptist Church, which met initially in the Marks' home, met in this unit for a period of time.*

Ira Marks Directs Construction of a Little Brown Chapel. *The chapels were assembled from panels that were bolted together on the mission site. The panels could be disassembled and loaded onto a flatbed truck. Here Missionary Ira Marks (right) directs assembly of a little brown chapel to start a new mission. Many western churches started in chapels built on railroad cars, mobile chapels, and units like the little brown chapels.*

SIGNIFICANT CHANGES

THE DECADE OF THE 1960S

The 1960 U.S. census reported that 667,191 people lived in Idaho, 285,278 in Nevada, and 890,627 in Utah. The population of the three states combined grew by 404,960 people to 1,843,096, a gain of 28 percent during the decade of the 1950s.

UISBC Employs Medford Hutson as Pastoral Missionary (Utah)
The HMB and UISBC employed K. Medford Hutson as the pastoral missionary to Cedar City FSBC and Richfield FBC on January 1, 1960. Hutson was born February 21, 1928, at Forest, Texas. He trusted Christ at age nine through the influence of his parents, and was baptized by Forest, Texas, FBC. He wrote:

> As a junior boy I sat on the back row Sunday mornings to talk and play during the sermon. I didn't hear the words the preacher said, but when the invitation was given, I was scared. I ran to a second pew where Dad sat, told him my feelings, and Dad led me to know Christ. Going forward was one of the great moments of my life. Christ was real to me. I was baptized four weeks later along with my mother.

Hutson graduated from Lon Morris Junior College, East Texas Baptist College, and SWBTS. He married Dorothy Faye Slaton, and they had three children. He wrote, "God called me to serve at age sixteen at Alto Frio, Texas, youth camp. I surrendered to preach at age twenty-two during a youth revival at Jacksonville, Texas, Central Baptist Church." He pastored Texas churches at Jefferson, Atlanta, Queen City, Lufkin, and Bertram. After his selection as the "outstanding pastor in the Church Development Program of TXBC," the HMB and UISBC employed him as a missionary. While at Richfield, Hutson served as a volunteer chaplain for Sevier Valley Hospital and Utah State Youth Detention Center. He led community devotions on radio, announced the Richfield High School football games, and served as Richfield area Chamber of Commerce president. He served as associational missionary for the Mid-State, Gideon, and Rainbow Canyon associations (1967–1972). After twenty-seven years of service in Utah, the Hutsons retired on December 31, 1992, to pastor the Bertram, Texas, FBC.

God Calls LaVern Inzer to Winnemucca

According to Don Ledbetter, Leonard Sigle enlisted LaVern Inzer to serve as Winnemucca, Nevada, pastor in a unique way. Inzer, a Turlock, California, pastor, received a personal visit from Sigle who asked, "Would you mind if I prayed and asked God to send you to Winnemucca?" Inzer replied, "No, but where is Winnemucca?" Sigle took a Nevada map and made a cross with a line underneath. "There is Winnemucca, Nevada," he said, "where we have a small church and a field that covers 40,000 square miles." Then Sigle prayed, "Dear Lord, I pray in the Name of Jesus that you will send LaVern Inzer to Winnemucca. In the Name of Christ I pray." Then Sigle began to weep. Inzer reported, "My reaction was that he did not give God a chance to say no." Ledbetter wrote that the Inzers soon moved to Winnemucca, Nevada. Inzer worked two years at a lumberyard while he pastored the Winnemucca church. During an eleven-year pastorate with the church, he started missions at Jungo, Battle Mountain, Reese-Antelope Valley, Crescent Valley, McDermitt, Paradise Valley, Getchell Mine, Denio, Bottle Creek, and Pumpernickle Valley (Ledbetter, *History of Nevada Southern Baptists*, VII, 21–24).

Fallon, Nevada, First Southern Baptist Church

The Hawthorne, Nevada, Calvary Baptist Church organized the Fallon, Nevada, FSBC in January 1960. Ray Mendenhall of the U.S. Air Force started the mission in 1955. The new church affiliated with Nevada association and the SBGCC. Early pastors were Joe Zeiglar, Glen Gurley, Adrian Foster, Jesse Wall, Robert Kock, H. C. Verna, Walt Mercer, Charles Ferrell, Al Tremayne, Walter Alexander, Mike Procter, Glen Murphey, and Ted Wakeman. Mercer, who pastored the Fallon FSBC for seven years, had been picked up while hitchhiking by E. W. Hunke Jr. near Globe, Arizona, many years earlier. When Hunke learned that he was running from the call of God to preach, he took him home to Phoenix and enrolled him as a GCC ministerial student.

North Tahoe, California, First Baptist Church

South Lake Tahoe, California, FBC organized the North Tahoe FBC in 1960. The church affiliated with the Nevada association and SBGCC. Len Koster, a GGBTS student from Canada, served as the first pastor. Early pastors were Charles Anderson and Dan Holzer. When NVBC was formed in 1978, North Tahoe FBC chose to continue its affiliation with California.

SBGCC Employs Foy King as Pastoral Missionary (Nevada)

After the BGCA and the SBGCC agreed to divide Nevada north and south, rather than east and west, the HMB and SBGCC employed Foy Ottis King as the pastoral missionary to Ely, Nevada, and northeastern Nevada on January 1, 1960. He was born on April 8, 1907, at Morgan Mill, Texas, to Henry Allen and Betty (Roquemore) King and had three brothers and seven sisters. King was saved at age nine on June 20, 1915, baptized by Morgan Hill, Texas, Missionary Baptist Church in 1917, and ordained by Abilene, Texas, University Baptist Church in May 1930. After he graduated from the Merkel, Texas, High School, HSU, and SWBTS, he attended GGBTS.

King served as an Army chaplain in World War II (1942–1946). He married Lela Fay Mathis on September 1, 1936, at Mart, Texas, and they had two children. He pastored at Sheffeld, Texas, and at

Firebaugh, Keyes, Tulare, Mojave, and Corona, California. After he served Ely, Nevada, FBC (1960–1964), King was transferred by the HMB to Hawaii to pastor churches at Pukalani, Lanai City, and Kaunakakai (1964–1981). He did not serve as an associational missionary, but the remote fields he served demanded that dedication. King retired at Riverside, California. His wife died on March 13, 1993. King died October 31, 1994, at the age of eighty-seven.

Emmett, Idaho, Baptist Mission

The Nampa, Idaho, FSBC started the Emmett, Idaho, Baptist Mission on January 21, 1960. Emmett affiliated with Boise Valley association and the BGCA. The early pastors were A. L. Webster, Walter Bode, Robert Tomsett, Dan Walker, Dale Mitchell, Richard Alkire, James Arndt, and Ritchie Weers.

BGCA Employs Bill Barker as Missionary (Nevada)

After Jack Maben resigned as the Lake Mead association of Nevada missionary, the HMB and BGCA employed Willie Allen Barker on March 1, 1960. His territory stretched along the Colorado River from Las Vegas, Nevada, to Yuma, Arizona. Long distances made the arrangement very difficult. Barker was born September 26, 1925, in Maury County, Tennessee, to Clyde and Annie (Hardison) Barker. He was saved at age nine, and baptized by the Columbia, Tennessee, Rock Springs Baptist Church. He graduated from Columbia, Tennessee, High School and Carson Newman College, attended SWBTS, and worked two summers as a Tennessee Baptist Convention summer missionary. His wife wrote, "Bill surprised us all by announcing his plans to enroll as a ministerial student while standing in the registration line. Barker questioned God's wisdom because he experienced severe seasonal asthma during summer months. Can God use a preacher who has an insufficient supply of breath?" After teaching Bible and high school math for one year, Barker left Tennessee in 1949 to find a place to improve his health. He attended the Oklahoma City SBC and journeyed to Phoenix, Arizona. After completing seminary, he married Emily Peoples, and they had four children. He pastored churches in Tennessee, and at Tucson, Tombstone, Wickenburg, Kingman, and Sierra Vista, Arizona. The HMB and BGCA employed him as missionary to Yuma, Mohave, and Lake Mead associations (1960–1961). When health failed, he retired from the active ministry on January 30, 1974, the twenty-fifth anniversary of his ordination. Barker died September 13, 1978, in the Tucson Medical Center at the age of fifty-three.

Cedar City, Utah, First Baptist Church

Harold Dillman, a HMB/BGCA pastoral missionary, organized the Cedar City, Utah, FBC on Friday, January 26, 1960, in the Escalante Hotel ballroom with eighteen charter members. Persons assisting in the organization were Lewis Arnold, Harold and Opal Dillman, Roger Baxter, Bob Wayman, Bill Rounds, Mayo Brown, Ira Marks, and Robert and Dot Lowe. The church affiliated with Salt Lake association and the BGCA. The church purchased property on March 26, 1958, and immediately began construction of a church plant. Early pastors were Harold Dillman, Medford Hutson, Rodger Russell, M. K. Wilder, Roy Worthley, Robert Marshall, and David Carver.

Granger, Utah, First Baptist Church

Kearns, Utah, FBC organized Granger, Utah, FBC March 3, 1960, in the Joe Eubanks' home with twenty-six charter members. The new church affiliated with Salt Lake association and BGCA. Charlie Tague built the first unit on three acres of land that belonged to the association, and dedicated it in October 1962. Early pastors were Joe Eubanks, Mayo Brown, Russell Whetstone, J. N. Foreman, Burton Greenwood, Louis Demster, Steve Hayes, Glenn Munkres, Wallace Miller, and Fred Kirkland. The church sponsored the SLC, Utah, Shiloh, and Magma Antioch Baptist missions.

Utah-Idaho Churches Report Significant Events

Idaho Southern Baptists met at the Cathedral Pines Camp facilities in June 1960 for their annual camp. Sidney Maddox,

Hopkinville, Kentucky, FBC pastor served as the camp pastor, and Delbert Fann, the Brigham City Indian Center pastor, served as the missionary. Missionary Roy Ferguson reported 144 registered, twenty-five saved, and forty-two rededications, with seven for special service.

Utah Baptists purchased a twenty-acre site at Wallsburg, Utah, for a permanent camp facility. William and Bessie Fleming paid off the $5,780 balance due to buy the land located about five miles off Highway 189 between Provo and Heber City.

Otis Edwards, Blanding, Utah, FBC pastor, started a mission at Blanding for the six hundred Southern Ute Indians cut off from the reservation. A woman who trusted Christ opened her living room for services. A front porch VBS enrolled twenty Indian young people.

Pocatello, Idaho, FSBC started a new mission at Georgetown, Idaho, on August 14, 1960, under the direction of Raymond Glass, BGCA pastoral missionary at Soda Springs, Idaho. The new mission affiliated with Eastern Idaho association and the UISBC.

Clyde Barrow, Idaho Falls Calvary Baptist Church pastor and Utah-Idaho Southern Baptist Fellowship (UISBF) president, died at a SLC hospital on September 3, 1960, from heart failure. The Kentucky pastor served the Northwest in Oregon, Washington, and Idaho.

The Intermountain BSU convention met at the Logan, Utah, FBC on November 19–20, 1960, in a historical first. Program leaders were William Preston Hall (BSSB), C. E. Archer (BGCA), and Roland Smith of SLC.

Fred McCaulley retired as the HMB western field-worker on December 31, 1960. He and his wife worked alongside SBGCC leaders in promoting the HMB Tentmaker program. Mrs. McCaulley served as California WMU president for several years.

Evanston, Wyoming, Hillcrest Baptist Church

Ogden, Utah, Calvary Baptist Church organized the Evanston, Wyoming, Hillcrest Baptist Church on June 17, 1960. The church affiliated with Golden Spike association and BGCA. Jimmy Floyd served as the first pastor. The church purchased an entire city block in the Hillcrest addition of Evanston. Charlie Tague completed the new building on July 6, 1961. Early pastors were Jimmy Floyd and Jack Goldie.

Utah-Idaho SBC Leadership Meets at Boise

The UIRMC met September 28–30, 1960, at Boise, Idaho, Mountain View Baptist Church with Charles Ray presiding. After scripture, prayer, and missionary reports, the UIRMC considered mission funds, progress evaluation, committee organization, and promotion of work. The BGCA associate executive/mission director, E. W. Hunke Jr., worked with UIRMC to take their recommendations to the BGCA executive board. The UISBF established four working committees: programs, plans, and policies; finance; and nominating. The UIRMC elected Arthur Nunn as president, Darwin Welsh as vice-president, and Robert Lowe as secretary. Committee members were Charles Ray, Andy Underhill, Robert Schreckenburg, Clyde Godfrey, and J. C. Farrington.

Messengers from the Utah-Idaho churches convened September 29–30, 1960, the first time without representation from the Nevada churches, for a seventh annual session at Boise, Idaho, Mountain View Baptist Church. The committee took time to thank Charles L. McKay and the BGCA for the help they provided. While meeting for information, fellowship, and inspiration, the group discussed all aspects of their joint endeavor. The program personalities were A. B. Cash, HMB; Charles McKay and E. W. Hunke Jr., BGCA; Ira I. Marks, Harold Dillman, and Charles Ray, Utah; and Roy Ferguson and E. J. Jenkins, Idaho.

When the UIRMC met at SLC, Utah, Rose Park Baptist Church December 1–2, 1960, the agenda included committee organization, election of promotional officers and approved workers, program of work, new mission work, and missionary reports. The UIRMC set up three committees: nominating/calendar (Welsh, Schreckenburg, Wickes); denominational cooperation/finance (Godfrey, Farrington, Lowe); and operations/missions (Ray,

Underhill, Nunn). Darwin Welsh reported that the SLC Rose Park Baptist Church had three children, two grandchildren, and one great-grandchild. They had started the Kearns FBC, SLC Highland Baptist Church, and Glendale FBC; Kearns started Granger FBC; SLC Highland started Holladay Baptist; and Holladay started the Cottonwood Baptist Mission. Rose Park had plans to start new work at Heber City and Midvale.

Bountiful, Utah, First Southern Baptist Church

Clearfield, Utah, FBC organized the Bountiful FSBC on November 20, 1960, with thirty charter members at the American Legion Hall. The SLC, Utah, Rose Park Baptist Church started the mission in the home of L. C. Roots in 1956. The church affiliated with Golden Spike association and the BGCA. After the new church purchased property in 1961, Charlie Tague constructed their first unit, and the members dedicated it December 2, 1962. The early pastors were Logan Roots, Milton Simmons, John Dixon, Ike Jorgensen, and David Martin.

UIRMC Organizes and Considers Reports

UIRMC president Arthur Nunn, Pocatello, called the committee to order on February 8, 1961. Members present were Robert Lowe, Andy Underhill, and Homer Wickes. W. E. Greene, Walter White, Bill Thornton, and Harold Dillman signed as visitors. The BGCA employees included Roy Ferguson of Idaho, Ira Marks and Roland Smith of Utah, E. W. Hunke Jr. of Phoenix, and Harold Bennett from the BSSB. The BGCA staff gave reports; the UIRMC discussed mission opportunities; and Harold Bennett discussed the 30,000 Movement. Hunke reported that the HMB allocated $41,450 for Utah and Idaho for 1961.

In 1961 the HMB and BSSB updated the policy giving minimum requirements for a new state convention to qualify for financial aid from the SBC: five years of cooperation, fifty churches with ten thousand members, 10 percent of church receipts to the Cooperative Program, two years association as a regional fellowship, and a fund to begin operating a new convention.

The nine SLC area churches participating in the SBC Baptist Jubilee revivals on April 16–30, 1961, reported thirty-nine saved and thirty-eight additions by letter.

SBGCC Employs Grady Cothen as Executive Secretary

Since northern Nevada SBC churches affiliated with the SBGCC, Nevada pastors and people watched the selection of a new executive secretary with great interest. Birmingham, Alabama, FBC pastor, Grady C. Cothen, followed S. G. Posey as the SBGCC's fourth leader. Cothen immediately called the SBGCC board to prayer, saying, "Our constant intercession with the God of our fathers is that he will send an awakening to us and ours in our time." Cothen, a forty-year-old Poplarville, Missouri, native, came from a long line of Baptist preachers. His father and two of his brothers responded to God's call to Christian ministry. Cothen served as a U.S. Navy chaplain in World War II and pastored SBC churches in Tennessee, Oklahoma, and Alabama. He was greatly admired, loved, and respected for his outstanding preaching and denominational service in state and national conventions. He and his wife, Bettye, and two children moved to Fresno, California, on February 10, 1961.

Utah-Idaho Summer Camps Reach People for Christ

The Utah Baptist camp met in July 1961 at Wallsburg, Utah, and reported 270 registered, ninety-four visitors, twenty saved, forty-one rededications, and seven for special service. Pastor W. W. Robbins of High Point, North Carolina, served as the camp pastor; Dorothy Hicks, FMB worker, served as the missionary; and Marshall Price of Ft. Worth, Texas, led recreation. The Idaho Baptist camp, which met in July 1961 at Cathedral Pines campgrounds, reported 152 registered, ten saved, thirty-six rededications, and six for special service. The Iowa Park, Texas, Faith Baptist Church pastor, John Klappenbach, served as the camp pastor, and Lawrence Stanley of Phoenix, HMB missionary to Chinese, served as camp missionary.

Milford, Utah, First Baptist Church

Cedar City, Utah, FBC organized the Milford Baptist Church on July 1, 1961, with Bob Irmen as the first pastor. Irmen said, "My call to ministry and my call to Utah were simultaneous." The new church affiliated with Salt Lake association and the BGCA. An item in *The Salt Lake Tribune*, dated September 7, 1963, told of the GCC Wings for Christ ministry at Milford. After their building was destroyed by fire in January 1964, Wings for Christ ministerial students did not permit the church to miss a service. The early pastors were Brent Baxter and Vernon Whaley.

Searchlight, Nevada, Baptist Mission

Boulder City, Nevada, FBC started Searchlight Baptist Mission on October 18, 1961. The work affiliated with Lake Mead association and the BGCA. Thomas Riggs served as the first pastor. Wings for Christ preachers provided pulpit supply each week for the new Searchlight mission. C. E. Wilbanks, former HMB staff evangelism leader and SBGCC state evangelism secretary (1945–1950), retired at Searchlight to serve as pastor. After this second retirement, he moved to Waco, Texas, and wrote:

> Sometimes I get so hungry to see you again that I feel like hitchhiking to Atlanta. Your successes in the Lord's work are a constant joy and pride to me. Your birthday greetings cheered me on at age 90. I feel no different except my knees are giving me static. For the life of me I do not know where to lay the blame—from kneeling so much or from lack of kneeling, RUST. From the noise I am forced to say the trouble is rust. . . . Yours is the 34th birthday greeting I have acknowledged, all in writing (Wilbanks, letter to Hunke, 4/28/85).

Ft. Hall, Idaho, Baptist Indian Mission

The Blackfoot (Ft. Hall), Idaho, Baptist Indian Mission held its first service in December 1961 in a log cabin which belonged to charter member Emma Dann. The new Indian mission affiliated with Eastern Idaho association and the BGCA. Early pastors were Eugene Branch, Earl Jackson, Mike McKay, and Tom Mendez.

Sunset, Utah, Baptist Mission

Roy, Utah, FBC started the Sunset, Utah, Baptist Mission on December 14, 1961. The mission affiliated with the Golden Spike association and BGCA. The mission met each week at the Sunset Elementary School until they purchased three acres and built the first building.

Nevada Leaders Meet with UIRMC

The UIRMC met at Glorieta Baptist Assembly August 7, 1961. The members attending were Clyde Godfrey, Robert Lowe, Charles Ray, D. E. Acker, and Homer Wickes. Visitors present were Ira Marks, Roy Ferguson, Leonard Sigle, Rev. and Mrs. E. J. Jenkins, Ray Wallace, John L. Smith, Ronald Siebert, Harold Dillman, and Foy King. E. W. Hunke Jr. led a planning session for a 1962 missionary-moderator meeting. Sigle and King discussed Nevada work with the group. A. B. Cash, HMB pioneer missions secretary, discussed the committee relationships with the HMB. Even though Nevada churches no longer sent representatives to Intermountain West fellowships, their leaders remained in close contact.

Marks reported that the HMB and BGCA language missions director, Irvin Dawson, had completed building plans and authorized construction of a new mission building on the Ute Indian Reservation at White Rocks, Utah. Charlie Tague completed the construction in 1961.

Wings for Christ Targets Pioneer Mission Field

GCC faculty advisor, James McNett, and GCC ministerial students met with Charles McKay and E. W. Hunke Jr. at the BGCA Baptist building to discuss incorporation of the GCC club named "Wings for Christ." The club proposed to fly students to Utah and southern Nevada mission points to supply pulpits. Many of the students were skilled pilots, mechanics, or instructors who served in the U.S. Air Force during the Korean War. Wings for Christ secured eight planes which they dedicated to the Lord's work. McNett also piloted the planes.

Wings for Christ elected Keith Hull as president, Dan White as secretary, Harold Jenkerson as vice-president, and Dick Sanders as treasurer. The preachers who piloted the planes were Keith Hull, Dan Hull, Ron Kelsch, Bob Dienhart, Bob Fetter, David Baker, Waldo Wilt, Charles Schauf, Melvin Owens, and Roger Hober. The preachers who did not pilot the planes but were flown to preaching points to preach were Floyd Lacy, Jim Richards, Gary Reynolds, Jim Barnes, Al Buehring, Harold Jenkerson, Harold Hambley, Dale Parker, Roy Gene Edge, Les Roberts, Andy Nutima (Navajo interpreter), Bob Wallace, Dick Sanders, Tony Anaya, John Smith, Troy Wilkerson, Harold Pope, Charles Heistand, and Sam Moses.

Hunke contacted the BGCA missionaries each week to pinpoint pulpit supply needs in Arizona, Nevada, and Utah. The planes left Phoenix Deer Valley Airport on Sunday mornings loaded with students who were dropped off along the way. Students gave the honorariums into a Wings for Christ treasury and were reimbursed for expenses. The group dedicated a Piper Tri-Pacer to the Lord in a service at Deer Valley Airport September 23, 1962. Thirty-five people listened as Hunke preached the dedication message. Members raised one thousand dollars and borrowed four thousand dollars to pay for the plane, which was put into service immediately. Wives of the members organized an auxiliary group to aid their husbands in preaching Christ. Dan Hull recalled some experiences:

> Keith mentioned one time that we had started or re-opened over one hundred churches and missions from 1961 to 1964. I flew north from Phoenix into northern Arizona and southern Utah. Other pilots went south, east, and west. I don't remember all the places where Keith and the other pilots flew. We had four Piper Tri-pacers, one Cherokee 10, one Cherokee 6, a Piper Cub Trainer, and a Twin Beechcraft. We had thirty-five seats and they were filled every week. Our purpose in

Wings for Christ was to serve as many Southern Baptist churches as possible. After we started or re-opened a church, we supplied them with a preacher until they were strong enough to call a pastor. We also supplied, held revivals, and helped in crusades. I flew planes to Searchlight, Nevada; Window Rock and Zuni, New Mexico; Blanding, Toquerville, Cedar City, Hurricane, St. George, Richfield, Beaver, Milford, and many other places.

We served at Agua Caliente, Texas Hill, Sommerton, Wellton, Tacna, Winterhaven [CA], Gila Bend, Maricopa, Buckeye, Aguila, Salome, Yarnell, Bullhead City, Bagdad, Chino Valley, Ashfork, Seligman, Lake Mohave Ranchos, Cottonwood, Camp Verde, Chevelon, Heber, Young, Pinetop, White River, Snowflake, St. Johns, Clifton, Safford, Sells, Huachuca City, Pearce, St. James, Bisbee, Douglas, Winslow, Leupp, Dilkon, and Ganado in Arizona (Dan Hull, letter to Hunke, 3/7/97).

BGCA Changes Name to Arizona Southern Baptist Convention

When the BGCA closed its thirty-third annual session on November 17, 1961, at Phoenix FSBC, the name had been changed to the Arizona Southern Baptist Convention (ASBC). The convention reported that 1,163 registered from the Idaho, Nevada, Utah, and Arizona churches.

Boise, Idaho, Highlands Baptist Church

Boise, Idaho, Mountain View Baptist Church organized the Boise Highlands Baptist Church on December 3, 1961. Because it met in an old Episcopal chapel, the mission was called the Old Chapel Baptist Mission. At the groundbreaking service the oldest charter member, Augusta Hinshaw, held the handles of an old turning plow as members pulled it forward with ropes. At the first prayer meeting in the new building on February 20, 1963, members sat on bales of insulation. The church affiliated with Boise Valley association and the ASBC. The early pastors were Norfleet Wheeler, Harry Johnson, P. L. Merilott, Doug Robinson, Lewis Demster, George Hess, and Dan Skinner.

BGCOW Employs Fred Moseley as Executive Director

After Robert Milam retired as the BGCOW executive director in 1961, the BGCOW employed Fred B. Moseley, the HMB city mission secretary, to serve Idaho, Oregon, Washington, and western Canada. Moseley, a Gloster, Mississippi, native, received a formal education at Mississippi College and NOBTS. He pastored Baptist churches in Mississippi, Alabama, and Louisiana and served as the LBC associate executive director. After completing five years with BGCOW (1961–1965), he returned to Atlanta to serve as HMB associate executive director. The Moseleys retired first in Mississippi but returned later to Oregon where they both died.

Blackfoot, Idaho, Emmanuel Baptist Church

Idaho Falls, Idaho, Calvary Baptist Church organized the Blackfoot Emmanuel Baptist Church January 7, 1962, with twenty-one charter members. On October 6, 1957, Clyde Barrow, Ed Fast, Skeets Benson, and Ben Cowell drove from Idaho Falls to meet with Andy Kotzian and his family to make plans to start the mission. Ed Fast and Ralph Miller served as supply. The church affiliated with Eastern Idaho association and the UISBC. The early pastors were Gale Walters, Raymond Glass, George Hill, Billy Swindler, James Jamieson, Archie Phillips, Lu Gilman, Robert Fields, Glenn Munkres, Dennis Bridge, Frank MacKey, and Brian Harrison.

Bill Thornton Leads UIRMC Sessions

President Bill Thornton called the UIRMC into session at the SLC Rose Park Baptist Church on February 6–7, 1962. The members present were Bill Thornton, Bob Lowe, Richard Mobley, Darwin E. Welsh, Homer Wickes, George Eichler, and Bev Greer. The visitors were Charles McKay, Roy Sutton, W. E. Greene, John Smith, Charles Ray, C. O. Estes, Bob Wayman, Bill Rounds, Roger Baxter, and Harold Dillman. Greene discussed ways he used laymen in Colorado revivals, and McKay told of experiences in Arizona revivals. A. B. Cash called to say that Atlanta pastors could lead October 1963 simultaneous revivals in Utah. The

UIRMC recommended employment of Charles Ray as the Utah general missionary.

Salt Lake City, Utah, Holladay Baptist Church

SLC, Utah, Highland Baptist Church organized the Holladay Baptist Church in April 1962 with fifty-six charter members. When the mission started on May 19, 1957, in a department store basement, the Oklahoma City Olivet Baptist Church promised to send seventy-five hundred dollars annually and pray. The Olivet pastor, Grady Cothen, later became the SBGCC executive director. The church affiliated with Salt Lake association and the ASBC. After the church bought land in 1958, Charlie Tague completed a first unit brick-veneer building with a long porch and ornamental iron posts. The church dedicated the new building April 12, 1959. Pastor Homer Wickes was killed in an August 1969 auto accident. Early pastors were Charles Ray, Homer Wickes, Chester Bunch, Steve Hayes (int.), and Andy Hornbaker.

Las Vegas, Nevada, College Park Baptist Church

Las Vegas, Nevada, Nellis Baptist Church organized the Las Vegas College Park Baptist Church on May 24, 1962, with forty-three charter members. The new church affiliated with Lake Mead association and the ASBC. The mission had started November 15, 1959, in a second-story office suite with Virgil Clubb as mission pastor. Early pastors were Virgil Clubb, Lewis McClendon, Bob VanHook, Jerrell Griffin, A. G. Pervis, Dan Raley, Adrian Hall, and Bob Norvell.

ASBC Employs Charles Ray as Missionary (Utah)

After Ira I. Marks resigned on November 7, 1961, to become the Aberdeen, South Dakota, pastoral missionary, the HMB and ASBC employed Charles Albert Ray as the Utah missionary effective June 15, 1962. Marks had served the Idaho, Nevada, and Utah churches for eleven years. He found four churches when he arrived and left twenty-six churches and eighteen missions.

Ray was born May 21, 1919, at Prattville, Alabama, to Samuel Alonzo and Docia Ophelia (Thompson) Ray. He was saved at the age of eleven, baptized by the Prattville, FBC in 1930, and ordained by the Birmingham, Alabama, Pike Avenue Baptist Church in 1944. He graduated from Autauga County schools, Auburn, and SWBTS. He never married. He wrote, "I surrendered for full-time Christian service at Ridgecrest, North Carolina, in 1942 and dedicated my life to Utah at an HMB conference near Pacific Grove, California, in 1950." He pastored Baptist churches at Ft. Towson, Oklahoma; and at Roosevelt, Dragerton, and SLC (Rose Park, Millcreek, and Holladay), Utah. The HMB and ASBC employed him as the missionary to Gideon (1962–1967), Golden Spike, Salt Lake, and Utah associations (1962–1969). Ray edited the Salt Lake association newsletter which became the *Utah-Idaho Southern Baptist Witness*. After retiring, he moved to Alabama.

ASBC Employs Donald Loving as Missionary (Nevada)
Because of serious health problems, Bill Barker resigned from the missionary position in southern Nevada and Arizona. The HMB and ASBC employed Donald Lee Loving as his successor May 1, 1962. Loving was born at Stilwell, Oklahoma, to George and Iris M. Loving on August 6, 1931. He had four brothers and three sisters. He was saved at the age of ten through his parents' influence, baptized by the Wilburton, Oklahoma, Calvary Baptist Church in August 1941, and ordained by the Concord, California, Bethel Baptist Church December 30, 1952. He wrote, "The Lord spoke to me during a revival that my father conducted. . . . Several weeks later I committed my life to Christ in a Sunday evening service at the Calvary Baptist Church."

He graduated from Bakersfield, California, East High School, Valley College, OBU, and GGBTS (Th.D.). Loving married Patsy Brown August 12, 1955, at Gadsden, Alabama, and they had three children. He wrote:

> I dreamed of being a professional baseball player, but God had better things in mind for me. While serving as East Contra Costa association youth president, I did things I never dreamed of doing such as public speaking, teaching

SS, and speaking out for my Lord. I felt He wanted me in ministry.

He pastored churches at Wilburton, Oklahoma; Brentwood, Needles, and Stockton, California; and Las Vegas, Nevada. The HMB and ASBC employed him as missionary to Lake Mead, Mohave, and Yuma associations in 1962 and 1963. He resigned to pastor the Las Vegas Redrock Baptist Church.

Idaho Baptist Encampment Meets at Cathedral Pines

Idaho Southern Baptists gathered at Cathedral Pines Baptist Encampment thirteen miles north of Ketchum, Idaho, for the annual state assembly on June 17, 1962. The 225 campers from fourteen SBC churches and seven missions included twenty-three Shoshone-Bannock Indians brought by Eugene Branch, a missionary. Sweetwater, Texas, Lammar Street Baptist Church pastor, J. L. Cartrite, served as camp pastor, and Branch served as missionary. They reported twenty-nine saved, twenty-two rededications, and twenty-four for special service. The program leaders were Walter Bode, George Eichler, Billy Swindler, Robert Schreckenburg, Sue Harbour, the Clyde Godfreys, the E. J. Jenkins, the Lavoid Robertsons, the Roy Fergusons, and the W. Wisels. Bill and Naomi Hunke represented the ASBC at the encampment.

"World in My Heart" Conferences Conducted in Utah-Idaho

The UISBF promoted six "World in My Heart" conferences using Ecclesiastes 3:11, Philippians 1:7, and 2 Corinthians 6:11 as texts. F. Milton Gage and Carl Halverson led the conferences that were held at Price, Granger, and Brigham City, Utah, and at Blackfoot, Kimberly, and Boise, Idaho.

Montezuma Creek, Utah, Calvary Baptist Church

Blanding, Utah, FBC organized the Montezuma Creek Calvary Baptist Church in a home on September 23, 1962, with twenty-eight charter members. The new church leased property for thirty years in 1959 and constructed its first building. Missionary Ray said that

Montezuma Creek was the twenty-eighth SBC church in Utah. The new church affiliated with Gideon association and the ASBC. The organizational council members were Charles Ray, Tom Parks, Eugene Ege, Chris Woodard, Dick Gay, James Stone, and James Brown. The early pastors were Don Seigler, Thomas Parks, Donald Forbes, John Bishop, Brent Baxter, Wayne Fults, and Ken Prewett.

Ninth UISBF Session Convenes at Idaho Falls

The UISBF met at the Idaho Falls Calvary Baptist Church on November 5–6, 1962, for its ninth annual session. President Bill Thornton, Boise, Idaho, Mountain View Baptist Church pastor, led the sessions. The theme, "My Church's Task," placed an emphasis on prayer, missions, and evangelism. The program used the state convention format which included reports as well as inspiration and instruction. The participants were A. B. Cash, HMB; Charles McKay, ASBC; T. A. Patterson, TXBC; and E. N. Patterson, GCC. After the conference, Bill Thornton, president, led the UIRMC in a business meeting. Committee members present were Andy Underhill, Clyde Godfrey, Bob Schreckenburg, Darwin E. Welsh, S. E. Cearley, John Smith, George Eichler, Richard Mobley, and Lavoid Robertson.

Tremonton, Utah, Bear River Valley Baptist Church

Ogden, Utah, Ben Lomond Baptist Church organized the Tremonton Bear River Valley Baptist Church on December 9, 1962, with twenty-two charter members. The church affiliated with the Golden Spike association and the ASBC. Pastor James Sollie and Ira Marks, who had visited with Benny Cherko, started the mission at the Garland, Utah, public library. The church met in the fire station until it purchased a home for meetings. Early pastors were C. O. Estes, Daryl Golding, W. E. Greene, Frank Edwards, and Audie Cathey.

Truckee, California, First Baptist Church

Missionary Leonard Sigle visited in Truckee, California, in 1963 and organized the Truckee FBC. Bob Duffer served as the first pastor. The new church affiliated with Nevada association and the SBGCC. Early pastors were Douglas Low, A. L. Tremayne, C. B. Dean, and Bill Burkett. When the NVBC constituted in 1978, the Truckee church opted to continue affiliation with the SBGCC.

Crescent Valley, Nevada, Baptist Church

Winnemucca, Nevada, FBC organized the Crescent Valley, Nevada, Baptist Church on July 16, 1973. The new church affiliated with Nevada association and the SBGCC. When Crescent Valley, Nevada, received word they would receive a new post office building in 1963, an eighty-year-old retired Baptist minister called "Doctor John" Hawkins asked for a post office box for a Baptist church when there was none. Doctor John saw the spiritual need and decided a new Baptist church was needed. Hawkins came out of his retirement, secured help from local residents, and restored the house given by the railroad company to start the Baptist church. Early pastors were L. B. Sigle (int.), Harvey Broadway, LaVern Inzer (int.), Tom White, and Dale Broadway.

Orangeville, Utah, Baptist Mission

Price, Utah, FBC organized the Orangeville Baptist Mission in January 1963, according to an ASBC report in November 1963. The new mission affiliated with Utah association and the UISBC.

Las Vegas, Nevada, Desert Hills Baptist Church

Las Vegas, Nevada, Sunrise Baptist Church organized the Las Vegas Desert Hills Baptist Church January 6, 1963, with thirty-three charter members. The mission started on September 2, 1962, in a second-floor room of a commercial building. Gerald Marshall served as the first pastor. The church affiliated with Lake Mead association and the ASBC. After purchasing property, they built the first unit of their building in 1963. Early pastors were Gerald Marshall, Horace Duke, Bill Thompson, Don Wilson, Dick Higley, Wayne McCutcheon, Tom Propelka, Bob McDuffie, and David Brown.

First Southern Baptist Church of Las Vegas

Las Vegas FSBC organized on June 26, 1955, in the IOOF Hall. FSBC met at the Carpenter's Hall for services under the direction of Pastor Charles Ashcraft who left Los Alamos (NM) FBC to start the Nevada mission under the sponsorship of Henderson FSBC.

Thirty-three charter members organized Las Vegas FSBC (not all are pictured here). Pastor Charles Ashcraft (top right), and his wife Sarah (below Ashcraft), led FSBC from 1955 to 1965 when he became the first UISBC state executive director.

Las Vegas FSBC began construction on its first church building in 1958. Ray Cutright, a layman, served as chairman of the building committee. Charlie Tague helped develop plans for the building. A fourteen-thousand-square-foot educational plant was completed in November 1971.

Provo Sponsors Work at Cedar City

Harold Dillman led some Roosevelt, Utah, Baptist Church members in a 1948 survey of Provo. During the summer, A. B. Barnes, missionary from Phoenix, Arizona, and two HMB summer missionaries led VBS. The Provo FBC organized August 23, 1948. Because of a severe snowstorm in November 1950, the church members traveling to Roosevelt to help organize Utah Baptist Association could not get through the snow. The picture above shows Provo FBC meeting in a home.

Provo, Utah, FBC organized its Cedar City mission into a church on January 22, 1960 (pictured above), with Harold Dillman as mission pastor. Bottom center: pastoral missionaries Robert E. Wayman of Richfield and Harold Dillman of Cedar City; Ira I. Marks, missionary (left—second from bottom); Opal Dillman (left side SS record—second from top); Roger Baxter, Bill Rounds, Dot Lowe, Mayo Brown, and Bob Lowe (five on top right).

Jerome, Idaho, Baptist Mission

Burley, Idaho, FBC started the Jerome Baptist Mission on January 6, 1963, in the home of pastor Oval Walker. Eleven people attended the first service. The new mission affiliated with Magic Valley association and the UISBC.

Utah-Idaho SBC Evangelism Conference Meets at SLC

The Utah-Idaho SBC evangelism conference met on February 4–6, 1963, at the SLC, Utah, FSBC. Out-of-state speakers were David C. Hall, Vernon Yearby, C. E. Archer, Ed Packwood, and W. D. Lawes. The local participants were Charles Ray, Bob Compere, Roland Smith, and Darwin E. Welsh. Ray announced that William Fleming of Ft. Worth, Texas, a millionaire who had blessed many SBC lives on the mission fields of western U.S.A. and Canada, had died.

Orofino, Idaho, First Baptist Church

The Lewiston, Idaho, Orchards Baptist Church started its fifth mission at Orofino, Idaho, on March 17, 1963, under the leadership of associational missionary Ed Byers. The church held services in the community building for eighteen months until a new building was occupied in the spring of 1965. The church affiliated with Lewis-Clark association and the BGCOW. Holt Sodeman served as the first pastor. Early pastors were Darnell Archie, Ray Bowen, Bob Parker, William Dawkins, Grover Garrett, and Gene Dempsey.

UIRMC Asks SBC to Waive Membership Rules

The UIRMC met on May 7, 1963, at Twin Falls, Idaho, FSBC. Members present were Bill Thornton, Darwin E. Welsh, John Smith, George Eichler, Lavoid Robertson, Richard Mobley, and Alton Thomas. The visitors were Roy Ferguson, Idaho; Charles Ray and Roland Smith, Utah; and E. W. Hunke Jr., Phoenix. Darwin Welsh presented a resolution addressed to the HMB and ASBC asking that membership guidelines be waived and the Utah-Idaho SBC churches be permitted to constitute a new state convention on November 5–6, 1964, with operations to begin on January 1, 1965. Unanimous approval followed. Ray and Ferguson reported on Utah and Idaho SBC work. Hunke discussed missionary housing, funds spent for pastoral support, and schools of missions schedules. Thornton discussed a possibility of Utah-Idaho sponsoring a booth at the SBC in 1964. John Smith asked that a joint Utah-Idaho Southern Baptist camp be considered.

David C. Hall, the ASBC member of the HMB directors, led HMB directors in lively discussion about the future of the Utah-Idaho Southern Baptist work during the mid-year Glorieta meeting. Hall said a minimum requirement of ten thousand members to attain convention status was not realistic for the Utah-Idaho SBC churches. George Bullard led opposition, and insisted that the HMB follow adopted guidelines. The HMB waved membership requirements, but insisted on fifty churches giving 10 percent to the Cooperative Program. The HMB action brought a burst of enthusiasm to the forty-four struggling Utah-Idaho SBC churches. The UIRMF targeted January 1, 1965, as the date to begin operation.

Las Vegas, Nevada, Central Baptist Church

Las Vegas, Nevada, Sunrise Baptist Church organized the Las Vegas Central Baptist Church on June 16, 1963, with twenty-six charter members. The new church affiliated with Lake Mead association and the ASBC. Gene Mockerman, the sponsoring church pastor, noted that this new church was the third mission started by the Sunrise Baptist Church in 1963. Early pastors were Ray Lyons and Marvin E. Hammond.

Salt Lake City, Utah, Central Baptist Church

SLC, Utah, Highland Baptist Church organized the SLC Central Baptist Church on June 23, 1963, with twenty-two charter members. Missionary Charles Ray moderated the organizational service. The organizational program participants were Bryan Luttrell, James L. Cooper, W. C. Rounds, Roger Baxter, and Mayo Brown. The church affiliated with Salt Lake association and the ASBC. The mission had begun in the YWCA building in downtown SLC about five blocks from the Mormon Temple and later moved to the Ike Jorgensen home at 951 Lake Street. The evening services were held at the Tabor Lutheran Church which had been built in 1909. The HMB bought the Lutheran building with a loan underwritten by the Amarillo FBC, Dallas Oakcliff Baptist, and Denton FBC. The daily commercial tours took people to see a stained-glass window which had been brought to Utah from Denmark. Early pastors were Charles Ray (2), James McFatridge (2), M. E. Stevens, Robert McCullar, and Carl Holden. Mary Wigger started a Concern Center in the downtown facility in 1968.

Fifteenth Utah Baptist Encampment Meets at Wallsburg
The fifteenth annual Utah Baptist Encampment met July 22–27, 1963, at the Wallsburg, Utah, campsite. Utah missionary Charles Ray reported 215 registered, sixteen saved, and thirty-one for special service. Moscow, Idaho, pastor Dick Turner served as the camp pastor and Samuel Hernandez as the missionary.

SBGCC Employs Ralph Longshore as State Mission Director
Following Edmond Walker's resignation in September 1963 to become the Hawaii Baptist Convention executive secretary, the HMB and SBGCC employed Ralph E. Longshore, Alabama Baptist Convention evangelism secretary, to succeed him. Longshore was born in 1923 in Alabama. He graduated from Howard College and SBTS, and pastored churches in Alabama, Indiana, Tennessee, and Oklahoma. The BSSB employed him as a staff member. When Grady Cothen resigned as SBGCC executive director in April 1966, the SBGCC state executive board asked Longshore to serve as the interim director. After the SBGCC state board employed Robert Hughes as executive director in October 1966, Longshore remained on the SBGCC state staff as the associate executive/state mission director.

Soda Springs, Idaho, First Baptist Church
Pocatello, Idaho, FSBC organized the Soda Springs FBC on October 13, 1963, with nine charter members. The new church affiliated with Eastern Idaho association and the ASBC. Early pastors were Raymond Glass, William Jones, Ron Seibert, Bennie Wright, Larry Angel, and Kenneth Jackson.

Twin Falls, Idaho, Trinity Southern Baptist Church

Twin Falls, Idaho, Trinity Southern Baptist Church organized on October 13, 1963, at the Disabled Veterans Hall with seventeen charter members. Charles Leonard Sr. served as the first pastor. Leonard, an emeritus China missionary, said, "This is the first time I have taken part in the organization of a church, including China, Manchuria, Hawaii, or America, where every one of the members tithed." The church affiliated with Magic Valley association and the UISBC. In 1957 the church bought property and a building from the Church of Christ. Early pastors were Charles Leonard, Robert Schreckenburg, Louis Demster, and Orville Welshhon.

UISBF Begins Process to Constitute a State Convention

The UISBF met for its tenth annual meeting from October 31 to November 1, 1963, at the SLC, Utah, FSBC with Bill Thornton, UISBF president, presiding. The associational progress reports named "Possessing the Land" were given by Walter Bode, Boise Valley; Lavoid Robertson, Magic Valley; John L. Smith, Golden Spike; Gary Christopherson, Eastern Idaho; Lee Bullard, Salt Lake; and Harmon Popham, Utah. Messages were preached by Charles McKay, ASBC; Chester Quarles, Mississippi; Loyd Corder, HMB; and Bill Thornton, Boise. Thornton reported on events in 1963: the HMB pastors' retreat at the SLC Temple Square Hotel in January; UISBF booth at the Kansas City SBC; and twenty-five church simultaneous revivals led by Atlanta pastors in September. Welsh noted that the Utah-Idaho SBC church letters reported 373 baptisms, 5,078 members, $361,178 receipts, $32,552 Cooperative Program, and $5,568 association missions.

The UIRMC met on December 17, 1963, at the SLC, Utah, FSBC to finalize organizational plans and establish committees needed to attain state convention status. The members of an expanded eighteen-member committee were Bill Thornton, Homer Wickes, Bob Compere, Darwin Welsh, James Aldrich, Mel White, John L. Smith, Ed Fast, Gary Christopherson, John Embery, Lavoid Robertson, Mayo Brown, Rolan Bell, George Eichler, and Riley McCall. The guests present were Charles Ray and Roland Smith of

Utah; Roy Ferguson of Idaho; and E. W. Hunke Jr., Phoenix. Ray, Ferguson, and Smith gave reports on the work.

Hunke reported that every needed action was in motion: the ASBC was setting aside 15 percent of Utah-Idaho Cooperative Program gifts; the BSSB was notified of plans to constitute; the HMB budget plans needed to be finalized; twenty-six new churches had been organized during the 30,000 Movement; and the HMB made the necessary program changes. He responded to questions about the size and nature of a state staff and HMB funding procedures. Smith discussed BSSB funding procedures. Thornton announced the committee assignments for 1964: Homer Wickes, John Smith, John Embery, James Aldrich, George Eichler, Gary Christopherson, and Al Starbuck would serve on an operations and missions committee (constitution and bylaw); Darwin Welsh, Lavoid Robertson, Edwin Fast, Bob Compere, and Mel White would serve on the finance and denominational cooperation committee (budget); and S. E. Cearley, Mayo Brown, Rolan Bell, Lewis Warren, and Riley McCall would serve on the calendar and nominating committee (plans and calendar).

The UIRMC met on February 5, 1964, at SLC, Utah, FSBC under the direction of president Bill Thornton. The committee members present were Embery, Robertson, Thornton, Wickes, Welsh, Brown, Compere, Fast, Bell, White, Eichler, Christopherson, Cearley, Smith, and McCall. The visitors present included Charles Ray and Roland Smith, Utah; Roy Ferguson, Idaho; E. W. Hunke Jr., ASBC; James Thrasher, a layman; and Raymond Cearley. Committee reports were approved. The HMB agreed to fund the expenses necessary to constitute a state convention. Hunke announced that Leonard G. Irwin, HMB survey specialist, and Harold Graves, GGBTS president, would lead a series of conferences in the two-state area and suggested that members preserve history materials. Charles McKay, ASBC, promised to notify other conventions.

The UIRMC met on April 29–30, 1964, at the SLC, Utah, FSBC under the direction of president Bill Thornton. Members present were Thornton, Embery, Robertson, Wickes, Welsh, Compere, Brown, Fast, Eichler, Smith, White, and McCall.

Visitors were A. B. Cash, HMB; J. M. Crowe, BSSB; Roy Ferguson, Idaho; Roland Smith and Charles Ray, Utah; and E. W. Hunke Jr., ASBC. Pastors present were Russell Whetstone, E. J. Jenkins, and Roy Worthley. Cash reviewed procedures to constitute a convention. The committee chairmen presented reports: Homer Wickes (constitution), Darwin Welsh (budget), and Mayo Brown (calendar). Crowe discussed how the BSSB related to new state conventions. The UIRMC approved a third draft of the constitution. Welsh said the proposed budget was set at $133,000. Forty-eight churches and eighteen missions were to meet October 29–30, 1964, to constitute a new convention. The eight ASBC employees in Utah and Idaho had doubled efforts to meet the fifty-church requirement.

Inzer Establishes Baptist Missions Foundation and Trust, Inc.

LaVern Inzer incorporated the Baptist Missions Foundation and Trust, Inc. of Nevada in 1964 with thirty-five dollars. The Battle Mountain, Nevada, FBC received the first loan of one thousand dollars in 1966. On January 1, 1997, Inzer reported that foundation assets reached $1,058,392.51.

Payette, Idaho, First Southern Baptist Church

Caldwell, Idaho, FSBC organized the Payette, Idaho, FSBC on February 16, 1964, with twenty-four members. The new church affiliated with Boise Valley association and the ASBC. The early pastors were J. B. Greer (int.) and A. D. Reed.

Nevada Pastors Meet for First Nevada Baptist Fellowship

A. B. Cash, HMB pioneer missions secretary, called a meeting of Nevada, California, and Arizona SBC leaders at the 1963 HMB week at Glorieta. Aware that the Utah-Idaho churches would constitute their convention on October 29, 1964, Cash felt that northern and southern Nevada SBC leaders needed to know each other. Those who attended the informal meeting were Leonard Sigle, Sparks; Ralph Longshore, Fresno; Don Loving, Las Vegas; and E. W. Hunke Jr., Phoenix. The group agreed that fellowship between the northern and southern Nevada churches would be beneficial. Sigle agreed to invite the southern Nevada pastors to northern Nevada in 1964, and Loving agreed to invite northern Nevada pastors to southern Nevada in 1965. The first Nevada Baptist Fellowship (NVBF) met at Sparks, Nevada, Temple Baptist Church in April 1964, during the one-hundredth anniversary of Nevada statehood. SBC leaders who attended were A. B. Cash, HMB; E. W. Hunke Jr., ASBC; and Wade Armstrong, SBGCC. Missionary Don Loving, who had resigned, and Leonard Sigle directed the 1964 program. Pastors scheduled the second NVBF for Las Vegas in 1965.

ASBC Employs Milton Gage as Missionary (Nevada)
After Don Loving resigned as missionary to pastor Las Vegas Redrock Baptist Church, the HMB and ASBC employed Freddie Milton Gage on April 15, 1964, as missionary to Lake Mead association. Gage was born July 5, 1927, at Roosevelt, Oklahoma, to Fred and Rae (Hawkins) Gage. He had one brother and one sister. Gage was saved at age fourteen, baptized by Reydon, Oklahoma, FBC in 1941, and ordained by Shawnee, Oklahoma, FBC. A neighbor, Kenneth Ballard, who served as the Reydon church music director, led him to trust Christ. He graduated from the Ft. Cobb, Oklahoma, High School, OBU, and SWBTS. Gage married Mary Lee Henry on March 25, 1951, at Erick, Oklahoma, and they had four children. He wrote, "God impressed on me for more than a year that He wanted me to preach the Gospel. I have that assurance daily." He pastored Oklahoma Baptist churches at Mangum, Cheyenne, and Olustee, and Arizona SBC churches at Sierra Vista, Phoenix, and Queen Creek. While pastor at Sierra Vista, Gage led the church to start seven new missions. The HMB and ASBC employed him as the missionary to Lake Mead association of Nevada (1964–1969) where he constituted five new churches one year and started nine new church-type missions the next. The Gages moved back to Oklahoma to rear their children. After retirement they spent winters in Arizona to serve the churches.

Gooding, Idaho, First Southern Baptist Church

The Kimberly, Idaho, FSBC organized the Gooding FSBC on May 3, 1964, with eighteen charter members and forty enrolled in SS. The mission, which began on September 15, 1963, met at the White Chapel Seventh Day Adventist Church. Clay Coursey served as the first pastor. The church affiliated with Magic Valley association and the ASBC. An earlier church, which had organized in Gooding on November 20, 1952, ceased functioning. The church met in the home of the pastor who supported himself by teaching school until he went to Africa as a foreign missionary. Roy Ferguson reported that Gooding was the seventeenth SBC church in Idaho. The early pastors were Clay Coursey, Roy Myers, Gordon Watson, John Rolfe, Vic Walker, Paul Jackson, and Richard Rhodes.

Boise, Idaho, Calvary Baptist Church

Mountain Home, Idaho, FSBC organized Boise Calvary Baptist Church June 14, 1964, with nineteen charter members. The mission started with prayer in Ransom Southerland's home on July 14, 1960, with the first service in Harold Powell's home on July 17, 1960. James Martin served as the first pastor. Organizational council participants were missionary Roy Ferguson, Norfleet Wheeler, Bill Thornton, Ransom Southerland, N. S. New, Raymond Cearley, and Bill Thornton. The new church affiliated with Boise Valley association and the ASBC. Calvary church started the downtown Boise University Baptist Church in July 1971. The early pastors were James Martin, Scott New, Joseph Peterson, Tom Prevost, Louis Demster, John Embery, and Stephen Kern.

Idaho Baptist Encampment Meets in the Sawtooth Mountains

The Idaho Baptist Encampment met at the Cathedral Pines campgrounds in the Sawtooth Mountains on June 21–27 and June 28–July 4, 1964. Caldwell FSBC pastor, Frank Boydstun, preached the first week, and C. E. Archer (ASBC) preached the second week. Missionary Blanche Simpson of Brazil served as camp missionary for both camps. The camps reported 331 registered with sixty-one decisions.

HMB Reports Changes in Evangelism

The HMB and ASBC employed Bruce and Bea Conrad as the new missionaries to the Brigham City, Utah, Indian work on July 15, 1964. The Conrads had completed twelve years at Chilocco Indian School in Oklahoma. Wade Armstrong resigned as the SBGCC state evangelism director on August 1, 1964, and was succeeded by an FMB missionary Eugene Grubbs. Other state evangelism leaders were Lewis Steed (BGCOW), who served northern Idaho, and W. D. Lawes (ASBC), who served southern Nevada, Idaho, and Utah. C. E. Autrey led the HMB evangelism division at Dallas, Texas.

Orem, Utah, Baptist Mission

Provo, Utah, FBC started the Orem, Utah, Baptist Mission on August 2, 1964. James Barger and Brenda Matlock, student summer missionaries, began the work with a VBS. Abernathy, Texas, FBC gave a $121 offering for VBS expenses. The mission affiliated with Salt Lake association and the ASBC. Charles Ray reported that Roy Worthley resigned Provo FBC to lead the Orem mission.

Wings for Christ Completes a Mercy Mission

Wings for Christ completed one of its many mercy missions on August 26, 1964, when they flew Jerry Webb, age twenty-two, from Canyon City, Colorado, to Coolidge, Arizona. Webb, the son of Arizona missionaries Truman and Lena Webb, had suffered a broken upper right leg and fractured pelvis in a serious auto accident involving five college students. The students were traveling from Canyon City to Cripple Creek where they worked as summer employees of Imperial Hotel. Ron Kelsch piloted the Wings for Christ plane.

Cottonwood, Utah, Baptist Mission

SLC, Utah, Holladay Baptist Church started the Cottonwood Baptist Mission on September 6, 1964, at Cottonwood Mall in the SLC area. The new mission affiliated with Salt Lake association and the ASBC. Missionary Charles Ray led the first service.

Raymond Cearley Reports Progress at Mountain Home

Raymond Cearley, the Mountain Home, Idaho, FSBC pastor wrote the ASBC office on October 11, 1964, saying:

> We had a great start for the new year yesterday with 333 in SS, 185 in Training Union, six baptized, and three additions by letter. We praise God for this especially since we lost one hundred and fifty of our faithfuls due to military transfer during summer months. In spite of this we are running ahead of the attendance for the same period of time last year. Thank you for all your help and prayers as we labor for the Lord in Mountain Home.

Salt Lake City, Utah, Southeast Baptist Church

The SLC, Utah, Holladay Baptist Church organized SLC Southeast Baptist Church October 25, 1964, with twenty-two charter members. The new church affiliated with Salt Lake association and the UISBC. Holladay started the mission in the basement of Ted Osborne's home and later rented a bank basement for services. After the church secured a fifty-thousand-dollar HMB loan, Atlas Construction completed a church building on the three-and-one-half acre location owned by the church on July 1, 1969. Early pastors were Charles Ray, Charles Clarke, Mayo Brown (int.), Jeff Rousseau, Ron Parker, and Mike Gray. Southeast church emerged as the strongest church in the UISBC in the 1990s.

Utah-Idaho Southern Baptists Finalize Plans

Two days before the constitution of the UISBC, on October 26–27, 1964, the women met at the SLC, Utah, FSBC to finalize plans to organize a state WMU. Two WMU leaders from the ASBC led the event: Almarine Brown, the WMU executive secretary, and Mrs. H. E. Martin, WMU president. They conducted sessions with the associational WMU presidents and were assisted by Bernice Elliott of the Birmingham, Alabama, SBC/WMU office.

The UIRMC met on October 28, 1964, for its final session. The members present were Bill Thornton, John Embery, Mel White, George Eichler, Bob Compere, John L. Smith, Edwin Fast, Mayo Brown, Darwin E. Welsh, Gary Christopherson, and Homer Wickes. The visitors were Courts Redford, HMB; Charles Ashcraft, Las Vegas, Nevada, FSBC pastor and ASBC president; and E. W. Hunke Jr., Roy Ferguson, Roland Smith, Dick Turner, Raymond Cearley, E. J. Jenkins, John Upchurch, and Kelly Lawson. UIRMC chairmen, Mayo Brown (calendar), Darwin Welsh (budget), and Homer Wickes (constitution), gave reports. President Thornton appointed the time, place, and preacher and resolutions committees.

The first annual UISBC pastors' conference met on October 28, 1964, at the SLC, Utah, FSBC. The program committee members were Gary Christopherson, chairman; Darwin Welsh; and E. W. Hunke Jr., a former Vernal, Utah, FBC pastor. The speakers included Harold Graves, GGBTS president; George Eichler; John Smith; John Embery; Homer Wickes; and Gary Christopherson. The conference elected John Embery as the first president, George Eichler as vice-president, and Lavoid Robertson as secretary.

Utah-Idaho Southern Baptist Convention Constitutes

The fifty-two Utah-Idaho SBC churches sent 363 messengers and visitors to constitute the twenty-ninth SBC state convention at the SLC, Utah, FSBC on October 29, 1964. The constituting churches were affiliated with seven associations in Utah and Idaho: Eastern Idaho, Boise Valley, Magic Valley, Golden Spike, Salt Lake, Utah, and Gideon. Messengers, who represented sixty-five hundred members, voted to begin operations on January 1, 1965, to adopt a $149,821 budget, to raise $59,200 Cooperative Program dollars in 1964, and to elect a state executive board.

A. B. Cash, HMB pioneer missions secretary, led in organizing the executive board. The UISBC board elected Charles Ashcraft, Las Vegas, Nevada, FSBC pastor, as the first executive secretary. The constitution of the new UISBC state convention established a new set of problems for work in Utah and Idaho. The ASBC staff, who had helped the pioneer churches in the North since 1944, would no longer work in the two states. The churches would now depend on a small, overloaded UISBC staff. The UISBC executive director was asked to shoulder the task of evangelism.

Ira Marks Pays Tribute to the Pioneers

After reflecting on the historical past, former missionary Ira I. Marks listed reasons why the work grew: (1) God called, ordained, and sent consecrated pastors and families to work in Utah; (2) the HMB and ASBC assisted the churches with pastoral aid; (3) student summer missionaries helped with VBS and survey; (4) pastors who served in Utah remained in the West; and (5) the churches located in the South and East helped by co-sponsoring work and helping pay pastors' salaries.

Marks paid tribute to former student summer missionaries and pastors who pioneered Utah work. The student summer missionaries were Lewis Martin, Bob King, Cecil Morgan, Joe Gish, Mr. and Mrs. Milt Hughes, Roger Lovett, Frances Bryant, Elsa Dean Gish, Wade Robertson, Dan White, Cassie Henderson, Dwight Dudley, Jimmy McCoy, Logan Roots, Glen Blaisdell, Jean Graham, Linda Lyons, Sid Baskin, and C. W. Bryant. The pioneer pastors were Nolan Beaird, W. W. Fordham, Bill Trow, J. E. Akin, E. W. Hunke Jr., David Pate, Paul Cauethon, Myron Crawford, N. T. James, Roy Leverette, Leon Maxwell, W. R. Ward, Fred Higginbotham, Fred Marks, and others he did not name.

Ogden, Utah, Valley View Baptist Church

Ogden, Utah, Calvary Baptist Church organized the Ogden Valley View Baptist Church on November 8, 1965, the first new church to be organized in the UISBC. The mission started on May 3, 1964, with three families under the leadership of missionary Charles Ray. The church affiliated with the Golden Spike association and the UISBC. The early pastors were B. J. Hall, Meredith Davis, and David Duncan.

ASBC Thirty-Sixth Annual Session Welcomes UISBC Leaders

The SBC churches in Nevada and Arizona sent 443 messengers and visitors to the thirty-sixth annual ASBC at Phoenix Central Baptist Church on November 11–13, 1964. No messengers from Utah and Idaho registered for the first time in eighteen years. The ASBC had been reduced to 251 churches and 127 missions. Charles Ashcraft, ASBC president, introduced two representatives from the UISBC: Darwin Welsh, UISBC vice-president, and Charles Ray, Utah missionary. The ASBC received the two men enthusiastically.

UISBC Employs Charles Ashcraft as Executive Secretary

Charles Ashcraft, ASBC president, stunned the ASBC executive board when he resigned to become the first UISBC leader effective on January 1, 1965. Ashcraft, who was known for his preaching, grace, charm, and kindness, had discouraged Nevada churches from the continuing relationship with Utah-Idaho Southern Baptists. He now led the new UISBC without help from the Nevada churches.

ASBC Describes 30,000 Movement as a Success

Phil Jones of the HMB reported that fifteen new churches organized in a five-year period from 1960 to 1964 in Idaho, Utah, and Nevada. The SBC 30,000 Movement ended December 31, 1964. The ASBC described the effort as a glorious success. Utah, Idaho, Nevada, and Arizona requested 407 awards for new work during the campaign: 287 for new missions and 120 for churches. In 1964 the ASBC hit its targeted goal of "sixty-four in sixty-four." From June 1, 1956, to December 31, 1964, the new churches grew from zero to 12,541 members, 14,052 in SS, $955,588 in receipts, and $81,462 in Cooperative Program gifts. The ASBC had constituted the UISBC and four new associations (Apache, White Mountain, Troy Brooks, River Valley) during the emphasis.

Tonopah, Nevada, First Baptist Church

Hawthorne, Nevada, Calvary Baptist Church organized Tonopah FBC in 1965. Layman Harvey Francis started the mission as a Bible study. James Minnis served as the first pastor. The new church affiliated with Nevada association and the SBGCC. The early pastors were James Minnis, Laughlin Mackay, E. C. Duncan, R. L. Shannon, Ron Hibpschman, Harvey Broadway, Lewis Davis, Larry Dickey, Paul Ray, and Tim Shields.

Walker, California, First Baptist Church
Yerington, Nevada, FBC organized the Walker, California, FBC in 1965. The new church affiliated with Nevada association and the SBGCC. Greg Rodman served as the first pastor. The early pastors were Melvin Jones, Bob Wells (int.), Frank Kriz, LaVern Inzer, David Seifert, Tom Bishop, Cameron Irwin, and Bill Smith.

Wendover, Utah, First Baptist Church
Ely, Nevada, FBC organized the Wendover FBC in 1965. An earlier mission started by Utah missionary Ira Marks had ceased to exist. Don Ledbetter preached the organizational sermon for Foy O. King, Ely pastoral missionary. The new church affiliated with the Nevada association and the SBGCC. The early pastors were Don Ledbetter (int.), Milford Cooper, Glenn Swarthout, Edward Renfro, Carroll Schroeder, Earl Speakman, and Mack Cole. The church later affiliated with Salt Lake association and the UISBC.

Las Vegas, Nevada, Parkdale Baptist Church
The Las Vegas, Nevada, Parkdale Baptist Church organized in 1965. The new church affiliated with Lake Mead association and the ASBC. The early pastors were A. Towns, Robert Foster, Dennis Vaughn, Jim Vernon, Dan Raley, and Robert Walker. When the church ordained Vaughn as a minister in October 1972, Don Mulkey preached the sermon.

HMB Starts the Christian Service Corps and US-2 Programs
The HMB initiated the Christian Service Corps and the US-2 programs in 1965. The corps provided a means for laypersons to volunteer for mission service. No educational requirements were

established. Persons thirty-five years of age and over gave from two to ten weeks of service. The US-2 program used college grads twenty-seven years of age or younger willing to give two years of mission service. The board provided travel, housing, and modest salary. The associational missionaries directed the activities of both the Christian Service Corps and the US-2ers.

HMB Employs Arthur Rutledge as Executive Director

When Courts Redford retired as the HMB executive director in 1964, the HMB employed Arthur Bristow Rutledge. Rutledge was born on April 30, 1911, at San Antonio, Texas, to Abram Burl and Sarah Priscilla Graham Rutledge. He was saved, baptized, called to the ministry, and ordained by the San Antonio Central Baptist Church. He attended Briscoe and Crockett grade schools, Washington Irving Junior High, and Breckenridge High School. He graduated from Baylor University, SBTS, and SWBTS (Th.D.). While preaching at a Latin-American Baptist mission, Rutledge met volunteer worker Vesta Mae Sharber and married her at Somerset, Texas, on June 8, 1936. They had three children. During his twenty-seven-year pastoral ministry he pastored nine churches. The native Texan began his HMB tenure at age fifty-three, served twelve years, retired on December 31, 1976, and died November 27, 1977. He and his wife are buried in Newnan, Georgia.

UISBC Employs Darwin Welsh as State Mission Director

The HMB and UISBC employed Darwin E. Welsh, SLC, Utah, FSBC pastor, as associate executive/missions director on March 1, 1965. Welsh had served seven years on the ASBC executive board and five years on the UIRMC. Welsh was born on October 31, 1923, in Taylor County, Iowa. He was saved and baptized at age nine. He graduated from Denton, Texas, High School, and attended North Texas State and HPC. Welsh served in the U.S. Air Force (1942–1947). He married Zula M. Meredith, and had three sons. Welsh pastored Texas Baptist churches at Denton, El Dorado, Trent, and the Coleman County Echo Baptist; Artesia, Colorado; and SLC, Utah, FSBC. His call to Colorado came when a cowboy evangelist, George Havens, preached at Artesia, Colorado. Havens's mother shared the information with her pastor, Darwin Welsh, at the Trent, Texas, FBC. After several phone talks with the Gillory family, he drove to Artesia to eat Christmas dinner with the Gillorys and preach. He moved his family to snow-covered Colorado in a U-Haul trailer. Welsh taught fourth and fifth grades at school and opened the Rangely, Colorado, Baptist Mission in the Saddle Club building by the river. He served as the school principal (1956–1957) while he pastored at Artesia and Rangely. Prior to his election as UISBC state mission director, he pastored the SLC, Utah, FSBC. He served as the UISBC executive director for twenty years. After his retirement in 1990, he married Anita Lemke and pastored churches in Arizona at the Village of Oak Creek and Sedona. The Welshes moved back to Utah to serve as the Alta Canyon Baptist Church pastor in Sandy, Utah.

Las Vegas, Nevada, Twin Lakes Baptist Church

Las Vegas, Nevada, FSBC organized the Las Vegas Twin Lakes Baptist Church on April 4, 1965. Don Mulkey, founding pastor, had established the Edmonton, Alberta, Dovercourt Baptist Church before moving to Las Vegas. The new church affiliated with Lake Mead association and the ASBC. While meeting in Twin Lakes Plaza Shopping Center, the church reported seventy-two additions, 135 in SS, and ninety in Training Union. Mulkey stayed for sixteen years and led three building programs. Twin Lakes was one of six new SBC churches organized in Las Vegas in 1965. The early pastors were Don Mulkey, Robert Hunn, and David Doyel.

Charlie and Virginia Tague Leave the Intermountain West

When Larry, Charlie and Virginia Tague's eight-year-old son, died on April 14, 1965, the Tagues moved to California to continue their church building ministry. He built new church buildings at San Diego and Carlsbad in California, and Tijuana, La Paz, San Lucas, San Felipe, and Ojos Negro in Mexico. After they retired from the building ministry, they lived at Encinitas, California, until they moved to Chino Valley, Arizona, in 1997.

General Missionaries in the 1950s and 1960s

Jack Knox Maben, HMB/BGCA missionary to Nevada (1958–1959).

Roy and Dorothy Ferguson, HMB/BGCA missionary to Idaho (1959–1984).

James Edwin Byers, special missionary to Idaho (1959–1972).

Foy and Lela King, HMB/SBGCC missionary to Nevada (1960–1964).

Bill and Emily Barker, HMB/BGCA missionary to Nevada (1960–1961).

LaVern A. Inzer, HMB/SBGCC missionary to Nevada (1960–1986).

General Missionaries in the 1960s

Charles Albert Ray, HMB/ASBC missionary to Utah (1962–1969).

Donald Lee Loving, HMB/ASBC missionary to Nevada (1962–1963).

F. Milton and Mary Lee Gage, HMB/ASBC missionary to Nevada (1964–1969).

K. Medford and Dorothy Hutson, HMB/ASBC missionary to Utah (1969–1982).

Mayo and Celia Brown, HMB/ASBC missionary to Utah (1969–1984).

Robert A. and Sara Wells, HMB/SBGCC missionary to Nevada (1969–1982).

North Las Vegas, Nevada, First Southern Baptist Church

Las Vegas, Nevada, Twin Lakes Baptist Church organized the North Las Vegas (Community College) FSBC in 1965. The church affiliated with Lake Mead association and the ASBC. Don Wright served as the first pastor. The church celebrated the beginning of Wright's eighth anniversary and the church's seventh on September 26, 1972. After the church reverted to mission status, Don Mulkey filled the pulpit as pastor. The early pastors were Wright, Bob Dorsey, David Wallace, Cal Collins, and Al Turrill. In 1988 the church merged with Las Vegas Frontier Baptist Church and took the name Frontier Community College Baptist Church. Karel Sylvanus served as the pastor.

Nevada Pastors Meet for Second Nevada Baptist Fellowship

Boulder City, Nevada, FBC, the oldest SBC church in southern Nevada, hosted the second annual NVBF in Boulder on April 28–29, 1965. To familiarize the northern Nevada pastors with their churches, each session met at a different location: the Lake Mead association office and Twin Lakes, Nellis, and Redrock Baptist churches. The program personalities were A. B. Cash, HMB; Crile Dean, Sparks Temple Baptist Church pastor; Charles Day, Hawthorne Calvary Baptist Church pastor; Milton Gage, Lake Mead association missionary; Leonard B. Sigle, Nevada association missionary; and Nevada governor Grant Sawyer, who spoke on the theme "Nevada, Today and Tomorrow." Others in attendance were Don Loving, James Minnis, Don Mulkey, Hugh Hamilton, Walt Oman, William Singleton, I. B. Wilson, and LaVern Inzer. SBC workers present were Lewis Newman, HMB; E. W. Hunke Jr., ASBC; and Ralph Longshore, SBGCC.

Henderson, Nevada, Faith Baptist Church

The Henderson, Nevada, FSBC organized the Henderson Faith Baptist Church on April 29, 1965, with thirty-eight charter members. The new church affiliated with Lake Mead association and the ASBC. Jim Reid served as the first pastor. The early pastors were Herbert Hughes, Louis Nimmo, Terry Starkey, and Jim Motshagen.

Indian Springs, Nevada, First Baptist Church

Las Vegas, Nevada, Nellis Baptist Church organized the Indian Springs FBC on May 2, 1965. The church affiliated with Lake Mead association and the ASBC. The mission started November 15, 1964, with forty-three present. Seventy-seven enrolled in Bible study. Bill Thornton served as the first pastor. The early pastors were Bernard Ford, Charles Ghormley, Owen Overton, Ronald Wagner, Hollis Lockeby, Robert Pierson, James Vernon, Denver Copeland, Arnold Kelly, Nathan Huff, Walter Goad, Russell Dains, and Bill Gibbons.

Las Vegas, Nevada, First Mexican Baptist Mission

The Las Vegas, Nevada, First Mexican Baptist Mission started in August 1965 with SS, Training Union, Thursday evening service, and two worship services in the sponsoring church. The mission affiliated with Lake Mead association and the ASBC.

Las Vegas, Nevada, Bethel Baptist Church

North Las Vegas, Nevada, Calvary Baptist Church organized the Las Vegas Bethel Baptist Church September 26, 1965. Jaffus Haley served as the first pastor. The new church affiliated with Lake Mead association and the ASBC.

Weippe, Idaho, Baptist Church

The Orofino, Idaho, First Baptist Church organized the Weippe FBC in October 1965. Pastor Holt Sodeman taught a Thursday evening Bible study in the community building until the people asked for a Sunday service. The church met in a Seventh Day Adventist building in January 1966 with missionary Ed Byers leading. Douglas Hopper served as the first pastor. The new church affiliated with Lewis-Clark association and the BGCOW.

Las Vegas, Nevada, East Las Vegas Baptist Church

Las Vegas, Nevada, Nellis Baptist Church organized the East Las Vegas Baptist Church on October 10, 1965, in a store building on the Boulder highway. The church affiliated with Lake Mead association and the ASBC. Early pastors were Larry Railes, Darwin Crow, and Dale Tullock. The church did not grow and reverted to mission status under Las Vegas Sunrise Baptist Church.

Nevada Association Celebrates Its Tenth Anniversary

Nevada association celebrated its tenth anniversary at the annual meeting at Sparks, Nevada, on October 15–16, 1965. The messengers paid tribute to missionary Leonard and Edrie Sigle for years of faithful service to Nevada Baptists. Nevada association divided into three zones: (1) Sierra (Carson City, Reno, Lake Tahoe); (2) Lahontan (Lovelock to Hawthorne); and (3) Humbolt River (Winnemucca to Ely).

Melvin Owens Dies in Wings for Christ Tragedy

Melvin Owens, a member of GCC Wings for Christ, was killed on December 2, 1965, when his plane crashed on the way home from his Sunday services. A news report described the tragedy:

> In a sermon shortly before he was killed in a plane crash, a Phoenix minister-school teacher told his small congregation he was prepared to die. The body of the Rev. Melvin Owens, forty-one, was found in the kneeling position near the wreckage of his single engine plane in southwestern Utah. A Bible, with his name engraved in gold letters, was on the ground between the victim and the wreckage. "If I had one hour to live, I'm ready to go," the minister in the Wings for Christ group of the Southern Baptist church told about thirty persons Sunday morning in a mission service at Milford, Utah. Owens left Milford, in central Utah, about 1:45 p.m. Sunday on an eighty-five mile trip to pick up three GCC student ministers at Hurricane who had made a religious survey of the community. Dr. James L. McNett, pastor of University Baptist Church in Phoenix, said he learned the

plane missed the top of a hill by about ten feet. A rain storm covered the area when the plane crashed on Sunday afternoon. McNett said the crash was the first involving any of the Wings for Christ planes during 500,000 hours of flying. This particular plane, purchased through the redemption of 5,472 trading stamp books, had been used for several life-saving mercy missions during the year.

Eureka, Nevada, Diamond Valley First Baptist Church

Ely, Nevada, FBC organized the Eureka Diamond Valley Baptist Church in 1966. George Thomason, the first pastor, served the congregation for ten years. The church affiliated with Nevada association and the SBGCC. Early pastors were Jerry Holmes, David Morrison, Arthur Wickes, James Wright, Wayne Cathey, and Dan Kirk.

Layton, Utah, Bi-Lingual Baptist Church

Layton, Utah, Bi-Lingual Baptist Church organized in 1966 and affiliated with Golden Spike association and the ASBC. The early pastors were Ernest Silvas and Salvador Fernandez.

BGCOW Employs Roland Hood as Executive Director

The BGCOW executive board employed state mission director, Roland Parks Hood, in 1966 as its third executive director. Hood had served the BGCOW since 1948 when the HMB and SBGCC employed him as general missionary to succeed H. A. Zimmerman in Oregon and Washington. Hood led the convention until retirement in 1968.

Sponsoring Conventions Continue Evangelism Emphasis

After leading the ASBC state evangelism conference in January 1966, W. D. Lawes moved to Atlanta to join the HMB evangelism staff. The HMB and ASBC employed Irving Childress to succeed Lawes April 1, 1966. The ASBC evangelism director continued to serve Lake Mead churches in southern Nevada. SBGCC evangelism director Eugene Grubbs served northern Nevada, and BGCOW evangelism director Lewis Steed served northern Idaho.

SBGCC Employs Robert Hughes as Executive Secretary

SBGCC, which had been on a plateau for several years, employed Robert D. Hughes as its fifth SBGCC executive secretary in 1966. SBGCC president Clyde Skidmore spoke to the convention about the decline, and urged that 107 new missions be started in 1967. R. L. Patillo, the SBGCC/SS secretary, reported that 40 percent of the churches had a SS enrollment loss in the years 1963–1965. Hughes was born on August 1, 1919, at Glenwood, Arkansas. He graduated from AOBU and SWBTS, married Ruth Williams, and they had three children. He pastored two Arkansas Baptist churches, three Texas churches, and two California churches. He served as missionary for the Arkansas Carey Baptist Association in 1942, pastored the Ventura, California, FSBC for ten years, and Long Beach FSBC for eight years. He served as SBGCC president, long-range planning committee chairman, executive board chairman for three terms, and the total program committee chairman.

St. Anthony, Idaho, Upper Valley Baptist Church

Idaho Falls, Idaho, Calvary Baptist Church organized the St. Anthony Upper Valley Baptist Church in February 1966 following a census of Rexburg. The church met in Veterans Memorial building, Old Hansen Memorial Chapel, a home, V.F.W. Hall, and two mobile chapels. The new church reported thirty-one resident members and thirty-three baptized. It affiliated with Eastern Idaho association and the UISBC. The early pastors were George Eichler, Kenneth Parker, and Chuck Joyner.

Nevada Pastors Meet for Third Nevada Baptist Fellowship

After having met at Sparks and Boulder City, Nevada, for the first two fellowships, Nevada association invited southern Nevada pastors to meet at Hawthorne Calvary Baptist Church, the oldest SBC church in Nevada, on April 14–15, 1966. Ledbetter discusses this session as the first annual meeting saying that the first two meetings of the pastors were preliminary. The program participants were Larry Lewis, LaVern Inzer, James Minnis, Don Loving,

Leonard Sigle, Milton Gage, Crile Dean, Ralph Longshore, Irvin Dawson, Grady Cothen, Jerrell Griffin, and A. B. Cash.

Moscow, Idaho, Trinity Baptist Church

The Moscow, Idaho, Trinity Baptist Church organized in May 1966. The new church affiliated with Lewis-Clark association and the BGCOW. Roy L. Johnson, Northwest Baptist historian, reported that the city of Moscow fascinated Southern Baptists because of the university located there. Mission services, which began in a home in September 1959, later met in the American Legion cabin and the Seventh Day Adventist church. The church completed its church plant in January 1963. Richard Turner served as the first pastor.

ASBC Reorganizes after Hunkes Move to Alaska

The HMB and ASBC employed Roy Sutton to succeed E. W. Hunke Jr. in 1966. The ASBC executive board assigned the Trust and Memorial Fund responsibilities to Bill Parker. Irvin Dawson, the ASBC language mission director since May 1, 1957, resigned to go to an HMB language mission position. With the departure of both ASBC mission leaders, the convention realigned the state staff and reassigned responsibilities. The HMB and ASBC employed the Las Vegas FSBC pastor Dan Carmichael Stringer Jr. as the associate mission director on December 1, 1966.

Las Vegas, Nevada, New Jerusalem Baptist Church

After the Lake Mead association credentials committee and its missionary, Milton Gage, met with the messengers from Las Vegas New Jerusalem Baptist Church, they recommended that they be seated at the October 1966 annual meeting. The black church served with the association and the ASBC faithfully.

West Jordan, Utah, First Baptist Church

Kearns, Utah, FBC organized the West Jordan FBC on November 13, 1966, with twenty-five charter members. The mission started August 9–20, 1965, with a VBS and revival led by

Benny Farmer, of Louisiana, and Sid Baskin. The church affiliated with Salt Lake association and the UISBC. After having met at the Daughters of Utah Pioneer Hall, the church purchased five acres of land and sold three acres to pay off the debt. The early pastors were Joe Eubanks, Olan Gooch, Ruel Cook, David Arnette, James Akin, John Blake, Dewayne Thompson, Rhett Durfee, and Myron Adams.

Las Vegas, Nevada, West Oakey Baptist Church

Las Vegas, Nevada, Redrock Baptist Church organized the Las Vegas West Oakey Baptist Church in 1967. The mission, which had begun in November 1965, had twenty-three present for the first service. The church affiliated with Lake Mead association and the ASBC and sponsored four new missions. The early pastors were Don Shumake, Lock Mackay, Tom Popelka, Neal Myers, Walker Campbell, and Michael Rochelle. Rochelle, who had been saved, baptized, and called to preach at Las Vegas Twin Lakes Baptist Church, led West Oakey to become Nevada's largest SBC church.

Reno, Nevada, Second Baptist Church

Reno, Nevada, Grace Baptist Church sold its church property to Reno Second Baptist Church and ceased to exist in 1967. The Second Baptist Church, a black congregation, affiliated with the Nevada association and the SBGCC on October 13–14, 1967. Pastor William Webb led the church to participate faithfully in the associational program of Nevada Baptists.

Nevada Baptists Find New Ways to Evangelize

The NVBF elected a nine-member steering committee in 1967 to work with HMB leaders in exploring new ways to evangelize Nevada. When Leonard Sigle came to retirement age the following year, the HMB agreed to use him as pastoral missionary. After retirement, Sigle started new SBC work at Beatty, Nevada, and Kings Beach.

Lake Mead association of Nevada reported that twenty-four VBSs enrolled 2,684 pupils, led 116 to Christ, and raised $834 for the Cooperative Program. After having organized six new Las Vegas churches in 1965, the association reported starting nine new missions in 1967: Spanish, Paradise, Mt. Pass, Searchlight, Mt. View, Beatty, Alamo, Mt. Charleston, and West Oakey.

Rainbow Canyon Baptist Association Constitutes (Utah)

Messengers from four SBC churches in southwestern Utah and in northern Arizona organized the Rainbow Canyon association in 1967: St. George, Cedar City, Milford, Utah, and Page, Arizona. SBC churches located at Richfield and Panguitch affiliated later. The Rainbow Canyon association celebrated its twenty-fifth anniversary in 1992.

Nyssa, Oregon, Park Avenue Baptist Church

The Nampa, Idaho, FSBC organized Nyssa, Oregon, Park Avenue Baptist Church on May 21, 1967, with thirty-one charter members. The new church affiliated with Boise Valley association and the UISBC. The mission had started on November 4, 1963, with William Hyslop as the first pastor. When attendance declined until no one attended services except Mrs. E. J. Jenkins, Asheville, North Carolina, Grassy Branch Baptist Church pastor, Jay Blankenship, led his church to pay off the Park Avenue church debts. Early pastors were Jimmy Williams, Delbert Smith, Roy Kilby, Ralph Tisdial, Jerry Branson, Charles Williamson, Roy J. Ferguson, Dale Mitchell, John Henry, James Dobbs, Thomas Moore, John Blake, and Jim Erickson. Delbert Smith's wife became ill and died across the state line in Idaho as he tried to get medical help.

Salt Lake City, Utah, University Baptist Church

SLC, Utah, Highland Baptist Church organized the University Baptist Church on September 17, 1967, with twenty-nine charter members. The SLC mission met at 316 University Street. Two US-2 couples led in the work: Ken and Mildred Mathias of Tennessee, and Jim and Polly Coleman of Mississippi. The church affiliated with Salt Lake association and the UISBC. The early pastors were Joe Conway, Joe Music, C. E. Autrey, Terry Minchow-Proffitt, Kevin Sigsby, and Lynn Weston. The church started missions at Murray-Midvale, Heber, and SLC Chinese.

SBGCC Annual Meeting Convenes at Reno in 1967

Northern Nevada's eighteen churches and thirteen missions hosted the twenty-seventh annual SBGCC annual meeting at Reno in November 1967. The convention registered 953 messengers and 376 visitors. California Southern Baptists met outside California for the first time. Nevada churches had 408 Nevadans present. Ralph Longshore, SBGCC cooperative missions division director, shared that the SBGCC missionaries organized eleven new churches and started twenty-four new missions in 1967. He expressed hope that the HMB's "Project 500" emphasis would encourage SBGCC churches to start fifty new works each year.

On October 1, 1967, the HMB had launched "Project 500," a two-year program to plant five hundred new churches. The emphasis continued through September 30, 1969.

HMB Pioneer Solomon Dowis Dies at Atlanta

Solomon Franklin Dowis (1891–1967) died at Atlanta, Georgia, on November 5, 1967, one week after completing his last interim pastorate at Doraville, Georgia, FBC. Dowis led Southern Baptist advance in the West from 1943 to 1958. Friends described Dowis as a great pioneer, outstanding mission strategist, powerful preacher, careful organizer, master negotiator, and efficient administrator. He understood people, their abilities and needs, and how to use their talents for God and mankind. In 1998 the Hunkes continued to write Frances Dowis, a former secretary who became his wife, at her Gatlinburg, Tennessee, home.

Battle Mountain, Nevada, First Baptist Church

Winnemucca, Nevada, FBC organized the Battle Mountain FBC in 1968. LaVern Inzer started the mission with Thursday night Bible studies. The church affiliated with Nevada association and the SBGCC. Early pastors were Thomas Underwood, Calfrey Collins (2), Ron Hill, Tom Bacon (int.), Danny Henderson, Adrian Hall (int.), Rudy Duett (int.), Quinton Montgomery, and Ken Cox.

Mid-State Baptist Association Constitutes (Utah)

Mid-State association of Utah constituted in 1968 when the messengers from two central Utah Baptist churches met and decided to reduce travel time. The following year the churches reported six baptisms, 244 members, $11,058 in receipts, and $832 to the Cooperative Program. Medford Hutson served the association until it disbanded in 1969 at the annual associational meeting.

BGCOW Employs Eugene Grubbs as Executive Director

The BGCOW employed William Eugene Grubbs as its executive director to succeed Roland P. Hood in 1968. Grubbs served the Idaho panhandle, Oregon, Washington, and western Canada. Grubbs, a native of Foley, Alabama, grew up in Florida and graduated from Stetson University and NOBTS. He pastored Baptist churches in Florida, Alabama, Missouri, and Mississippi. The FMB sent him to the Philippines as a missionary. Grubbs had served as SBGCC evangelism secretary (1968–1970) with responsibilities in both northern Nevada and California. After he completed his work with the BGCOW, he returned to the FMB.

BGCOW Employs Howard Ramsey as Missionary (Idaho)

After missionary Joe Theo Howard retired in 1967, he moved to Kerrville, Texas. The HMB and BGCOW employed Howard H. Ramsey on January 1, 1968, as missionary to Inland Empire association. He led SBC work in northern Idaho and the Spokane area. Ramsey was born on October 1, 1928, at Tulia, Texas, to Paul and Dessa Mae (Keller) Ramsey. He had two sisters. He served in the U.S. Army Airborne (1946–1948). After trusting Christ at age twenty-seven, he was baptized by the Amarillo, Texas, South Lawn Baptist Church August 26, 1955. The Roby, Texas, Liberty Baptist Church ordained him December 15, 1957. He wrote:

> My home was non-Christian. At the age of six I responded to an invitation, and was immersed by the Tulia, Texas, FBC, but did not know Christ. At age twenty-five I began to search for meaning in life by attending church. While I was searching for peace, my pastor showed me how to be saved and led me to Christ and baptism.

He graduated from Tulia High School, Texas Tech College, HSU, SWBTS, and Southwest Baptist University (DST). He married Lawanda Gay Sewell at Tulia, Texas, October 14, 1949, and they had three children. He wrote:

> In 1962 I preached a revival for the Spokane, Washington, Pines Baptist Church. Pastor Frank Barnes said fewer than thirty percent of people in the Northwest were church members, but I found great openness for witnessing. On my return to Texas, I asked my people to pray for God to send personal soul-winning preachers to the Northwest, and seven months later I responded to the call from Kennewick, Washington.

Ramsey pastored churches at Roby, Mineral Wells, and Lipan, Texas. The HMB and BGCOW employed him as missionary to Inland Empire association (1968–1971) and state evangelism secretary (1972–1979). He directed the HMB direct evangelism division.

Riggins, Idaho, Baptist Mission

The Cottonwood, Idaho, Baptist Church started the Riggins Baptist Mission in 1968 after James and Patsy Myers, Harley Wendt, and others surveyed the community in the summer of 1968. The mission asked Cottonwood, Idaho, Emmanuel Baptist Church to serve as their sponsor. The mission affiliated with Whispering Pines association and the UISBC. Irvin Derry served as the first pastor.

Beatty, Nevada, First Southern Baptist Church

When Leonard Sigle retired as Nevada association missionary on December 31, 1967, he was employed by the HMB and SBGCC to serve as pastoral missionary at Beatty, Nevada. The mission affiliated with Nevada association and the SBGCC. After six months, Sigle led the Beatty mission to call Don Wilson as pastor. The early pastors were Don Wilson, Curtis Bellomy, Fred Loer, and Reese Morrow.

New Meadows, Idaho, Baptist Mission

The Cottonwood, Idaho, Baptist Church organized New Meadows Baptist Mission on July 14, 1968, with seven people present. On the following day the Cottonwood church sent pastor James Myers, his two sons Bart and Matt, Robin Addleman, the Harley Wendts, and summer missionaries Caroline Hodge and Mary Lee Aden to survey New Meadows. On July 20 an organizational session was held in the home of Oris Tinsley. The mission bought and remodeled an old home for services in 1968. The new church affiliated with Treasure Valley association and the UISBC.

Salt Lake City, Utah, Shiloh Baptist Church

The Granger, Utah, FBC organized the SLC, Utah, Shiloh Baptist Church March 10, 1968, with thirteen charter members. The church affiliated with Salt Lake association and the UISBC. J. N. Foreman of Granger and Ira Martin of Shiloh led services. Black church pastors who affiliated with the SBC helped white pastors know how to respond when Martin Luther King Jr. was assassinated on April 4, 1968, at Memphis, Tennessee. Prentiss Ware poured foundations for a new church building which Shiloh dedicated June 11, 1972. The UISBC elected Ira Martin to the UISBC executive board, a first for black Baptists in Utah. Early pastors were Ira Martin, Lafayette Moseley, and H. J. Lilly.

ASBC Employs Jess Canafax as Associate Mission Director

After Dan Stringer resigned as the ASBC associate missions director August 31, 1968, to pastor Scottsdale, Arizona, Coronado Baptist Church, the HMB and ASBC employed Jess Lee Canafax, the missionary of Central association, as the ASBC state mission director (1968–1982). Canafax was born at Ardmore, Oklahoma, on April 27, 1924, to William and Mary Ann Canafax. His pastor led him to Christ at the age of twenty-five. Ada, Oklahoma, Trinity Baptist Church baptized him Easter Sunday April 17, 1949, and Ardmore Emmanuel Baptist Church ordained him on July 21, 1951. He served in the U.S. Navy.

Canafax graduated from Ardmore High School, Murray State College, and East Central State in Oklahoma, and he attended SWBTS. Grand Canyon University (GCU) bestowed a D.D. degree on him. He married Joyce Arvetta Setzer on September 4, 1947, and they had two children. He pastored churches at Tulsa and Mounds, Oklahoma, and Glendale, Arizona. He left the ASBC in 1982 to serve as TXBC new work director. After retirement, they returned to Tulsa, Oklahoma, where he continued to serve as an interim and supply pastor.

HMB Faces Major Evangelism Changes

The HMB faced major changes in its evangelism program as the decade of the 1960s closed. When C. E. Autrey retired in 1969, HMB associates carried on the program. Eugene Grubbs, the SBGCC state evangelism director, resigned to become BGCOW executive director, and Lewis Steed, the BGCOW state evangelism director, retired the following year. Irving Childress continued to lead ASBC evangelism in southern Nevada. The HMB and SBGCC employed Harry D. Williams to replace Grubbs in 1969. The UISBC used its executive director to promote evangelism. The HMB initiated a mission youth program in 1969. High school and college-age students traveled with their sponsors as mission choirs to hold Backyard Bible Clubs (BYBC) and lead out in evangelism. In 1977, 350 groups involving 14,000 young people worked across the United States.

Pullman, Washington, Emmanuel Baptist Church

Moscow, Idaho, Trinity Baptist Church organized the Pullman Emmanuel Baptist Church in 1969 with two college professors and their families. Bill Peters served as the first pastor. Peters wrote, "In 1968 I saw Roy Owen at the Southern Baptist Convention in Houston. He introduced me to the HMB Project 500 and I signed up. Ed Byers called me about Pullman, and we decided God was in it; we came, and never looked back." The church affiliated with Lewis-Clark association and the BGCOW. In 1969 the Emmanuel church reported fifty-nine members and five baptisms. Clint Ashley followed Peters as pastor.

Elko, Nevada, Calvary Baptist Church

The Elko, Nevada, Calvary Baptist Church organized on July 12, 1969, with thirty-three members. The church affiliated with Nevada association and the SBGCC. Robert D. Hughes, the SBGCC executive director, preached the organizational service. Early pastors were Arthur Blessitt, John Randolph, and Don Ledbetter, who served the church seventeen and one-half years. The church established missions at Carlin, Wells, Mountain City, Spring Creek, Wildhorse, Tuscarora, Murphy's Hot Springs, Jackpot, Three Creek, Contact, Jarbidge, and Wendover.

Salt Lake City, Utah, Millcreek Baptist Church

The SLC, Utah, Holladay Baptist Church organized the SLC Millcreek Baptist Church on March 16, 1969, with twenty charter members. The church affiliated with Salt Lake association and the UISBC. After first meeting in the Herb Smith home, the Millcreek church met at Marlowe Manor School. A gift from the Skaags family enabled the church to buy property at 155 East 4500 South. The early pastors were Charles Ray, Michael Donahoo, and John Cook.

UISBC Employs Mayo Brown as Missionary (Utah)

After Charles Ray resigned as a missionary in 1969 to return to the pastorate, the HMB and SBGCC employed Myles Mayo Brown as the missionary to Utah (1969–1972), Golden Spike (1969–1976), and Salt Lake (1969–1984) associations. Brown was born in Copiah County, Mississippi, October 16, 1922, to Myles Mayo and Minnie Mabell (Howell) Brown. He had six sisters. He was saved at age nine through his parents' influence. The Jackson, Mississippi, Griffith Memorial Baptist Church baptized him October 18, 1931, and ordained him November 4, 1945. Brown wrote, "I became increasingly aware of my need of forgiveness and salvation. After talking with parents and pastor, I made a decision to give my heart to Christ on a Sunday afternoon and made a public profession of faith that evening." After serving in the U.S. Air Force (1941–1945), he married Celia Elizabeth Voggs on April 3, 1945, at Jackson, Mississippi, and they had five children. He graduated from

Jackson Central High School and Mississippi College and attended NOBTS. Brown pastored Antioch and Calvary Baptist churches in Lincoln County, Center Ridge and Bethlehem in Yazoo County, Pleasant Ridge in Holmes County, and Ethel, Mississippi. He pastored SBC churches at Provo and Granger, Utah; Las Vegas, Nevada; and Mt. Home, Idaho. Lou Gehrig's disease forced Brown to take disability retirement in 1984. The Browns moved to Phoenix, Arizona, and continued to teach SS and minister to senior adults. When Brown's health failed in 1993, Baptist Village of Arizona opened its doors with a promise to care for them the rest of their lives. He died April 21, 1997.

St. George, Utah, First Southern Baptist Church
Cedar City, Utah, FSBC organized the St. George FSBC on June 8, 1969, with twenty-two charter members. Pastor Medford Hutson, Morris Lee, and Nell Bass had begun a Bible study which developed into a mission. The mission, which met at the fire station, Elks Lodge, and library, affiliated with Rainbow Canyon association and the UISBC. FSBC bought a building, called T. J. Gamble (2) as the first pastor, and used GCC Wings for Christ students to fill the pulpit. Early pastors were Jack Edwards, Mel White, Rhett Durfee, and David Howell.

Meridian, Idaho, Cherry Lane Baptist Mission
Nampa, Idaho, FSBC started Meridian, Idaho, Baptist (Cherry Lane) Mission on August 10, 1969. The new mission affiliated with Boise Valley association and the ASBC. The early pastors were Gale Walters, Willis Blair, Huron Polnac, and Dan Campbell.

Kamiah, Idaho, Pine Ridge Baptist Church
Cottonwood, Idaho, Baptist Church organized Kamiah Pine Ridge Baptist Church on September 7, 1969, with eleven charter members. The new church affiliated with Boise Valley association and the UISBC. Members of a nine-member survey team to determine the need for a Baptist church in Kamiah were James and Patsy Myers, Pam and Robin Addleman, Mrs. Gene McIntyre, the Harley Wendts, and HMB summer missionaries Carolyn Hodge

and Mary Lee Aden. The church met first in the Anderson home and later in the V.F.W. Hall. The aggressive missionary work of the Myers made it possible for the church to start new missions at Cottonwood, Grangeville, Nez Perce, and Weippe, and Bible studies at Kooskia, Stites, and Pierce. A "Monday school" started in one logging town. Early pastors were James Myers, Larry Maxwell, Charles Alderman (int.), Jack Azbill, Bill Webster (int.), and Steve Ruth.

Cottonwood, Idaho, Emmanuel Baptist Church
The Cottonwood, Idaho, Emmanuel Baptist Church organized in the Joseph Addleman home with seventeen charter members September 7, 1969. The Addleman, Myers, and Reynolds families withdrew from Cottonwood Baptist Church for the purpose of starting a Southern Baptist Church. The new church affiliated with Whispering Pines association and the UISBC. The church met in the community hall, a renovated home on East and Myrtle Streets, and a Methodist church building. A new unit was constructed in 1984–1985. James Myers served as the first pastor. The Riggins, Idaho, Baptist Mission asked the church to serve as its sponsor in October 1969. Earlier attempts in 1958 by W. C. Carpenter of Lewiston, Idaho, to start the Cottonwood mission did not produce a church. The early pastors were James Myers, Roger Pigg, James Arndt, Larry Maxwell, Larry Jones, Austin Laverty, Randy Myers, and Mike Dugan.

SBGCC Employs Robert Wells as Missionary (Nevada)
After the retirement of Leonard B. Sigle in 1969, the HMB and SBGCC employed Robert August Wells as the missionary to Nevada association (1969–1977). He later served the Northern Nevada and Spooner (1977–1982), and Truckee River (1979–1982) associations. Wells was born on August 11, 1917, at Ratcliff, Arkansas, to Hal and Ricca Wells. He had two brothers and one sister. He was saved at age thirteen through the influence of his parents. The Ratcliff, Arkansas, Baptist Church baptized him in 1930 and later ordained him. He wrote, "When a converted Jewish preacher led a brush-arbor revival in Branch, Arkansas, my father

witnessed to me during the invitation, and I responded." Wells graduated from the Ratcliff, Arkansas, High School, AOBU, and SWBTS. He married Sara Louise Biggs on December 16, 1943, and they had three children. He pastored SBC churches at Raland, Natural Steps, and Pine Bluff, Arkansas; Cleburne, Tell, and Tyler, Texas; Lomita, California; and Longview, Washington. Wells wrote:

> My parents encouraged children to get the best available education in their chosen fields. One seminary chapel speaker spoke on the theme "Go West Young Man, Go West and Grow Up with the Westward Movement." When I finished seminary in 1950, we came west to visit family and preach. The Lomita church called me; I stayed twelve years and grew a church from 100 to 1,200 members. My greatest joy was having a part in starting over fifty new churches in western U.S.A.

Wells helped the Nevada SBC churches prepare for formation of the NVBC. After his retirement in September 1982, the family returned to California. He served as American Bible Society representative, started five new churches, pastored three churches (int.), worked as Long Beach Harbor association missionary (1984–1985), and served as California Baptist Foundation estate planning consultant. He loved sports, played golf, and won fifty-eight Senior Olympic (mostly gold) medals. He died on November 4, 1995, after running a race where he had won the silver medal. He was buried at Newhall, California, with Don Ledbetter officiating.

SBC Agencies Report Continuing Growth

GGBTS of Mill Valley, California, celebrated its twenty-fifth anniversary in 1969. Two churches launched the seminary on March 31, 1944. The SBGCC adopted GGBTS in November 1944 and the SBC in 1950. The three presidents who served GGBTS were Isam B. Hodges, Benjamin O. Herring, and Harold K. Graves.

As the 1960s decade closed, the HMB announced that "Project 500," a program to start 500 new churches (1968–1969), resulted in 211 new churches and new missions. Phil Jones, an HMB researcher, reported that twenty-three SBC churches started during the effort in the Intermountain West during the five-year period (1965–1969): Idaho (5), Nevada (10), and Utah (8).

Groundbreaking Services in the Intermountain West

C. E. Archer of Phoenix breaks ground for the North Las Vegas Calvary Baptist Church in 1958.

Pastor Roy J. Ferguson breaks ground for the new Kearns (UT) FBC building in 1958.

Twin Falls (ID) FSBC breaks ground for its first building in 1956 on the corner of Washington and Filer Streets. The new building, built with hired and volunteer labor, was completed in July 1956. FSBC later reorganized as the Magic Valley Baptist Church.

Layman Don Hansen breaks ground for the Las Vegas (NV) Sunrise Baptist Church in 1961.

Pastor Don Mulkey (R) breaks ground for the Las Vegas Twin Lakes Baptist Church in 1966.

Important Directions

THE DECADE OF THE 1970S

The U.S.A. Census Bureau reported that 944,127 people lived in Idaho, 488,738 in Nevada, and 1,059,273 in Utah in 1970. The population in the three states grew by 649,042 in the 1960s to 2,492,138, a gain of 35 percent in one decade.

Coeur d'Alene, Idaho, Emmanuel Baptist Church

Trentwood, Washington, FBC organized Coeur d'Alene Emmanuel Baptist Church in 1970. The church affiliated with Inland Empire association and BGCOW. Early pastors were John Jeffries, Wendel Jansen, Tom Vance, Randall Thetford, Butch Tanner, and Dan Brandel.

Wells, Nevada, First Baptist Church

Elko, Nevada, Calvary Baptist Church organized the Wells FBC in 1970. The new church affiliated with Nevada association and the SBGCC. In 1975 Wells FBC reported fourteen members, six baptisms, and $3,567 in total receipts. The early pastors were Douglas Graves, Willie Deiss, and Arthur Wicks.

Ft. Duschesne, Utah, Emmanuel Baptist Church

Ft. Duschesne, Utah, Emmanuel Baptist Church was organized in 1970, according to a study by Phil Jones. The mission started with a Bible study led by John Blake at the American Legion Hall. Blake, an HMB and UISBC employee to Ute Indians, pastored the two churches. The church affiliated with Utah association and the UISBC. When the Mormon church wanted the Baptists' location for a motel, they traded a half block for the land and helped the Baptists construct their new building. Early pastors were John Henry, Carter Furrh, Louis Belcher, John Henry, and Ed Hillman.

Las Vegas, Nevada, Koinonia Baptist Church

Henderson, Nevada, Faith Baptist Church organized Las Vegas Koinonia Baptist Church in 1970 under the direction of pastor Jim Reid. The church ministered to casino workers and showgirls on the strip. The HMB employed Reid as resort missionary.

Reid spoke to a GGBTS class about his ministry. After the *New York Times* reported his activities, the article was reprinted in the *Atlanta Constitution* October 12, 1973. It created a problem situation in Southern Baptist circles. The wild-west lifestyles continued to shock southern culture. Ministers of God tried to find ways to reach people who did not darken church doors:

> Nearly every night you'll find Jim Reid back-stage talking to nude show girls, many of whom he knows by their first names. He wears show clothes and talks show biz with the stars, card sharks, and stage hands of this gambling and resort city where roulette wheels spin and liquor flows twenty-four hours a day. . . . When Reid proposed a Bible study on stage between shows for the performers, he was told, "You're out of your mind"; nevertheless, fifteen persons showed up for the first session. . . . In addition to his services and regular Bible studies in several hotels, Reid has five prayer therapy groups, does personal counseling, and teaches English reading.

Tommy Starkes, a former HMB staff member, followed Reid as pastor of Koinonia in 1978. The church changed its name to Tropicana Christian Fellowship, and affiliated with the Southern Nevada association and the NVBC.

ASBC Employs Leroy Smith as Missionary (Nevada)

After Milton Gage resigned to return to Oklahoma, the HMB and ASBC employed Francis Leroy Smith of Billings, Montana, as missionary to Lake Mead association. Smith was born on March 23, 1914, at Waco, Texas. He was saved in August 1929 and baptized into South Plains, Texas, Baptist Church. He graduated from Lockney, Texas, High School and Baylor University, and attended WBC and the SWBTS. He married Claudine Thornton June 18, 1933, at Clovis, New Mexico, and they had two children. When his wife's mother died of pneumonia in 1937, the Smiths reared her three small children. Smith surrendered to preach under the ministry of Willis Ray and pastored churches at Lamesa, Osage, and Monahans, Texas, and El Dorado and Ruston, Louisiana. His wife wrote:

> The Ruston WMU president asked Leroy to teach the HMB book on mission work in the West in March 1948. He could never get peace in the pastorate after that experience. We traveled to California and coming home through Arizona, Leroy noticed that every town had a Catholic Church, but very few had a Baptist church. God called him to the pioneer fields.

The HMB and BGCA employed him as state evangelism secretary in July 1948 and as the GCC president (1950–1952). In three years he led GCC to move from Prescott to Phoenix, to buy an eighty-acre campus, to build nine buildings, to pay off a crushing debt, and to earn full accreditation from the University of Arizona and the Arizona Department of Education.

The Smiths moved to Denver, Colorado, with Willis J. Ray on January 1, 1956, to help organize the new CBGC. The HMB and CBGC employed Leroy Smith as the half-time state mission director and half-time Denver, Colorado, missionary (1956–1965). He also served as missionary to five Montana associations from 1966–1970: Treasure State, Glacier, Hi-Line, Yellowstone, and Triangle. He served the Old Faithful association of Wyoming (1966–1970). The HMB and ASBC employed him as missionary to

Lake Mead association (1970–1971) and Central association of Arizona (1971–1977). During his ministry, he started 115 missions and churches and preached many revivals. He reported five hundred additions a year. After he retired, he hoped to visit churches he helped start but he died at the Phoenix St. Joseph Hospital. Smith was buried in the Glendale, Arizona, Rest Haven Cemetery.

SBGCC Employs LaVern Inzer as Pastoral Missionary (Nevada)

The HMB and SBGCC employed Winnemucca, Nevada, FBC pastor, LaVern Inzer, on August 1, 1970, as northeastern Nevada pastoral missionary. Inzer, who had pastored the Winnemucca church for ten years, was given the title "mountain missionary." Inzer was born on December 15, 1924, at Sayre, Oklahoma. He graduated from Mississippi College and attended GGBTS and Fresno State College. He married Elva Hand, and they had four children. He served in the U.S. Navy (1943–1946), pastored part-time work in Louisiana, worked as a missionary to migrants (1949–1956), and pastored the Turlock, California, West Avenue Baptist Church (1956–1959). After Leonard Sigle enlisted his services, he moved his family to Winnemucca, Nevada, where he pastored the FBC. The HMB and SBGCC employed Inzer as a missionary to the same area he had served for more than a decade.

Charles McKay Resigns as ASBC Leader

Charles McKay, the ASBC executive secretary since October 1, 1956, resigned to pastor the Scottsdale, Arizona, FSBC September 3, 1970. The ASBC executive board, by standing vote, invited McKay to retain his position. He declined but agreed to serve as a consultant through October 31, 1970. The ASBC elected Roy F. Sutton, the associate executive/missions secretary, to serve as interim. When McKay arrived in the West, many said that he had broken the Texas barrier. E. W. Hunke Jr., his associate for eight years, wrote about McKay's boundless energy:

> When McKay arrived at his office in the morning, he got on forty horses at the same time and rode off in different directions. He had so many things going it was difficult to solidify

all his gains of the day. McKay emphasized that each staff member was to train someone to do his job to prepare the future leaders. McKay trained a generation of ASBC state board members to serve as the next generation of executive directors: Bill Hunke and Bill Duncan for Alaska; Roy Sutton for Arizona; Charles Ashcraft for Utah-Idaho and Arkansas; Darwin Welsh for Utah-Idaho; Roy Owen for Northern Plains; Dan Stringer for Northwest, Florida, Arizona, and New York; Otha Winningham for Minnesota-Wisconsin; Glen Braswell for Colorado; Ernie Myers for Nevada; and John Sullivan for Florida.

ASBC Employs Roy Sutton as Executive Director

Because Nevada SBC churches continued the long relationship with the SBGCC and ASBC, they demonstrated great interest in the leadership of the two sponsoring conventions. The ASBC employed Roy Fortson Sutton as the successor to Charles McKay on September 3, 1970. He was born November 7, 1908, near Dubberly, Louisiana, to Mr. and Mrs. Martin F. Sutton. When he was five, his father died of heart disease; his mother reared the family. He was saved, baptized, and joined the local church at age fifteen. He surrendered to preach at age twenty-two. After graduation from Baylor and the SWBTS, he pastored Dallas, Texas, Hampton Place Baptist Church. Doctors advised Sutton to move to a drier climate because of his health problems. The HMB and BGCA employed him as field-worker to Tucson on November 1, 1946. With exception of five years in New Mexico and Colorado, he spent his ministry serving Arizona Southern Baptists. As the ASBC executive director (1970–1978), he helped constitute NVBC and lead the ASBC through its fiftieth anniversary celebration.

BGCOW Employs Dan Stringer as Executive Director

The HMB and ASBC employed Dan Carmichael Stringer Jr. as associate executive director/state mission director on December 1, 1970. After serving six months, he resigned to become BGCOW state executive director. Stringer related to southern Nevada as Las Vegas FSBC pastor and to northern Idaho as the BGCOW leader.

He was born on November 7, 1927, at Cordell, Oklahoma, to Avie Lola (McArthur) and Dan Carmichael Sr. He had three sisters. He was saved at age seven in a revival through his parents' influence, baptized by the Erick, Oklahoma, FBC, and ordained in 1948 by the Albuquerque, New Mexico, FBC. Stringer married Harriet Elizabeth Rogers of Lisbon, Florida, on November 11, 1948, and they had two children. He graduated from the Albuquerque High School, Baylor University, and SBTS. He served as a U.S.A. Marine in World War II (1945–1946) and pastored churches at Scottsdale and Buckeye, Arizona, and at Las Vegas, Nevada. He served as the executive director for four conventions: Northwest (1971–1979), Florida (1979–1989), Arizona (1990–1995), and New York (int.) (1996). He received honorary doctorates from CBC and Stetson. The Stringers retired at Scottsdale, Arizona.

BGCOW Changes Name to Northwest Baptist Convention

On January 1, 1970, Baptist General Convention of Oregon-Washington became Northwest Baptist Convention (NWBC). The change of names was proposed in 1969 during the administration of executive director Eugene Grubbs. Grubbs continued to serve the BGCOW until Stringer arrived on the field to succeed him.

UISBC Employs Darwin Welsh as Executive Director

After Charles Ashcraft resigned in 1970 to become Arkansas Baptist Convention executive director, the UISBC executive board employed Darwin E. Welsh as its executive director on January 1, 1971. Welsh, the former Artesia, Colorado, FBC and SLC, Utah, FSBC pastor, had served as the UISBC state mission director under Ashcraft since March 1965.

St. Maries, Idaho, College Avenue Baptist Church

The Spokane, Washington, Pines Baptist Church organized St. Maries College Avenue Baptist Church in 1971 with Scott Creach as the first pastor. Creach, who worked at a Spokane dairy, started the St. Maries work and led the church to buy an old building. The new church affiliated with Inland Empire association and the

BGCOW. The church renovated its church plant in 1996. The early pastors were Wayne Creach, J. B. Greer (2), Larry Akins, Don Pemp, Herman Mullis, and James Ashurst.

HMB Begins Major Emphasis on Volunteers

In 1971 the HMB initiated two volunteer missions programs: (1) Semester Student Missions and (2) Campers on Mission. The student program, designed like student summer missions, allowed students to serve during the school months. The campers program provided information to campers about U.S. mission work needing a Christian witness and appointed them to specific locations for two week assignments. Eleven thousand families were at work in the SBC camping program in 1977.

On September 11, 1971, the UISBC conducted a commissioning service at the SLC FSBC for four young people who had committed themselves to a two-year mission under the sponsorship of parents and friends, a concept patterned after that of the Mormons. The four young people were Diana Rhodes and Sharon Phillips of North Little Rock, Arkansas, and Benton Welsh and Sam Ashcraft of SLC, Utah. Luman Gilman read the scripture and led the prayer; Joe Music led the orientation; and Darwin Welsh preached a message. After presentation of the students, the service closed with prayer.

HMB Reorganization Places a New Emphasis on States

As financial fortunes of the HMB improved, additional funds reached the western states. In 1970 the HMB allocated $176,484 for Utah and Idaho. The HMB channeled Nevada funding through the SBGCC and ASBC, sponsors of the work. Kansas-Nebraska Southern Baptists extended thanks to the UISBC for special assistance during their difficult days of debt. Twelve newer SBC state conventions and seven "old South conventions" sent more than $300,000 to help the Kansas-Nebraska convention when it faced financial disaster.

UISBC and HMB leaders met at SLC, Utah, on May 6, 1970, for the cooperative missions conference. Persons present were Darwin

Welsh, Mayo Brown, M. K. Wilder, Lavoid Robertson, and Anita Lemke from the UISBC; Quentin Lockwood, W. R. Grigg, Warren Woolf, Irvin Dawson, Travis Lipscomb, and Hugo Culpepper from the Atlanta HMB staff. The leaders discussed the status of work in the UISBC and projected budget needs for 1971.

The HMB returned to a mission process initiated in 1871, one hundred years earlier, when it employed three secretaries to relate to state convention leaders. The HMB reorganization on January 1, 1971, initiated a planning and coordination section with a director and four regional coordinators. Leonard Irwin served as section leader with Gerald Palmer (East), J. N. Evans (East-Central), Wilson Brumley (West-Central), and E. W. Hunke Jr. (West) serving as the regional coordinators. Hunke, who had served as Vernal FBC pastor and ASBC missions director, was sent to the Intermountain West for the third time.

The HMB regional coordinator served as the liaison between the HMB president and the state executive director. He coordinated development of a long-range plan, developed priorities and action plans to reach specific goals, and developed a cooperative budget to implement the plans. The coordinator met with state executive directors and their missions/evangelism staff three times a year. Only a few of these meetings are included in this history.

The ASBC and HMB cooperative planning conference for 1972 met on January 26, 1971, at Phoenix, Arizona, Baptist building. Persons present included Roy Sutton; Dan Stringer Jr.; Mary Jo Stewart; Bill Parker; Dewey Barlow, HMB board member; and E. W. Hunke Jr., HMB coordinator. The group reviewed the agreements, procedures, plans, policies, relationships, and 82 percent HMB and 18 percent ASBC ratio of participation. They employed nine associational missionaries and twenty-six language missionaries. Other work included pastoral aid for Nevada ($4,606) and Arizona ($17,000) and twenty-two summer missionaries. The HMB supported language missionaries on eleven Spanish and eight Indian fields. Spanish camp at Paradise Valley Baptist Ranch registered 139 and reported twenty-six saved.

The UISBC and HMB cooperative planning conference for 1972 met on January 28, 1971, at the SLC Baptist building located at 986 South Fourth East. Persons present were Darwin Welsh, executive secretary; Ruel Cook, UISBC president; Anita Lemke, bookkeeper; and the HMB coordinator. Welsh reported the Cooperative Program receipts for 1970 were only $722 more than in 1969; that there was no possibility to reach a $67,000 goal for 1971 ($14,000 increase); that Arkansas provided $2,500 and the ASBC $2,598 in 1970; and that a $15,000 HMB advance had been depleted. He said there were 30,000 unemployed people and 53,000 on welfare in Utah.

The SBGCC and HMB cooperative planning conference for 1972 met on January 29, 1971, at the Fresno, California, Baptist building. Persons present were Robert Hughes, Ralph Longshore, Jack Combs, Alma Bray, David Oglesby, Jack O'Neal, and E. W. Hunke Jr. Plans for work in northern Nevada were considered. The HMB and SBGCC employed Charles Clayton as the Tahoe resort ministries director and Kings Beach, California, FBC pastor. Barry St. Clair, who had spent two months visiting the Tahoe area, led twenty-eight people to Christ.

Robert D. Hughes, SBGCC executive secretary, said that the SBGCC task was described in the words of a message John Williams preached at the 1970 Baptist World Alliance: "It is the whole duty of the whole church to give the whole gospel to the whole world."

Evangelist Clyde Billingsley Moves to Utah

Clyde Billingsley, his wife Judy, and two children, Charles and Lisa, moved from Clovis, New Mexico, to SLC, Utah, in early February 1971. Billingsley, who graduated from the University of Tennessee and SWBTS, served eight years as vocational evangelist. He had preached so many revivals in Utah and Idaho that he and his family decided to live at SLC (1971–1972). The offerings from his revivals were supplemented by Pioneer Evangelism, Inc., to provide living expenses and enable him to devote full time to evangelism in the pioneer areas. In 1972 the Billingsleys moved back to New Mexico to pastor Carlsbad FBC. UISBC loved this pioneer evangelist. When a position on the state staff opened in 1974, the convention asked the Billingsleys to return to SLC.

Nevada Baptists Make Significant Advances in 1971

The NVBF steering committee met January 29, 1971, at Reno, Nevada, FSBC. Following supper, president Don Leo Wright called the meeting to order. Members present were Don York, Bob Wells, Gary Rothchild, Ralph Marchbanks, Karel Sylvanus, Leroy Smith, Walt Mercer, Darrell Evenson, and Carrol Haskins. The committee worked on mailing lists, permits, mission priorities, population, road maps, constitution, educational workers, and missionaries.

The NVBF met at North Las Vegas, Nevada, on April 30, 1971, for the sixth annual session. The officers were as follows: Don Wright, president; William Webb, vice-president; Ralph Marchbanks, treasurer; and Darrell Evenson, secretary. After the Las Vegas mayor, Gene Echols, welcomed the group, Ralph Longshore and Robert D. Hughes led Bible study. ASBC president C. E. Archer and SBGCC president Levi Price preached. Bob Wells of northern Nevada and Leroy Smith of southern Nevada gave missionary reports. The GCC choir sang, and Don Leo Wright delivered the president's message.

The NVBF steering committee met October 29, 1971. Members present were Don Leo Wright, Don Wilson, Don Shumake, Dan Beltz, Walter Mercer, and Cal Collins. After dinner, served by the host church, Wright called the meeting to order and Walt Mercer led the opening prayer. The nominating committee reported that Don Shumake filled the vacancy created when Karel Sylvanus moved. They elected Shumake as secretary, Wilson as missions committee member, and approved minutes of the last meeting. The committee received reports on insurance, incorporation, and the Caliente mission; appointed a committee to investigate the possibility of securing a campsite; requested twelve hundred dollars from the HMB rather than the usual three hundred dollars; approved Gary Rothchild as the NVBF resident agent; and asked the NVBF president to attend the California and Arizona conventions with expenses paid. The NVBF requested that 10 percent of the Nevada Cooperative Program gifts be retained for the forming of a Nevada convention. The committee authorized Shumake to sign checks in the absence of the treasurer. After announcing the date for the next meeting on January 28, 1972, the committee adjourned.

Nevada Baptist Forerunner noted that Lake Mead association lay evangelism schools enrolled 291 people from thirteen churches with an average attendance of 249. More than two hundred went out into homes on Thursday evening to win people to Christ.

Las Vegas, Nevada, FSBC reported one thousand enrolled in SS November 21, 1971. Pastor Darrell Evenson reported that records improved as the church raised fifteen thousand dollars to construct a debt-free fourteen thousand-foot two-story "miracle educational building." During the financial campaign, FSBC reported that 431 attended SS one Sunday, fifteen made professions of faith, and eighteen united with the church by letter.

Don Leo Wright, NVBF president, reported in the December 15, 1971, *Nevada Baptist Forerunner* that "the SBGCC was not quite as peaceful as the ASBC, but that a delicate and thorny issue was handled in a very fine manner and with a good spirit." Nevadans Crile Dean, L. E. Chism, and Bill Webb appeared on SBGCC program. Wright congratulated Redrock Baptist Church and the pastor Don Loving for a $1,036.17 check received by the fellowship. He noted that Irving Childress, ASBC evangelism secretary, planned to conduct a state evangelism conference at Las Vegas, Nevada, on January 14–15, 1972, prior to the Arizona evangelism conference.

Kings Beach, California, First Baptist Church

Tahoe City, California, FBC organized the Kings Beach, California, FBC in June 1971 with fifty-three charter members. The new church affiliated with Nevada association and the SBGCC. Leonard Sigle started the work in November 1968 in a rented home. The HMB and SBGCC employed Charles Clayton as resort missionary. Early pastors were Don Wilson, Ted Wakeman, and Frank Tenoreo.

Boise, Idaho, University Baptist Church

Boise, Idaho, Calvary Baptist Church organized the Boise University Baptist Church in July 1971 with Dan Brandell as the first pastor. The new church affiliated with Boise Valley association and the ASBC. Early pastors were Farrell Massey, John Embery, Oval Walker (int.), Dan Robinson, and Dan Walker.

Ogden, Utah, Second (Emmanuel) Baptist Church

Sixteen charter members led by J. H. Speach organized the Ogden Second (Emmanuel) Baptist Church on September 21, 1971. The church affiliated with Golden Spike association and the UISBC, bought a Mormon ward building for services, and conducted a radio ministry. The early interims were Darwin Welsh, Mayo Brown, and Guy Ward. Early pastors were C. L. Gafford, C. H. Carter, William Monroe, James Gates, Willie Martin, and Charles Petty.

UISBC Hears Reports and Honors Retiree

UISBC state staff and missionaries held a three-day planning retreat at Friday Harbor, San Juan Island, Washington, August 16–18, 1971. John Allen, HMB church extension associate, and E. W. Hunke Jr., regional coordinator, participated in the retreat.

On October 28, 1971, the HMB and UISBC reported twenty-six missionaries employed by the two agencies: six in language work, one in Christian social ministries, two in church extension, one in special ministry, and sixteen pastors on salary supplement.

UISBC met for its seventh annual session at the Pocatello, Idaho, FSBC on November 8–10, 1971. Jack Stanton, the associate evangelism secretary, represented the HMB.

Former Utah pastor, John L. Smith, completed his twenty-year ministry of preaching and teaching against Mormon doctrines. He believed that Mormonism was foreign to traditional Christianity, and that it should be compared with Islam or Buddhism rather than Christianity. The Smiths took three hundred days to travel from coast-to-coast in 1971 to speak 350 times in seventeen states. He warned the SBC churches about fourteen thousand Mormon missionaries and sought help for the two hundred Utah towns without any non-Mormon church. Smith, founder of Utah Missions, Inc., reported he had spoken three thousand times in thirty-seven states and in more than a hundred colleges and seminaries on the subject of Mormonism.

ASBC Forty-Third Annual Session Meets in Phoenix

Messengers from southern Nevada SBC churches met with the ASBC for its forty-third annual session at Phoenix FSBC, November 9–11, 1971. Alex Davila preached on "Living the Spirit of Christ in Expectancy." Wiley Henton led prayer. The Wednesday evening session featured the GCC choir and a message by F. Leroy Smith entitled "Murder by Consent." NVBF president, Don Leo Wright, reported on progress in Nevada. The ASBC reported five new churches organized and sixteen new missions started. Statistical tables listed 232 churches, fifty church-type missions, and 139 Bible fellowships in the convention.

Don Leo Wright Challenges NVBF Committee

The NVBF steering committee met January 28, 1972, at Sparks, Nevada, Temple Baptist Church. The members present were Don Leo Wright (chairman), Crile Dean, Dan Beltz, Bill Webb, Walt Mercer, Gary Rothchild, Don Ledbetter, Robert Wells, and Don Wilson. The subcommittees met and reported at a general session. The NVBF considered calendar, budget, annual meeting mission features, camp, and set a goal to have three hundred in attendance at the annual meeting. Chairman Wright reported that Roy Owen, the HMB associational services associate, would attend the annual meeting April 28, 1972. On March 15, 1972, Wright wrote this letter:

> Can the Southern Baptists really make an impact on Nevada for Christ? This is a question we will seek to answer at our seventh annual session [Capital Rally] at Carson City. Remember to elect your messengers. Soon my two years as your NVBF president will be completed. It has been an enjoyable experience—one that I will always treasure. My prayer for your new president is that he will use accomplishments during the first seven years; that he will lead to greater accomplishments; that he will love Nevada; and that he will

work toward a Nevada state convention. We now have a group of men at the HMB who will work with us to this end.

ASBC Employs M. E. McGlamery as Missionary (Nevada)

The HMB and ASBC employed M. E. McGlamery on March 7, 1972, as the missionary to Lake Mead association of Nevada. McGlamery succeeded Leroy Smith. He was born October 18, 1913, at Pickton, Texas, to Marshall and Daisy McGlamery. He had four brothers and five sisters. He was saved at age eleven through the influence of his parents and pastor and baptized in Emmet Minter's pond by Pickton, Texas, Bethel Baptist Church in 1924. He wrote, "I was saved on Monday night in a revival, the only one converted during the week, and the church baptized me the following Sunday along with one who was waiting baptism and one from another church." He graduated from the Ada, Oklahoma, Horace Mann High School, Baylor University, and SWBTS. McGlamery married Sarah Juanita Deering on March 2, 1935, at Pickton, Texas, and they had two children and two guardian children. He pastored Texas churches in Rehoboth association and at Wills Point. After a pastorate at Tucson, Arizona, he served as missionary to Southern Nevada association (1977–1980). When the McGlamerys retired in 1980, they returned to Texas.

Whispering Pines Baptist Association Constitutes (Idaho)

Twenty-one messengers from three Idaho churches constituted Whispering Pines association on April 25, 1972. Time factors, distance, and mountains prevented Idaho panhandle churches from participating in the Boise Valley association meetings. Churches constituting the association were Cottonwood, Emmanuel; Kamiah, Pine Ridge; and Grangeville, Mountain Shadows. Larry Maxwell pastored at Kamiah, and James Myers pastored the Cottonwood and Grangeville churches. Roy Ferguson moderated the service which was held in an old Cottonwood home that was remodeled for the church services. Maxwell was elected as the first moderator.

NVBF Seventh Annual Session Meets at Carson City

The NVBF met on April 28, 1972, at Carson City, FSBC for its seventh annual session. President Don Leo Wright moderated this "Capital City Rally." The theme "Getting It All Together," taken from Esther 4:14, provided the focus. The Nevada governor, Michael O'Callaghan, welcomed messengers to the Capital City. Featured speakers were Charles Ashcraft, former Las Vegas FSBC pastor and Arkansas Baptist Convention executive secretary; Robert Hughes, SBGCC executive secretary; E. W. Hunke Jr., HMB western regional coordinator; Donald McGregor, *California Southern Baptist* editor; James Staples, CBC president; and Jess Canafax, ASBC associate executive/missions secretary. HMB staff members Roy W. Owen and Leonard G. Irwin visited the sessions. The NVBF reported thirty-eight churches, eight missions, 136 baptisms, and 237 additions to the churches. The NVBF elected Gary Rothchild as president and Dan Beltz vice-president.

Leonard Irwin, planning and coordination section director of the HMB, sent the following memo to HMB leaders Rutledge, Belew, Moseley, and Corder:

> At a NVBF that Hunke, Owen, and I recently attended, a need was expressed for an HMB representative to meet with the fellowship steering committee for counsel. The three of us concur that Roy Owen should sit with the committee and be the HMB contact person in future relations to this committee.

NWBC Employs Bill Peters as Missionary (Idaho)

On June 6, 1972, after Howard Ramsey resigned to become NWBC evangelism secretary, the HMB and NWBC employed William Kenneth Peters as missionary to Inland Empire association. Inland Empire included SBC churches located in the Idaho panhandle. Peters was born on October 14, 1925, at Kansas City, Missouri, to John Henry and Georgia Peters. He had five brothers. He was saved at age twelve through the influence of his mother and pastor, both baptized in 1937 and ordained on March 23, 1952, by the Independence, Missouri, Maywood Baptist Church. He wrote, "My mother kept us in SS. I had good teachers and a loving pastor [W. E. King]. A deacon led me to Christ at church." Peters served in the U.S. Air Force (1943–1945). He graduated from William Jewell College, Central Baptist Theological Seminary, and GGBTS, where he earned the D.Min. degree. He married Alice Esther Hall, and they had four children. Peters pastored churches at Whitesville, Ludlow, and Kansas City (2) in Missouri, and at Pullman, Washington. He wrote:

> I preached a revival in 1966 at Grand Junction, Colorado. Roy Owen, the area missionary, invited me to help on the western slope, but since I was building at Kansas City, I declined. In 1968 I saw Owen at the Houston SBC; he introduced me to Project 500, and I signed up. Pullman, Washington, was the possibility. After missionary Ed Byers called me, we looked into it, decided God was in it, so we came and never looked back. It has been a wonderful journey.

The HMB and NBC employed Peters as missionary to Lewis-Clark association of Idaho and Inland Empire of Washington (1972–1977). He served as the NWBC associate executive and missions director (1977–1986), interim NWBC executive director (1979–1980), and the GGBTS Northwest Baptist Center director. After his retirement in 1992 he pastored the Hong Kong International Baptist Church for seventeen months. He wrote, "On January 14, 1996, I flew to Spokane, preached three times, and flew back home that night and felt great! At 3:45 the next morning I woke up very ill. Friday it was a firm diagnosis, acute myelogenous leukemia; by Saturday I was undergoing chemotherapy." He journeyed to Houston, Texas, for treatment. Medical science did not help him; he died on September 12, 1996. The Portland, Oregon, Mill Park Baptist Park memorial service remembered him for his years of faithful service to the Northwest.

HMB Report Describes the UISBC Mission Field

The HMB western regional coordinator was required to submit a report on the status of each state convention each year and to pinpoint the needs and opportunities. On June 19, 1972, Hunke wrote about Idaho, Nevada, and Utah. Region IV is a designation for seven western state conventions which cover an area of 1.7 million square miles, one-half of the land area of the United States. The conventions include thirteen states: Idaho, Nevada, Utah, Alaska, California, Arizona, Hawaii, Montana, North Dakota, Washington, South Dakota, Oregon, and Wyoming. The UISBC works in Utah and southern Idaho. Churches are located along the arc of the Snake River, in Great Salt Lake Basin, and in rural areas of the two states. The highly irregular land mass is dominated by Idaho's Sawtooth Mountains and Utah's Wasatch Range.

Baptists began growing churches in the Mormon Empire when new people moved in to service the petroleum industry, military bases, and new business ventures. Churches have developed at Boise, Twin Falls, Pocatello, Idaho Falls, Ogden, Provo, and SLC. Reaching the area requires patience and dedication. The heavy building debts, small church memberships, difficult cultural settings, few Southern immigrants, and scarcity of trained SBC leadership are monumental problems. Mission work with Spanish, Orientals, and Indians has been initiated.

UISBC Employs Richard Ashworth as Missionary (Utah)

After the UISBC reassigned Medford Hutson as the Richfield pastoral missionary, the HMB and UISBC employed Richard Lee Ashworth on September 1, 1972, as missionary to Gideon (1972–1991), Rainbow Canyon (1972–1987), Utah (1972–1990), and Color Country (1985–1990) associations. Ashworth was born on October 2, 1924, at Pasadena, California, to S. L. and Helen Fee (Dodson) Ashworth. He had no brothers or sisters. He was saved at the age of twenty-two through the influence of a pastor and friend, baptized in the Arkansas River in April 1947, and ordained on January 25, 1951, by the Muskogee, Oklahoma, Hyde Park Baptist Church. He wrote, "On one Sunday morning in 1946 I overcame my timidity and surrendered completely to the will of God as I understood it. I had believed in God, the Bible, and Jesus since a child, but I did not make a commitment until out of the Navy and planning marriage."

Ashworth married Ruby Lee Stockwell at Muskogee, Oklahoma, in 1947, and they had three children. He felt the Holy Spirit call him to preach at age twenty-five while teaching in a public school sixth-grade class. He wrote:

> I had become more involved in church activities and was our Sunday School director. Church Training helped me to get feelings in order. I surrendered to do anything but preach and was willing to go anywhere. When I did agree to preach, I found the peace I sought! I continue to find God's peace and assurance in my place of service.

He graduated from Muskogee Central High School and Oklahoma Northeastern State University. He attended OBU, Colorado College, and SWBTS. He wrote, "At age thirty-three while attending SWBTS, I felt God's leadership to pioneer missions in the West." Ashworth pastored Oklahoma Baptist churches at Muskogee, Haskell, Kinta, and Guthrie, and at Caldwell, Idaho. After retirement in 1989, he remained in Utah to serve as the Gideon associational missionary. In 1991 the Ashworths moved to Boise, Idaho, where he served as an interim pastor, and started the Boise Silver Sage Baptist Church in his family room. He led the small group to buy a 4.87 acre church site and make plans to build.

Lemmon Valley, Nevada, Fellowship Baptist Church

Sparks, Nevada, Temple Baptist Church organized the Lemmon Valley Fellowship Baptist Church in October 1972 with Gilbert Cook as the first pastor. The new church affiliated with Nevada association and the SBGCC. The early pastors were Jesse Wall, Pat Riley, Dave Marke, Charles Anderson, James Smith, Don Mulkey (int.), Murray Day, Ernest B. Myers (int.), Don Lewis, Arnold Shavers, and William Webb.

Weippe, Idaho, Prairie Baptist Church

Cottonwood, Idaho, Emmanuel Baptist Church started Weippe Prairie Baptist Mission August 14, 1972, when Larry Maxwell and James Myers led thirty-six young people from Georgia to hold a VBS and revival in the community to revive the church. The new church affiliated with Whispering Pines association and UISBC. Maxwell led Sunday evening services at the Seventh Day Adventist building until February 19, 1978, when the church purchased an acre of land with an old saw shop and remodeled it for church services. Early pastors were Larry Maxwell, Doug Hopper, Hale Anderson, Gordon Mills, Don Fowler, George Hopson, Gary Snyder, and Allen Snyder.

Las Vegas FSBC Ordains David Wallace

Las Vegas, Nevada, FSBC ordained David Truett Wallace to the ministry September 3, 1972. Pastor Darrell Evenson said, "Many have been licensed by our church, but David is the first one who grew up in the church and was licensed and ordained to preach by First Southern. We count it a landmark and blessing." Speakers were Don Loving, Don Mulkey, Ellen Clay, Les Grantham, Virginia Rae, John Shillington, and M. E. McGlamery. Flagstaff, Arizona, pastor, Bill May, preached the sermon. Wallace graduated from Las Vegas Rancho High School, Northern Arizona University, and GGBTS. He and his wife, Janie, and three children led churches in California, Arizona, and Nevada.

Minden-Gardnerville, Nevada, First Baptist Church

The Minden-Gardnerville, Nevada, FBC was organized in the fall of 1972 with Paul Ray as pastor. The church affiliated with Nevada association and the SBGCC. Early pastors were Paul Ray, David Boos, and Ed Jordan.

UISBC Plans Joint Ventures with the HMB

UISBC and HMB leadership met at the SLC, Utah, Baptist building, on October 25–26, 1972, to plan joint ventures for 1974. Persons present were Darwin Welsh, Anita Lemke, and Mary Wigger (UISBC), and E. W. Hunke Jr. (HMB). The UISBC reported eight associations, sixty-two churches, 9,916 members, $148,489 gifts for missions, and $835,437 in total receipts.

The UISBC met for its eighth annual session at Provo, Utah, FBC on November 7–8, 1972, under the direction of president M. K. Wilder of Page, Arizona. E. W. Hunke Jr. represented the

HMB at the sessions. The UISBC received a $25,581 inheritance and used the funds to establish the Utah-Idaho SBC Loan Fund. The UISBC loaned money to four churches and used the balance to buy the Baptist building mortgage in order to pay interest to themselves.

Idaho SBC Pastor Captures Armed Men

Ron Mitchell, age thirty-one, graduated from GCC in Phoenix, Arizona, and took a job serving as the Henderson, Idaho, marshall and pastor of its only church. He and his wife had six children. In 1972 the sheriff called saying that two dangerous armed men were on the way to the east shore of Coeur d'Alene Lake. The clergyman halted their auto, disarmed the men, and took them into custody. As church time arrived, he asked a duck hunter with a shotgun to stand watch over his prisoners while he went to church to preach.

Ririe, Idaho, Ririe Baptist Church

Idaho Falls, Idaho, Calvary Baptist Church organized Ririe Baptist Church in 1973. Bruce Gardner, Calvary Baptist Church pastor, had begun a weekday Bible study in the community which led to the mission's start. The church affiliated with Eastern Idaho association and the UISBC and purchased two and a half acres of land and a building from the Presbyterians. The early pastors were Henry Wright and Donald McCown.

NBVF Leaders Study Options for the Future

The NVBF steering committee met at Fallon, Nevada, October 27, 1972. Roy W. Owen, HMB associational missions associate, met with the committee. Nevada reported thirty-one churches, 8,384 members, $81,718 for missions, and $759,362 in total receipts.

The NVBF study committee met at Las Vegas, Nevada, Showboat Hotel January 17–18, 1973, to consider Nevada study data and to plan for the future. Persons who attended were Paul Lewis, M. E. McGlamery, Robert Wells, Crile Dean, Don Loving, Walt Mercer, Don Leo Wright, Robert Hughes, Roy Sutton, Darwin

Welsh, E. W. Hunke Jr., and Tommy Coy. Chairman Roy W. Owen was not able to attend this meeting.

The *Nevada Baptist Forerunner* reported that the SBC had more churches in Nevada than any other denomination. President Garry Rothchild reported that the NVBF steering committee approved a committee to study Nevada in its October 1972 meeting. The study committee was composed of five Nevada members elected by the NVBF and representatives from the ASBC, SBGCC, and HMB. The steering committee met at Boulder City, Nevada, FBC January 26, 1973, with HMB leaders Roy Owen and E. W. Hunke Jr. On June 5, 1973, Owen, the NVBF study committee chairman, wrote to committee members to suggest three possible approaches: (1) historical and statistical background presentations with panel discussion; (2) presentation to an annual fellowship meeting; and (3) exploration of renewed fellowship with Utah-Idaho Southern Baptists.

Richfield, Utah, First Baptist Church

Cedar City, Utah, FBC organized the Richfield FBC on January 1, 1973, with sixty-four charter members. The church affiliated with Rainbow Canyon association and the UISBC. The mission began with four people February 4, 1967, the third attempt since 1957 to build a church. After the Amarillo, Texas, FBC choir took a census, the Tyler, Texas, FBC choir enrolled 135 children in VBS. On January 2, George Sanders, a member of the trio that sang at the constitution, died. His burial was the first in the new church's history. Sanders, a new Christian called the "first fruit," was awaiting baptism. Early pastors were Ira Marks (int.), Bob Wayman, Keith Hull, K. Medford Hutson, and members of Wings for Christ.

UISBC Initiates New Evangelism and Men's Meetings

W. D. Lawes, HMB evangelism associate, preached to 850 people at a UISBC rally in SLC. The 150 member UISBC youth choir sang the musical *Encounter* under direction of Bill Anderson of the BSSB.

Idaho, Nevada, and Utah Southern Baptists had their first opportunity to attend a national SBC when it met at Portland,

Oregon, June 12–14, 1973, under the direction of president Owen Cooper of Mississippi. The SBC registered 8,871 messengers and many visitors.

UISBC Baptist Men gathered for a retreat at the Box Elder campground near Brigham City, Utah, on July 2–3, 1973, under the direction of Darwin Welsh, UISBC executive secretary. Retreat speakers were David Barnes, Shu Okumura, and A. V. Farr. Tommy Coy and E. W. Hunke Jr., of the HMB attended the retreat.

The UISBC and Salt Lake association sponsored a fifth Sunday meeting at the Salt Palace Little Theater at SLC, Utah, September 30, 1973. The "Sounds of Now" youth choir, sponsored by the Hill Air Force Base chapel, brought special music. E. W. Hunke Jr., HMB western regional coordinator, preached on the theme "Our God Is a Consuming Fire."

The UISBC and HMB initiated long-range planning at the SLC, Utah, FSBC, on October 1–2, 1973. The UISBC planning group consisted of the executive secretary, state staff members, three associational superintendents, three state board committee chairmen, three state task force chairmen, and one from each of the seven listening groups in Utah and Idaho. HMB staff members, E. W. Hunke Jr. and Tommy Coy, represented the HMB.

Nevada Baptists Celebrate SBC Growth

The Nevada evangelism conference met at Carson City FBC on February 15–16, 1973. The program featured A. V. Washburn, BSSB; Vander Warner, Richmond, Virginia, Grove Avenue Baptist Church pastor; John Havlik, HMB evangelism associate; Jack Taylor, San Antonio, Texas, Castle Hills Baptist Church pastor; James Draper, Del City, Oklahoma, FSBC pastor; and several musicians.

Roy W. Owen, HMB associational services associate, met with Nevada missionaries Robert Wells and M. E. McGlamery in Las Vegas, Nevada, on April 26 prior to a NVBF meeting at the Las Vegas Twin Lakes Baptist Church on April 27–28, 1973. The participants and visitors attending the sessions represented the HMB, SBGCC, and ASBC. The conference format was for fellowship, information, and inspiration, but Nevadans talked about a state convention.

Nevada association messengers gathered for the eighteenth annual session at Hawthorne, Nevada, on October 12–13, 1973, to celebrate the twenty-fifth (silver anniversary) of the founding of Hawthorne (Babbitt), Nevada, FSBC (Calvary). Speakers for the special session were the Ben Felts; the Leonard Sigles; Fred Beck Jr., FMB missionary from Indonesia; and Robert D. Hughes, SBGCC executive secretary. Bernard Ford, the host church pastor, preached the annual sermon. Missionary Bob Wells reported that the four new churches added in 1973 raised the number of churches to twenty-four. Missions were started at Dayton and South Reno.

Post Falls, Idaho, Baptist Church
Lloyd Garrison, his wife, and two student missionaries led a VBS under pine trees at Post Falls, Idaho, on property owned by the HMB in June 1973. The VBS enrolled 182 boys and girls. One student missionary preached his first sermon at the commencement, and Garrison realized God called him to start the new Post Falls mission. They met under pine trees from July to September 1973 and moved into a funeral home chapel. Frontiers for Baptist Men builders constructed the building, and the first service on January 20, 1974, had sixty in attendance. The church affiliated with Inland Empire association and the NWBC. Garrison baptized sixty-nine people at Post Falls in twenty months. The HMB and BGCOW employed him as a pastoral missionary with the assignment to start one new church each year. He served ten years and started nine new churches. Early pastors were George Scantlan, Carvel O'Dell, and Paul Logue.

Crescent Valley, Nevada, Baptist Chapel
Winnemucca, Nevada, FBC organized Crescent Valley Baptist Chapel on July 16, 1973. The mission started under the direction of Leonard B. Sigle and LaVern Inzer. Harvey Broadway served as the first pastor. The new church affiliated with Nevada association and the SBGCC. Early pastors were LaVern Inzer (int.), Tom White, Ace Sliger, Reese Morrow, Opal Douthit, Ed Farr, Tom Bacon (int.), Alfred Tremayne, and Dale Broadway.

Summer Camping in Utah and Glorieta

A. B. Barnes and family prepare to spend the summer in Utah camps and VBSs (1945–1949).

Utah SBC camp committee (L-R) Top: Ray, Rounds, and Wickes. Bottom: Smith, Lowe, Thornton.

The 1961 Utah Baptist Encampment registered 270 campers and ninety-four visitors. The picture above shows people who made a decision for Christ during the camp near Wallsburg, Utah. There were twenty saved, forty-one rededications, and seven for special service.

Top (L-R): Dillman (shirt), Ray, Henton. Second row: Opal Dillman (glasses), Sutton, and Marks. John Smith (center).

Center row (L-R): Glass, Hunke, Ferguson, and Sigle (below Ferguson). Photo taken at Glorieta, New Mexico.

Wings for Christ in Nevada and Utah

Keith Hull, Wings for Christ founder/pilot (1961–1968), shown here beside a Wings for Christ plane.

Wings for Christ began in 1961 and secured eight planes to serve the small Utah and Nevada churches.

Wings for Christ provided a way for the GCC ministerial students to preach for small churches. The skilled pilots and mechanics flew for the U.S. Air Force during the Korean War. Here eighteen ministerial students prepare for departure on one weekend in the 1960s.

Keith and Dan Hull of Tucson were members of West Phoenix Baptist Church while in GCC.

Dan and Eleanor Hull served as presidents of WFC women's and men's organizations.

Reno, Nevada, South Reno Baptist Church

Reno, Nevada, FSBC organized the South Reno Baptist Church in 1974. Missionary Bob Wells started the mission in the Elks Club lodge hall with help from Shreveport, Louisiana, Broadmoor Baptist Church. The church affiliated with Nevada association and SBGCC. The early pastors were Toby Adair, Randy Houston, James Fox, Don Ledbetter (int.), Harold Green, and Barry Campbell.

Nevada Baptists Struggle with Relationships

On February 23, 1974, eastern Nevada SBC pastors met at the Austin, Nevada, American Legion Hall. The pastors who attended were Cal Collins, Walt Mercer, Ron Hibpschman, Earl Hosea, George Thomason, Tom Bacon, Jim Tilley, and LaVern Inzer. Twenty-eight people in attendance elected Collins as the moderator and Inzer as the clerk. The discussion centered on their isolation from western and southern Nevada, failure of programs to meet church needs, the need for another association, and the possibility for fellowship among the churches in eastern Nevada. The clerk wrote the HMB to ask for a new missionary to serve eastern Nevada. The representatives in the meeting were from Fallon, Tonopah, Ely, Battle Mountain, Diamond Valley, Hawthorne, and Walker Lake.

On April 26, 1974, the NVBF adopted three proposals from its study committee: (1) that the same structures and relationships be maintained with SBGCC and ASBC; (2) that the annual meetings of NVBF be continued with emphasis on fellowship; and (3) that NVBF recognize that it is inadvisable to form a state convention at this time in our history. The new officers were Quinton Montgomery, president; Tom Bacon, vice-president; Louis Nimmo, secretary; Don Mulkey, treasurer; and Don Loving, historian.

SBGCC Adopts Plan to Start New Churches

SBGCC adopted the two-year program presented by executive director Robert Hughes named "1,006 by 76." The SBGCC wished to push the number of churches over one thousand. The SBGCC theme for 1974, "Sharing Christ through Mission Action," sought to involve churches in mission action, increase Bible teaching and enrollment, increase the number of baptisms, and increase mission gifts from the churches. The SBGCC executive board approved the emphasis as it stood to honor its executive director in May 1974. During the 1975–1976 church year, the number of new churches organized doubled the annual average of the past few years.

HMB researcher Phil Jones reported that extant SBC churches organized from 1970–1974 were located in Idaho (7), Nevada (8), and Utah (4). The HMB allocated $278,780 for work in Utah and Idaho in 1975. The HMB continued to budget mission funds for use in Nevada through the SBGCC and ASBC.

Midvale, Utah, First (Alta Canyon) Baptist Church

The SLC, Utah, University Baptist Church organized Midvale FBC on August 25, 1974. The mission had begun in 1974 with a home Bible study led by Robert Fuelling, Clyde Billingsley, Joe Music, and Darwin Welsh. The church affiliated with Salt Lake association and the UISBC. C. E. Autrey served as the first pastor. The SBC youth who helped establish the work were Diana Rhodes and Sharon Phillips of Arkansas, Allen Wilcoxon, Lorenzo Silvas, Robert Westberry, James Killian, Carol Lindsay, Diana Gipson, and Pam Wilson. When Midvale FBC closed in September 1977, members met for three months in the Good Shepherd Lutheran facilities and in Carol Browning's home. The church purchased two acres with two homes in August 1982 and changed its name to Alta Canyon Baptist Church. Others who assisted the church were Buck Buchanan, John Blake, and Darwin Welsh.

Jackpot, Nevada, Southern Baptist Church

Twin Falls, Idaho, Eastside Baptist Church organized the Jackpot Southern Baptist Church under the leadership of pastor Robert Schreckenburg in September 1974. The church affiliated with Magic Valley association initially and later with Nevada association. E. J. Jenkins, the French Broad association of North Carolina missionary, raised funds and constructed the building in

1973. Jenkins had served as a Nampa, Idaho, pastoral missionary with the HMB and ASBC earlier. Ray Forrest served as the pastor.

Idaho Panhandle Churches Choose Affiliations

Problems related to affiliation with two state conventions serving in Idaho surfaced on September 10, 1974. Some Idaho panhandle churches chose to affiliate with the NWBC while others chose to affiliate with the UISBC. HMB leaders decided to make subsidies to the Idaho pastors through both state conventions. In 1974 two NWBC associations served northern Idaho churches—Inland Empire and Lewis-Clark. Panhandle churches choosing to relate to the UISBC affiliated with Boise Valley association.

Pioche, Nevada, Berean Baptist Church

Las Vegas, Nevada, Parkdale Baptist Church organized the Pioche Berean Baptist Church on September 22, 1974, with twenty-four charter members. The new church affiliated with Lake Mead association and the ASBC. Two Baptist church families had asked M. E. McGlamery, missionary from Las Vegas, to preach in Pioche once a month. The two families led eight people to Christ and readied them for baptism. Early pastors were R. A. Walsh, Gene Simpson, Clarence Smith, and Sam Stanton.

Fernley, Nevada, First Baptist Church

Fallon, Nevada, FSBC started the Fernley mission in 1970, after surveying the community. After its organization, the church affiliated with Nevada association and the SBGCC on October 18, 1974. Gary Gibson, an SBC pastor who was stationed in Nevada while in military service, led the church to affiliate. Early pastors were Roy Young, Sam Newell, and Kevin White. After his Air Force retirement, Gibson returned to pastor the church.

UISBC Tenth Annual Session Meets at SLC

The UISBC met for its tenth annual session on November 12–13, 1974, at the SLC FSBC under direction of president Luman

Gilman. Darwin E. Welsh, UISBC executive secretary, spoke using "Decade of Blessings, Future, and Hope" as the theme. The guest speakers were Charles Ashcraft of Arkansas; Arthur Rutledge and E. W. Hunke Jr., HMB; B. J. Chenault, Annuity; Roland Smith, BSSB; Ron Tonks, Historical Commission; and Von Worten, FMB.

C. E. Autrey, a former HMB evangelism secretary, arrived at SLC in May 1974 to serve as the UISBC state evangelism consultant for one year. After one year, he returned to his home in Florida. Ren Adams arrived at SLC in November 1974 to serve as the HMB and UISBC director of Christian social ministries. Harlan Capps arrived in January 1975 to direct language missions.

ASBC Forty-Sixth Annual Session Meets at Las Vegas

The ASBC met for its forty-sixth annual session at the Las Vegas Convention Center November 12–14, 1974, under the direction of president Henry Wooten. Governor O'Callaghan welcomed the 730 guests (392 messengers) to Nevada. The ASBC reported that five new churches organized and fifteen missions were started in 1974. Paradise Valley Baptist Ranch reported 1,477 persons attended ten weeks of camping, 111 trusted Christ, and thirty-nine surrendered to special service. The ASBC reported 5,530 baptisms, 85,375 members, $9,521,993 total receipts, $658,181 Cooperative Program receipts, and $42,341,000 in church property. The new officers for 1974–1975 were Henry Wooten, president; Donald Mulkey, first vice-president; Nathan Pillow, second vice-president; and C. L. Pair, recording secretary.

HMB Helps Fund Associational Workers

In 1975 the HMB helped fund two missionaries in each of the three Intermountain states: Bill Peters in northern Idaho (NWBC) and Roy Ferguson in southern Idaho (ASBC); Mayo Brown in northern Utah (ASBC) and Richard Ashworth in southern Utah (ASBC); and Bob Wells in northern Nevada (SBGCC) and M. E. McGlamery in southern Nevada (ASBC). The HMB helped fund state mission directors for the conventions: Jess Canafax, ASBC; Ralph Longshore, SBGCC; and Darwin Welsh, UISBC. The three executive directors were Darwin Welsh in Utah-Idaho, Roy Sutton in southern Nevada and Arizona, Robert Hughes in northern Nevada and California, and Dan Stringer in northern Idaho, Oregon, and Washington.

East Carbon, Utah, First Baptist Church

The East Carbon, Utah, FBC organized in 1975. The church affiliated with Utah association and the UISBC. Early pastors were John Watson, Mike McGuire, Roy Southern, and Warren Osburn.

Gabbs, Nevada, First Baptist Church

The Fallon, Nevada, FSBC organized the Gabbs FBC in 1975 with Sam Crum as the first pastor. The church affiliated with Nevada association and the SBGCC. The early pastors were Doyle Wheat, Doyle Broadway, and Samuel Crum.

Fallon, Nevada, Faith Baptist Church

The Fallon Faith Baptist Church was organized in 1975 by the members of Fallon FSBC who withdrew for that purpose. The church affiliated with Nevada association and the SBGCC. Early pastors were Carol Garrett, H. G. Holmes, and Walter Alexander. When the members resolved their differences, they reunited with FSBC.

Writers Explain Phenomenon of Western Growth

Everett Hullum and Kim Watson wrote a feature article titled "SBC Pioneer Movement: The Move West" in January 1975 saying, "A parochial, isolationist SBC denomination was loosely structured, theologically insecure, and largely ignorant of the nation-wide religious conditions until 1942." They described SBC religious expansion into the West as being the most rapid in U.S.A. church history. The BGCA alone served one-fourth of the U.S. land area. The article reported:

> The advance on dual axles, Arizona and California, moved forward with the "lean, clear-eyed, weathered Texan named

Willis J. Ray" at the wheel. Ray said SBC work in Idaho began when the American Baptists fired Idaho pastor Charles Shipp and he started an SBC church; in Wyoming and Montana when the oil workers from Oklahoma moved in search of work started new SBC churches; in South Dakota when a U.S.A. military chaplain started an SBC church at Rapid City; in Colorado when two Bryant brothers came as pastors; and in Utah when two transplanted SBC deacons started an SBC church in a Mormon community (*California Southern Baptist*, 1/9/1975).

SBC Growth in Western U.S.A. Staggers the Researchers

The BSSB research services department released the 1974 church letter statistical data in February 1975. In thirty-five years (1940–1974) SBC work in the West grew from the two small state conventions in New Mexico and Arizona to ten state conventions, 145 associations, 2,201 churches, 35,387 baptisms, and 681,139 members. Westerners reported $331,822,000 in church property, $72,413,000 in receipts, and $10,994,097 in mission gifts to SBC mission causes.

Robert A. Wells, the Nevada missionary wrote, "In 1950, two hundred SBGCC churches gave $99,785 through Cooperative Program channels. At that time the Hawthorne church was the only SBC church in Nevada. In 1975 the forty-two churches in Lake Mead and Nevada associations gave more than $100,000 to missions."

Grangeville, Idaho, Mountain Shadows Baptist Church

The Cottonwood, Idaho, Emmanuel Baptist Church organized the Grangeville Mountain Shadows Baptist Church on January 19, 1975, with forty-one charter members. Pastor James and Patsy Myers and other Cottonwood members surveyed the community, and held the first service on September 7, 1969, in the Grangeville Episcopal Church. The church affiliated with Whispering Pines association and the UISBC. On July 26, 1974, the mission bought land for fourteen thousand dollars. A building was constructed in

1976–1977, and the first service was held on February 6, 1977. Early pastors were James Myers, Doug Robinson, Steve McFall, and Steve Hall.

UISBC Employs Clyde Billingsley as State Mission Director

On February 4, 1975, the UISBC state board met in a called meeting between sessions at the state evangelism conference to employ Clyde Billingsley as the UISBC state mission director and William H. Souther as UISBC state music director. UISBC voted to purchase 4.288 acres of land in Taylorsville, Utah, from the HMB for a future church site.

The growth of Utah-Idaho SBC work led the HMB and UISBC to employ Carlsbad, New Mexico, pastor Clyde Billingsley as the state mission director. Billingsley was born on June 2, 1940, to Col. Clyde and Glenna (Mattern) Billingsley. He had two sisters and one brother. He was saved at age eight, baptized by the Greenville, South Carolina, Poinsett Mills Baptist Church, and ordained by Knoxville, Tennessee, Church Well Avenue Baptist Church. Billingsley wrote, "My father, who served as a pastor, led me to Christ one evening during our regular family altar." He graduated from Knoxville Central High School, University of Tennessee, and SWBTS. He was called to preach at eighteen years of age during a youth revival in Knoxville. He volunteered to serve as a foreign missionary. Billingsley married Judy Kirkland in 1975 while a student in SWBTS, and they had two children. He pastored churches at Knoxville, Tennessee; Lajunta, Texas; and Carlsbad, New Mexico. The HMB and UISBC employed him as state mission director on March 1, 1975. After serving two years, he resigned to go to Northern Plains Baptist Convention. The NWBC and Florida Baptist Convention employed him as the evangelism secretary. When Darwin Welsh retired in 1989, Billingsley moved back to SLC, Utah, to serve as the UISBC executive secretary. He later directed the Montana Southern Baptist Fellowship.

UISBC Holds Meetings at Idaho Falls and SLC

The UISBC met for its eleventh annual session on November 11–12, 1975, at the Idaho Falls, Idaho, Calvary Baptist Church under the direction of president Chester Bunch. W. H. Souther led the music with Ann Clapp at the organ and Camille Lass at the piano. James Minnis, Glenn Munkres, Don Kimbrough, and Neal Foster read the scriptures and led the prayers. The out-of-state speakers were Meeler Markham, HMB; Phillip Harris, BSSB; Ray P. Rust, seminaries; Kenneth Nicholson, FMB; and I. D. Maricle, Annuity. Local speakers were Darwin Welsh, Wayne Harlow, Clyde Billingsley, and Logan Thomas. UISBC staff members were Darwin E. Welsh, executive director; Anita Lemke, executive assistant; Clyde Billingsley, missions; Guy Ward, education; Gernice Ward, WMU; and William Souther, music.

An "energy corridor" conference convened at the SLC Temple Square Hotel on December 18–19, 1975. Extensive oil field and oil shale developments in the Intermountain West led HMB leaders to hold conferences to discuss growth in impacted areas. Leaders from Utah, Idaho, Wyoming, Colorado, New Mexico, and Arizona were invited. The speakers were Bennie Delmar, Wyoming; R. A. Long, New Mexico; Clyde Billingsley, Utah; and Roy Owen, Colorado. Tommy Coy, James Nelson, and E. W. Hunke Jr. of the HMB spoke on the program. Phil Jones reported that the new churches organized from 1970 to 1975 were in Idaho (7), Nevada (8), and Utah (4). A January 29, 1976, report listed Nevada with forty-four churches, twenty church missions, 876 baptisms, 7,549 members, $5,702,215 church property, $1,461,878 receipts, and $80,936 in Cooperative Program gifts.

Fruitland, Idaho, First Baptist Church

Fruitland, Idaho, FBC organized in 1976 and affiliated with Boise Valley association and the UISBC. Early pastors were Roy Kilby, Richard Carlson, Randall Thetford, Travis McKinney, and Bennie Wright.

Salt Lake City, Utah, Chinese Baptist Mission

SLC, Utah, FSBC started the SLC Chinese Baptist Mission in 1976. Sarah Ashcraft, wife of UISBC executive secretary Charles H. Ashcraft, conducted activities that led to formation of the mission, which affiliated with Salt Lake association and the UISBC. The mission, which owned no property, conducted services in the SLC Millcreek Baptist Church. Early pastors were Yam Yee Lee and Jack Lee, the first to be baptized.

Nampa, Idaho, Valley (Victory) Baptist Church

Nampa Valley Baptist Church organized in 1976 and affiliated with Boise Valley association and the UISBC. Early pastors were Leo Sullivan, Doug Robinson, and Charles Alderman.

Heber City, Utah, Heber Valley Baptist Church

The SLC, Utah, Holladay Baptist Church started Heber Valley Baptist Church in 1976 with Ken and Sissy Mathias, two HMB US-2 missionaries. The first meeting convened above the fire station under the direction of Darwin E. Welsh. Jim and Polly Coleman, also HMB US-2 missionaries, followed the Mathias family. The new work affiliated with Salt Lake association and the UISBC. After the church organized and purchased property and a building, they reverted to mission status in 1990. The early pastors were Ken Mathias, Jim Coleman, Robert Fuelling, Tom Ernst, Jack Craig, and Buck Buchanan.

Murray, Utah, Korean Baptist Mission

John Lee, a HMB and UISBC missionary, started Murray Korean Baptist Mission in 1976. Lee retired from the HMB but continued to serve in 1997 as the mission's first and only pastor. The new mission affiliated with Salt Lake association and the UISBC.

UISBC State Evangelism Conferences Meet at Boise and SLC

The UISBC state evangelism conference met at Boise, Idaho, Rodeway Inn on February 1–3, 1976. The speakers were Jaroy Weber, SBC president; Ernie Adams, BSSB; Roy Fish, SWBTS; Manuel Scott, Los Angeles Calvary Baptist Church pastor; D. L. Lowrie, North Ft. Worth Baptist Church pastor; Bob Sena and E. W. Hunke Jr., HMB; Ron and Pat Owens, Houston, Texas; and Harry Taylor, Kansas-Nebraska Baptist Convention. The UISBC conducted two evangelism conferences in February 1976. The

Boise conference attracted 725 participants and the SLC conference reported 963 attending. Utah and Idaho youth singing in the youth musicals numbered 258.

Plans to Constitute Nevada Baptist Convention Initiated

State executive directors Robert D. Hughes of California and Roy F. Sutton of Arizona met with Leonard Irwin and E. W. Hunke of the HMB at the San Francisco St. Francis Hotel February 9, 1976, to discuss the future of Nevada Southern Baptist work. After two hours of consultation, the group agreed that: (1) no meetings would be held prior to the NVBF meeting on April 29–30, 1976; (2) Hughes would travel with two northern Nevada leaders, missionary Bob Wells and moderator Don Ledbetter, to discuss the grassroot feelings toward constituting a new Nevada SBC state convention; (3) Sutton would provide information to southern Nevada; (4) any discussion about establishing a committee or sending SBC workers would be deferred; (5) Irwin would discuss an educational worker with Comish or Cothen at the BSSB; (6) Hughes and Hunke would be present at a planned Reno conference; (7) Sutton would send J. L. Canafax to represent Arizona at Reno; and (8) any future meetings would involve the missionaries and moderators.

The NVBF met for its eleventh annual session April 29, 1976, at Reno, Nevada. SBC pastors and people from both northern and southern Nevada attended the meeting. Local personalities were Nevada governor O'Callaghan, Rudy Duett, William Webb, Robert D. Hughes, Bud Stengell, Judy Holland, Don Loving, and president Don Ledbetter. Missionaries Bob Wells of Reno and M. E. McGlamery of Las Vegas spoke. Other guests were Harold Green and J. L. Canafax of Phoenix; W. A. Criswell of Dallas; E. W. Hunke Jr. of the HMB; and the CBC musicians from Riverside, California.

SBC Volunteers Respond to Idaho Distress Call

On June 5, 1976, the Teton Dam in eastern Idaho broke under extreme water pressure, and downstream results were disastrous. When the SBC Brotherhood sent out a distress call, volunteers from across the United States responded to meet the physical and spiritual need. The HMB and UISBC collected funds for the Red Cross and sent out $12,565 to SBC pastors to help with the recovery.

UISBC Employs Earl Jackson as Missionary (Utah-Idaho)

Because of the population growth in Utah and Idaho, the HMB and UISBC employed Earl Vernon Jackson as missionary to Golden Spike and Eastern Idaho associations on June 1, 1976. Jackson was born on August 9, 1931, at Sumter, South Carolina, to Joseph and Mary Jackson. He had seven brothers and one sister. He was saved at age twelve, baptized in an old cold-water, under-pulpit baptistry by Privateer Community, South Carolina, Bethel Baptist Church in 1943, and ordained November 10, 1957, at Augusta, South Carolina, by Bell Ridge Baptist Church. Jackson wrote, "My Sunday School teacher had a profound influence, but my mom was the living example of a true Christian. During our annual July third week revival, I went forward with my younger brother Frank to trust Jesus as my Savior and Lord." He graduated from Sumter Edmunds High School, North Greenville College, William Carey College, and NOBTS. He married Peggy Still on November 26, 1954, at Barnwell, South Carolina, and they had four children. Jackson pastored churches at Gibson and Stapleton, Georgia, and Sumrall and Baxterville, Mississippi. He wrote:

> I felt called to missions during the Ben Lipper [Mountain of Trust] Bible conference. I stayed in touch with Peter and Lily Kok because they encouraged me. When I married Peggy, we made our final surrender to missions under Clarence Hanshew. We got the real feel for missions on a mission trip to Cuba, New Mexico, with the Hanshews to lead VBS and revival among Navajo Indians.

The HMB and UISBC employed Jackson to serve the Ft. Hall, Idaho, Indian Baptist Mission (1967–1976), and Eastern Idaho and Golden Spike associations (1976–1997). He preached three weeks at Siberia in Russia in 1995. The Jacksons retired on August 30, 1997, after completing thirty years of HMB ministry in Idaho and Utah.

Meyers, California, Tahoe Paradise Baptist Church

South Lake Tahoe Baptist Church celebrated the two-hundredth anniversary of the United States July 4, 1976, by organizing Meyers Tahoe Paradise Baptist Church with Paul Wallace as the first pastor. The new church affiliated with Nevada association and the SBGCC. Early pastors were Paul Wallace, Bill Bibbins, Len Sullivan (2), Walter Stinett, James Reno, Mike Davis (int.), and Tom Johnson.

HMB Employs Bill Tanner as Executive Director

The HMB employed OBU president William G. Tanner as the HMB executive director on July 21, 1976, to succeed Arthur Rutledge on his December 31, 1976, retirement. Tanner was born March 10, 1930, at Tulsa, Oklahoma. He graduated from Baylor, University of Houston, and SWBTS. He earned, or was awarded, the following degrees: Ed.D., Th.D., Ph.D., L.L.D., D.M., D.D., and L.H.D. He married Ellen Sampey Yates, and they had four children. Tanner pastored churches at Wheelock, Cleburn, and Houston, Texas, and at Gulfport, Mississippi. He served as president of the Mary Hardin-Baylor and Oklahoma Baptist universities. He resigned from the HMB to serve as Oklahoma Baptist Convention executive director in 1987.

UISBC Twelfth Annual Session Meets at Granger

The UISBC met for its twelfth annual session November 9–10, 1976, at the Granger, Utah, FBC, under the direction of president Chester Bunch. William Souther, Judy Billingsley, and Maria McCown led the music which featured John Chandler, Baptist Hour choir, the Granger FBC choir, Clyde and Judy Billingsley, Dale Shaw, John and Margaret Blake, and Bi-Centennial Choir. Charles Fowler, Phil McCown, Don Barr, Gene Crewse, and John Lee read the scriptures and led the prayers. The speakers were Gomer Lesch, BSSB; Edward Wheeler, HMB; John Ward, Annuity;

James McAtee, FMB, Indonesia; Albert McClellan, SBC Executive Committee; and Glendon McCullough, Brotherhood. The HMB budgeted $378,576 for the UISBC in 1977, an increase of $74,641 over the 1976 budget. The new officers were Bruce Gardner, president; Louis Demster and Carroll Reynolds, vice-presidents; and Jon Engstrom, recording secretary.

Heartache and Tragedy Strike SBC Leaders

Michael Lee McKay, Ft. Hall, Idaho, missionary to Indians, wrote:

> Pray for our health and spiritual power for Christ among the Indian folk. I am limited to Sunday School and worship for the time being. I am getting stronger slowly but surely, thanks be to God for His mercy and love. My last four years in Alaska with responsibility to pastor two missions, plan new ministries, and direct camps broke me. I praise the Lord for the kindness of the HMB, and support from Anita and Darwin who stood by us until we could recover.

E. W. Hunke in a memo to HMB staff (23 February 1977), wrote:

> Two tragedies this week have struck West Coast SBC leadership: (1) Monday, February 21, a daughter-in-law of Dr. and Mrs. Robert Hughes was buried in California. He was called home from the SBC state executive directors' meeting at Charleston, South Carolina. Sandy, age 30, had been living with Hodgkins Disease for several years. In addition to her husband, Sandy left two children ages eight and three. (2) Wednesday, February 23, a grandson of the W. C. Carpenters, was killed at Pasco, Washington. Carpenters' daughter, Mary, who lived with her husband in Salem, Oregon, was visiting in Pasco today when the 18 month-old child was killed.

Topaz Lake, Nevada, First Baptist Church

Minden-Gardnerville, Nevada, FBC organized the Topaz Lake FBC of Topaz Ranch Estates in 1977 with Larry Rothchild as first pastor. The church affiliated with Nevada association and the

SBGCC. The mission met first in a fire station and later in a mobile home placed on three acres purchased by the church. Early pastors were Ray Hand (2) and Mitchell Bryant.

Goldfield, Nevada, First Baptist Church

Goldfield FBC organized in 1977 with Bob Mann as pastor. The new church affiliated with Nevada association and the SBGCC.

Clarkston, Washington, Heights (Sonrise) Baptist Mission

Lewiston, Idaho, Orchards Baptist Church reported that its Clarkston Heights Baptist Mission had three added by baptism and six by letter in 1977. The new mission affiliated with Lewis-Clark association and the BGCOW. Harold Morgan served as pastor.

Lewis-Clark Association Reports New Missions

The Moscow, Idaho, Trinity Baptist Church reported missions at Bovill and Potlatch, Idaho, in 1977. Pastors Terry Posey and David Palmer served Bovill mission, and Jim Young served Potlatch. Ronald Seibert's attempt to start the Lewiston Valley Baptist Mission did not produce a continuing work.

Horseshoe Bend, Idaho, Baptist Church

Bend, Idaho, Baptist Church organized in 1977 and affiliated with Boise Valley association and the UISBC. Early pastors were David Hodgdon, Dale Mitchell, Richard Derby, and Richard DeBriae.

Kaysville, Utah, Wasatch Baptist Church

William Jones started the Kaysville Wasatch Baptist Church in 1977. The new church affiliated with Salt Lake association and the UISBC. Early pastors were William Jones and Lynn Weston.

Nevadans Consider Implications of Convention Status

Nevada association voted to recommend the constitution of a Nevada SBC state convention at their 1976 annual session. Nevada association sent representatives to the Lake Mead association annual meeting on October 18–19, 1976, to discuss the proposal. Southern Nevada SBC churches concurred.

On January 19–20, 1977, the NVBF representatives met with leaders of their two sponsoring state conventions at the Las Vegas, Nevada, Lake Mead associational office. The group asked seven questions: (1) What are advantages and disadvantages for Nevadans in a new state convention? (2) What are minimum SBC requirements for constitution (qualification) for denominational funds? (3) What kind of organization and budget can the new convention support? (4) Will the sponsoring SBGCC and ASBC vote to constitute a new Nevada state convention? (5) How can we best share information about a new Nevada SBC state convention with churches? (6) How can the ASBC be assured that church loans in Nevada will be repaid? (7) What steps and time tables need to be set so that churches may proceed in an orderly way toward constitution?

The participants were Hughes and Longshore, SBGCC; Canafax and Sutton, ASBC; Wells and McGlamery, Nevada missionaries; Bacon and Holmes, Nevada moderators; Stanley Unruh, NVBF president; and E. W. Hunke Jr., HMB. Hunke was elected to moderate the meeting. The SBC work in Nevada was twenty-five years old, and the HMB was budgeting more than $100,000 annually for Nevada. The ASBC board voted "to look with favor on the SBC churches in southern Nevada voting to withdraw from the ASBC to organize a new Nevada state convention."

The NVBF met at the North Las Vegas, Calvary Baptist Church on April 27, 1977, under the direction of president Stan Unruh. Gerald Palmer, HMB vice-president, led three Bible studies, and Peter McLeod, Waco, Texas, FBC pastor, preached feature messages in the morning and evening sessions. Executive directors Robert Hughes (SBGCC) and Roy Sutton (ASBC) spoke. Missionaries Robert Wells of northern Arizona and M. E. McGlamery of southern Nevada provided reports. Nevada pastors discussed the theme "Working Together in Nevada." Panel members were Robert Holmes, Quinton Montgomery, Donald Ledbetter, and Tom Bacon. Following special music by the Las Vegas, Nevada, Twin Lakes Baptist Church, HMB leaders Gerald B. Palmer and E. W. Hunke Jr.

spoke. GCC musical groups sang at each session. Officers elected for the new year were Rudy Duett, president; Tom Propelka, vice-president; Evelyn Newell, secretary; and Don Mulkey, treasurer. Missionary M. E. McGlamery, reported that the southern Nevada churches had 242 baptisms, 5,816 in SS enrollment, and $67,943 in mission gifts in the church year.

UISBC Evanglism Conference Meets at Salt Palace

The UISBC evangelism conference met January 30 to February 1, 1977, at the Salt Palace in SLC, Utah. The meeting featured music under the direction of William, Harold, and Billy Souther. Program participants were Jaroy Weber, Lubbock FBC; Emmanuel McCall, HMB; Theo Patnaik, Clovis, California; E. W. Hunke Jr. and Carter Bearden, HMB; Rodney Webb, Mississippi Baptists; and Darwin Welsh, UISBC executive secretary. Hunke taught four Bible studies.

HMB Employs A. C. Queen as Evangelism Consultant

The HMB, in keeping with a long tradition, sent A. C. Queen as an evangelism consultant to help the Nevada Southern Baptists prepare for their new convention and help strengthen the UISBC churches. Alonzo and Mildred Queen moved to Carson City, Nevada, on May 9, 1977. Queen was born on August 21, 1915, at St. Louis, Missouri, to Benjamin Calvin and Mary Alice (Larkin) Queen. He had a brother and three sisters. Queen was saved at age eighteen through the influence of a high school teacher, baptized by the DeSoto, Missouri, FBC in February 1934, and ordained by DeSoto Oakland Baptist Church in 1940. He wrote, "A teacher challenged me to read through the New Testament. I became a believer before I ever attended church." He graduated from DeSoto High School, Southwest Baptist College, William Jewell College, and SWBTS. He married Mildred Louvena Lake in 1941 at Bolivar, Missouri, and they had two children. He served in the U.S. Navy in World War II and as a Civil Air Patrol major. He pastored SBC churches in Missouri, Texas, and California, and served as a

BSU worker in Missouri, Illinois, and Cuba, where he pastored Havana, Cuba, FBC. The HMB and NWBC employed him as a missionary to Siskiyou, Douglas, and Klammath associations in Oregon (1970–1973). The HMB employed him as the Nevada/Utah/Idaho regional evangelism director (1977–1980). GGBTS employed him as adjunct professor of ministry and director of its SLC, Utah, extension center (1981–1982). Queen died February 19, 1989.

A. C. Queen wrote, "I have had good meetings with leadership in SLC and some specific plans are under consideration for 1978–1979. Can Utah-Idaho count on the HMB enlisting the eighty preachers and song leaders needed to help in the April 15–22, 1979, meetings in the churches?"

HMB, State Conventions, and Seminaries Cooperate

The HMB initiated the Mission Service Corps in 1977, largely in response to an appeal from President Jimmy Carter of Georgia. The program was designed for persons twenty-one years of age and older who agreed to provide their own support and to serve a two-year mission. The HMB set a goal of five thousand missionaries.

The HMB, SWBTS, and the UISBC joined together in a summer 1977 internship program for seminary students. The following served: Barbara Hawkins, Linda Spear, and Roy Burkett at Boise; Chris Kutin and August Miller at Alta Canyon; and Song and Ian Sakai at SLC Japanese. The HMB/BSU student summer missionaries were Brenda Hughey, Peggy Cryar, Patricia Poucher, David Wood, Ted Holmes, Daryl Coats, Donna Jarvis, Cheryl Christensen, David Soto, John Burleigh, Cathy Williams, James Logan, and Connie Cone.

Wallace, Idaho, Baptist Church

Kellogg, Idaho, FBC started the Wallace Baptist Mission in June 1977 with a VBS. The small Idaho mining town, located near Fourth of July Pass, had eighteen taverns, two grocery stores, and eighteen hundred people. The SBC services were held in a downtown store building in Wallace. The new church affiliated with Inland Empire association and the NWBC. One student summer missionary, Michael Passmore of Hawkinsville, Georgia, labored alongside the Lloyd Garrisons all summer. The SS averaged forty in attendance, and services averaged forty-eight. Garrison baptized twenty-one people. Lee Layman also pastored the Wallace church.

Nevada Southern Baptists Move toward New Convention

NVBF president Rudy Duett wrote to each northern Nevada SBC church on July 1, 1977, asking the church to vote yes or no on a proposal to constitute the new Nevada state convention. Three teams of workers came from Shawnee, Oklahoma, Indian churches to witness to Indians in the Battle Mountain, Nevada, area on July 11–18, 1977.

The NVBF steering committee met at Tonopah, Nevada, on September 8, 1977, to plan for a Nevada convention. Participants were Tom Propelka, Don Mulkey, Don Loving, Stanley Unruh, Robert Holmes, and M. E. McGlamery from Lake Mead association in southern Nevada, and Rudy Duett, Tom Bacon, Sam Worley, Don Wilson, and Paul Lewis from Nevada association. Rudy Duett, NVBF president, reported that eighteen letters of intent to affiliate with the new convention had been received. The chairmen of the program, personnel, and finance committees provided reports.

The NVBF committee adopted five proposals: (1) constitute a new convention in the fall (1978) to begin operation on January 1, 1979; (2) adopt dates at the annual associational meetings next month; (3) recognize NVBF elected officers as a functional executive board; (4) ask all the churches to send the official messengers to an April 27, 1978, NVBF meeting to approve initial recommendations; and (5) request the ASBC and SBGCC to set aside some NVBF 1978 Cooperative Program funds to begin operation in 1979. The constitution committee met October 6, 1977, at Reno FSBC to study constitutions of newly formed state conventions and draft the new constitution.

Nevada Association Changes Name to Northern Nevada

Nevada association changed its name to the Northern Nevada Baptist Association at the October 7, 1977, annual meeting. The Northern Nevada association reported twenty-eight churches with 5,137 members. Rudy Duett, NVBF president, met with Lake Mead association to recommend that the Nevada convention be organized in the fall of 1978 and begin operations January 1, 1979. The proposal was adopted.

NVBF Structure and Function Committee Sets Agenda

The NVBF structure and function committee met on October 11, 1977, at Tonopah FBC. Persons attending were president Rudy Duett, Robert Holmes, J. Paul Lewis, Stanley Unruh, Don Mulkey, Don Wilson, Don Ledbetter, M. E. McGlamery, Robert A. Wells, A. C. Queen, and David Wallace. At the request of the committee, E. W. Hunke Jr. had mailed a hand-drawn proposal detailing structure, Cooperative Program funding, total budget, HMB support, and state convention gifts to the SBC, using the Alaska and Northern Plains conventions as models. The committee set annual associational meetings on October 6–7, 1978 (Northern Nevada), and October 9–10, 1978 (Lake Mead). Jimmy Allen, SBC president, was asked to speak at the constitutional session.

The HMB separated NVBF funding from ASBC and SBGCC budgets for the first time in 1977. The 1977 NVBF allocation of $99,876 required a $15,216 ASBC/SBGCC subsidy and $84,660 from the HMB. A projected 1978 budget of $137,400 required $16,572 from SBGCC and ASBC, and $120,828 from the HMB. The HMB coordinator spent one month in Nevada and Utah-Idaho in 1977.

Lake Mead Association Changes Name to Southern Nevada

Lake Mead association voted to change its name to Southern Nevada Baptist Association on October 17, 1977. The association reported twenty-two churches, six missions, 636 baptisms, 9,445 members, $1,585,420 receipts, and $354,863 mission gifts in 1979. The association elected representatives to serve on the NVBF steering committee and provisional executive board, to plan the program, write the proposed constitution and bylaws, and form an organizational nucleus to complete the myriad of tasks needed to establish a state convention. The Northern Nevada and Southern Nevada Baptist associations hosted a world mission conference on January 22–29, 1978.

UISBC Thirteenth Annual Session Meets at Boise

UISBC met for its thirteenth annual session November 8–9, 1977, at the Boise, Idaho, Mountain View Baptist Church, under the direction of president Bruce Gardner. Dale Shaw, Bob Tate, and W. H. Souther directed the music featuring the Idaho Baptist choir, Maxine Souther, and the Boise Baptist youth choir. Bea and Bruce Conrad, Edie and Huron Polnak, Margaret and John Blake, Virginia and Mike McKay, and Neomi and Richard Vera read the scriptures and led the prayers. The speakers were Wayne Evans, seminaries; James Powell, SBC Executive Committee; Larry Crisman, Annuity; Jerry Scruggs and A. C. Queen, HMB; Richard Horn, FMB; and Lloyd Householder, BSSB. The newly elected officers were Bruce Gardner, president; George Eichler and Carroll Reynolds, vice-presidents; and Jon Engstrom, recording secretary.

Cothen Shares BSSB Policy with the NVBF

The HMB, BSSB, ASBC, SBGCC, and NVBF agreed to establish the Nevada date of constitution as October 16–17, 1978, with the new convention to begin operations on January 1, 1979. Grady Cothen, the BSSB executive director, wrote to NVBF president Rudy Duett on November 10, 1977, as follows:

> It is the policy of the BSSB to cooperate with sponsoring state conventions, in this case Arizona and California, to be sure that we in no way interfere with the orderly processes which have been adopted by these appropriate Baptist bodies. I have said to Brother Hunke and to Dr. Hughes and Dr. Sutton that when it is felt desirable, we will make a contribution of $10,000 a year to provide an education worker prior to formation of a new convention. The SBGCC and ASBC would be expected to subsidize BSSB funds to make a worker possible.

Associational Missionaries in the 1970s

Francis Leroy Smith, HMB/ASBC missionary to Nevada (1970–1971).

M. E. and Juanita McGlamery, HMB/ASBC missionary to Nevada (1972–1977).

William Kenneth Peters, HMB/NWBC missionary to Idaho (1972–1977).

Richard and Ruby Ashworth, HMB/UISBC missionary to Utah (1972–1991).

Earl and Peggy Jackson, HMB/UISBC missionary to UT/ID (1976–1997).

Donald Kersey Laing, HMB/NWBC missionary to Idaho (1978–1987).

The Utah-Idaho Southern Baptist Convention

The UISBC state staff met for an annual retreat to plan their work. Staff (L-R) in 1971: Clyde Billingsley, missions; John Allen, HMB; Darwin Welsh, executive director; Gernice Ward, WMU; Mayo Brown, Utah missionary; Guy Ward, education; Anita Lemke, executive assistant; Medford Hutson, Utah missionary; Roy Ferguson, Idaho missionary; and E. W. Hunke Jr., HMB.

First UISBC Baptist Building, Salt Lake City, Utah.

Second UISBC Baptist Building, Sandy, Utah.

UISBC staff in 1982 (L-R): Lavoid Robertson, evangelism; Bruce Gardner, missions; Guy Ward, education; W. H. Souther, music; Gernice Ward, WMU; Darwin Welsh, executive director; and Anita Lemke, executive assistant.

UISBC Reports Two Historic Events

UISBC called attention to two significant happenings during November and December 1977: (1) Boise, Idaho, SBC churches built a new library for their Chair of Bible at the university and named it for Charles Ashcraft. Ashcraft, the first UISBC executive director who now served as the Arkansas Baptist leader, flew to Boise to dedicate the new facility. (2) The UISBC employed John Baker, the retired Northern Plains Baptist Convention state executive director, to serve as the interim state missions director until July 1978.

Spirit Lake, Idaho, Baptist Church

In 1978 pastor George Scantlan of Post Falls and an evangelist from Missouri found Missouri Mule Cafe while visiting. The owner, Maggie Poland, indicated interest in starting a Baptist church at Spirit Lake. The mission started with a Bible study in the cafe after closing time and later moved to an empty Seventh Day Adventist building used as an antique shop. Spokane Lakes Baptist Church organized the Spirit Lake Baptist Church May 20, 1990. The church affiliated with Inland Empire association and the NWBC. Early pastors were Steve Blachurst, John Panther, Steve Reno, Arnold Kenney, and Lloyd Garrison.

Jordan Valley, Oregon, Village Baptist Church

The Jordan Valley Village Baptist Church organized in 1978 and affiliated with Boise Valley association and the UISBC. The early pastors were Bill Elliott and John Richards.

Weiser, Idaho, Calvary Baptist Church

Weiser Calvary Baptist Church organized in 1978 and affiliated with Boise Valley association and the UISBC. Early pastors were Richard Carlson, Travis McKinney, and Lloyd Barney.

Tahoe Southern Baptist Association Constitutes (SBGCC)

Two Southern Baptist churches located on the California side of Lake Tahoe chose not to affiliate with the Nevada convention.

Messengers constituted the Tahoe Southern Baptist Association of California in 1978 to retain the relationship with the SBGCC.

UISBC Conducts Two Evangelism Conferences

The annual UISBC evangelism conference met January 29, 1978, at the SLC, Utah, Salt Palace Little Theater. Ebbie Smith, the SWBTS missions professor, led Bible studies. The speakers were William Schweer, GGBTS evangelism professor; Edward Wheeler, Rodney Webb, and John Havlik, HMB; and Adrian Rogers, Memphis, Tennessee, Bellevue Baptist Church pastor. The music was directed by Billy Souther of Florida and Harold Souther of Missouri. A. C. Queen, the HMB regional evangelism consultant, helped plan the meeting. With a few exceptions, the same speakers led an Idaho evangelism conference on January 30–31, 1978, at Boise, Idaho, Mountain View Baptist Church. The added program personalities in Idaho were C. E. Autrey and John Baker of SLC, and E. W. Hunke Jr., HMB.

Logan, Utah, Maranatha Baptist Church

The Logan, Utah, Maranatha Baptist Church organized with one hundred charter members in February 1978. James Herod, Logan FBC associate pastor, believed that Logan FBC had left historic SBC doctrines for the charismatic movement. After a discussion with missionary Earl Jackson and Logan FBC, an agreement was reached to have "Pledge a New Work Sunday." One hundred people left the Logan FBC to organize the new Maranatha Baptist Church. The new church affiliated with Golden Spike association and the UISBC. The early pastors were James Herod and Don Emerson.

Nevada Missionaries Send Glowing Reports

Southern Nevada association churches supported the Greater Las Vegas Billy Graham Crusade on February 19–22, 1978. M. E. McGlamery wrote:

> I think you will be pleased to learn that the Las Vegas, Nevada, Billy Graham Crusade was very successful.

Cumulative attendance was 63,000 for the five services and 3,144 people made commitments for Christ. Jim Reid participated very actively in the crusade. In a special service held at 3 p.m. on Saturday, February 4, there were about 1,000 present with forty-three decisions.

Missionary Robert Wells of the Northern Nevada association wrote the southern Nevada SBC pastors to welcome them to northern Nevada, and to ask that they speak in the churches on Wednesday evening April 26, 1978, on their way to the last NVBF. Some pastors stopped at churches on the way to Carson City to speak and spend the night. Wells wrote:

> Southern Baptist work in northern Nevada grew very rapidly in an eight year period [1970–1978]. In 1970 the association reported nineteen churches with 1,554 members, and twenty pastors—eleven bivocational. The largest church had fewer than 125 persons in services on Sunday and a budget less than $26,000 a year. By 1978, Nevada association had forty-one churches and forty-one pastors, each with pastoral support. Each church had secured property. The churches baptized 500 people. The association reported one church 530 miles from South Lake Tahoe in the same association. The SBC now has more SBC churches and missions in Nevada than any other denomination. This happened in thirty years.

HMB, ASBC, and SBGCC Finalize Plans for Nevada Convention

State executive directors Robert Hughes (SBGCC), Roy F. Sutton (ASBC), and E. W. Hunke Jr. (HMB) met at the Nashville Ramada Inn on February 20, 1978, to confirm plans for the Nevada convention and finalize the 1979 budget. Hunke provided future dates and time lines. Hughes reported that church pastoral aid problems in the Lake Tahoe area were resolved. Sutton noted that the Nevadans' relationship to two separate state conventions and lack of experience with board procedures prevented emergence of a single unifying personality. The effort to use the evangelism consultant was not readily accepted. Hughes said that the SBGCC spent as much money in the northern Nevada area as it received and expected no budget pressure. Sutton reported that the ASBC received sixty thousand dollars in Cooperative Program money from the southern Nevada churches and anticipated severe pressure on its budget. To help Nevadans launch the convention, the SBGCC planned to give one thousand dollars per month for the first year. The ASBC designated its 1978 state mission offering to Nevada, an anticipated thirty thousand dollars.

NVBF Meets to Officially Confirm Constitution Plans
The NVBF annual meeting convened at the Carson City, Nevada, FBC on April 27, 1978. Honorable Mike O'Callaghan, the Silver State of Nevada governor, welcomed the church messengers from all across Nevada to Reno. Bill Pinson, the GGBTS president, led two Bible studies. The Reno FSBC pastor and NVBF president, Rudy Duett, gave a presidential address. Reports were given by Robert D. Hughes, SBGCC; Roy Sutton, ASBC; Robert Wells, Reno; M. E. McGlamery, Las Vegas; and Harvey Broadway, Tonopah. President Grady Cothen, BSSB, preached the morning and evening messages. E. W. Hunke Jr., HMB, spoke on the theme "Working Together to Make a Dream Come True" to close the afternoon session. A signed document entitled "A Request for Recognition to the SBC Boards, Agencies, and State Conventions" was approved:

> WHEREAS, Southern Baptist work in the state of Nevada is approaching the thirtieth anniversary, and
>
> WHEREAS, Nevada Baptist Fellowship is attaining the minimum qualifications for the state convention status prescribed by the Baptist Sunday School Board and Home Mission Board, and
>
> WHEREAS, both the Northern Nevada and Southern Nevada Baptist associations are requesting the privilege of working together in reaching Nevada for Christ, and

WHEREAS, the Nevada Southern Baptist regional committee is completing the initial recommendation for a Nevada Baptist State Convention constitution, bylaws, structure, budget, and

WHEREAS, an official date for the constitution of the Nevada Baptist State Convention is being confirmed for October 16–17, 1978:

WE UNDERSIGNED, ELECTED MESSENGERS FROM SOUTHERN BAPTIST CHURCHES AND MISSIONS IN THE NEVADA AREA, DO HEREBY RESPECTFULLY REQUEST:

That the board of directors of our two sponsoring state conventions, Arizona Southern Baptist Convention and Southern Baptist General Convention of California, officially recognize this expressed desire and send representatives to assist in the constitution of a new Southern Baptist state convention, and

That the board of directors of Southern Baptists' two principal funding boards, the Baptist Home Mission and Sunday School boards, officially recognize this expressed desire and send representatives to assist in the constitution of a new Nevada Southern Baptist state convention, and

That other state conventions, fraternal organizations, and other SBC boards, agencies, and institutions be represented at this historic meeting.

APPROVED ON THIS TWENTY-SEVENTH DAY OF APRIL, NINETEEN HUNDRED AND SEVENTY-EIGHT.

Final Preparations Initiated by NVBF Committees

The NVBF organized to make final preparations for the new state convention. The NVBF elected northern Nevadans Evelyn Newell, Don Ledbetter, Paul Lewis, Tom Bacon, Mike Procter, and

Rex Langston; and southern Nevadans Robert Holmes, Don Mulkey, Stanley Unruh, Tom Propelka, Don Loving, and Bruce Castleberry to complete the constitutional plans. The steering committee set up three committees: (1) a search committee to find an executive director to lead the new convention with Don Mulkey (chairman), Don Ledbetter, Stanley Unruh, and Paul Lewis; (2) a location committee to find the best location for the convention offices with Tom Bacon (chairman), Bruce Castleberry, Rex Langston, Robert Holmes; and (3) a constituting committee to develop the program, budget, and constitution with Tom Propelka (chairman), Mike Proctor, Evelyn Newell, and Don Loving. On May 3, 1978, the HMB western regional coordinator wrote the following memo to HMB executive director Bill Tanner:

> David Benham and I attended the NVBF meeting in Carson City on April 27, 1978. Paul Adkins and James Barber visited briefly in connection with another meeting scheduled in the area. The meeting was most enthusiastic and in excellent spirits. This was the last fellowship meeting scheduled prior to convention constitution. Fellowship meetings date back to the first one held at Sparks, Nevada, in 1957. Even though Northern Nevada and Southern Nevada associations have affiliated with two different state conventions, they have had twenty-one years association through these fellowship meetings.

On May 26, 1978, the HMB western regional coordinator wrote the following letter to Grady Cothen, BSSB executive director:

> Rudy Duett, NVBF president called to report that 156 messengers from thirty-eight churches attended the annual meeting at Carson City, Nevada, on April 27. Visitors did not register. Forty-six SBC churches have agreed to affiliate and eight additional church-type missions plan to constitute in the next year—minimum qualifications will be met. Every single SBC church in Nevada is now committed to the new convention.

Rathdrum, Idaho, Baptist Church

The Post Falls, Idaho, Baptist Church started the Rathdrum Baptist Church in 1978 with a family baptized at the Post Falls church. Lloyd and Marjorie Garrison moved their mobile home to the community to begin the work. They rented a store building adjacent to the tavern, painted the interior, and cleaned out the coal room for the nursery. Services began with several classes outside under the trees. While ten buckets caught rain coming through the roof, Eddie Freeman of Texas preached the May revival with one hundred in attendance. After the Dumas, Texas, FBC choir conducted the VBS, the Wichita Falls, Texas, FBC work team framed the building. The Wichita Falls and Kalispell, Montana, church groups camped on the property and completed the new building. The Garrisons baptized thirty-six new converts at Rathdrum. The church affiliated with Inland Empire association and the NWBC. Early pastors were Charlie Hodges, John Henry, and Ronald Houghtaling.

Walker Lake, Nevada, Baptist Church

Hawthorne, Nevada, FSBC organized the Walker Lake Baptist Church on June 30, 1978. Arlis Hibbard, mission pastor, started the mission on June 1, 1972. The new church affiliated with Northern Nevada association and the SBGCC. The church sponsored SBC work at Schurz and Mason Valley. The early pastors were Jim Tilley, Sean Lathrop (int.), Ernest Hewett, John Ashcraft, Tom Bacon (int.), E. L. Eudy, and Hale Anderson. Tilley and Ashcraft left the church to serve as SBC foreign missionaries. James Hamilton pastored the Mason Valley mission.

UISBC Employs Bruce Gardner as State Mission Director

After Clyde Billingsley resigned, the HMB and UISBC employed Bruce Gardner, Idaho Falls, Idaho, Calvary Baptist Church pastor as the state mission director on July 1, 1978. Gardner was born at Albuquerque, New Mexico, April 14, 1930, to M. B. and Louise (Hannah) Gardner. He had two brothers. He was saved at age eight through his mother's influence, baptized by Second (Fruit Avenue) Baptist Church, licensed in March 1959, and ordained ten years later by the Fruit Avenue church. He reported:

> My mother sent me to church around the corner, and I was too timid to give my name. When I was six years of age, someone followed me home and led my mother and father to Christ. When I was eight, my mother knelt in front of me, looked me in the eyes, and asked me to accept Christ as my personal Savior. As a child I considered being a medical doctor or a lawyer but reasoned that I was too timid. When I was thirteen it dawned on me that God had a business. At first I resisted serving as a minister, but later surrendered to God's call.

Gardner graduated from Albuquerque High School, HSU, and SWBTS, and served in the U.S. Air Force. Gardner married Berniece Bell at Albuquerque on January 6, 1952, and they adopted two sons. After serving as a religious education director, he pastored churches at Gallup, New Mexico, and Idaho Falls, Idaho. He served as the UISBC state mission director from July 1, 1978, until he retired December 31, 1992, at Thoreau, New Mexico.

Gardner reported that fifteen student missionaries were at work in Utah and Idaho during the summer of 1978: Kathy Smith, Ted Holmes, James Smith, Peggy Ray, Frankie Bagley, Denise Donovan, Jami Cartwright, Jayne Barry, Nancy Beatty, Cyndi Vincent, Joseph Chambers, Joy Fortenberry, Myra Tripp, and David Jay.

Carson City, Nevada, Capital City Baptist Church

Carson City, Nevada, FBC started the Carson City, Capital City Baptist Mission on July 2, 1978, in the Elks Club with Paul Ray serving as the first pastor. The church organized in 1978 and affiliated with Northern Nevada association and the NABC. The church moved to the Seventh Day Adventist church in May 1984 and into their own facility in May 1987. The early pastors were Paul Ray and Larry Rothchild.

NWBC Employs Don Laing as Missionary (Idaho)

After Bill Peters resigned, the HMB and NWBC employed Donald Kersey Laing as missionary on August 1, 1978. The association included churches in the Idaho panhandle. Laing was born

October 23, 1933, at Tipton, Oklahoma, to John Spurgeon and Cassie Laing. He had four brothers and one sister. He was saved at age nine at the Hobbs, New Mexico, FBC, baptized by the Tipton, Oklahoma, FBC, in 1942, and ordained by the Hobbs, New Mexico, Rock Chapel Baptist Church in August 1953. He wrote:

> While I was spending a summer with an older brother in Hobbs, New Mexico, my best friend Edwin was saved one Sunday while I was away visiting my mother in the hospital. Edwin told me what happened to him and wanted me to talk with pastor W. C. Carpenter. We talked after SS, and I accepted the Lord as my Savior. I waited to be baptized by my Oklahoma country church.

He married Barbara Ruth Clark in 1942 at Hobbs, New Mexico, and they had four children. He graduated from Hobbs High School, HSU, SWBTS, and GGBTS (D.Min.). Laing pastored churches at Winters, Dunn, Alvarado, and Colorado City, Texas; and at Urbana, Arkansas. The FMB appointed the Laings as missionaries to Brazil (1967–1977). The HMB and NWBC employed him as missionary to Inland Empire association (1978–1987), and the HMB and SBGCC to Long Beach Harbor association (1987–1994). After he retired, he pastored Long Beach Truett Memorial Baptist Church.

NVBF Location Committee Recommends Reno for Offices

The NVBF location committee met September 27, 1978, at Reno, Nevada, FSBC. Chairman Tom Bacon read letters from the churches offering office space. A letter from Grady Cothen, executive director of the BSSB, suggested the group settle on one location and not two. After Phil Jones, an HMB researcher, reported on the study requested by the committee, they recommended Reno as the location for the state convention office for these reasons: (1) closer to Nevada state capital; (2) better airline connections inside Nevada because of government business; (3) location of the main university campus; and (4) convenient highway travel.

E. W. Hunke Jr.

Nevada Governor Proclaims "Southern Baptist Week in Nevada"

The Nevada governor officially participated in formation of the new Nevada Area Baptist Convention by proclaiming October 15–21, 1978, as Southern Baptist Week.

STATE OF NEVADA EXECUTIVE DEPARTMENT: proclamation by the Governor:

WHEREAS, SBC churches of Nevada now include more than 12,000 members with 65 churches and missions; and

WHEREAS, these congregations have gathered to plan an association of Nevada Baptist churches which no longer requires affiliation [support from] Southern Baptist state conventions in other [neighboring] states; and

WHEREAS, Nevada Baptist Area Convention will have its constituting meeting in mid-October;

NOW, THEREFORE, I, MIKE O'CALLAGHAN, Governor of the State of Nevada, do hereby proclaim the week of October 15–21, 1978, in Nevada as SOUTHERN BAPTIST WEEK.

Nevada Area Baptist Convention Constitutes

About three hundred Nevada SBC church messengers gathered at the Las Vegas, Nevada, Redrock Baptist Church on October 16–17, 1978, to constitute the new Nevada Area Baptist Convention (NABC). The first session featured GCC "Jubilation Singers," Rex Langston, Stanley Unruh, Rudy Duett, governor Mike O'Callaghan, Wayne North, Bill Hahn, Mike Proctor, Tom Propelka, Robert Hughes, Roy Sutton, Lester Hampton, Brooks Wester, and Don Loving. The second session featured Cecil Deas, Harvey Broadway, Roy Sutton, Robert Hughes, Robert Holmes, Robert Lee, Don Mulkey, E. W. Hunke Jr., and Steve Neesley. Music was provided by GCC singers and the Las Vegas Twin Lakes Baptist Church choir. The third session featured Doug Wooten, Tom Bacon, Don Ledbetter, Helen Fling, Charles Ashcraft, and

Sam Newell. The music was provided by the GCC singers and the Las Vegas West Oakey Baptist Church choir. The fourth and final session featured the California Singers, Keith McRevy, Jim McLeroy, M. E. McGlamery, Bob Wells, Bill O'Brien, Willis J. Ray, and a message by Ernest Myers, the newly elected NABC executive director. The ASBC gave sixteen churches, eight thousand members, $11,250 from the James P. Bridges fund, $15,000 from the state mission offering, and funds contributed from Nevada churches to ASBC for the last three months of 1978. The SBGCC planned to give $11,120 from 1976 and 1977 state mission offering overages, to return Nevada gifts received in the 1978 SBGCC state mission offering, and to receive a special offering on February 4, 1979.

E. W. Hunke Jr. wrote this memo to William Tanner, the HMB president:

> On Monday morning, October 16, 1978, prior to NABC sessions, I met with NVBF president Rudy Duett, budget committee chairman Robert Holmes, and Ernest B. Myers to review the budget. All items were in order. At 5 p.m. I hosted the HMB fellowship dinner and invited various SBC board and agency representatives. I extended your personal greetings and provided SBC president, Jimmy Allen, an opportunity to speak to the group. Constitution sessions followed the proposed program. Several items deserve emphasis. The vote to constitute was the highlight. Following the vote, the messengers seemed suddenly to realize what they had done. They sat in stunned silence; Duett wept and was unable to speak. Mrs. Robert Fling suggested that we stand and sing the doxology—beautiful! Lester Hampton, oldest deacon in point of service from the oldest Nevada SBC church at Hawthorne, led the dedication prayer. Tom Bacon, Hawthorne, Nevada, FSBC pastor, read highlights of the church's beginnings and affiliation with the SBC about a year later. Bacon said that Fred McCaulley, an HMB employee, explained SBC structure, doctrine, and work to the church

when a vote to affiliate was taken in 1948. On October 21, 1978, the church will observe its thirtieth anniversary.

Seven state executive secretaries attended the constituting sessions: Hughes, Sutton, Owen, Stringer, Welsh, Lee, and Ashcraft. State and SBC representatives were too numerous to mention here. Communications in one form or another were received from most state conventions. Some issues were debated or questioned: the "Area" in the name of NABC; election of state directors from the floor rather than by board action; and the budget (BSU director). Opposition to the location of the state office in Reno did not materialize. The southern Nevada brethren are to be commended for an all-out effort to be cooperative. Executive secretary-elect Ernest B. Myers used some statistics in his fifteen minute presentation. He said there were seventy-five churches/missions, 14,000 members, 750 baptisms, and 10,000 enrolled in Bible study in NABC. Rudy Duett, the NVBF president for two years, was elected as the first president. The convention elected the NVBF executive committee as the first board of directors. A three-year rotation was set. A 320 acre land tract near Pioche, Nevada, was offered to NABC with no strings, but with hopes it might become the assembly grounds. The estimates of value ranged from $95,000 to ten times that amount. No appraisal was noted, but it apparently is an excellent location with a year round running stream, mountains, trees, etc. The spirit was excellent with little argumentation. The constituting sessions ended Tuesday night. On Wednesday morning, October 18, 1978, I sat in on the first official NABC executive board meeting to be a resource. Mission personnel in the work sheets, with the exception of Worley, were employed by NABC directors. The board adopted a NABC/HMB cooperative agreement. I clarified Queen's relationship to the NABC executive director, who will most likely serve as state evangelism director (Hunke, memo to Tanner, 10/20/78).

NABC Employs Ernest Myers as First Executive Director

The newly elected NABC state executive board employed Ernest Boyd Myers of Phoenix, Arizona, as the first executive director and treasurer on October 16, 1978, at Las Vegas, Nevada.

Myers was born on June 21, 1925, at Dockery, Mississippi, to Chester and Alma (Dubard) Myers. He had four brothers and one sister. He was saved at age thirteen and baptized and ordained by the Boyle, Mississippi, FBC. Myers said, "While walking out in the cotton field, I made a decision to go forward on a Friday night in our July revival. Three made decisions that night. My mother was influential in my decision to trust Christ." Myers graduated from Darling High School, Mississippi College, and NOBTS. GCC bestowed an L.L.D. degree on him. During World War II, he served in the U.S. Navy in the South Pacific, and received a Commendation Award and Purple Heart. He felt called to preach at age nine before he trusted Christ, and he made it public in college. Myers married June McKay, and they had two children. He pastored Baptist churches at Gautier, Sunflower, and Byram, Mississippi, and at Cross Plains and Nashville, Tennessee. The ASBC employed him as Training Union and SS secretary, and the BSSB as the church building consultant to forty-three hundred churches. He returned to Arizona in May 1975 to direct the ASBC conference center at Prescott, Arizona. He led Nevada Baptists for thirteen years (1978–1992). After retirement on June 30, 1992, he served as the New England Baptist interim executive secretary for fourteen months. The Myers retired at Phoenix, Arizona.

NABC Executive Board Organizes for Work

NABC executive board met for the first session at Sambo's Restaurant in Las Vegas on October 18, 1978. NABC president Rudy Duett called the meeting to order. The terms of the first board members were drawn: Don Mulkey, Bruce Castleberry, Rex Langston, and Paul Lewis for one year; Stanley Unruh, Evelyn Newell, Tom Bacon, and Robert Holmes for two years; and Don Ledbetter, Don Loving, Tom Propelka, and Cal Collins for three years.

On November 21, 1978, the NABC executive board met at Las Vegas, FSBC to conduct official business. NABC operation was set to begin January 2, 1979. The NABC leased space for one year at Sparks, Nevada, Temple Baptist Church for $250 per month. Ernest Myers, executive director, reported that $47,500 in budget funds were in hand and available for operation.

UISBC Fourteenth Annual Session Meets at Salt Lake City

UISBC met for its fourteenth annual session November 14–15, 1978, at the SLC FSBC under the direction of George Eichler. The elected president, Bruce Gardner, had accepted a position on the UISBC staff. W. H. Souther directed the music which featured the Intermountain Baptist Choir, Camille Ladd, John Enloe, and the Southeast Baptist Church choir. Tom Vance, Ted Fields, Don Barr, Joyce Wright, and Betty Demster read the scriptures and led in the prayers. The speakers were Delos Miles, seminaries; Curtis Dixon, FMB; Reggie McDonough, BSSB; and Van Nichols, HMB. Willis Blair preached the convention sermon. The officers were George Eichler, president; Jeff Rousseau and Carroll Reynolds, vice-presidents; and Jon Engstrom, recording secretary. The GGBTS established an SLC seminary extension center with Fred Fisher, a GGBTS faculty member, teaching the Sermon on the Mount and C. E. Autrey teaching evangelism of the early church (Acts).

Kanab, Utah, Victory Baptist Church

A Nampa, Idaho, truck driver spent the night in Kanab several times and became concerned about its spiritual condition. After the driver surrendered to Christian ministry and graduated from Grace Bible Institute in 1979, he called on missionary Richard Ashworth. Ashworth suggested that he move to the field and rent a home. The driver received help from a Portsmouth, Virginia, Baptist church to buy a newly constructed building at a thirteen-thousand-dollar discount. He led in organizing Kanab Victory Baptist Church. The church affiliated with Rainbow Canyon association and the UISBC. The early pastors were Larry Molt, Mark Baker, Charles Hatcher, and M. K. Wilder.

Carson City, Nevada, Hispanic Baptist Mission

Carson City, Nevada, FBC started the Carson City Hispanic Baptist Mission in 1979 with Mike Roberts as pastor. The new work affiliated with Northern Nevada association and the NVBC.

Salt Lake City, Utah, *Mision Bautista El Sembrador*

Initial attempts in 1979 to start a Spanish-speaking church named SLC *Primera Iglesia Bautista* did not produce a continuing ministry. In 1995 SLC Alta Canyon Baptist Church sponsored Ramon Rodriquez in a second effort. *Iglesia Bautista El Sembrador* was organized with forty-eight members and affiliated with Salt Lake association and the UISBC. Early pastors were George Ramirez and Salvador Cano. Ramon Rodriquez continued to pastor in 1997.

Burley, Idaho, *Primeria Iglesia Hispana*

In 1979 several Spanish families who attended the Burley FBC contacted Paul Rodriquez about starting a Spanish-speaking work. Rodriquez, a bivocational field-worker, moved to Rupert, Idaho, and rented an unused church building for services. In 1980 the church purchased a building in Burley for regular worship and SS services. The church affiliated with Magic Valley association and the UISBC. Rodriquez still pastored the church in 1997.

Mina, Nevada, Baptist Chapel

Hawthorne, Nevada, FSBC started Mina Baptist Chapel in 1979. The new mission affiliated with Northern Nevada association and the NVBC. In 1987 the mission reported sixteen members, thirty-five in VBS, and $8,767 in receipts. The early pastors were J. R. Sammons, Troy Gourley, and Allen Hopkins.

Ely, Nevada, Victoria-Currie Baptist Mission

The Ely, Nevada, FBC started Victoria-Currie Baptist Mission in 1979. The mission affiliated with Northeast association and the NVBC. In 1982 the mission reported one baptism, nineteen enrolled in SS, and $1,313 in total receipts. Early pastors were George Thompson and James Hardcastle.

Northern Nevada Association Breaks Ties with SBGCC

Northern Nevada association discontinued its ties with SBGCC on January 1, 1979, to affiliate with the NABC. Missionary Bob Wells wrote in the associational newsletter:

> It seems strange that after more than twenty-five years as pastor and then the director of missions, I am no longer associated with the California convention. I have personally written to express appreciation for what they have meant to me. It was an effort to say thanks to Robert D. Hughes and the state staff. They will make an effort in February to help by giving us an offering received from the churches. Thanks California Southern Baptists for your mission work in Nevada.

NABC Begins Official Operations in January 1979

On January 2, 1979, NABC executive director Ernest Myers and secretary-bookkeeper, Jan Crockett, opened the offices at 9 A.M. in the Sparks Temple Baptist Church. When the administrative committee had their first meeting on January 18, 1979, they set the date of the NABC annual meeting at Hawthorne FSBC on October 29–30, 1979. E. W. Hunke Jr. flew from Atlanta to Reno to spend three days, January 24–26, 1979, with Ernest B. Myers. He helped establish administrative procedures for the new convention.

NABC sponsored an evangelism conference at the Las Vegas FSBC on January 22–23, 1979. Participants in the first official conference were Roger Barrier, Ray Buford, Adrian Hall, Roy Fish, Robert Holmes, Gary Gleason, Earl Hosea, Don Ledbetter, Nathan Pillow, Paul Lewis, Don Mulkey, Ginger Mulkey, Jim McLeroy, A. C. Queen, and Roy Fish. Bob Wells wrote, "An evangelism emphasis for the first NABC sponsored event is a great way to start."

On January 23, 1979, the NABC state board employed Mel C. Craft, the Tylertown, Mississippi, pastor as the church services director; Vern Miller as the NABC editor; and Charles McKay, CBC professor of Bible, as the state missions director. On June 1, 1979, the NABC board employed Roy Sutton as the public relations director and Ruth Wood as the administrative assistant. A. C. Queen, HMB regional evangelism consultant, continued to work with the Nevada churches in evangelism.

The *California Southern Baptist* reported that SBGCC churches raised $24,000 in the special February 4, 1979, love offering for Nevada. The gift represented half the $47,666 anticipated income promised by the SBGCC and ASBC. HMB missions leader James Nelson met with NVBC and Northern Nevada associational leaders to divide the work into four associations.

Athol, Idaho, Baptist Mission

Post Falls, Idaho, Baptist Church started the Athol Baptist Mission in the summer of 1979 with a VBS led by Marjorie and Lloyd Garrison. Sam Reddell, a graduate of GGBTS, and his wife, Joni, drove fifty miles each Sunday to assist in the work. A Thursday night Bible study was held in the Bayfield community on Lake Pend Oreille each week. Garrison baptized four people. The new mission affiliated with Inland Empire association and the NWBC. The early pastors were Charles Hodges, Rodney George, and Larry Parker.

Reno, Nevada, Granite Hills Baptist Church

Reno, Nevada, FSBC organized the Reno Granite Hills Baptist Church on July 1, 1979, with Howard Bell as first pastor. The church affiliated with Northern Nevada association and the NABC. The early pastors were Adrian Hall (int.), Rudy Duett (int.), James Thompson, and Howard Bell. The church, which met in the Stead Air Force Base theater chapel, established six Bible study groups with 110 enrolled and averaged 100 in Sunday School.

Pierce, Idaho, Majestic Mountain Baptist Church

The Kamiah, Idaho, Pine Ridge Baptist Church organized Pierce Majestic Mountain Baptist Church on September 9, 1979, with eleven charter members. The new church affiliated with

Whispering Pines association and the UISBC. Larry Maxwell and James Myers had visited the community and begun services on February 4, 1977. The mission bought property and had a groundbreaking service on August 12, 1979. The first services, held December 21, 1980, in the new building, featured a Christmas program. The church affiliated with Lewis-Clark association and the NWBC in 1983. The early pastors were Larry Maxwell, Hale Anderson, Garry Snyder, Wayne Ladner, and Curtis Dellosy.

Pahrump, Nevada, First Southern Baptist Church

Las Vegas, Nevada, West Oakey Baptist Church organized the Pahrump FSBC on September 30, 1979, with George Montgomery as first pastor. The new church affiliated with Southern Nevada association and the NABC. Early pastors were Roger Bannerman, Reese Morrow, Robert Pearson, Ronald Trummell, and Calvin Post. The church reorganized in 1986.

Lahontan Baptist Association Constitutes (Nevada)

The messengers from fourteen Northern Nevada association churches and missions constituted Lahontan association of Nevada on October 19, 1979, after Nevada association voted to dissolve and form four new associations. Pastor John Ashcraft served as first moderator. The churches were located at Fallon, Hawthorne, Gabbs, Walker Lake, Lovelock, Tonopah, Yerington, Silver Peak, Fish Lake, Goldfield, Mina, Schurz, Kingston Canyon, and Round Mountain. In 1980, ten churches and four missions reported fifty-three baptisms, 1,384 members, $210,106 in total receipts, and $29,319 in mission gifts.

Northeast Baptist Association Constitutes (Nevada)

The messengers from eighteen Northern Nevada association churches and missions constituted Northeast association of Nevada on October 19, 1979. Cal Collins served as the first moderator. The churches were located at Battle Mountain, Crescent Valley, Diamond Valley, Elko, Twin Falls, Winnemucca, Austin, Carlin, Mountain City, Wells, Wildhorse, Sunnyside, Victoria-Currie, Ely, Paradise Valley, Reese-Antelope, Jackpot, and

McDermitt. Nine churches and eleven missions reported 103 baptisms, 837 members, $299,617 in total receipts, and $70,947 in mission gifts in 1980.

Spooner Baptist Association Constitutes (Nevada)

Messengers from eight Northern Nevada association churches and missions constituted the Spooner association of Nevada on October 19, 1979. Paul Lewis served as the first moderator. The churches were located at Carson City, Capital City, Gardnerville, South Lake Tahoe, Tahoe Paradise, Topaz Lake, Dayton, and Walker. Eight churches and missions reported 178 baptisms, 1,537 members, $292,638 total gifts, and $33,807 in mission gifts in 1980.

Northern Nevada Baptist Association Constitutes (Nevada)

Messengers from nine Northern Nevada association churches and missions constituted a new association on October 19, 1979, and voted to retain the name of the old association. Pastor Gene Edwards served as the first moderator. Churches were located at Fernley, Silver Springs, Granite Hills, Kings Beach, Sun Valley, Lemmon Valley, Sparks Temple, Reno First Southern, Reno Second, South Reno, and Steamboat Springs. In 1980, nine churches and two missions reported 127 baptisms, 1,724 members, $318,853 in total gifts, and $55,792 in mission gifts. Charles L. McKay reported that two Arkansas SBC churches had agreed to sponsor work at Las Vegas and Steamboat Springs. The name Northern Nevada was changed to Truckee River in 1982 and Sierra in 1986.

NABC Celebrates First Year of Service

The NABC met for its first annual session on October 30–31, 1979, at Hawthorne, Nevada, FSBC, the oldest church in the NABC. The speakers were Harold Bennett, SBC Executive Committee; Sue Lindwall, FMB missionary to Guatemala; and William Tanner, HMB. Stephen Neesley, John Babb, Dan Raley, William Webb, and Richard Sanders read the scriptures and led the prayers. The welcome was extended by Raymond Maysako, Mineral County Chamber of Commerce president. Mona and Keith McRevy, Ray

Buford, the GCC Jubilation Singers, Paul Stanley, Rex Langston, Ruth Wood, Crystal Stanley, and CBC Rhapsody Singers provided music for the convention. NABC removed the word "Area" from its name to become Nevada Baptist Convention (NVBC). Don Mulkey was elected president and Adrian Hall vice-president. The NVBC reported forty-eight churches and twenty-six missions with 13,859 members. Don Ledbetter listed these church-type missions as having started in the 1970s: Wells, Mina, Jackpot, Mountain City, Wildhorse, and Manhattan.

The NVBC executive board met on November 20, 1979, to elect Pamela Phinney as part-time BSU worker at University of Nevada, Las Vegas. The board elected Rudy Duett as Church Training director with responsibilities beginning on December 1, 1979. The HMB and NVBC employed Don Mulkey to succeed Charles McKay as the missions director. Adrian Hall succeeded Mulkey as the NVBC president.

The NVBC moved into permanent office space in December 1979. A beautiful Victorian house located at 895 North Center Street in Reno, a former residence for University of Nevada presidents, was bought for $74,500 and remodeled. The building was located at the university entrance gate.

UISBC Celebrates Its Fifteenth Anniversary at Pocatello

The UISBC met for its fifteenth annual session on November 13–14, 1979, at Pocatello, Idaho, FSBC under the direction of president George Eichler. W. H. Souther directed the music. Personalities on the program were Billy Barton, Willis Blair, Donald Douglass, Bruce Gardner, Jon Engstrom, Laverne Fisher, Luman Gilman, James Herod, Camille Ladd, Richard Graham, Earl Jackson, Mike McKay, Pete Owen, James Myers, Ronnie Parker, Donna Powell, Carroll Reynolds, Eugene Soulsby, William H. Souther, Guy D. Ward, Darwin E. Welsh, and Bob Williams. SBC leaders reporting to the UISBC were Fred M. Chapman, Stewardship; Winston Crawley, FMB; Bryant W. Hicks, SBTS; Frank G. Schwall, Annuity; David P. Turner, BSSB; E. W. Hunke Jr., HMB; and Ronald A. Tonks, Historical Commission.

Strategies to Reach the Intermountain West

***Orofino, Idaho**—The Lewis-Clark Baptist Association held regular fifth-Sunday singspirations. The Orofino FBC overflowed with the many Southern Baptists at this 1980s meeting.*

***SLC, Utah**—Nine HMB/BSU student summer missionaries pause for this photo in front of HMB/UISBC missionary Mayo and Celia Brown's home before moving on to their places of service in Utah and Idaho to lead BYBCs, VBSs, surveys, and to build buildings, etc.*

***Priest River, Idaho**—The entire UISBC state staff participated in a citywide tent revival on August 20–24, 1986, on their way to the annual UISBC staff retreat at Friday Harbor, Washington.*

Meaningful Developments

THE DECADE OF THE 1980S

During the fifty-year period (1940–1990), the population of Idaho, Nevada, and Utah grew from 1,185,430 to 3,931,162 people. Because the HMB followed Southern Baptists to the West in the 1940s, it developed a nationwide denomination. Even though the churches grew slowly, a median SBC church in the Intermountain West numbered one hundred resident members, enrolled ninety in SS, received $23,826 in offerings, and baptized twelve.

Salt Lake City, Utah, Japanese Baptist Mission

Elizabeth Taylor Watkins, a returned FMB missionary from Japan, started Japanese work in SLC in 1980. The new mission affiliated with Salt Lake association and the UISBC. The early pastors were John Kamiyama, Robert Jones, John Lee, and Katsuhiko Sugiuchi. Watkins began work with the Japanese people in Utah in 1980 with several thousand dollars she had saved from her small pension. The UISBC state staff celebrated her eightieth birthday April 21, 1980, at the SLC, Utah, Chuck-A-Rama Restaurant. She was born on April 21, 1900, at Camden, South Carolina, and graduated from Judson College, Columbia University, and the WMU Training School. Her career took her into Virginia, Tennessee, Oklahoma, and Grenfell, Newfoundland. In 1928 Watkins launched a foreign mission career in Japan. The emperor of Japan recognized Watkins's contributions to Japan and gave her a fifth-class Order of the Precious Crown. She retired as a missionary and moved to SLC in August 1970. When she died in 1983, she left possessions and the residue of her estate to the FMB and UISBC for work with Japanese people.

NVBC Employs Don Mulkey as State Mission Director

After Charles L. McKay resigned, the HMB and NVBC employed Donald W. Mulkey on January 1, 1980, to succeed him. Mulkey and his wife, Anne, had served in Canada before they arrived to start Las Vegas Twin Lakes Baptist Church. He was born at Amarillo, Texas, July 17, 1928; graduated from the University of New Mexico, and GGBTS; and received an honorary D.D. degree from GCU. Mulkey married Anne Spalding of San Jose, California, and they had six children. He served in the U.S. Army (1946–1948); as the music director at Albuquerque, Novato, and Alameda, California; and as the pastor at Albuquerque and Mountainair, New Mexico, and Graton, California. After starting an Edmonton, Alberta, Baptist church, the Mulkeys moved to Las Vegas to start a mission in their home. Twenty-one attended the first service. The HMB and NVBC employed him as the state mission director (1980–1990). After retiring in 1990, he served as HMB contract missionary at Kapaa, Kauai, Hawaii. They retired at Arkadelphia, Arkansas.

NVBC Employs Tom Bacon as Missionary (Nevada)

The HMB and NVBC employed Tom Lee Bacon as missionary to the Lahontan and Northeast Baptist associations on March 1, 1980. He was born on September 14, 1936, at Mt. Vernon, Texas, to Tom and Lois Bacon. He was saved at age twelve, baptized by Winnsboro, Texas, Missionary Baptist Church, and ordained by the Riverside, California, FSBC (Sunnyslope) in October 1962. Bacon wrote, "I was convicted of my sin at a VBS, and two months later I prayed to receive Jesus Christ while in the privacy of my own room at home." Bacon married Thelma Clamp on June 11, 1955, at Anaheim, California, and they had four children. He graduated from the Lynwood, California, High School, California State

University at Hayward, and GGBTS. He felt called to missions in 1951 at age seventeen. He wrote:

> Allen Barnes was instrumental in my call to missions. During my freshman year at college, the interests which claim an uncommitted young man swirled around me. I had difficulty with my Christian witness on weekends. One night as I read my Bible in the dorm room a roommate made fun of me. I went outside to be alone, and to promise God that I would preach.

He pastored in California at Riverside, Belmont, and Chino, and at Hawthorne, Nevada (1973–1980). The HMB and NVBC employed him as missionary to northeastern Nevada (1980–1992), and state mission director for the NVBC in 1992.

Pioneer Ira Marks Makes His Last Move

Ira I. Marks, HMB pioneer missionary to Utah, Idaho, and Nevada (1950–1961), wrote on March 4, 1980:

> Because of circumstances and what we believe to be the will of the Lord, we have moved to make our home in Lee Haven of Lee's Summit, Missouri, for the rest of our lives. I do hope we will not have to move again. My first choice of something to do is to help churches to start some more mission churches. There are three associations in northwest Missouri, an association in northeast Kansas, and churches in Iowa forming a new convention in 1980–1981. Surely this is the place God wants me to spend the rest of the twenty years that I asked him to give me when I prayed in October 1977.

NWBC Employs Cecil Sims as Executive Director

After Dan Stringer resigned, the NWBC employed Cecil Charles Sims on June 1, 1980, as executive director. The NWBC continued to work with Idaho panhandle churches. Sims was born on February 8, 1928, at Mineola, Texas, to Cecil and Mamie Sims.

He had one brother. He was saved at age seven through the influence of his parents, baptized in June 1935, and ordained by Mineola, Texas, First Baptist Church in December 1948. Sims wrote, "I came to an awareness of my sin and knew I was lost. I made my decision at a Sunday morning service as a child responding out of his need to trust Christ's provision. I trusted Him as my personal Saviour." He graduated from Mineola, Texas, High School, Baylor University, and SWBTS. He married Billie Jeannine Becker, and they had four children. Sims wrote:

> I expressed my call publicly at a church camp at age fourteen; I have never deviated from the conviction that God called me. R. E. Milam was instrumental in my call West. Several southern families wanted a church like the one back home. The state convention gave them my name; the church had me come in view of a call; and I went to Wenatchee, Washington, and stayed ten years.

He pastored churches at Mart, Clarksville, Gilmer, and Simpsonville, Texas; and at Wenatchee, Richland, and Tacoma, Washington. The HMB and NWBC employed him as missionary to four provinces in western Canada (1978–1980). The NWBC elected him as executive director (1980–1994). He was honored as a distinguished alumnus by SWBTS in 1985 and by Baylor University in 1994. After retirement in 1994 at Portland, he led in constructing a new state office complex on property he had secured during his administration.

Youth Lead Utah-Idaho Summer Missions
The HMB and BSU students who assisted in Utah and Idaho in the summer of 1980 were Kathy Gould, Patty Atchley, Jenny Jobe, Joel Flowers, Judy Bolton, Rochelle Lyles, David Weeks, Daryle Morse, Susan Goodroe, Debbie Kirkpatrick, Virginia Tatum, Christy Catazano, Marshall Pierce, and Kent Barnes. Ramona Conrad and Diane Townsend, local students, also helped in outreach through VBSs, BYBCs, and surveys in Utah and Idaho.

Salt Lake association's two-week camp at the Pinecliff Camp Grounds met on June 9, 1980, and reported 215 campers and staff in attendance. Troy Richardson directed youth week and Berniece Gardner directed children's week.

Pioneer Fred McCaulley Enters Home for Aging
Fred McCaulley, HMB western field-worker from 1946 to 1960, was moved to Dallas, Texas, Buckner-Trew-Ryburn Complex for the Aging in 1980. McCaulley, a powerful influence on SBC growth in the West, was presented a bound volume of letters from friends by his pastor, James E. Coggin, of Ft. Worth, Texas, Travis Avenue Baptist Church. E. W. Hunke Jr. wrote:

> My memories go back to Baylor days in Waco, Texas, when I first learned of the work you and your wife did for the Lord in home missions. Naomi attended the first SBGCC BSU retreat in August 1946 and remembers you first in that context. That conference convened just the week before we were married in her Fresno home. Our visits with you at Glorieta HMB week and at various conferences in western U.S.A. helped us know your concern for the work in Arizona. You recommended excellent pastors [like Byron Bruce] to lead our ASBC churches. Hundreds of your "Tentmakers" in California enriched our lives. Personal letters and Christmas greetings keep us interested and concerned about you and your continuing ministry. We love you in Christ and wish you His very best.

Pioneer Harold Dillman Dies on June 22, 1980
Utah Southern Baptist pioneer Harold Dillman, founder of the first SBC church in the Intermountain West at Roosevelt, Utah, died June 22, 1980. The Utah native had given his heart and life to serve Christ and reach Mormon people. Mayo Brown, Salt Lake association missionary, wrote:

> Harold was a pioneer in the truest sense; he will be missed by all of us. His faith and commitment to God's will; his

willingness to pay the price of faithfulness to our Lord; his concern for lost people; and his love for missions are a lasting legacy that will be an inspiration to all who worked with him, knew him, and loved him.

Las Vegas, Nevada, Paradise Valley Baptist Church

Las Vegas, Nevada, FSBC organized the Las Vegas Paradise Valley Baptist Church on June 29, 1980, with Ralph Hall as the first pastor. Paradise Valley began as a mission in 1974 in the Camelot Shopping Center. The church affiliated with the Southern Nevada association and the NVBC. Sponsoring FSBC helped dedicate Paradise Valley's beautiful new building in an afternoon service during its own twenty-fifth anniversary celebration. The early pastors were Ewan Settlemoir, Ralph Hall, Jerry Scott, and Johnny Hughes.

HMB Employs Lloyd Garrison as Pastoral Missionary (Idaho)

The HMB and NWBC employed Thomas Lloyd Garrison as a church starter missionary August 20, 1980. He and his wife, Marjorie, spent their lives serving northeastern Washington and northern Idaho. Garrison was born October 17, 1919, at Channing, Texas. He graduated from WBC and SWBTS and received an honorary doctor of humanities degree from Mary Hardin Baylor University for his work in reviving and building churches. He married Marjorie Farnsworth of Canadian, Texas, and they had four children. Prior to his move to the Northwest, he pastored Texas Baptist churches (1939–1955). He pastored churches at the Dalles in Oregon and at Yakima, Spokane (2), Nine Miles Falls, and Deer Park, Washington. During his time as Idaho missionary, he pastored SBC churches at Post Falls, Otis Orchards, Wallace, Rathdrum, and Sandpoint.

Dayton, Nevada, Calvary Baptist Church

The Carson City, Nevada, FBC organized the Dayton Calvary Baptist Church at Dayton town hall in 1980 with Gerald Peterson as the first pastor. The church, which affiliated with Northern

Nevada association and the NVBC, met in a mobile chapel from June 7, 1978, until August 1980 when they occupied a new building.

NVBC Second Annual Session Meets at Las Vegas

The NVBC met for its second annual session on October 28–29, 1980, at Las Vegas, Nevada, FSBC under the direction of president Adrian Hall. The GCC Jubilation Singers and CBC Rhapsody Singers provided the music. Don Ledbetter preached the annual sermon. The out-of-state guests were Lewis Myers and Eloise Cauthen, FMB; Catherine Allen, WMU; W. C. Fields, SBC Executive Committee; E. W. Hunke Jr., HMB; and Ronald Tonks, Historical Commission. NVBC honored retiring missionary M. E. McGlamery for his eight years of service and Charles McKay for two years of service, and employed Nancy Hall as half-time WMU director. The convention reported fifty-two churches, twenty-six missions, 15,299 members, and gifts of $208,496 for the Cooperative Program. NVBC elected Adrian Hall as president and Beverly McLeroy as vice-president. Work teams from Mississippi, South Carolina, Oklahoma, and Texas constructed several new church buildings.

On November 5, 1980, Ernest Myers, NVBC executive director, proposed that the BSSB and HMB jointly fund a person as secretary of SS and evangelism work. Since BSSB and HMB assignments and methods of subsidy differed, and the HMB had employed A. C. Queen to work in evangelism, the HMB chose not to participate. After Queen resigned in 1982 to work full-time at GGBTS, the NVBC executive board agreed to employ Adrian Hall as NVBC Bible teaching director and Don Ledbetter as the state evangelism secretary for Nevada.

UISBC Sixteenth Annual Session Meets at Clearfield

The UISBC met for its sixteenth annual session on November 10–11, 1980, at the Clearfield, Utah, FBC under the direction of president Louis Demster. The Clearfield and Roy FBC choirs, Earl Geiszler, Bonnie Phillips, and Jon Enloe, sang. Dorothy Hutson,

Kerna Young, Mike Eaves, Glenn Bower, and Joyce Wright opened the sessions with Bible readings and prayers. The speakers were Gene Daniel, Annuity; Carolyn Weatherford, WMU; Kenneth Evenson, FMB; William Schweer, seminaries; Howard Foshee, BSSB; Lyndon Collings, HMB; Tim Headquist, Executive Committee; and Charles Ashcraft, Arkansas Baptist Convention. Dewayne Thompson preached the annual sermon. Newly elected officers were Louis Demster, president; Carroll Reynolds and Bill Warren, vice-presidents, and Eric Frye, recording secretary. C. E. Autrey, the SLC extension center of GGBTS director, reported that Raymond Keathley of GGBTS taught Romans in July, and Autrey taught three classes.

Bruce Conrad Baptizes a Seminole Indian

Bruce Conrad, an HMB missionary to the Indians at Brigham City Indian School wrote about a typical experience in his life:

> Last Sunday night I baptized a young Seminole lady. It was a long time in coming. Her Christian father, who now works in Alaska and is separated from her mother, had a great deal to do with her becoming a Christian. He came to visit her and her roommate several days. Then he had to go. He told them goodby and left to catch a plane at SLC. On the way something told him to stop and go back to Linda's apartment. He did not want to go home without Linda making a decision to invite Jesus into her life. When he told Linda of his concern and gave her the plan of salvation, she prayed and invited Christ to come into her life.

Elk City, Idaho, Baptist Church

Kamiah, Idaho, Pine Ridge Baptist Church organized the Elk City Baptist Church in 1981 with Larry Maxwell as the first pastor. After Maxwell and James Myers had visited the community and found people wanting services, Maxwell started a Bible study in 1967. Mr. and Mrs. Gwen Shearer donated land for a building in 1978, and construction started in August 1979. The church affiliated with Whispering Pines association and the UISBC. Early pastors were Larry Maxwell, Billy Sutton, Roy McKenzie, Leo Porter, Hal Crawford, Richard Lynch, and Mike Rickman.

Ogden, Utah, Bilingual Baptist Mission

The Ogden, Utah, Bilingual Baptist Mission started in 1981 and affiliated with Golden Spike association and the UISBC. The early pastors were Salvador Fernandez and Herman Chacon.

Eight Associational Missionaries Serve in 1981

The missionaries serving in Idaho, Nevada, and Utah in 1981 were Arlie McDaniel, Lewis-Clark; Don Laing, Inland Empire; Roy Ferguson, Boise Valley and Whispering Pines; Earl Jackson, Golden Spike (Utah) and Eastern Idaho (Idaho); Mayo Brown, Salt Lake; Richard Ashworth, Rainbow Canyon, Gideon, and Utah (Utah); Robert Wells, Northern Nevada, Spooner, and Truckee River; Tom Bacon, Lakontan, and Northeast; and David Meacham, Southern Nevada.

Tonopah, Nevada, Fish Lake Baptist Mission

Tonopah, Nevada, Fish Lake Baptist Mission started in 1981 and affiliated with Lahontan association and the NVBC. The early pastors were Harold Cary and Ed Pratt.

Payson, Utah, First Baptist Church

The Provo, Utah, FBC organized the Payson FBC in 1981. The work began as a storefront mission and affiliated with Salt Lake association and the UISBC. The early pastors were Neal Henry and Donald Carter.

Reno, Nevada, Steamboat Baptist Church

The South Reno, Nevada, Baptist Church organized the Reno Steamboat Baptist Church in 1981. The mission had started with a Bible study in November and services in December 1979 at Via Blanca Mobile Home Park. Jim Meek, the first pastor, moved from Louisiana to Scottsdale, Arizona, where he became a

Coronado Baptist Church charter member. At age eleven he knew he wanted to start churches. The church affiliated with Sierra association and the NVBC, bought a two-story building at 1480 Geiger Grade, and purchased adjacent property in 1985. It built a sanctuary to seat 350 worshipers, and started a new mission in East Sparks.

Carlin, Nevada, First Baptist Church
Winnemucca, Nevada, FBC organized the Carlin FBC on March 30, 1981. The mission had started in 1974 with Arthur Blessitt as the first pastor. LaVern Inzer led the mission, which met at the IOOF Hall, to organize and construct a new building. The church affiliated with Northeast association and the NVBC. The early pastors were Don Ledbetter (int.), Larry Henderson, Tom Bacon (int.), James Hopkins, Dan Nicholson, and LaVern Inzer (2).

NWBC Employs Arlie McDaniel as Missionary (Idaho)
After W. C. Carpenter retired, the HMB and NWBC employed Arlie Leo McDaniel Sr., February 1, 1981, to serve as the missionary for Lewis-Clark association. McDaniel was born October 7, 1915, at Lonoke, Arkansas; saved at age fourteen through an evangelist's influence; baptized in England, Arkansas, Clear Lake in 1930 by the Coy, Arkansas, Timberline Baptist Church; and ordained May 9, 1937, by Roby, Texas, Liberty Baptist Church. He wrote, "When I was at the mourners' bench, my mother came out of the choir and helped me understand that I simply needed to accept Jesus and He would save me." He served as a U.S. Air Force chaplain in World War II (1942–1946). McDaniel graduated from Baylor University and attended HSU and GGBTS. CBC honored him with a D.D. degree. He married Ella Mae Owens, and they had seven children. He led churches at Mt. Ida; Toby, Texas; and Mena, Arkansas. He wrote, "I was pastor of the Mena FBC, when Fresno, California, Harvard Terrace Baptist Church called me sight unseen. Three SBGCC state workers, Wilbanks, Porter, and Looney, recommended me. After one week of prayer I accepted. We moved to

Fresno on July 1, 1952, in a U-Haul trailer." He pastored churches at Fresno, Richmond, Barstow, Ventura, Escondido, and Orange, California, and served as California Baptist Foundation executive director (1960–1962). The HMB and NWBC employed him as the missionary to Lewis-Clark association of Idaho (1981–1991). When the McDaniels retired in 1992, they moved to Victorville, California.

Intermountain West Features Evangelism
On February 1, 1981, eight hundred people attended a UISBC evangelism rally at SLC, Utah, Salt Palace. Maxine Souther and Jon Enloe led the music; James Eaves of SWBTS preached the message; and 174 Utah-Idaho young people sang the musical *Light-Shine*.

UISBC conducted its evangelism conference on February 2–3, 1981, at SLC FSBC. Bob Anderson of San Bruno, California; Jon Enloe of SLC; Billy Souther of Richmond, Virginia; and William and Maxine Souther of Kellogg, Idaho, provided the music. The speakers were C. E. Autrey, Louis Demster, Mayo Brown, Frances Davis, Donald Douglas, Eric Frye, Bruce Gardner, Bonita Ortiz, and Ronnie Parker. Other speakers were William Pinson, GGBTS; James Eaves, SWBTS; William Schweer, GGBTS; and Bill Hogue and E. W. Hunke Jr., HMB.

After A. C. Queen retired January 31, 1981, Ernest Myers led the NVBC evangelism program. The 1981 evangelism conference met at Las Vegas Desert Hills Baptist Church to emphasize "spiritual awakening." The speakers were Franklin Paschal, Nashville FBC pastor; Louis Drummond, SEBTS professor; and John Havlik, HMB. A third annual youth evangelism conference at Carson City attracted 250 Nevada youth.

Darwin Welsh, UISBC executive director, took the state staff and evangelism conference speakers into rural Idaho on March 6–7, 1981, for an area conference at Kamiah, Idaho, Elementary School. Arlie McDaniel, the Lewis-Clark associational missionary, joined with the Whispering Pines association pastors, UISBC staff, and the speakers in the conference. T. J. and Karen Calvin of Priest River, Idaho, provided the music. The speakers were Howard

Ramsey, J. D. Ellis, Herman Rios, and E. W. Hunke Jr., of the HMB. The northern Idaho pastors, most of whom were bivocational, had been unable to make a six-hundred-mile round-trip to SLC, Utah, for the evangelism conference each year.

Tennessee pastors and Arkansas music directors led thirty-five NVBC churches in the first simultaneous revivals in Nevada, April 5–12, 1981, since forming the new convention in 1978.

C. E. Autrey Proves that Evangelism Works

On May 14, 1981, the *Rocky Mountain Baptist* published an article telling of the remarkable growth of SLC, Utah, University Baptist Church:

> After three years under 76-year-old C. E. Autrey's leadership, a mission in the heart of Mormon country is filled to overflowing. He reported that thirty-four people joined the church Easter Sunday: twenty-nine by profession of faith; twenty-six of them adults. These decisions represent the resurrection his leadership gives. When he was called as pastor, University Baptist had five members, and two moved away before he arrived. Now SS attendance averages 140, and the membership has increased to 213. He makes about 400 visits or contacts every month. His revival calendar is full of revival engagements. He studies five hours a day for seminary extension classes he teaches, some at the University of Utah. Almost every afternoon he dons his red cap and jogging shoes and walks briskly through the community. His accomplishments are as extraordinary as the man; he preached to an estimated 50,000,000 persons in his long ministry with about 300,000 decisions for Christ during tent revivals and crusades. The SLC University Baptist Church touches a dozen nationalities, mostly students working on post-graduate degrees. Half of the members are foreign—from Bolivians to Malaysians. The church sponsors a mission for the eighty-five Cantonese-speaking Chinese and has launched out to the Vietnamese. His loving involves

visiting, calling, and writing letters to those who visit his church. The corner stone of his ministry is continuous contact with new converts.

NVBC Employs David Meacham as Missionary (Nevada)

After M. E. McGlamery retired, the HMB and NVBC employed David Franklin Meacham, August 1, 1981, as the new missionary to Southern Nevada association. Meacham was born on May 17, 1945, at Renton, Washington, to Samuel Gaines and Edith (Adair) Meacham. He had no brothers or sisters. He was saved on Easter Sunday at the age of ten through the influence of his parents, baptized in April 1956 by Atlanta, Georgia, FBC, and ordained February 22, 1970, by the New Orleans, Louisiana, Valence Street Baptist Church. He graduated from Rosemead, California, High School, Pasadena City College, San Diego State University, and NOBTS. Meacham married Linda Sue Cox on July 12, 1969, at New Orleans, Louisiana, and they had three children. He wrote, "Earl Crawford was instrumental in my call to missions at age twenty-nine. I attended high school in the West and was pastor of Sunnymead, California, FBC, when I felt called to do mission work at Big Bear Lake." Meacham served as the mission pastor at Big Bear Chapel (1975–1977) and church extension director in Puget Sound association in Washington (1978–1981). The HMB and NVBC employed him as the missionary to Southern Nevada association (1981–1992). The NVBC executive board employed him as the NVBC state executive director on April 1, 1992.

Clearwater, Idaho, First Baptist Church

The Clearwater, Idaho, FBC, which was organized by pioneer Baptist preacher J. B. York on Christmas Day 1887, affiliated with the Whispering Pines association and the UISBC on August 8, 1981. Because of the comity agreements, Baptist leaders had asked York to affiliate with Northern Baptists. After the building burned, Jane Cowling gave property to the church in 1903. A new building was constructed in 1950. The early Southern Baptist pastors were Larry Maxwell, Bob Mulkey, Ken Bliven, and Bill Horn.

Austin, Nevada, Baptist Church

Crescent Valley, Nevada, Baptist Church organized the Austin Baptist Church in October 1981 in an old fire station with Don Ledbetter preaching the first sermon. The church affiliated with Lahontan association and the NVBC. After the church purchased a recreational vehicle park, they used the clubhouse for services. Early mission pastors were Tom White, Reese Morrow, Ace Sliger, John Ramsey, LaVern Inzer (int.), and Larry Wiley (int.).

Silver Springs, Nevada, Lakeview Baptist Church

Fernley, Nevada, FBC organized the Silver Springs Lakeview Baptist Church in October 1981. The new church affiliated with Lahontan association and the NVBC. The early pastors were Bill Adkin, John Dwyer, Grover Goodner, Lee Haywood, and Troy Gourley.

Priest River, Idaho, Southern Baptist Church

Sandpoint, Idaho, Boyer Baptist Church organized the Priest River Southern Baptist Church on October 11, 1981. Pastor Barry Sherwood led services at Priest River Legion Hall in July 1978. The church affiliated with Silver Lakes association and the UISBC. After property was purchased in 1983, the church constructed a new building and held their first service in the building in October 1986. The early pastors were Barry Sherwood, T. J. Calvin, Dave Huffman, and Tim Morris.

NVBC Third Annual Session Meets at Carson City

NVBC met for its third annual session on October 27–28, 1981, at the Carson City, Nevada, FBC, under the direction of president Beverly McLeroy. Jim McLeroy, J. L. Sammons, David Doyel, Paul Ray, and Arthur Wicks read the scriptures and led in prayers. The CBC Rhapsody Singers and Carson City FBC choir provided special music; Ruth Wood played the piano; Ernest B. Myers preached the convention sermon; and Joe Ingram, of Oklahoma, gave the inspirational message. The out-of-state speakers were Darold Morgan, Annuity; James Crane, FMB;

Jimmy Allen, Radio/TV; Tim Hedquist, SBC Executive Committee; Connie Regener, American Bible Society; Jim Lewis, HMB; and Grady Cothen, BSSB. Ernest Myers, NVBC executive secretary, introduced David Meacham as the new Southern Nevada association missionary. The NVBC reelected Beverly McLeroy as the president and Stanley Unruh as vice-president. NVBC reported fifty-one churches, forty-one missions, 15,946 church members, 1,123 baptisms, and $243,282 Cooperative Program receipts.

UISBC Seventeenth Annual Session Meets at Boise

The UISBC met for its seventeenth annual session on November 10–11, 1981, at Boise Calvary Baptist Church under the direction of president Louis Demster. Special music was provided by T. J. and Karen Calvin, Caldwell FSBC choir, Eugene Soulsby, Duane Barnes, Lon Sitton, Tom Gorman, and the Boise Calvary Baptist Church choir. Gordon Mills, Wadell Schronk, Andy Hornbaker, Pete Mayse, and Roger Stacy read the scriptures and led the prayers. The speakers were John Dillman, FMB; Larry Haslam, BSSB; Wendell Belew, HMB; Harvey Kennedy, Annuity; and Leonard Hill, Executive Committee. Donald Douglass preached the convention sermon. The UISBC elected Carroll Reynolds as president, John Embery and Lavoid Robertson as vice-presidents, and Carol Browning as secretary.

Goldfield, Nevada, Baptist Church

Tonopah, Nevada, FBC organized the Goldfield Baptist Church in December 1981 with Harold Carey as the first pastor. The new church affiliated with Lahontan association and the NVBC. Early pastors were John Shearer (int.) and Bobby Mann.

Salt Lake City, Utah, Cambodian Baptist Mission

The SLC University Baptist Church started the SLC Cambodian Mission in 1982 under the direction of C. E. Autrey. The mission affiliated with Salt Lake association and the UISBC. The early pastors were Earl Geiszler and Sy Thang Chhea.

Ontario, Oregon, First Southern Baptist Church

Caldwell, Idaho, FBC organized the Ontario, Oregon, FSBC in 1982. The mission, which started with Tuesday night Bible study led by Louis Demster, affiliated with Boise Valley association and the UISBC. The church bought a building and remodeled it for services. Later the people bought an adjacent lot, removed an old house, and developed a parking lot. Early pastors were Dan Robinson, Ray Reese, and Randy Martindale.

Mt. Home, Idaho, Emmanuel Baptist Church

Forty members from the Mt. Home, Idaho, FSBC withdrew to form Mt. Home Emmanuel Baptist Church in 1982. The work, which had no sponsor, affiliated with Boise Valley association and the UISBC. Missionary Roy Ferguson led the organizational service. The church purchased property on the highway and constructed a beautiful new building. Early pastors were Harry Johnson (int.) and Marvin Reece.

Boise, Idaho, Trinity Baptist Church

Boise, Idaho, Calvary Baptist Church organized Boise Trinity Baptist Church in 1982 with fifteen charter members. The church, which affiliated with Boise Valley association and the UISBC, met initially in a theater and schoolhouse. The association later constructed a movable building on property previously purchased with an HMB site loan.

Rose Lake, Idaho, Baptist Mission

Kingston, Idaho, Kingston Baptist Church started the Rose Lake Baptist Mission in 1982 with Carl Estes as the first pastor. The mission affiliated with Whispering Pines association and the UISBC. The church affiliated later with the NWBC.

Midvale, Utah, *Mision Capilla Betel*

Midvale, Utah, FBC started the Midvale *Mision Capilla Betel* in 1982 under the direction of Salvador Cano, missionary. The new work affiliated with Salt Lake association and the UISBC. This

Spanish mission did not survive. In 1996 West Jordan, Utah, FBC started a new mission named *Primera Iglesia Bautista* to minister to Spanish people in the greater SLC area.

Challis, Idaho, First Baptist Mission

Blackfoot, Idaho, Emmanuel Baptist Church started Challis, Idaho, First Baptist Mission in 1982 with Bennie Wright as the pastor. The mission affiliated with Eastern Idaho association and the UISBC.

Murray, Idaho, North Fork Community Baptist Mission

Kingston, Idaho, Kingston Baptist Church started the Murray North Fork Community Baptist Mission in 1982 under the leadership of Carl Estes. The mission affiliated with Whispering Pines association and the UISBC. Bud Hall served as the first pastor.

Mt. Pleasant, Utah, First Southern Baptist Church

In 1982, after coal miners from Kentucky started a Bible study in Mt. Pleasant, Utah, a mission was started in the basement of the city hall. Pastor Perry Causey purchased ten acres of land, and a Lubbock, Texas, FBC work team constructed a new building. The new church affiliated with Rainbow Canyon association and the UISBC. Perry Causey continued to serve as pastor in 1997.

Salmon, Idaho, Salmon Valley Baptist Church

Idaho Falls, Idaho, Calvary Baptist Church organized Salmon Valley Baptist Church in 1982 with fifteen charter members. A member of the Idaho Falls church, Glenn Munkres, went to Salmon frequently to visit his mother. He started a Bible study in her home in 1968 and a mission later. The new church affiliated with Eastern Idaho association and the UISBC. After purchasing three-plus acres in southeast Salmon, the congregation constructed a log church building. The early pastors were Richard Burns, John Rebman, Bruce Miller, and Mike Palmer.

Delta, Utah, First Southern Baptist Church

The Delta, Utah, FSBC began with Bible study in 1982 and affiliated with Salt Lake association and the UISBC. After purchasing a city block, the congregation erected an impressive building. The early pastors were C. W. Brown, Mike McDowell, and Glenn Munkres.

Kingston, Idaho, Kingston Baptist Church

Priest River, Idaho, Southern Baptist Church organized the Kingston Baptist Church in 1982. Carl and Beverly Estes visited the community and found a Catholic woman who wanted a Bible study in her home. The church affiliated with Silver Lakes association and UISBC, bought property in 1982, and constructed a new church building (1987–1988). Early pastors were Dale Swink, Carl Estes, and Gordon Mills.

1982 Events Give Insight to Progress

Don Mulkey, NVBC state mission director, reported that eleven HMB and BSU student summer missionaries served in Nevada in 1981. NVBC churches established twenty-three new church starts during the 1980–1981 associational year.

NVBC executive board employed Rebecca Snyder as campus BSU director for University of Nevada, Reno, and Michael McCullough as Christian social ministries director on September 8, 1981. NVBC vice-president Beverly McLeroy first became NVBC president when president Adrian Hall resigned to become a NVBC employee.

The HMB reported thirty-three missionaries in Idaho, thirty-four in Nevada, and forty-one in Utah on January 1, 1982. The report included language, resort, church extension, association, and other categories of missionaries.

The UISBC sponsored a regional evangelism conference at the Vernal, Utah, FBC on March 5–6, 1982. The speakers were Dennis Bridge, Hermon Rios, Jack Stanton, A. C. Queen, and E. W. Hunke Jr., from the HMB. The local personalities were Darwin Welsh, Richard Ashworth, Kathi Morehouse, Rodger Russell, Howard Porter, Richard Overman, and the Utah associational choir.

On March 7, 1982, Granger, Utah, FBC celebrated its twenty-third anniversary by paying off all indebtedness and burning the note. The speakers were Minnette Rhodes, Darwin E. Welsh, Glenn Munkres, Mayo Brown, Burton Greenwood, and Joe Eubanks. The associational newsletter reported:

> The burning of a note of indebtedness is always a mark of accomplishment. It is evident that the Lord has blessed His people and that the people are responsive to the leadership of the Lord. Charlie Tague, the builder of the first unit, once lived at Vernal, Utah, and served as Training Union director. He gave his life to the Lord as a full-time builder of church buildings. He built 38 first unit buildings in the Rocky Mountain West.

Bruce Gardner, UISBC mission director, listed the following HMB and BSU student summer missionaries in Utah and Idaho in the summer of 1982: Cindy Troutman, Lois Smith, Crystal Walker, Angel Figgee, Beth Arthur, K. C. Butler, Craig McCue, Mike Abell, Linda Strange, David Brown, Brent Fields, Sharon Iskell, Vicki Gill, Rebecca Montgomery, Karrie Aguire, Amariles Morales, Allen Comer, and James Best. The NVBC reported seventeen student missionaries in Nevada with two SWBTS summer seminar teams.

On June 17, 1982, the *California Southern Baptist* reprinted an article written by a missionary, Bob Wells of Nevada:

> In 1969, at the request of Nevada association, I became director of missions. I went to the area feeling I was accepting a hard field of service. The task proved to be otherwise. Because of the vision and dedication of those on that pioneer mission field, it has proved to be a rewarding experience. I quickly learned their vision of the future. There have been forty new works added to the existing nineteen churches and eight missions. Five associations came from the one association. This means that one-third of all the work in northern Nevada started during this thirteen year period.

Murray, Utah, First Thrift and Loan Company defaulted July 2, 1982, and was closed by the Utah State Financial Institution Department. The UISBC had $117,081 of its funds deposited in the company. UISBC executive secretary, Darwin Welsh, wrote, "Funds in the bank were deposited in nine accounts. As far as we are able to determine, each account is insured up to $15,000." Five weeks later the UISBC staff and associational missionaries met Welsh at Boise for the annual staff planning retreat. When word came that Welsh's father suffered a stroke and had been hospitalized at Alta Vista Hospital, the workers canceled the meeting.

Price, Utah, FBC celebrated its thirtieth anniversary August 29, 1982. Maxine Boyd recognized the charter members. Trevor Whiteside gave a church history, and Art Martinez (Price mayor) presented an enlarged photo of the original building. After the church choir sang, pastor Neal Foster preached the message. The crowd of 145 people enjoyed the dinner and fellowship.

UISBC Employs Lavoid Robertson as Evangelism Director

After A. C. Queen resigned, the HMB and UISBC employed Lavoid Otha Robertson as state evangelism director on August 26, 1982. Robertson was born on May 31, 1926, at Weinert, Haskell County, Texas, to Arthur Chester and Molly Viola (Harris) Robertson. He had five brothers and five sisters. He was saved at age twenty-four and baptized and ordained by Curry Chapel Baptist Church near Haskell. He married Margie Geneva Drinnon on June 4, 1950, at Curry Chapel in Texas, and they had two sons. He wrote, "My wife, Geneva, was most responsible for my salvation. She was a wonderful person, fully committed to Christ. I was saved in our home fifteen months after we were married." Robertson graduated from HPC and attended the GGBTS extension center in SLC, Utah. Because he was so shy, he had difficulty making the decision to preach the gospel. He owned and operated a Pontiac auto agency. While a student, he attended the HPC revival in 1952 led by Otis Strickland, Decatur College president. Robertson committed his life to serve in the West. He pastored SBC churches at Blanket, Mattson, and Brownwood, Texas; Twin Falls, Idaho; and Clearfield, Utah. When the Robertsons retired at SLC, Utah, he pastored at Kearns. Following a trip to Russia in 1997, Robertson contracted Gullain-Barre disease, became paralyzed, and was hospitalized for long-term care.

NVBC Fourth Annual Session Meets at Las Vegas

NVBC met for its fourth annual session October 26–27, 1982, at Las Vegas FSBC with president Beverly McLeroy leading. Terry Arnold, Tom Wilson, Ritchie Weers, John Randolph, and Joe Stewart read the scriptures and led the prayers. Ruth Wood, Jan Prince, John Chandler, Paul Stanley, Norm Sahm, Greater Las Vegas Choir, GCC Jubilation Singers, and Mike Rodrigues led the music. Mayor William Briare welcomed the messengers, and John Babb preached the convention sermon. The guests were Pat McDaniel, Annuity; Bill Graham, BSSB; Reggie McDonough, Executive Committee; Bill Clark, FMB; Foy Valentine, Christian Life; Jack Redford, HMB; and Bill Nichols, Radio/TV. Both John Sullivan, Shreveport, Louisiana, Broadmoor Baptist Church pastor, and Dan Vestal, Midland, Texas, FBC pastor, preached. NVBC honored Bob and Sara Wells for thirteen years of service. Don Ledbetter, who had pastored Elko, Nevada, FBC seventeen years, was recognized as the NVBC state evangelism director. Adrian Hall, NVBC Bible teaching ministries secretary, received the J. N. Barnett and B. W. Spilman awards for the largest percentage SS enrollment gains and best ratio of new SS starts. The convention reported fifty-six churches, forty-six missions, 16,285 members, $261,974 in Cooperative Program gifts, 12,393 in SS enrollment, and 1,233 baptisms. The board approved a plan for NVBC to enter a partnership with Louisiana Baptist Convention (LBC).

NVBC executive board met on October 27, 1982, at Las Vegas FSBC. Beverly McLeroy, outgoing chairman, introduced Neal Myers as the NVBC president and executive board chairman. Jan Norvell, Tom White, and Jerry Peterson served as new board members. The president named Robert Holmes as the programs, plans, and policies committee chairman, and J. R. Sammons as the missions committee chairman. Neal Myers led the executive committee.

Darwin Welsh Describes Optimism of the UISBC

Executive director Darwin E. Welsh described the state of the UISBC in his column "Comments":

> The annual associational meetings this year were a good experience. There is a note of optimism; people are catching a vision; we have entered a new day. We have had a slow, and sometimes painful infancy; but as one voiced it in an associational meeting, "Where there is no battle, there is no victory." Several UISBC associations celebrated twenty-fifth anniversaries this year: Golden Spike, Boise Valley, and Eastern Idaho. Joe King, member of Elk City FBC who was a town drunk until he accepted Christ as Saviour, rejoices because Southern Baptists came to his town. He reminded me that we should rejoice over one who is found and not lament about the struggle (*Utah-Idaho Southern Baptist Witness*, 11/82).

UISBC Eighteenth Annual Session Meets at Granger

UISBC met for the eighteenth annual session November 9–10, 1982, at the Granger FBC under the direction of president Carroll Reynolds. The Roy FBC trio, Southeast Baptist Church choir, Dick Hamm, John and Margaret Blake, and the Holladay Baptist Church ladies ensemble provided the special music. Gene Crewse, Richard Overman, Bob Copeland, Lafayette Moseley, and Buck Buchanan read scriptures and led the prayers. The speakers were Odell Crowe, BSSB; Reggie McDonough, SBC Executive Committee; Jack Redford, HMB; Rudy Fagan, Stewardship; David Young, FMB; and Dave Borders, Annuity. Bruce Conrad preached the convention sermon. Newly elected officers were Carroll Reynolds, president; Bill Warren and Ron Parker, vice-presidents; and Carol Browning, secretary. The UISBC board adopted a long-range plan for 1983–1987. The mission statement read:

The UISBC mission is to assist and encourage cooperating churches to fulfill the great commission: (1) by presenting the gospel to all persons and providing the opportunities for participation in fellowship and ministry; (2) by providing encouragement and resources churches need to develop mature discipleship, mission education, stewardship, family, and ethnic leadership; and (3) by providing the support system for pastors and other staff and their families to meet peculiar needs of those serving in Utah and Idaho.

Corning, California, Baptist Church
Sun Valley, Nevada, FBC organized the Corning Baptist Church in 1983 with Charles Anderson serving as the first pastor. The new church affiliated with Truckee association and the NVBC.

Salt Lake City, Utah, Korean Baptist Mission
SLC Korean Baptist Mission started in 1983 and affiliated with Salt Lake association and the UISBC. The early pastors were Ki Byung Chung, Jong Soo Ham, and Paul Jun.

Round Mountain, Nevada, Smokey Valley Baptist Church
The Tonopah, Nevada, FBC organized the Round Mountain Smokey Valley Baptist Church in 1983. The early pastors were Harvey Broadway, Ace Sliger, LaVern Inzer (int.), John Ramsey, Terry Carrington, and Opal Douthit.

West Jordan, Utah, First Baptist Church
West Jordan, Utah, FBC organized in 1983 and affiliated with Salt Lake association and the UISBC. Early pastors were Dewayne Thompson, Rhett Durfee, and Brian Davis.

Tonopah, Nevada, Silver Peak Baptist Mission
Tonopah, Nevada, FBC started the Silver Peak Baptist Mission in 1983. It affiliated with Lahontan association and the NVBC. The early pastors were Harvey Broadway, Bob Mann, and Ron Trummell.

Buildings in Idaho, Nevada, and Utah

Mountain Home, ID, FSBC met at the American Legion building when organized March 15, 1957.

Mountain Home FSBC completed a sanctuary and occupied it on the Sunday before Easter in 1961.

Brigham City, UT, FBC met at the War Memorial building when picture taken September 8, 1957.

North Las Vegas, NV, Com/College Baptist Church was organized in 1957. First building pictured above.

The HMB bought this SLC Tabor Lutheran building in 1963—most photographed church in SLC.

Buildings and People in Nevada

The Dayton, NV, Calvary Baptist Church organized and completed its first building in 1980.

South Reno Baptist Church with missionary Bob Wells, Ann Adair, and pastor Toby Adair.

Nevada Area Baptist Convention constituted at Las Vegas on October 16, 1978. Ernest Myers, the new NABC executive director, is pictured with ASBC state staff members (L-R): Myers, Canafax, Sutton, Goss, Stringer, and Parker. Myers had previously served on the ASBC staff.

North Las Vegas, NV, Calvary Baptist Church building on its completion in December 1958.

J. L. Dugger organized the Sun Valley, NV, FBC in 1958. FBC met in this building in 1970.

SBC Leaders Seek Ways to Resolve a Conflict

Because associations overlapped in the Idaho panhandle, some conflicts developed. On February 18, 1983, the following SBC leaders met at Seattle, Washington, to discuss problems between the NWBC and the UISBC: Cecil Sims and Bill Peters, NWBC; Bruce Gardner and Darwin Welsh, UISBC; and Gerald B. Palmer and E. W. Hunke Jr., HMB. Palmer read a paper and discussed rationale for drawing a line across Idaho to divide territory. The leaders agreed on four items: overlapping causes problems; churches wish to continue the existing relationships; every county seat now has a Baptist church; and we have more work to do than all of us can do together. All believed churches were autonomous and that they were free to affiliate where they wished.

Sandpoint, Idaho, Faith Baptist Church

The Bonners Ferry, Idaho, FBC started the Sandpoint Faith Baptist Church in 1983 when Lloyd and Marjorie Garrison moved a mobile chapel and their mobile home to the community. After the difficult first year, three men and the pastor built a log church building. The church affiliated with Inland Empire association and the NWBC. The early pastors were Barry Sherwood and Lloyd Garrison.

Don Mabry Initiates NVBC/LBC Partnership

The NVBC executive board met March 3, 1983, to hear LBC state mission director Don Mabry challenge them to have two hundred churches with 20,000 Southern Baptists by 1989. He reported that Joannie and Norma Armstrong would visit Nevada on July 17–31, 1983, to develop a list of needs and opportunities in Nevada for communication to Louisiana Baptist churches.

Las Vegas, Nevada, Spring Valley Baptist Church

The cosponsoring Las Vegas West Oakey and Redrock Baptist churches organized the Las Vegas Spring Valley Baptist Church on March 23, 1983. Spring Valley mission had begun in 1974. The church affiliated with Southern Nevada association and the

NVBC. Early pastors were Don Loving (int.), Huel Waddell, Arnold Kelly, Carey Smith (int.), Dan Boler, and Johnny Nantz.

NVBC Employs Neal Myers as Missionary (Nevada)
After Bob Wells retired, the HMB and NVBC employed Neal Joe Myers May 15, 1983, to serve as missionary to Spooner and Truckee River associations. Myers was born on April 20, 1928, at West Plains, Missouri, to Nathaniel James and Mary Catherine (Cole) Myers. He had one sister. Myers was saved at age twelve through his parents' influence, baptized by the Oklahoma City Southside Baptist Church in 1940, and ordained by the Shawnee, Oklahoma, University Baptist Church August 16, 1950. He wrote, "My father went forward to commit his life to Christ, and my sister and I followed him. Mother was already a member of the church." Myers married Martha Eva Muller on December 19, 1948, at Ironton, Missouri, and they had four children. He graduated from Oklahoma City High School, OBU, GGBTS, and Luther Rice Seminary (D.Min.). He wrote:

> GCC president Leroy Smith sent us to Sanders, Arizona, FBC and to the Navajo Mission at Ganado where we served as summer missionaries. We filled in for Bill Crews who left with his ill wife. We lived in a modern hogan with plumbing, no roof hole, and a concrete floor. I worked at the gas station, pastored the Sanders church in the school, and preached at an El Paso Natural Gas Company pump station and Ganado Navajo Indian Mission.

Myers pastored churches at Campbell, Missouri; Phoenix and Scottsdale, Arizona; and Boulder City and Las Vegas, Nevada. He served as Scottsdale Baptist Hospital chaplain (1970–1971). The HMB and NVBC employed him as the missionary to Truckee River and Spooner (1983–1986) and Sierra (1986–1990) associations. He resigned on December 31, 1990, to pastor South Lake Tahoe, Nevada, FBC. When he retired, he moved to West Plains, Missouri. In 1996 he wrote, "We are fine and enjoy Ozark living, but we still miss the West."

Southern Baptists Plan for the Future

On June 3, 1983, the UISBC bought the building at 8649 South 1300 East in Sandy, Utah, for $259,378. The convention sponsored a regional evangelism rally at Kamiah, Idaho, August 19–20, 1983, under the direction of Lavoid Robertson. The local speakers were Jack Azbill, Carl Estes, and Larry Jones. HMB church extension director, Jack Redford, preached three times. Robertson taught "The Pastor's Prayer Life."

The Northern Nevada association changed its name to Truckee River Baptist Association in 1983. It later merged with Spooner association to form Sierra association. The NVBC executive board assigned Mike McCullough the task of editing *The Nevada Baptist* along with Christian social ministries in May 1983.

On September 12, 1983, the NVBC executive board convened at Reno FSBC with president Stanley Unruh presiding. Ernest Myers asked the board to prepare carefully for simultaneous revivals to be led by LBC pastors and music directors. Charles Harvey, the LBC state evangelism director, and Calvin Cantrell, assistant, met with the NVBC staff.

Las Vegas, Nevada, Lone Mountain Baptist Church

Las Vegas, Nevada, Redrock Baptist Church organized the Las Vegas Lone Mountain Baptist Church in the fall of 1983 with Roy Worthley as pastor. The church affiliated with Southern Nevada association and the NVBC. The building was dedicated debt free.

NVBC Fifth Annual Session Meets at Reno

NVBC met for its fifth annual session October 25–26, 1983, at Reno FSBC with president Stanley Unruh leading. Hoyt Savage, Clarence Smith, James Thompson, Murray Day, Bob Walker, and Paul Chambliss read the scriptures and led the prayers. Ruth Wood, Bennett Cook, Helen Clare, Genie Matthews, Janice Bordigioni, GCC, and CBC led the music. Charles Grisham preached the convention sermon. The speakers were Landrum Leavell, NOBTS; Bennett Cook, HMB; Gene Daniel, Annuity; Don

Kammerdiener, FMB; James Staples, CBC; Brooks Faulkner and James Draper, BSSB; and William Hinson, New Orleans FBC pastor. Vern Miller retired as editor and Mike McCullough replaced him with Anne Mulkey as the assistant. NVBC elected a layman, Jerry Johnston, as the president. Robert Lee, LBC executive director, discussed the LBC/NVBC partnership. Don Ledbetter, state evangelism director, reported that he moderated his first state evangelism conference, directed a youth conference, trained pastors and missionaries, and prepared churches for the 1984 simultaneous revivals. The state missions director Don Mulkey reported that the NVBC began operations with sixty-five churches and missions in 1978, that these increased to 112 in 1983, and that forty-nine NVBC churches participated in the world mission conferences to hear twenty-three home and foreign missionaries. The NVBC reported fifty-six churches, fifty-six missions, 17,242 members, 1,171 baptisms, and $306,563 Cooperative Program gifts.

UISBC Nineteenth Annual Session Meets at Boise

UISBC met for the nineteenth annual session at the Boise, Idaho, Mountainview Baptist Church, on November 8–9, 1983, under the direction of president Carroll Reynolds. Music was provided by William Souther, Kevin Booe, Jan Crowl, and John and Margaret Blake. Local speakers were Glenn Bower, Roberta Edwards, John Embery, Bruce Gardner, Larry Jones, Huron Polnac, Lon Sitton, Troy Richardson, Lavoid Robertson, Dan Robinson, Gernice and Guy Ward, Bill Warren, Darwin Welsh, and Joyce Wright. SBC agency representatives were Clay Coursey, FMB; W. C. Fields, Executive Committee; E. W. Hunke Jr., HMB; Gomer Lesch, BSSB; W. B. Tolar, SWBTS; Betty Whitlock, Annuity; and Mike Davis, Brotherhood. Lavoid Robertson, UISBC state evangelism director, reported that eighteen people from Utah and Idaho traveled to Korea to help in Korean partnership simultaneous revivals in 1983. The former UISBC executive director, Charles Ashcraft, International Baptist Bible Institute development vice-president, addressed the messengers.

Huntington, Utah, Mountain View Baptist Church

Price, Utah, FBC organized Huntington Mountain View Baptist Church in 1984. Two Utah coal-fired power plants in the area had attracted non-Mormon workers to the Mormon community. After the Baptists located a vacant Christian church building, they started a Bible study. The church affiliated with Utah association and the UISBC. Early pastors were Charles Hatcher and Randy Thames.

Wellington, Utah, First Baptist Church

After graduation from Criswell Bible College in 1984, Warren Osburn moved to Wellington, advertised Baptist services in the local paper, and started Wellington FBC with twenty-two members. Dallas, Texas, FBC sent a work team to construct the new building, and a layman gave thirty-five thousand dollars to the project. The church affiliated with Utah association and the UISBC. The pastor reported that he baptized forty former Mormons into the church.

Las Vegas, Nevada, Eastern Heights Baptist Mission

Las Vegas, Nevada, Parkdale Baptist Church started the Las Vegas Eastern Heights Baptist Mission in 1984. The following year, the mission reported thirty members, fifty-three in VBS, and two baptisms. The mission affiliated with Southern Nevada association and the NVBC.

Rupert, Idaho, Colonial Baptist Church

Burley, Idaho, FBC organized Rupert Colonial Baptist Church in 1984 with four members under the direction of Willis Blair, who had returned to Idaho from Texas to start the new mission. The church affiliated with Magic Valley association and the UISBC. The old Burley hospital facility was rented until a new building could be constructed.

Pocatello, Idaho, Christian Life Fellowship

Members from Pocatello Gate City Baptist Church started the Pocatello Christian Life Fellowship in 1984 with Donald Bishop as the pastor. The church affiliated with Eastern Idaho association and the UISBC.

Nevada Baptists Enlarge Work in 1984

The NVBC executive board convened on January 20, 1984, at the Reno Baptist building. The board voted to purchase the KOLO building at 406 California Avenue for $350,000. The board spent $112,000 to improve the site and renovate the structure. When completed, the convention building was valued at $600,000. LBC gave $60,000 toward this project.

NVBC churches entertained 240 LBC preachers, laypeople, and music directors for the March 25–30, 1984, simultaneous revivals. Don Ledbetter reported that the churches had 350 professions of faith in the revivals. The evangelistic teams, serving under the direction of Charles Harvey of the LBC state staff, were one part of the 1984 Nevada/Louisiana partnership in missions projects.

The NVBC executive board met September 6, 1984, at the Reno FSBC. Rudy Duett, the NVBC state BSU director, introduced Mickie Adee as the new University of Nevada at Reno campus BSU director. Mike Fidler served as the University of Nevada at Las Vegas BSU director. The LBC invited Ernest Myers to go to Korea and assist in a 1985 Korean mission. The NVBC executive board voted to give $3,100 to help their executive director make the mission trip.

Priest River Baptists Build a New Sanctuary

Priest River, Idaho, Baptist Church helped the UISBC state staff understand problems and opportunities faced by the isolated Idaho churches through a monthly bulletin in 1984:

> Praise the Lord! What a month this has been. We signed the deed for our church property. We have two acres in front of the high school, a prime location both for the community and high school students. . . . Last month we signed a contract saying that we will tear down an old church building in town and use

as much of that material as we can. We had work teams to call expressing an interest in coming to help us tear it down and begin building our first unit. In March we participated in a Pioneer Penetration Week with SWBTS students. What a week! We had seven people accept Christ as Saviour. One lady was eighty years old, and others were high school students. One committed her life to Christ and another to special service. Last Sunday we had five people who attend regularly to join the church—three by letter and two by baptism.

J. T. Calvin, Priest River, Idaho, Southern Baptist Church pastor, mailed this newsletter on June 20, 1984:

We have been busy the past two months demolishing an old church building in town. It was given to us if we tore it down by the end of September. It is hard work, but our architect said there was enough material to frame our first unit. We will get a furnace with duct work, plumbing fixtures, windows, cupboards, lights, and pews. The savings of these items alone is worth our time and effort. Yesterday we broke ground for our foundation. How exciting to see something happening! We plan to have a foundation in by the time the building team, Carpenters for Christ, arrives from the Lamar County and Fayette County associations of Alabama. Right now we have loose ends to tie together like permits, power, water, etc. Pray for God's help! We know we are running months behind, but our goal is to be in our own building this fall. The Carpenters for Christ arrive on July 7. A week before that a team from Tate Street Baptist Church, Corinth, Mississippi, will be doing visitation, BYBCs, Bible clubs, Bible studies, and choir concerts. Churches from our own association will join us in outdoor services.

Stites, Idaho, Southern Baptist Church
Independence Flat, Idaho, Baptist Church organized Stites Southern Baptist Church in the 1890s under the direction of

J. B. York of Georgia. This church, one of nineteen organized by the early SBC pioneer, affiliated with Whispering Pines association and the UISBC on April 4, 1982, and Larry Maxwell served as pastor. Early pastors were John Raymond, Robert Mulkey, Thomas Downer, and Ralph Tarrant.

Missionary Mayo Brown Contracts Lou Gehrig's Disease
When the UISBC executive board met on May 3, 1984, at a new Sandy, Utah, Baptist building with fifteen members present, they accepted a letter of resignation from Mayo Brown with regret and with the promise of prayer support as he dealt with complications and deterioration caused by Lou Gehrig's disease. Brown took an early retirement and moved to Phoenix, Arizona. When the Baptist Foundation of Arizona learned of his plight, they moved Brown to Baptist Village at Youngtown, Arizona, and promised to care for him the rest of his life through the Grace Minnell Graves Fund. A visit to the veteran missionary in March 1997 revealed that he had astounded doctors with his determination to live. The Browns continued to bless people until his death on April 25, 1997.

Grass Valley, Nevada, Baptist Church
Winnemucca, Nevada, FBC organized the Grass Valley Baptist Church in June 1984 with nine charter members. The church met at the fire station, an airport pilot training room, the hangar, and a mobile chapel placed on three acres. It affiliated with Nevada Northeast association and the NVBC. Early pastors were Tom Bacon (int.), Darrell Regensberg, Gary Kuskie, and Charles Grisham.

UISBC Employs Louis Demster as Missionary (Idaho)
After Roy Ferguson retired, the HMB and UISBC moved Louis Everett Demster Jr. on June 1, 1984, from a pastoral missionary position to serve as missionary to Magic Valley, Boise (Treasure) Valley (1984–1991), Whispering Pines (1984–1988), and Silver Lakes Baptist associations (1987–1988). He was born on

April 15, 1928, at Lamar, Missouri, to Louis Everett and Elsie (Stoltz) Demster Sr. He was saved at age fourteen through the influence of his SS teacher, baptized by Lockwood, Missouri, FBC, in Rail Road Pond, and ordained by Twin Falls Trinity Baptist Church in 1963. He graduated from Lockwood, Missouri, High School, GCC, and attended seminary extension classes. He pastored churches at Phoenix, Arizona; Granger, Utah; and Caldwell and Boise, Idaho. He wrote, "I led two churches I pastored to start four missions; three of these are now churches. I reestablished two churches that closed their doors and have been involved in starting twelve missions, some of which are language." After retirement in 1991, Demster pastored the Boise, Idaho, Pierce Park Baptist Church.

Bruce Gardner Lists Students Serving in 1984

Bruce Gardner, UISBC mission director, reported the following HMB and BSU student summer missionaries at work in Utah and Idaho in 1984: Walter Clayton, Terry Crosby, Lynda Davis, Jill Queener, Merri Reeves, Larry Robinson, Lisa Shockley, Tim Allen, Jeffery Barnes, Jonnie Ferguson, Raymond Johnson, Wallace Keck, Bret Roberts, David Lane, Fran Rowley, Lenora Salley, Stephen Smith, Sherri Lee, Lisa Pickering, Rhonda Murphy, Stanley Minchow, and William Myers.

Fallon, Nevada, St. James Missionary Baptist Church

The Fallon, Nevada, St. James Missionary Baptist Church affiliated with Lahontan association and the NVBC in October 1984. Pastor Eddie Hill led the black church into fellowship with Southern Baptists. He developed a strong prison ministry.

Schurz, Nevada, Walker River Baptist Church

The Walker Lake, Nevada, Baptist Church organized the Schurz Walker River Baptist Church on October 7, 1984, with thirty-seven charter members. Walter Sinclair served as the first pastor. It affiliated with Spooner association and the NVBC. The church, located on Walker River Indian Reservation, dedicated a building September 7, 1987. The early pastors were John Ashcraft (int.), Lee Eudy, Walter Sinclair, and Robert Hogner.

NVBC Sixth Annual Session Meets at Las Vegas

NVBC met for the sixth annual session October 23–24, 1984, at Las Vegas College Park Baptist Church, under the direction of president Jerry Johnston. Alphonse Harris, Ibelize Veitia, Bob Stringer, Ed Jordan, Ed Farr, and David Ketchand read the Bible and led in prayers. Genter Stephens, Carol Jensen, Dodie Morgan, Ruth Wood, Linda Johnston, CBC Rhapsody Singers, Las Vegas FSBC choir, Paul Stanley, GCC, and Las Vegas College Park Baptist Church choir provided music. Bob Norvell preached the convention sermon. The speakers were Dennis Daniel, Brotherhood; Sandra Hayashida, FMB; Tim Hedquist, SBC Executive Committee; Don Mabry, LBC; Gary Cook, BSSB; Bill Williams, GCC; and David Bunch, HMB. Wayne Ward provided theme interpretations. Jess Moody, Van Nuys, California, FBC pastor, and Jaffus Hailey delivered the messages.

The NVBC established Nevada Baptist Foundation with Ernest Myers, director; Jerry Johnston, president; Walker Campbell, vice-president; and William Matthews, secretary. The NVBC board voted to develop the foundation charter and constitution and bylaws in 1985. The convention elected Jerry Johnston as the president and Robert Holmes as vice-president. Don Mabry reported on the LBC partnership and simultaneous revivals. The NVBC reported sixty churches, fifty-four missions, 1,241 baptisms, 17,451 members, and $308,130 Cooperative Program gifts from the churches in 1984. Myers announced that the staff now occupied new NVBC offices at 406 California Avenue in Reno.

NVBC executive board convened on October 24, 1984, at the Town Hall Room of the Las Vegas Silver Nugget Hotel. The board elected J. R. Sammons as vice-chairman. The NVBC president, Jerry Johnston, appointed Steve Neesley as programs, plans, and policies committee chairman; Michael Hogue as missions committee chairman; and Jerry Johnston as executive committee chairman. They invited HMB and BSSB leaders to guide them through a long-range planning process on November 8–9, 1984.

The HMB and NVBC employed Rudy and Diana Aguila as missionaries to the ethnic groups of Nevada in 1984. The Aguilas started missions with Korean, Hispanic, and Chinese, and second language classes in a number of churches.

UISBC Twentieth Annual Session Meets at Layton

UISBC convened the twentieth annual session on November 13–14, 1984, at the Layton, Utah, FBC under the direction of president Bill Warren. Mark Langley and GCC provided music for the convention. Ralph Bowen, Terry Minchow-Proffitt, Ernest Silvas, Gail Graves, and Herb Stoneman read scriptures and led in prayers. The speakers were Richard Farr, Annuity; Fred Chapman, SBC Executive Committee; Wendell Belew, HMB; Robert Turner, BSSB; Joy Cullen, FMB; and Larry Cox, Brotherhood. Medford Hutson preached the convention sermon. The newly elected officers were William Warren, president; Huron Polnak and Rodger Russell, vice-presidents; and Carol Browning, recording secretary.

Fillmore, Utah, First Baptist Church

The Richfield, Utah, FBC organized the Fillmore FBC in 1985. The chapel ministered to Laotians, Hmongs, and Piute Indians who worked in the mushroom fields. Messages were interpreted for the people. Pastor Kenneth Kuhlman constructed a chapel inside an old bus which traveled to the community for services. The church affiliated with Rainbow Canyon association and the UISBC. Early pastors were Ken Kuhlman, Glenn Munkres, and J. D. Stevens.

Hurricane, Utah, First Southern Baptist Church

St. George, Utah, FSBC organized the Hurricane FSBC in 1985 with twenty-three charter members. Twenty years earlier, a plane crash on December 2, 1965, killed Melvin Owens, a Wings for Christ pilot, on his way to Hurricane to pick up three GCC students who were surveying the community. The mission started with a Bible study in a rented motel room. The Lubbock, Texas, FBC sent a 130-member work team to construct a building and furnish it. College-age youth led Bible clubs, VBS, and a revival. The new church affiliated with Color Country association and the UISBC. Early pastors were Mel White (int.), Rhett Durphee (int.), Frank Kriz, Emory Huey, and Robert Helms.

Laughlin, Nevada, Baptist Mission
Boulder City, Nevada, FBC sponsored Laughlin Baptist Mission in 1985 with Philip Workman as pastor. The mission affiliated with Southern Nevada association and the NVBC. In 1986 the mission reported five members, two baptisms, ninety-one in VBS, and total receipts of $20,728.

Las Vegas, Nevada, Cheyene *Bautista Mision*
North Las Vegas, Nevada, Community Baptist Church started the Cheyene *Bautista Mision* in 1985, and it affiliated with Southern Nevada association and the NVBC. The mission reported seven members, six baptisms, and twenty-five in SS in 1986.

Wendell, Idaho, Calvary Baptist Mission
Gooding, Idaho, FSBC started Wendell Calvary Baptist Mission in 1985 with six members. The new mission, which affiliated with Magic Valley association and the UISBC, first met at Grange Hall. Property was purchased. The early pastors were Glenn Munkres and Van Kierstead.

Kooskia, Idaho, Clearwater Baptist Mission
Kamiah, Idaho, Pine Ridge Baptist Church started the Kooskia Clearwater Baptist Mission with a Bible study in 1985 under the leadership of James Myers, HMB church starter. The mission affiliated with Whispering Pines association and the UISBC. Early pastors were Robert Mulkey and Kenneth Blevin.

Las Vegas, Nevada, *Segundo Bautista Iglesia*

Las Vegas, Nevada, Redrock Baptist Church organized the Las Vegas *Segundo Bautista Iglesia* in 1985. It affiliated with Southern Nevada association and the NVBC. In 1986 the mission reported ten members, one baptism, and ten in SS.

Chubbuck, Idaho, Chubbuck Baptist Church

The Pocatello, Idaho, Gate City Baptist Church organized the Chubbuck Baptist Church in 1985 with thirty charter members after Earl Jackson and Billy Barton had surveyed the community in 1980. They determined that a new church was needed, and Barton started a weekday Bible study. The church affiliated with Eastern Idaho association and the UISBC, purchased two acres of land, and built the first unit. Early pastors were Robert Williams, Tommy Hicks, Don Bishop, and M. L. Waters.

Green River, Utah, First Baptist Church

East Carbon, Utah, FBC organized the Green River FBC in 1985. The mission, which started with a Bible study led by the East Carbon pastor, affiliated with Gideon association and the UISBC. A remodeled storefront building served as the meeting place. The early pastors were Jim Boulden and Randall Myers.

Las Vegas, Nevada, Chinese Baptist Fellowship

Las Vegas, Nevada, Lone Mountain Baptist Church started the Las Vegas Chinese Baptist Fellowship in 1985. It affiliated with Southern Nevada association and the NVBC.

Lewiston, Idaho, Tammany View Baptist Church

The Lewiston Tammany View Baptist Mission started in 1985 with Tim Palmer as mission pastor. After meeting initially in Clarkston, Washington, the church relocated to the East Orchards area of Lewiston, Idaho. The mission affiliated with Lewis-Clark association and the NWBC. Pastor Palmer led Bible studies and tried to start missions at Asotin and Pomery, Washington.

Panguitch, Utah, New Beginnings Baptist Church

The Richfield, Utah, FBC organized the Panguitch New Beginnings Baptist Church in 1985 with twenty-eight charter members. It had started with a home Bible study led by Medford Hutson and Richard Ashworth. The church affiliated with Rainbow Canyon association and the UISBC. Services were held in an old Mormon building and a Catholic building until lots were purchased and a mobile chapel moved on the site. The early pastors were the new work starters from Kentucky, Jim Townzen and Leo Porter.

Torrey, Utah, Wayne County Baptist Church

The Richfield, Utah, FBC organized the Torrey Wayne County Baptist Church in 1985. After a woman at Capital Reef National Park expressed interest in a Bible study, an Arkansas volunteer had started the mission in a mobile home. A divorced family sold their partially completed log home to the church for eight thousand dollars. The church affiliated with Rainbow Canyon association and the UISBC. Early pastors were Grover Bozarth, John Watson, and Ken Kuhlman.

UISBC Employs Kenneth Chadwick as Missionary (Utah)

After Mayo Brown retired, the HMB and UISBC employed Alvin Kenneth Chadwick on March 1, 1985, as the missionary to Salt Lake and Rainbow Canyon associations. Chadwick was born October 26, 1936, at Witts Springs, Arkansas, to William Frank and Clara M. Chadwick. He had one brother and two sisters. He was saved at age eleven through the influence of his parents, baptized in a bayou in 1947 by Tilly, Arkansas, Baptist Church, and ordained in 1956 by the Compton, California, Grace Baptist Church. He wrote, "I was reared in a Christian home and wanted to trust in Christ. One night I prayed the prayer that my mother taught me and knew I was a sinner and needed to put my trust in Christ. After praying and asking Christ to forgive me and enter my heart, he did." He married Barbara Evalyn Brisco June 28, 1957, at El Paso, Texas, and they had four children. He graduated from the Witts Springs, Arkansas, High School, CBC, and GGBTS. Chadwick wrote:

While I was in Compton, California, serving as a Grace Baptist Church SS leader, God dealt with me about the preaching ministry. I discussed this with pastor Van Griffin and my parents. After praying two weeks, I made my commitment public in a Sunday morning service and began making plans to go to CBC.

He pastored California SBC churches at Woodcrest, El Monte, and Hanford. He attended language school at San Antonio, Texas, and was appointed as a language missionary to Las Cruces, New Mexico. He served on the HMB Atlanta staff. The HMB and UISBC employed him as missionary to Utah's Salt Lake and Rainbow Canyon associations (1985–1996). He wrote, "With the exception of three years on the HMB staff, I have worked in the West." The HMB and Alaska Baptist Convention employed him as the state missions director on February 1, 1996.

NVBC Organizes to Continue Mission Advance

NVBC executive board met on March 12, 1985, at Reno FSBC. The board asked Michael McCullough, HMB Christian social ministry director and *The Nevada Baptist* editor, to assume the business affairs and responsibilities along with his other duties. Business manager Ruth Wood had been employed by the ASBC to serve as its state WMU director, effective June 15, 1985. The executive board voted to publish *The Nevada Baptist* as an eight-page tabloid.

The HMB Christian Service Corps and LBC sent more than one hundred volunteers to serve in Nevada in the summer of 1985. The workers, who cared for their travel and personal expenses, spent ten weeks in VBSs, BYBCs, survey work, and revival. Eight HMB and BSU student summer missionaries also worked in Nevada.

The NVBC state board met on October 23, 1985, at Winnemucca, Nevada, Red Lion Hotel. The board elected Jim Meek as the vice-chairman of the board. President Jim McLeroy announced that Lara Dean Strunk would serve as missions committee chairman and John Randolph as programs, plans, and policies committee chairman. The constitution specified that president Jim McLeroy was to serve as chairman of the executive committee.

UISBC Employs James Myers as Missionary (Idaho)

The HMB and UISBC employed James Arthur Myers as the church starter and missionary to northern Idaho March 15, 1985. He had pastored in Idaho for twenty-two years. After the Silver Lakes association constituted in 1988, UISBC received HMB permission to use Myers in an associational missionary role. Myers was born September 19, 1934, at South Greenfield, Missouri, to Harold Melvin and Nina Elaine (Maxwell) Myers. He had one brother and one sister. He was saved at age eleven through the influence of his pastor and baptized by Gooding, Idaho, FBC. He wrote, "I was convicted of being lost when my pastor preached one Sunday. I met with him and four other boys on Sunday afternoon and he led us to Christ. Two of the boys were Larry and Bill Maxwell—my cousins." Myers graduated from Gooding, Idaho, High School and Wayland Baptist University, and attended Idaho State University. In 1953 he married Patsy Dean Sorelle, and they had two children. He worked as a brick mason, high school teacher, and coach. He wrote, "While I was on vacation from WBC, Larry Maxwell, Clay Coursey, and their families visited us at my uncle's cabin near Easeley's Hot Springs in Idaho. We prayed about my staying in Idaho to pastor or going to seminary. I felt led to remain in Idaho and pastor the Twin Falls, Idaho, Trinity Southern Baptist Church." Glenns Ferry, Idaho, FBC ordained him April 13, 1963. After the HMB and UISBC employed him as a church starter, Myers pastored churches and missions at Cottonwood, Kamiah, White Bird, Grangeville, New Meadows, McCall, Cascade, Sandpoint, and Hayden Lake in Idaho. The HMB and UISBC employed him as missionary to Whispering Pines and Silver Lakes associations in 1988.

Las Vegas, Nevada, Frontier Southern Baptist Church

Las Vegas, Nevada, Nellis Baptist Church organized the Las Vegas Frontier Southern Baptist Church in April 1985. The new church, which affiliated with Southern Nevada association and the NVBC, merged with Community College Baptists to form the Frontier Community College Baptist Church in 1988. Karel Sylvanus served as the pastor.

Cascade, Idaho, Cascade Baptist Mission

Boise, Idaho, University Baptist Church started the Cascade Baptist Mission on June 30, 1985. James and Patsy Myers met Ed and Linda Cimbalik, Lee and Kim Odell, Lou and Leah Coash, Mrs. George Buckley, and Dale and Betty Cowley in May and June 1985. The mission met for its first service in the Ponderosa Plaza. It affiliated with Treasure Valley association and the UISBC. On June 4, 1989, the church held a groundbreaking service and constructed its first building in 1989 and 1990. Early pastors were James Myers, Bill McKenzie, Earl Geiszler, and Tom Moore.

NVBC Employs Norman Lewis as Missionary (Nevada)

A new missionary position was added to Nevada in 1985 by dividing an area served by Tom Bacon. Bacon continued to serve Northeastern association. The HMB and NVBC employed Norman Lee Lewis to serve Lahontan association on June 15, 1985. Lewis was born on July 11, 1925, at Little Rock, Arkansas, to Lee and Opal (Davis) Lewis. His father pastored country churches for fifty-two years. He had six brothers and three sisters. He gave himself to Christian education, church administration, and music. He graduated from College of the Ozarks and SWBTS. Lewis married Pauline Grisham of Arkansas, and they had four children. He led churches at Ft. Worth, Texas; Duncan, Oklahoma; Midway City and Upland, California; Las Cruces, New Mexico; and Russellville and Little Rock, Arkansas. He was employed as a missionary to Ashly County Baptist Association. The HMB and NVBC employed Lewis as missionary to Lahontan association of Nevada (1985–1989).

Kingston Village, Nevada, Baptist Church

Tonopah, Nevada, FBC organized the Kingston Village Baptist Church on September 2, 1985. The church affiliated with Nevada's

Northeast association and the NVBC. The church met in a school building until Louisiana work teams constructed their building in 1985. The early pastors were Harvey Broadway, Lewis Davis, John Ramsey, and Charles Adams.

UISBC Employs Bea Conrad and James Stiles

The UISBC executive board met on September 5, 1985, at the Baptist building to approve a $1,446,189 budget for presentation to the annual convention. The convention employed Bea Conrad as the state WMU director and James Stiles as religious education director. The board, in a spirit of love and concern, objected to a decision by Gerald Palmer to draw a line across Idaho to prevent pastoral aid from going to UISBC churches.

Las Vegas, Nevada, Sunnyside Baptist Church

Las Vegas, Nevada, Sunrise Baptist Church organized the Las Vegas Sunnyside Baptist Church on September 8, 1985. The church affiliated with Southern Nevada association and the NVBC. When the church failed to grow, it reverted to mission status with Las Vegas Redrock Baptist Church as sponsor. Early pastors were Louis Nimmo and Allen Hopkins.

NVBC Seventh Annual Session Meets at Winnemucca

NVBC met for its seventh annual session on October 22–23, 1985, at the Winnemucca, Nevada, Convention Center under the direction of president Jerry Johnston. James Hopkins, Darrell Regensberg, Ted Kern, Glen Murphey, and Allen Hopkins read the scriptures and led the prayers. Music was provided by Linda Johnston, GCC, Mike Hogue, David Ketchand, Winnemucca FBC choir, CBC Rhapsody Singers, Norm Sahm, and Darrell and Beverly Regensberg. J. R. Sammons preached the convention sermon. Mayor Warren Scott of Winnemucca welcomed the messengers from the churches. The out-of-state speakers were Bobbie Sorrill, WMU; Don Mabry, LBC; Frank Pollard, GGBTS; Grady Cothen, BSSB; Steve Hayes, FMB; Elaine Elkins, Annuity; W. C. Fields, Executive Committee; and Helen Walker, CBC. The NVBC honored Adrian Hall, who had resigned to become

NWBC evangelism director, and his wife Nancy, who had served as NVBC state WMU secretary. Don Mabry announced that LBC had canceled a $60,000 debt owed by NVBC. NVBC reported sixty-three churches and fifty-three missions, 1,222 baptisms, 18,862 church members, and $312,702 in Cooperative Program gifts.

UISBC Twenty-First Annual Session Meets at Idaho Falls

UISBC met for the twenty-first annual session on November 12–13, 1985, at Idaho Falls Calvary Baptist Church under the direction of president William Warren. The music was provided by T. J. and Karen Calvin, Mark Langley, Ann Kriz, Eugene Soulsby, and Maxine Souther. Jay Edmondson, Gordon Mills, Salvador Cano, Tom Hicks, and Erik Frye read the scriptures and led the prayers. The speakers were Gwenn McCormick, BSSB; Gene Daniel, Annuity; James Dunn, BJC; Quentin Lockwood, HMB; and Jack and Gladys Martin, FMB. Andy Hornbaker preached the convention sermon. The newly elected officers were Andy Hornbaker, president; Huron Polnak and William Warren, vice-presidents; and Mike Gray, recording secretary.

Carson City, Nevada, *Iglesia Bautista Emanuel*

The Carson City, Nevada, FBC organized the Carson City *Iglesia Bautista Emanuel* on November 24, 1985, and it affiliated with Sierra association and the NVBC. Early pastors were Michael Roberts and Gary Smith.

American Falls, Idaho, Calvary Baptist Church

The Pocatello, Idaho, Gate City Baptist Church organized the American Falls Calvary Baptist Church in 1986 with twenty-eight charter members. Billy Barton and Earl Jackson had spent several days in American Falls in survey work. After discovering a need for a new mission, they started a Bible study. The new mission affiliated with Eastern Idaho association and the UISBC, bought an acre of land near the bypass, and constructed a new building in 1997. Raymond Runner served as the church's first pastor.

Washoe Valley, Nevada, Baptist Mission

Carson City, Nevada, Capitol Baptist Church started Washoe Valley Baptist Mission in 1986 with Hughes Bailey as pastor. The mission affiliated with Sierra association and the NVBC. In 1989 the mission reported ten members, two baptized, and $1,584 in gifts.

Imlay, Nevada, Baptist Mission

The Grass Valley, Nevada, Baptist Church started the Imlay Baptist Mission in 1986 with Darrell Regensberg as pastor. The new mission affiliated with Northeast association and the NVBC. In 1987 the mission reported five members and twenty-two in SS.

Blackfoot, Idaho, Mountain View Baptist Church

Blackfoot, Idaho, Emmanuel Baptist Church organized the Blackfoot Mountain View Baptist Church with twelve charter members in 1986. Roy Ferguson had led the church to start the mission among Shoshone-Bannock Indians in 1960. Eugene Branch, a Duke, New Mexico, Indian missionary, had moved to Idaho to pastor the mission (1961–1965). The church affiliated with Eastern Idaho association and the UISBC. Branch led in building the first unit on ten acres of reservation-leased land. Earl and Peggy Jackson also served as missionaries on the reservation (1967–1976). The church built a home for their pastor. Other early pastors were Tom Mendez, Mike McKay, and Ken Haynes.

Reno, Nevada, Reno Park Baptist Mission

Stead, Nevada, Granite Hills Baptist Church started the Reno Park Baptist Mission in 1986 with Jim Thompson as the pastor. The new mission affiliated with Sierra association and the NVBC.

Gerlach, Nevada, Empire Community Church

Fernley, Nevada, FBC organized the Gerlach Empire Community Church in 1986 with nineteen charter members and Gary Gibson as pastor. It affiliated with Sierra association and the NVBC.

Caliente, Nevada, Baptist Church

Pioche, Nevada, Berean Baptist Church organized the Caliente Baptist Church in 1986. The church affiliated with Southern Nevada association and the NVBC. Early pastors were Clarence Smith (int.) and Joe McQuiston.

Rose Lake, Idaho, Crossroads Baptist Church

Coeur d'Alene, Idaho, Emmanuel Baptist Church started the Rose Lake mission in 1986, and organized the Crossroads Baptist Church in 1994. It affiliated with Inland Empire association and NWBC. Early pastors were Ron Mitchell, Earl Stoval, and Curtis Bellomy.

Yomba, Nevada, (Indian) Baptist Church

Austin, Nevada, Baptist Church organized the Yomba (Indian) Baptist Church in 1986 under the leadership of Tom White. Kevin Brady served as the first pastor. The new church affiliated with Lahontan association and the NVBC.

Golconda, Nevada, Baptist Mission

Winnemucca, Nevada, FBC started the Golconda Baptist Mission in 1986 with Charles Grisham as pastor. The mission affiliated with Northeast association and the NVBC and reported sixteen members, seven baptisms, and seventeen in VBS.

NVBC Employs Cindy Still and Walker Campbell

NVBC executive board met on March 10, 1986, at Reno FSBC to elect Cindy Still as the state WMU director and Walker Campbell as state Bible teaching director. NVBC evangelism director, Don Ledbetter, reported that sixty-four NVBC churches participating in the April 1986 Good News America revivals had 192 professions of faith. He said, "The revivals were the best publicized in our Nevada history with extensive use of billboards, newspaper ads, television coverage, and radio spot announcements."

The SBC Executive Committee changed its long standing policy to permit the smaller state conventions to have representation on the SBC boards and agencies. NVBC executive director, Ernest B. Myers, had led the battle to change the policy. The new policy permitted NVBC to have representation on the Executive Committee when NVBC reached fifteen thousand members; on the HMB, FMB, and BSSB with twenty thousand members; and on other boards with twenty-five thousand members. The SBC approved the recommendation at its 129th convention June 10–12, 1986, at Atlanta, Georgia.

In 1986 Jackpot, Nevada, Baptist Mission reported that it affiliated with Magic Valley association. Robert Schreckenburg, the first pastor, had started new missions at Rogerson and Three Creeks, Idaho.

Mason Valley, Nevada, First Baptist Church

The Walker Lake, Nevada, Baptist Church organized the Mason Valley FBC on June 22, 1986, with thirty charter members. J. W. Hamilton served as the first pastor. The new church affiliated with Spooner association and the NVBC.

Priest River Baptists Conduct Citywide Tent Revival

The Priest River, Idaho, FBC erected a tent and conducted a citywide tent revival on August 20–24, 1986. The entire UISBC state staff participated in the revival. HMB leader E. W. Hunke Jr. preached, and T. J. and Karen Calvin led the music. After the revival the UISBC state staff met August 25–26, 1986, at Friday Harbor, Washington, for their annual state staff retreat under the direction of Darwin E. Welsh, UISBC executive director. Hunke and his wife, Naomi, led several conferences at the retreat.

Overton, Nevada, Lake Mead Baptist Church

North Las Vegas, Nevada, Community Baptist Church organized the Overton, Nevada, Lake Mead Baptist Church in September 1986 under the leadership of Cal Collins. The church affiliated with Southern Nevada association and the NVBC. The early pastors were David Brown and Marcus Ely.

Color Country Baptist Association Constitutes (Utah)

During the Rainbow Canyon association's annual meeting at Richfield in 1986, the messengers voted to divide the association to minimize travel and to serve the churches more effectively. Churches south of Milford and Cedar City formed the Color Country Baptist Association.

Boise, Idaho, First Korean Baptist Mission

Boise, Idaho, University Baptist Church started Boise First Korean Baptist Mission in 1986 under the leadership of Jong Soo Ham. The new mission affiliated with Boise Valley association and the UISBC. The mission met in the basement of its sponsoring church and maintained regular services in 1997. Ham started Mt. Home Korean Baptist Mission, but the mission left its SBC roots.

Glenns Ferry, Idaho, Spanish Baptist Mission

Glenns Ferry, Idaho, FBC started the Glenns Ferry Spanish Baptist Mission in 1986 with Spanish families who had been attending the services. Paul Rodriquez, who initiated weekday and Sunday night services with transit workers in the potato industry, led services which continued into 1997. The new mission affiliated with Magic Valley association and the UISBC.

Elko, Nevada, Spring Creek Baptist Church

The Elko, Nevada, Calvary Baptist Church organized the Elko Spring Creek Baptist Church in October 1986 with Ken Shaw as the pastor. The church affiliated with Northeast association and the NVBC. When missionary Tom Bacon served as the interim pastor, he led the church to complete its building.

Sierra Baptist Association Constitutes (Nevada)

Messengers from the Truckee River and Spooner associations met in a joint session on October 17, 1986, and disbanded the two associations to constitute a new one named Sierra association.

NVBC Eighth Annual Session Meets at Las Vegas

NVBC met for its eighth annual session October 21–22, 1986, at the Las Vegas Sunrise Baptist Church under the direction of president Jim McLeroy. Jaffus Haley, Don Lewis, Ron Trummell, Phil Workman, Robert Hogner, and Frank Lewis read the scriptures and led the prayers. Rick Branek, Paul Stanley, Mike Fiddler, Norm Sahm, Sheila Cutting, Beverly McLeroy, CBC Rhapsody Singers, Ray Young, Jan Smith, Edgar Williams, Las Vegas FSBC choir, Las Vegas College Park Baptist Church choir, and GCC provided the music. Las Vegas mayor Bill Briare welcomed the messengers from the churches, and Robert Holmes preached the convention sermon. Ernest B. Myers, the NVBC executive director, said:

> Nevada is growing at a rapid rate, and we will break the one million mark in population possibly this year. Eighty-five percent of our population does not profess any relationship to Jesus Christ as Saviour. We are a mission state. Our needs are great. . . . The battle is not over, and our work of the future must be strong and fruitful. I believe it will happen.

Other speakers were Doug Dickens, SBC seminaries; Orrin D. Morris, HMB; Frank Schwall, Annuity; Joe Stacker, BSSB; Reginald McDonough, SBC Executive Committee; O. K. Bozeman, FMB; Bill Williams, GCC; and Perry Sanders, the Lafayette, Louisiana, FBC pastor. NVBC approved the charter for the NVBC Foundation and elected these trustees: Jerry Johnston, William Matthews, Walker Campbell, David Overhouse, James Thompson, and Cal Collins. The trustees employed Cal Collins as the first executive director of the foundation. Don Mabry, LBC state mission director, reported that since the LBC/NVBC partnership started in September 1982, an average of five hundred Louisiana Baptists volunteered service in Nevada each year. NVBC elected Jim McLeroy as the president and Carey Smith as vice-president. The NVBC reported 19,603 members, sixty-eight churches and fifty-five missions, 891 baptisms, and $326,179 in Cooperative Program gifts.

Associational Missionaries in the 1980s

Tom Lee Bacon, HMB/NVBC missionary to Nevada (1980–1985).

Arlie L. and Ella McDaniel, HMB/NWBC missionary to Idaho (1981–1991).

David Franklin Meacham, HMB/NVBC missionary to Nevada (1981–1992).

Neal Joe Myers, HMB/NVBC missionary to Nevada (1983–1986).

Louis E. and Betty Demster, HMB/UISBC missionary to Idaho (1984–1991).

Kenneth and Barbara Chadwick, HMB/UISBC missionary to Utah (1985–1996).

Missionaries and Evangelists in the 1980s

Norman Lee Lewis, HMB/NVBC missionary to Nevada (1985–1989).

James A. and Patsy Myers, HMB/UISBC missionary to Idaho (1988–____).

Marion (Tom) and Brenda Vance, HMB/NWBC missionary to Idaho (1988–1994).

Mitchell W. and Sandra Bryant, HMB/NVBC missionary to Nevada (1989–____).

Donald H. Ledbetter, NVBC evangelism director (1982–____).

Lavoid O. Robertson, UISBC evangelism director (1982–1992).

NVBC State Board Organizes for New Year

NVBC executive board met October 22, 1986, at the Las Vegas Sahara Hotel, and elected John Randolph vice-chairman. President Jim McLeroy appointed Jim Meek as mission committee chairman and John Babb as programs, plans, and policies committee chairman. The NVBC constitution specified that president McLeroy serve as the executive committee chairman.

Don Mulkey, NVBC state mission director, reported that four UISBC missions had moved affiliation to the Northeast association and NVBC in 1986: Jackpot and Jarbidge in Nevada and Murphy's Hot Springs and Three Creek in Idaho. Elko, Nevada, Calvary Baptist Church assumed sponsorship of the four missions.

UISBC Twenty-Second Annual Session Meets at Salt Lake City

UISBC met for the twenty-second annual session on November 11–12, 1986, at SLC FSBC under the direction of president Andy Hornbaker. The local speakers were Buck Buchanan, Willis Blair, Bea Conrad, Mike Donahoo, John Embery, Bruce Gardner, Eric Frye, Luman Gilman, Barrett Lampp, John Meador, Gary Misener, Darwin Welsh, Lavoid Robertson, James Stiles Jr., and Herb Stoneman. Other speakers were James Clark, BSSB; Mel Torstrick, FMB; Mike Day, Brotherhood; Wanda Jackson, recording artist; Gary Floyd, music evangelist; Stanley Nelson, GGBTS; John Ward, Annuity; Ernest Standerfer, Stewardship; and E. W. Hunke Jr., HMB. The new officers were Andy Hornbaker, president; Huron Polnak and Willis Blair, vice-presidents; and Mike Gray, secretary. Lavoid Robertson, UISBC state evangelism director, reported that ten evangelism rallies attracted 1,386 people. Forty-eight people were saved in these meetings in 1986.

Pastors Explore Interest in an Idaho Convention

Two Idaho UISBC pastors, Gordon Mills of Kingston and Doug Robinson of Grangeville, wrote a letter on December 11, 1986, to Idaho pastors about the possibility of forming a convention.

Responses to the letter, which asked for a yes or no answer, determined that pastors were not interested in the fellowship.

> To pastors of SBC churches in Idaho: We are writing you to seek your mind and heart on a matter of interest to us. We believe that mission and ministry in the state of Idaho would prosper through a fellowship of Idaho churches. We believe the time has come to explore that possibility. We have discovered that one of the HMB guidelines to receive funding as a state convention is that churches be united in fellowship for several years. We would like to know how you feel.

Twin Falls, Idaho, Magic Valley Baptist Church

When the Twin Falls FSBC lost its serviceman pastor to an overseas assignment, the church decided to close its doors. Missionary Louis Demster found one member in 1987 who agreed to help restart the church. After advertising church services in a local newspaper, Baptists came, and the work revived with fourteen members. The church changed its name to the Magic Valley Baptist Church. Early pastors were Willis Blair and Fred Barton.

Caldwell, Idaho, *Primara Iglesia Bautista*

Caldwell, Idaho, FSBC organized the Caldwell *Primera Iglesia Bautista* in 1987 under the direction of Gale Graves. The new church called Napoleon Meynard as pastor, affiliated with Treasure Valley association and the UISBC, and purchased a building in the community to remodel for services.

Idaho Falls, Idaho, *Iglesia Bautista del Sur*

The Idaho Falls, Idaho, Calvary Baptist Church organized the Idaho Falls *Iglesia Bautista del Sur* in 1987 in its SS annex while Bruce Gardner served as the pastor. The church affiliated with Eastern Idaho association and the UISBC. The mission used two buildings, one for church services and the other for a rescue mission. Early pastors were Ernest Silvas and Lorenzo Silvas.

Las Vegas, Nevada, Palestine Baptist Church

The Las Vegas, Nevada, Palestine Baptist Church organized in 1987 from a mission that had started in 1982 and affiliated with Southern Nevada association and the NVBC. The new church reported sixty members, two baptisms, forty enrolled in SS, and $28,800 in total receipts.

HMB Employs Larry Lewis as Executive Director

After Bill Tanner resigned as the HMB executive director to become Baptist General Convention of Oklahoma executive director, the HMB employed Larry L. Lewis to replace him in 1987. Lewis was born on January 27, 1935. He graduated from Hannibal-LaGrange College, University of Missouri, SWBTS, and Luther Rice Seminary (D.Min.). He married Betty Jo Cockerell on February 28, 1964, and they had three children. He served as the associate pastor of three churches; pastored churches at Madison, Sturgeon, Ewing, Thompson, and St. Louis, Missouri; Snow, Oklahoma; Sulphur Springs, Texas; Columbus, Ohio; and Willingboro, New Jersey. The Baptist Convention of Pennsylvania-South Jersey employed him as the religious education director (1971–1974). After he served as Hannibal-LaGrange College president (1981–1987), Lewis was employed by the HMB as their executive director (1987–1997).

Nevada Baptists Begin Planning for 1989 SBC

NVBC executive board met on March 10, 1987, at Reno FSBC. Don Ledbetter, the NBC state evangelism director, reported on meetings he had met with HMB leaders to make plans for the Las Vegas SBC annual meeting in 1989. NVBC planned to utilize a personal witnessing blitz and simultaneous revivals to introduce "Here's Hope—God Cares for You." The HMB provided support in prayer, prospect discovery, and revival training. Don Mulkey, NVBC state missions director, reported that the HMB plans included planting twenty-five new churches in Nevada.

Southern Nevada association missionary, David Meacham, wrote that twenty-eight churches held a world mission conference from March 29 to April 5, 1987. Seven missionaries from each of the home and foreign mission fields helped the NVBC state workers and missionaries. The conferences reached 5,611 people.

NVBC executive board met September 10, 1987, at Reno FSBC. Ernest Myers, NVBC executive director, said that the SBC annual meeting at Las Vegas in 1989 could move Nevada work forward by twenty years. He believed revivals could produce two thousand baptisms. The sites for twenty-five new churches had been located.

A Las Vegas youth rally on December 3, 1987, reported six hundred young people in attendance and fifty professions of faith. Bailey Smith followed the youth meeting with a citywide crusade in Las Vegas on December 6–10, 1987, and reported three hundred professions of faith.

Bruce Conrad Becomes Laos Grandfather

Bruce Conrad, Utah Indian missionary, continued to write and share mission stories to give Southern Baptists an insight into Utah missions. On January 31, 1987, he wrote:

> Recently we made contact with a Laos family that I met last year. I was driving our Volks Rabbit at that time south of Salt Lake, and it quit running. I went to the house on the corner, and found this Laos family. He welcomed me with open arms and said, "Good, so now you can be our grandfather. We moved here from California, and we had a friend there who served as our grandfather." Last week Bea and I went to their home, and the Laos lady prepared us a noon meal. The food is very much like Thai food, and we really did enjoy it. The father told us of trouble his fifteen year old son had. When I was there the first time, I saw a FMB certificate on the wall. The FMB helped them get into the states as refugees.

UISBC Summer Program Touches New People

ASBC state evangelism director, Nathan Pillow, led a tent revival in Cascade, Idaho, in the summer of 1987 which resulted in twenty-two professions of faith. Pillow was assisted by the North Phoenix, Arizona, Baptist Church youth choir.

The ten HMB and BSU student summer missionaries who helped in the UISBC in the summer of 1986 were Matthew Atha, Daniel Burns, James Hord, Andon Johnson, Steve Johnson, Michelle Kent, Angela Lavvorn, Joe Marley, Carla Rogers, and Stacy Shelton. Others who assisted were Roger Lewellyn, Nathan Overstreet, Troy Wolff, Karen Carpenter, and Lauri and Sandra Hansen.

On June 16–18, 1987, the SBC in annual session at St. Louis, Missouri, elected A. B. Buck Buchanan and Bill Warren of the UISBC to its committee on boards. These two pastors met in March 1988 with the SBC committee to recommend the name of the first person in UISBC history to serve on the SBC Executive Committee. When the SBC met at San Antonio on June 14–16, 1988, for their 131st annual convention, the messengers elected Andy Hornbaker, the SLC Holladay Baptist Church pastor.

NVBC Ninth Annual Session Meets at Carson City

The NVBC ninth annual session met on October 20–21, 1987, at the Carson City FBC under the direction of president Jim McLeroy. Tim Gregory, Mitchell Bryant, Barry Campbell, Johnny Hughes, and Troy Gourley read the scriptures and led the prayers. Governor Richard Brian welcomed messengers to the state capital. Terry Arnold preached the convention sermon. Rudy Duett, Tim Shields, Miriam Lee, Jack Coldiron, Beverly McLeroy, CBC Rhapsody Singers and GCC Concert Choir, and a mass choir provided music. Ralph Smith of Austin, Texas, led the interpretations. President Jim McLeroy directed the NVBC business sessions. The NVBC approved an extension of the Nevada-Louisiana partnership through December 31, 1990, and commended Ellen Lamkin of Louisiana for faithfully coordinating the project.

The speakers were Helen Fling, WMU; Russell Tuck, CBC; Rudy Fagan, Executive Committee; William Crews, GGBTS; Frank Schwall, Annuity; Bob Bingham, HMB; James Smith, Brotherhood; Art Criscoe, BSSB; Sam Pittman, FMB; and Mark Short, LBC. The NVBC elected Terry Arnold as president, Bob Norvell and Lee Eudy as the vice-presidents, and reported 20,617 members in sixty-nine churches and fifty-nine missions, 13,063 enrolled in SS, 996 baptisms, and $342,891 Cooperative Program gifts. In 1987 three of the NVBC state staff members were elected to serve as leaders of their national organizations: Ernest B. Myers as president of the state executive directors; Rudy Duett as president of the state church training directors; and Don Ledbetter as president of the state evangelism directors.

NVBC executive board met October 21, 1987, at Carson City Ormsby House and elected Bob Norvell vice-chairman. President Terry Arnold appointed Mitch Bryant as the missions committee chairman and David Doyel as the NVBC programs, plans, and policies committee. The NVBC constitution specified that president Terry Arnold serve as chairman of the NVBC executive committee.

Norman Lewis Helps Ordain Three Men

Norman Lewis, Lahontan missionary, assisted in the ordination of Troy Gourley, Kevin White, and Kevin Brady in 1987. He wrote, "I traveled 23,323 miles across our association and have been in every church at least twice. I preached five revivals and led several Bible studies. It was a blessing to assist in dedication of Walker River building." Northeast missionary Tom Bacon said the LBC/NVBC link-up helped churches at Spring Creek, Wells, Crescent Valley, Battle Mountain, Wildhorse, Lamoille, and Kingston Village with camps, revivals, outreach, VBS, construction, resort ministry, and supply preaching.

UISBC Twenty-Third Annual Session Meets at Boise

The UISBC met for its twenty-third annual session at Boise, Idaho, Calvary Baptist Church on November 10–11, 1987, under the direction of president Andy Hornbaker. Local speakers were Ken Chadwick, Bruce Gardner, George Slaughter, Mark Langley, Lavoid Robertson, Bea Conrad, and Darwin E. Welsh. Out-of-state guests were Dan Robinson, Oklahoma chaplain; Tim Hedquist, SBC Executive Committee; C. Keith Mec, BSSB; Stanley Nelson, GGBTS; Mel Plunk, FMB; John Talbert, SWBTS student; and E. W. Hunke Jr., the Grand Canyon Baptist Association missionary. The new officers were John Embery, president; George Slaughter and Herb Stoneman, vice-presidents; and Mike Gray, recording secretary.

Salt Lake City, Utah, Central Indian Baptist Church

SBC missionary to the Indians, Bruce Conrad, began the new SLC Central Indian Baptist Church in 1988. The church affiliated with Salt Lake association and the UISBC. Conrad had retired as a missionary but continued pastoring the church in 1997.

Caldwell, Idaho, Sand Hollow (Purple Sage) Baptist Church

The Caldwell, Idaho, FSBC organized the Caldwell Sand Hollow Baptist Church in 1988 under the leadership of John Blake. The church, initially named Purple Sage, affiliated with Treasure Valley association and the UISBC. The church secured a building but later reverted to a mission status. Early pastors were William Schleifer and Chris Groom.

Boise, Idaho, Crane Creek (Highland) Baptist Church

HMB church starter George Wright opened the Bergeson Baptist Church in 1988. When Boise Highland Baptist Church ceased having services, the Bergeson church moved to the Highland facility, changed its name to Crane Creek Baptist Church, and affiliated with Treasure Valley association and the UISBC.

Brigham City, Utah, *Capilla Bautista*

The Brigham City, Utah, FBC started the Brigham City *Capilla Bautista* in 1988 when the government closed Intermountain Indian School at Brigham City. Missionary Earl Jackson worked with the Brigham City FBC missions committee to start the mission. The HMB Indian mission building, located on three acres of land, had been used for work with Indian students. The mission affiliated with Golden Spike association and the UISBC. Early pastors were Medardo Padilla and Jose Arechiga.

Sandpoint, Idaho, Trinity (Northside) Baptist Church

Sandpoint, Idaho, Northside Baptist Church organized in 1988 under the leadership of Barry Sherwood, and affiliated with Silver Lakes association and the UISBC. A Sandpoint church facility was purchased for services. The early pastors were Paul Travis and Billy Webster.

Incline Village, Nevada, First Baptist Church
Carson City, Nevada, FBC organized the Incline Village FBC in 1988. It affiliated with Sierra association and the NVBC. In 1989 the new church reported fifty members, sixteen baptisms, and $72,214 in total receipts. Henry Cannington served as pastor.

Centerville, Utah, First Baptist Mission
Richfield, Utah, FBC started Gunnison, Utah, Gunnison Valley Baptist Mission in 1988 under the leadership of Medford Hutson. The new mission affiliated with Rainbow Canyon association and the UISBC. After the mission ceased meeting, Jim Knowler moved to start the Centerville First Baptist Mission.

NWBC Employs Tom Vance as Missionary (Idaho)
After Don Laing resigned, the HMB and NWBC employed Marion Truett (Tom) Vance in 1988 as the Inland Empire missionary to serve the Idaho panhandle churches. Vance was born on December 7, 1945, at Doyle, Louisiana, to O. M. and Lola (Parsons) Vance. He was saved at age nine, baptized by Chute, Texas, Northside Baptist Church, and ordained in September 1968 by Westminster, Texas, FBC. Vance wrote, "My salvation experience came as a result of my parents' love. It was a natural decision in response to God's love." He served with the U.S. Marine Corps in Vietnam, and graduated from Southeastern Oklahoma State College, NOBTS, and GGBTS (D.Min.). He married Brenda Joyce Carpenter, and they had two children. He wrote, "My call to ministry came through aloneness in 1963. God made the scriptures in Timothy to preach come alive." While in seminary he pastored churches in Oklahoma, Texas, and Louisiana. He wrote, "At age twenty-nine I graduated from NOBTS. I had an extension telephone in our Mississippi barn. I received a call from the Brigham City, Utah, FBC pulpit committee chairman. The church asked us to come and our western adventure began." He pastored

churches at Brigham City, Utah; Coeur d'Alene, Idaho; and Redmond, Oregon. The HMB and UISBC employed him as the UISBC state mission director in 1994.

Mullan, Idaho, Mullan Baptist Mission

Kingston, Idaho, Kingston Baptist Church started the Mullan Baptist Mission as a Bible study in 1988, after Carl Estes and others surveyed the community and found interested families. Bud Hall served as the first pastor. The new mission affiliated with Whispering Pines association and the UISBC.

Sandpoint, Idaho, Selle Baptist Mission

The Priest River, Idaho, Southern Baptist Church started the Sandpoint Selle Baptist Mission on February 28, 1988. Billy and Cindy Barton and James and Patsy Myers surveyed, contacted some interested families, and held the first service at Selle Grange Hall with nine in attendance. The mission purchased the Grange Hall and remodeled it for services. The mission affiliated with Silver Lakes association and the UISBC. The early pastors were James Myers, Paul Travis, Dick Stephens, and Billy Webster.

Korean Baptists Employ Three UISBC Pastors

Seoul, Korea, Kangnam Baptist Association paid expenses for two UISBC state workers, Darwin Welsh and Bruce Gardner, and two pastors, Dan Walker and Jong Soo Ham, to participate in Korean revivals. The Kangnam association forged a sisterhood relationship with the UISBC May 31, 1988, and agreed to pay salaries for three Korean pastors to work in Utah and Idaho.

Nevada Baptists Sponsor Revivals and Fellowship

The NVBC churches hosted SBC preachers and musicians for the simultaneous revivals conducted on June 4–11, 1989, just prior to the Las Vegas SBC annual meeting. On the closing Sunday of the revivals, the HMB tried to start twenty-five new churches.

Nevada Baptist Indian Fellowship met for its first annual meeting on August 6, 1988, at Fernley FBC with representatives from Ione, Yomba, and Owyhee present. They elected Tom White of Austin as the official missionary to the Indians.

Las Vegas, Nevada, First Korean Baptist Church

Las Vegas, Nevada, West Oakey Baptist Church organized the Las Vegas First Korean Baptist Church June 26, 1988, with Dennis Kim as the first pastor. The new church met in the facilities of the West Oakey and Twin Lakes churches, and affiliated with Southern Nevada association and the NVBC.

Walker Campbell Dies at Age Fifty-Eight

James Walker Campbell, age fifty-eight, NVBC Bible teaching director, died of a heart attack on July 13, 1988. On July 15, 150 people gathered at the South Reno Baptist Church to celebrate his life.

Las Vegas, Nevada, Joshua Baptist Church

The Lone Mountain, Nevada, Baptist Church organized the Las Vegas Joshua Baptist Church July 10, 1988, under the leadership of Roy Worthley. The mission, which started in Charland Shopping Center with Walter Goad as pastor, affiliated with Southern Nevada association and the NVBC.

UISBC Reaches Out to New People in 1988

Fourteen HMB and BSU student summer missionaries worked in the UISBC during 1988: JeQuita Burch, Rob Lee, Rodney Robertson, Travis Howeth, Iona Pemberton, Michelle Sellers, Mary Francis, Lauriann Hansen, Roxan Clark, Kathy Nichols, Jon Patrick, Tracy Tweedell, Leigh Pinion, and Janet Whaley.

Lavoid Robertson, UISBC state evangelism director, reported that thirteen hundred people attended the ten regional evangelism rallies. The spring simultaneous revivals in forty-two churches, led by Texas, Tennessee, and Kentucky pastors, recorded forty-two professions of faith. Three churches conducted summer revivals in the UISBC tent in 1988.

McCall, Idaho, Calvary Baptist Mission

Boise, Idaho, Calvary Baptist Church started McCall Calvary Baptist Mission on September 15, 1988, under the leadership of James and Patsy Myers. The Myers led Bible studies and church services in McCall from March 1985 through August 1987. Early pastors were Jason Sidler and Chris Tiegreen. Treasure Valley association held a tent crusade at McCall in July 1995.

Fallon, Nevada, North Fallon Baptist Church

The Fallon, Nevada, FSBC organized the North Fallon Baptist Church on September 18, 1988. The mission had started April 15, 1986, in Vern Miller's home with Paul Ray as pastor. The church affiliated with Lahontan association and the NVBC. Early pastors were Wesley Hammond, Paul Ray, and John Ashcraft.

Hayden Lake, Idaho, Silverwoods (Silver Lake) Baptist Church

Priest River, Idaho, Southern Baptist Church started Hayden Silverwoods Baptist Church on September 22, 1988, with a Thursday night Bible study in the Meeters' home. After a survey of Hayden Lake on November 11, 1989, the first service was held on the next day with thirteen in attendance. The mission adopted the name Silverwoods at first, but later changed it to Silver Lake. The church affiliated with Silver Lake association and the UISBC. The church bought property in August 1992. Early pastors were James Myers, Jerry Johnson, Billy Burton (int.), and Rod Moerer.

Las Vegas, Nevada, First Baptist Church

Las Vegas, Nevada, FBC affiliated with Southern Nevada association and the NVBC in October 1988. FBC, which had related to Northern Baptists for sixty years, wanted a relationship with an evangelistic denomination. Bill Underwood served as pastor when the request for affiliation came.

Silver Lakes Baptist Association Constitutes (Idaho)

Messengers from four churches constituted the Silver Lakes Baptist Association of Idaho on August 29, 1988. The churches were Sandpoint Northside, Priest River Southern, Hayden Lake

Baptist (Silver Lake), and Kingston Baptist. The messengers, who had assembled at Priest River Southern Baptist Church, elected Billy Barton as the first moderator. Bruce Gardner preached the message. The pastors were Paul Travis, Sandpoint; Billy Barton, Hayden Lake; T. J. Calvin, Priest River; Doug Robinson, Kingston; and James Myers, Grangeville. UISBC state staff members present were Darwin Welsh, Bruce Gardner, and Lavoid Robertson.

NVBC Tenth Annual Session Meets at Las Vegas

The NVBC met for its tenth annual session at the Las Vegas West Oakey Baptist Church October 25–26, 1988, with president Terry Arnold presiding. Arnold Chavers, Marcus Ely, Romulo Soy, Rueben Harney, and Harold Rapp read the scriptures and led in the prayers. Las Vegas mayor Ron Lurie welcomed the messengers, and Russ Daines preached the convention sermon. Rick Branek, Ginger Alford, Steve Espinosa, David Leonard, Mary Geazell, GCU Chamber Singers, Renee Crites, Stan Lloyd, CBC Rhapsody Singers, Sheila Cutting, and West Oakey Alpha and Omega Choir provided the music. The speakers were John Hancock, Annuity; Ernest Myers Jr., FMB; David Bunch, HMB; Bill Graham, BSSB; Bill Crews, GGBTS; Jimmye Winter, WMU; and Bill Williams, GCC. The executive directors, Larry Lewis of the HMB and Mark Short of the LBC, addressed the NVBC. Ernest Myers led a tenth-anniversary celebration.

UISBC Twenty-Fourth Annual Session Meets at Salt Lake City

UISBC met for its twenty-fourth annual session on November 15–16, 1988, at SLC Southeast Baptist Church under the direction of president George Slaughter. David and Barbara Duncan, Lana Lustig, and the UISBC Singing Churchmen provided special music. The Joyful Noise Singers presented a musical concert in the final session. Lu Gilman, Andy Hornbaker, Warren Osburn, Ted Fields, and James Myers read the scriptures and led in prayers. Fermin Whittaker, HMB western regional coordinator, preached twice, and Rhett Durfee gave the convention sermon. Other speakers were Johnnie Goodwin, BSSB; and Ernest Standerfer, SBC Executive Committee. The officers were George Slaughter, president; Mike Gray and Herb Stoneman, vice-presidents; and Dan Walker, secretary.

Darwin Welsh announced his retirement as the UISBC executive director at a state board meeting November 16, 1988, at the SLC Southeast Baptist Church, effective with the close of the UISBC twenty-fifth annual session in 1989. The UISBC board elected George Slaughter as the vice-chairman and named these committee chairmen: Jim Harding, administrative; Carroll Reynolds, program; Lu Gilman, missions-evangelism; and Daryl Lyeria, education.

Las Vegas, Nevada, Green Valley Baptist Church

Las Vegas, Nevada, Green Valley Baptist Church organized in 1989 and affiliated with Southern Nevada association and the NVBC. The church reported 206 members, twenty-nine baptisms, and $135,265 in total receipts. The church valued its church plant at $298,000 in 1989. Early pastors were Donald English, Frank Lewis, and Bob Norvell.

Las Vegas, Nevada, Foothills Baptist Church

Las Vegas, Nevada, FSBC organized the Las Vegas Foothills Baptist Church in 1989 with Steve Davis as pastor. The church, which affiliated with Southern Nevada association and the NVBC, reported 204 members, thirteen baptisms, $550,000 property, and $109,760 total receipts. The early pastors were Steve Davis and Hoyt Savage.

Las Vegas, Nevada, Southwest Baptist Chapel

The Las Vegas, Nevada, FBC started the Las Vegas Southwest Baptist Chapel with two members in 1989 and Eric Griffin as the pastor. The chapel affiliated with Southern Nevada association and the NVBC.

Las Vegas, Nevada, University Baptist Church

The Las Vegas University Baptist Church organized in 1989 with Jeff Powell as pastor. The church affiliated with Southern Nevada association and the NVBC.

Sparks, Nevada, Neighborhood Baptist Church

The Sparks, Nevada, Neighborhood Baptist Church organized in 1989 with Lloyd Byers as pastor. The church affiliated with Sierra association and the NVBC.

Nephi, Utah, Nephi Baptist Mission

Perry Causey started the Nephi Baptist Mission in 1989. The mission affiliated with Rainbow Canyon association and the UISBC.

Las Vegas, Nevada, First Filipino Baptist Church

The Las Vegas, Nevada, *Iglesia Bautista Hispana* organized the Las Vegas First Filipino Baptist Church in 1989 with Romulo Soy as the first pastor. The new church affiliated with Southern Nevada association and the NVBC. In 1989 the church reported fifty-six members, fifty-one baptisms, and twenty-nine in VBS.

Owyhee, Nevada, Indian Baptist Church

Austin, Nevada, Baptist Church organized the Owyhee Indian Baptist Church in 1989 with Tony Marshall as pastor. The new church, which affiliated with Lahontan association and the NVBC, reported nineteen members and thirty-nine enrolled in SS.

Salt Lake City, Utah, Metro Spanish Mission

Salvador Cano started the SLC Metro Spanish Mission in 1989. The mission affiliated with Salt Lake association and the UISBC.

Henderson, Nevada, Highland Hills Baptist Church

The Henderson, Nevada, FSBC organized the Henderson Highland Hills Baptist Church in 1989 with Lewis Nimmo as pastor. The new church, which affiliated with Southern Nevada association and the NVBC, reported twenty-nine members, three baptisms, and receipts of $43,776.

Clearfield, Utah, Korean Baptist Church

The Clearfield, Utah, FBC organized the Clearfield Korean Baptist Church in 1989 with sixty-five charter members. John Lee,

SLC missionary to the Koreans, had started the mission in 1981 with Koreans at Hill Air Force Base who spoke no English. The church affiliated with Golden Spike association and the UISBC, purchased two and a half acres of land, and built a new building. Early pastors were John Lee and Kyung Tae Cha.

Minden, Nevada, Sierra View Baptist Church

The Minden, Nevada, Sierra View Baptist Church organized in 1989 with Bob Anderson as pastor. The church reported thirty-one members, ten baptisms, and property valued at $42,500. The work affiliated with Sierra association and the NVBC.

Las Vegas, Nevada, Monte Horeb Baptist Church

Las Vegas, Nevada, Palestine Baptist Church organized the Las Vegas Monte Horeb Baptist Church in 1989. The new church affiliated with Southern Nevada association and the NVBC. In 1989 the church reported forty members, eleven baptisms, and $6,212 in receipts.

SBC State Executive Directors Honor Welsh on Retirement

On February 21–22, 1989, the SBC state executive directors' association in annual session at San Diego, California, presented the following plaque:

> WHEREAS, Darwin E. Welsh will retire September 1, 1989, after twenty years as executive director-treasurer of Utah-Idaho Southern Baptist Convention; and
>
> WHEREAS, he participated in the organization of the Utah-Idaho Southern Baptist Convention in October 1964 by serving as chairman of the budget committee for the new convention; and
>
> WHEREAS, he joined the staff of the new convention on March 1, 1965, as associate executive director; and

WHEREAS, after four and one-half years of service as associate executive director, he was elected by the Utah-Idaho Southern Baptist Convention executive board to the position of executive director-treasurer, beginning his service on September 15, 1969; and

WHEREAS, during his nearly twenty-five years of service on that convention staff, he has served also at times as editor of the *Utah-Idaho Southern Baptist Witness*, missions and religious education director, business manager, stewardship and Brotherhood director; and

WHEREAS, he has led Utah-Idaho Southern Baptists in the past twenty years to grow from fifty-eight to ninety-four churches; from 8,452 to 18,295 members; from total receipts of $604,769 to $4,434,735; and church property from $2,892,900 to $19,832,620;

NOW THEREFORE BE IT RESOLVED, that members of the executive committee of the SBC, meeting in Nashville, Tennessee, February 20–22, 1989, express gratitude to God for the life and ministry of Darwin E. Welsh and express our deep appreciation to him for his long and faithful service to Southern Baptists; and

BE IT FURTHER RESOLVED, that this action be conveyed to his family and our fellow Southern Baptists of Utah-Idaho Southern Baptist Convention.

UISBC Employs Clyde Billingsley as Executive Director

The UISBC state executive board met at the SLC state office building on May 4, 1989, to employ Col. Clyde Billingsley as the state executive director. Billingsley arrived on September 1 to work one month with Darwin Welsh. He assumed the convention responsibilities on October 1, 1989. The executive board forged a five-year partnership with Kentucky Baptist Convention

(1990–1995) to link Kentucky churches and associations with the UISBC churches and associations.

First National SBC in Intermountain West Meets at Las Vegas

The SBC met for its one hundred thirty-second session at Las Vegas, Nevada, June 13–15, 1989, the first to meet in the Great Basin area of Intermountain West. The convention sessions, led by president Jerry Vines, were attended by 20,411 church messengers plus many visitors. Morris Chapman of Texas preached the sermon. Ernest B. Myers, NVBC executive director, was elected as the SBC second vice-president. NVBC state mission director, Don Mulkey, reported that eight churches constituted and eight church-type missions started in 1988–1989. NVBC state evangelism director Don Ledbetter reported that the eighty-six revival teams had been oriented at Las Vegas West Oakey Baptist Church on June 3. NVBC churches reported 525 professions of faith. The Las Vegas SBC, the sixth in the far West, attracted the largest attendance of the western meetings.

NVBC Employs Mitchell Bryant as Missionary (Nevada)

After Norm Lewis resigned, the HMB and NVBC employed Mitchell Wayne Bryant of the Topaz Lakes, Nevada, FBC (Topaz Ranch Estates) to serve as the missionary effective August 15, 1989. Bryant was born July 20, 1947, at Black, Missouri, to Lyle Joseph and Alice Geraldine (Shy) Bryant. He was saved at age thirteen through the influence of his SS teacher and pastor, baptized by the Festus-Crystal City, Missouri, FBC, and ordained in 1970 by Weir, Kansas, FBC. He wrote, "I attended church with my family all my life. When I realized my need to accept Christ as Saviour and Lord at age thirteen, I went forward during the Sunday morning invitation. My pastor led me to pray to receive Christ." He married Sandra Lynn Becknell, and they had two children. He graduated from the DeSoto, Missouri, High School, Pittsburg (Kansas) State University, and SWBTS. Bryant wrote:

> After completing my seminary work, I wanted to serve in pioneer missions work. God's timing opened doors to pastor

in Arkansas for a time. My heart has always been in new mission churches. I began my ministry at the Cherokee, Kansas, Baptist Chapel. In 1983 I led a revival for pastor Steven Neesley at Boulder City, Nevada, and felt a strong sense of God's leading to the West.

He pastored SBC churches at Cherokee, Kansas; North Crossett and Montrose, Arkansas; and Topaz, Nevada.

White Bird, Idaho, Pleasant View Baptist Church
The Grangeville, Idaho, Mountain Shadows Baptist Church organized the White Bird Pleasant View Baptist Church on October 15, 1989, with twenty-three charter members. After several of the families attended Grangeville service and the White Bird VBS, some were saved and baptized into the Grangeville church. James and Patsy Myers, Dave Niemeyer, Ken Carpenter, and Daniel Biggers led Monday night Bible studies at White Bird. The new church affiliated with Whispering Pines association and the UISBC, and bought an Assembly of God church building on December 24, 1981. A fellowship hall was built in August 1992. Early pastors were James Myers, Dave Niemeyer, Doug Robinson (int.), and Randy Myers.

NVBC Eleventh Annual Session Meets at Reno
The NVBC met for its eleventh annual session at Reno FSBC on October 24–25, 1989, with president Bob Norvell presiding. Mirio Whitley, Ken Cox, Lloyd Byers, John Babb, and Jim Thompson read the scriptures and led the prayers. Rudy Duett, the Winnemucca Born-Again Singers, Jim Griffiths, Nancy Owen, Mike Rodrigues, the GCU Ensemble, the CBC Light Singers, Jeoslyn Geras, and Melene Gibbons provided the music. The Las Vegas Green Valley Baptist Church pastor, Frank Lewis, led theme interpretation. Ted Kern preached the convention sermon. The speakers were Bill Williams, GCU; Frank Schwall, Annuity; Harry Bonner, Executive Committee; Don Wilton, NOBTS; Charles Chaney, HMB; Doug Anderson, BSSB; Jim Riddle, FMB; Russell

Tuck, CBC; and Mark Short, LBC. The NVBC reported 23,416 members, 1,410 baptisms, $43,246,317 property, 13,949 SS enrollment, $6,700,746 church receipts, and $414,287 Cooperative Program gifts.

UISBC Twenty-Fifth Annual Session Meets at Idaho Falls

The twenty-fifth annual UISBC session convened at the Idaho Falls, Idaho, Calvary Baptist Church November 14–15, 1989, under the direction of president George Slaughter. Clyde Billingsley, the newly elected executive director, preached on "This One Thing I Do," and "Prize of the High Calling of God." The twenty-fifth anniversary program was presented by Lavoid Robertson and Bruce Gardner of the UISBC state staff; E. W. Hunke Jr., former Vernal, Utah, FBC pastor (1953–1954); and Charles Ashcraft, the first UISBC executive secretary. The UISBC honored retiring executive director Darwin E. Welsh. The speakers were Dan Sanchez, SWBTS; Rudy Fagan, Stewardship; Ray Conner, BSSB; Mac Perkins, Annuity; and Larry Lewis, HMB. Blackfoot, Idaho, Emmanuel Baptist Church pastor, Brian Harrison, preached the convention sermon, and Mt. Home FSBC pastor, George Slaughter, delivered the president's message. Missionaries Earl Jackson, Richard Ashworth, Louis Demster, and Kenneth Chadwick spoke on the program. The new officers were Luman Gilman, president; James Harding and Paul Rodriquez, vice-presidents; and Dan Walker, secretary.

Dover, Idaho, Dover Baptist Mission

The Selle, Idaho, Baptist Church started the Dover Baptist Mission June 23, 1990, with eighteen present. Ten leaders from Silver Lakes association surveyed the community on Saturday, June 22, and began the mission on the following day. People taking the survey were Billy and Cindy Barton, James and Patsy Myers, Dave and Vicky Huffman, Jim Hammonds, Donna Brown, Lucille Allyson, and Mark Workam. An eighty-year-old former California pastor assisted in the survey. The ABC deeded the Dover church building to Sandpoint, Idaho, Northside Baptist Church. Early pastors were Billy Barton, Dick Stephens, Paul Corrick (int.), and Bill Webster.

Utah Pioneer Opal (Beaird) Dillman Dies June 22, 1993

Harold Dillman passed away on June 22, 1980. Opal Dillman, age eighty-three, died June 22, 1993, of heart failure at SLC, Utah, Alta View Hospital, after giving fifty years of sacrificial service to Utah-Idaho Southern Baptists. Opal remained active in Southern Baptist work and alert until her death. In the last letter she wrote to the Hunkes, she said:

> You are not forgotten! I just let the here and now take time that should be spent letting my old friends know they are as precious to me as the new ones. Harold was such a good person to fix things that I'm spoiled to have someone like that. My little income does not keep up with the outgo so I can't afford to hire work done. News about extending the seminary to southern California is interesting. If I ever leave Utah, I will be living near Dorothy [Visalia] or other relatives in the southern area. I am now being encouraged to spend my latter days writing the history of my life and Harold's here in Utah. If I am to do it, I think it will have to be soon—before my memories all leave me. Harold kept a diary of things for many years, but I do not find the many facts I need to go with my memory.

Southern Baptists arose from the devastation of Civil War in 1865 to become a powerful religious force in the United States and Canada. One must remember that the Arizona, California, New Mexico, and Northwest Southern Baptists set the stage for advance in the West with only a few struggling churches. The report of SBC churches in all of the western states on September 30, 1989, revealed that 2,820 churches affiliated with 148 associations, baptized 32,501 converts to Christ in 1989. The SBC had 1,356 missionaries at work in western states, American Samoa, and Canada December 31, 1989. Canada's 106 SBC churches had a membership of 6,000.

A Tribute to Home Mission Board Leaders

Solomon F. and Frances Dowis, HMB cooperative missions (1946–1958).

Amos B. Cash, HMB pioneer missions (1959–1967).

C. B. Hogue, HMB evangelism director (1973–1982).

Roy W. Owen, HMB associational missions (1968–1974).

William G. Tanner, HMB executive director (1977–1987).

Larry L. Lewis, HMB executive director (1987–1996).

APPENDICES

A. Chronological List of Associations — 339
B. Alphabetical List of Churches (By State/City) — 341
C. Chronological List of Missionaries — 355
D. Combined List of Associations and Missionaries — 357

Appendix A

CHRONOLOGICAL LIST OF ASSOCIATIONS

Idaho-Nevada-Utah

Constituted	Association	Convention
The Decade of the 1940s		
1942.03.02.AZ	Central	BGCA
1944.10.02.CA	Sacramento Valley	SBGCC
1946.08.29.AZ	Grand Canyon	BGCA
1948.10.00.CA	Sierra-Butte	SBGCC
The Decade of the 1950s		
1950.10.20.WA	Columbia Basin	BGCOW
1950.10.28.AZ	Mohave	BGCA
1950.11.18.UT	Utah	BGCA
1953.10.03.ID	Twin Buttes	BGCA
1953.10.08.CA	Feather River	SBGCC
1954.10.11.WA	Inland Empire	BGCOW
1955.07.20.NV	Nevada	SBGCC
1955.08.15.CO	San Juan	BCNM
1955.09.12.UT	Salt Lake	BGCA

Constituted	Association	Convention
1955.10.03.NV	Lake Mead	BGCA
1957.10.00.ID	Eastern Idaho	BGCA
1957.10.00.ID	Magic Valley	BGCA
1957.10.05.ID	Boise Valley	BGCA
1958.10.00.UT	Golden Spike	BGCA
1959.00.00.UT	Gideon	BGCA
1959.00.00.ID	Lewis-Clark	BGCOW

The Decade of the 1960s

1967.00.00.UT	Rainbow Canyon	UISBC
1968.00.00.UT	Mid-State	UISBC

The Decade of the 1970s

1972.00.00.ID	Whispering Pines	UISBC
1977.10.07.NV	Northern Nevada	SBGCC
1977.10.18.NV	Southern Nevada	BGCA
1979.10.19.NV	Spooner	NVBC
1979.10.19.NV	Lahontan	NVBC
1979.10.19.NV	Northeast	NVBC
1979.10.19.NV	Truckee River	NVBC

The Decade of the 1980s

1985.00.00.ID	Treasure Valley	UISBC
1985.00.00.UT	Color Country	UISBC
1986.10.17.NV	Sierra	NVBC
1988.00.00.ID	Silver Lakes	UISBC

APPENDIX B

ALPHABETICAL LIST OF CHURCHES

Idaho-Nevada-Utah (1940–1989)

Note: Association column lists initial affiliation of church or mission

Date	City, State, and Church Name	Association
	IDAHO	
1986	American Falls, Idaho, Calvary BC	Eastern ID
1979.06.00	Athol, Idaho, BM	Inland Emp
1989	Bergeson, Idaho, Bergeson BC	Treasure Val
1962.01.07	Blackfoot, Idaho, Emmanuel BC	Eastern ID
1961.12.00	Blackfoot, Idaho, Ft. Hall Indian	Eastern ID
1986	Blackfoot, Idaho, Mountain View BC	Eastern ID
1964.06.14	Boise, Idaho, Calvary BC	Boise Valley
1988	Boise, Idaho, Crane Creek BC	Treasure Val
1986	Boise, Idaho, First Korean BM	Boise Valley
1961.12.03	Boise, Idaho, Highlands BC	Boise Valley
1984	Boise, Idaho, Morning Wind BC	Boise Valley
1955.02.06	Boise, Idaho, Mountain View BC	Twin Buttes
1982	Boise, Idaho, Southeast Valley BM	Boise Valley
1982	Boise, Idaho, Trinity BC	Boise Valley
1971.07.00	Boise, Idaho, University BC	Boise Valley
1955.07.22	Bonners Ferry, Idaho, FBC	Inland Emp

Date	City, State, and Church Name	Association
1955.12.15	Burley, Idaho, FBC	Twin Buttes
1979	Burley, Idaho, *Primeria Iglesia*	Magic Valley
1955.09.06	Caldwell, Idaho, FSBC (Jordan Valley)	Twin Buttes
1987	Caldwell, Idaho, *Primera Iglesia*	Treasure Val
1988	Caldwell, Idaho, Purple Sage BM	Treasure Val
1988	Caldwell, Idaho, Sand Hollow BC	Treasure Val
1985.06.30	Cascade, Idaho, Cascade BM	Treasure Val
1982	Challis, Idaho, FBC	Eastern ID
1985	Chubbuck, Idaho, Chubbuck BC	Eastern ID
1977	Clarkston, Washington, Heights BC	Lewis-Clark
1958.11.00	Clarkston, Washington, Trinity BC	Inland Emp
1887	Clearwater, Idaho, FBC	Whisp Pines
1970	Coeur d'Alene, Idaho, Emmanuel BC	Inland Emp
1969.09.07	Cottonwood, Idaho, Emmanuel BC	Boise Valley
1959.07.00	Craigmont, Idaho, Highland BC	Inland Emp
1990.06.23	Dover, Idaho, BM	Silver Lakes
1981	Elk City, Idaho, Elk City BC	Whisp Pines
1960.01.21	Emmett, Idaho, FSBC	Boise Valley
1976	Fruitland, Idaho, FBC	Boise Valley
1960.07.14	Georgetown, Idaho, BM	Eastern ID
1957.06.00	Glenns Ferry, Idaho, Laird Mem (FBC)	Twin Buttes
1986	Glenns Ferry, Idaho, Spanish BM	Magic Valley
1964.05.03	Gooding, Idaho, FSBC	Magic Valley
1975.01.19	Grangeville, Idaho, Mountain Shadows	Whisp Pines
1988.09.22	Hayden Lake, Idaho, Silverwoods BC	Silver Lakes
1977	Horseshoe Bend, Idaho, Bend BC	Boise Valley
1987	Idaho Falls, Idaho, *Bautista del Sur*	Eastern ID
1951.03.26	Idaho Falls, Idaho, Calvary BC	Utah
1963.01.06	Jerome, Idaho, BM	Magic Valley
1978	Jordan Valley, Oregon, Village BC	Boise Valley
1969.09.07	Kamiah, Idaho, Pine Ridge BC	Boise Valley
1954.04.04	Kellogg, Idaho, FBC	Columbia B

Date	City, State, and Church Name	Association
1958.05.00	Ketchum, Idaho, FBC	Magic Valley
1950.08.00	Kimberly, Idaho, FBC	Columbia B
1982	Kingston, Idaho, BC	Silver Lakes
1985	Kooskia, Idaho, Clearwater BM	Whisp Pines
1953.08.02	Lewiston, Idaho, Orchards BC	Columbia B
1985	Lewiston, Idaho, Tammany View BC	Lewis-Clark
1988.09.15	McCall, Idaho, Mountain Pines BM	Treasure Val
1969.08.10	Meridian, Idaho, Cherry Lane BC	Boise Valley
1959.05.00	Moscow, Idaho, Trinity BC	Lewis-Clark
1982	Mt. Home, Idaho, Emmanuel BC	Boise Valley
1957.03.15	Mt. Home, Idaho, FSBC	Boise Valley
1987	Mt. Home, Idaho, Korean BM	Treasure Val
1953.06.00	Mt. Home, Idaho, Laird Memorial BC	Boise Valley
1988	Mullan, Idaho, Mullan BM	Whisp Pines
1982	Murray, Idaho, North Fork Comm BM	Whisp Pines
1957.12.17	Nampa, Idaho, FSBC	Boise Valley
1976	Nampa, Idaho, Valley (Victory) BC	Boise Valley
1968.07.20	New Meadows, Idaho, Meadows BM	Treasure Val
1967.05.21	Nyssa, Oregon, Park Avenue BC	Boise Valley
1982	Ontario, Oregon, FSBC	Boise Valley
1963.03.17	Orofino, Idaho, FBC	Lewis-Clark
1984	Parma, Idaho, Christian Life	Boise Valley
1964.02.16	Payette, Idaho, FSBC	Boise Valley
1979.09.09	Pierce, Idaho, Majestic Mountain BC	Whisp Pines
1958.01.05	Pocatello, Idaho, Central BC	Eastern ID
1984	Pocatello, Idaho, Christian Life	Eastern ID
1953.06.14	Pocatello, Idaho, FSBC (Gate City)	Utah
1984	Pocatello, Idaho, Grace Bible	Eastern ID
1983	Pocatello, Idaho, Spanish Mission	Eastern ID
1956.09.04	Polaris, Idaho, FBC	Inland Emp
1974.01.20	Post Falls, Idaho, FBC	Inland Emp
1959.05.21	Preston, Idaho, BM	Eastern ID

Date	City, State, and Church Name	Association
1981.10.11	Priest River, Idaho, Southern BC	Silver Lakes
1965.10.00	Pullman, Washington, Emmanuel BM	Lewis-Clark
1978	Rathdrum, Idaho, BC	Inland Emp
1959.05.14	Richfield, Idaho, BM	Magic Valley
1968	Riggins, Idaho, BM	Whisp Pines
1973	Ririe, Idaho, Ririe BC	Eastern ID
1989	Rogerson, Idaho, Rogerson BC	Magic Valley
1986	Rose Lake, Idaho, Crossroads BM	Whisp Pines
1984	Rupert, Idaho, Colonial BC	Magic Valley
1953.06.14	Rupert, Idaho, FBC	Magic Valley
1980	Rupert, Idaho, *Primera Iglesia*	Magic Valley
1982	Salmon, Idaho, Salmon Valley BC	Eastern ID
1983	Sandpoint, Idaho, Faith BC	Inland Emp
1988	Sandpoint, Idaho, Northside BC	Silver Lakes
1988.02.28	Sandpoint, Idaho, Selle BM	Silver Lakes
1963.10.13	Soda Springs, Idaho, FSBC	Eastern ID
1978	Spirit Lake, Idaho, BC	Inland Emp
1966.02.00	St. Anthony, Idaho, Upper Valley BC	Eastern ID
1971	St. Maries, Idaho, College Avenue BC	Inland Emp
1982.04.04	Stites, Idaho, Stites (Clearwater) BC	Whisp Pines
- - - -	Sun Valley, Idaho, Wood River BC	Magic Valley
1989	Three Creek, Idaho, Three Creek BC	Magic Valley
1957.10.13	Twin Falls, Idaho, Eastside (Trinity)	Magic Valley
1955.09.24	Twin Falls, Idaho, FSBC	Twin Buttes
1987	Twin Falls, Idaho, Magic Valley BC	Magic Valley
1958.11.00	Waitsburg, Washington, FBC	Inland Emp
1977.06.00	Wallace, Idaho, BM	Inland Emp
1965.10.00	Weippe, Idaho, BC	Lewis-Clark
1972.08.14	Weippe, Idaho, Prairie BC	Whisp Pines
1978	Weiser, Idaho, Calvary BC	Boise Valley
1985	Wendell, Idaho, Calvary BM	Magic Valley
1989.10.15	White Bird, Idaho, Pleasant View BC	Whisp Pines

Date	City, State, and Church Name	Association

NEVADA

Date	City, State, and Church Name	Association
- - - -	Alamo, Nevada, BM	Southern NV
1981.10.00	Austin, Nevada, BC	Lahontan
1989	Austin, Nevada, Owyhee Indian BC	Lahontan
1988	Battle Mountain, Nevada, Fellowship	Northeast
1968	Battle Mountain, Nevada, FBC	Nevada
1987	Battle Mountain, Nevada, Indian BM	Sierra
1968.07.00	Beatty, Nevada, FSBC	Nevada
1951.05.13	Boulder City, Nevada, FBC	Mohave
1981	Burns, Oregon, BM	Northeast
1986	Caliente, Nevada, BC	Southern NV
1981.03.30	Carlin, Nevada, FBC	Northeast
1978.07.02	Carson City, Nevada, Capital City BC	Northern NV
1985.11.24	Carson City, Nevada, *Emmanuel Bautista*	Sierra
1954	Carson City, Nevada, FBC	Feather Riv
1979	Carson City, Nevada, Hispanic BM	Northern NV
1986	Carson City, Nevada, Washoe Valley BM	Sierra
1988	Churchill, Nevada, Baptist Fellowship	- - - -
1983	Corning, California, BC	Truckee
1973.07.16	Crescent Valley, Nevada, BC	Nevada
1980.08.00	Dayton, Nevada, Calvary BC	Northern NV
1966	Diamond Valley, Nevada, BC	Northeast
- - - -	Eagleville, California, BM	Sierra
1989	East Sparks, Nevada, Neighborhood BM	Sierra
1969.07.12	Elko, Nevada, Calvary BC	Nevada
1986.10.00	Elko, Nevada, Spring Creek BC	Northeast
1955	Ely, Nevada, FBC	Utah
1975	Ely, Nevada, Sunnyside BM	Northeast
1966	Eureka, Nevada, Diamond Valley FBC	Nevada
1975	Fallon, Nevada, Faith BC	Nevada
1960.01.00	Fallon, Nevada, FSBC	Nevada

Date	City, State, and Church Name	Association
1988.09.18	Fallon, Nevada, North Fallon BC	Lahontan
1984.10.00	Fallon, Nevada, St. James Miss BC	Lahontan
1974.10.18	Fernley, Nevada, FSBC	Nevada
1981	Fields, Oregon, BM	Northeast
1975	Gabbs, Nevada, BM	Nevada
1986	Gerlach, Nevada, Empire Comm. BC	Sierra
1984	Gillman Springs, Nevada, BM	Lahontan
1986	Golconda, Nevada, BM	Northeast
1981.12.00	Goldfield, Nevada, FBC	Lahontan
1988	Goldfield, Nevada, Fish Lake BC	Lahontan
1984.06.00	Grass Valley, Nevada, BC	Northeast
1947.10.25	Hawthorne, Nevada, Calvary BC	Sacramento
- - - -	Henderson, Nevada, *Bautista Hispana*	Southern NV
1965.04.29	Henderson, Nevada, Faith BC (CF)	Lake Mead
1991	Henderson, Nevada, Gethsemane BM	Southern NV
1989	Henderson, Nevada, Green Valley BC	Southern NV
1989	Henderson, Nevada, Highland Hills BC	Southern NV
1954.01.10	Henderson, Nevada, Temple (FSBC)	Mohave
1985	Imlay, Nevada, BM	Northeast
1988	Incline Village, Nevada, FBC	Sierra
1965.05.02	Indian Springs, Nevada, FBC	Lake Mead
1983	Ione, Nevada, Indian BM	Sierra
1974.09.00	Jackpot, Nevada, SBC	Magic Valley
1986	Jackpot, Nevada, Spanish BM	Magic Valley
1971.06.00	Kings Beach, California, FBC	Nevada
1971	Kings Beach, California, *Christo Vive* BM	Sierra
1985.09.02	Kingston Village, Nevada, BC	Northeast
- - - -	Las Vegas, Nevada, *Betania Hispana* BM	Southern NV
1965.09.26	Las Vegas, Nevada, Bethel BC	Lake Mead
1987	Las Vegas, Nevada, *Bethel Bautista*	Southern NV
1963.06.16	Las Vegas, Nevada, Central BC	Lake Mead
1985	Las Vegas, Nevada, *Cheyene Bautista*	Southern NV

Date	City, State, and Church Name	Association
1985	Las Vegas, Nevada, Chinese BM	Southern NV
1962.05.24	Las Vegas, Nevada, College Park BC	Lake Mead
1963.01.06	Las Vegas, Nevada, Desert Hills BC	Lake Mead
1965.10.10	Las Vegas, Nevada, East Las Vegas BC	Lake Mead
1984	Las Vegas, Nevada, Eastern Heights BM	Southern NV
1988.10.00	Las Vegas, Nevada, FBC	Southern NV
1989	Las Vegas, Nevada, First Filipino BM	Southern NV
1988.06.26	Las Vegas, Nevada, First Korean BC	Southern NV
1965.08.00	Las Vegas, Nevada, First Mexican BC	Lake Mead
1987	Las Vegas, Nevada, Flamingo Road BM	Southern NV
1989	Las Vegas, Nevada, Foothills BC	Southern NV
1985.04.00	Las Vegas, Nevada, Frontier SBC	Southern NV
1955.06.26	Las Vegas, Nevada, FSBC	Mohave
1972	Las Vegas, Nevada, Foothills BC	Southern NV
1989	Las Vegas, Nevada, Green Valley BC	Southern NV
1965	Las Vegas, Nevada, Harbor CF	Southern NV
- - - -	Las Vegas, Nevada, Hope BC	Southern NV
1988.07.10	Las Vegas, Nevada, Joshua BC	Southern NV
1983.09.00	Las Vegas, Nevada, Lone Mountain BC	Southern NV
1989	Las Vegas, Nevada, Monte Horeb BC	Southern NV
- - - -	Las Vegas, Nevada, Morning Star BC	Southern NV
1986	Las Vegas, Nevada, Mt. Charleston BM	Southern NV
1990	Las Vegas, Nevada, Mt. Sinai Spanish	Southern NV
1956.01.22	Las Vegas, Nevada, Nellis BC	Lake Mead
1966.10.00	Las Vegas, Nevada, New Jerusalem BC	Lake Mead
1987	Las Vegas, Nevada, Palestine SBC	Southern NV
1980	Las Vegas, Nevada, Paradise Valley BC	Southern NV
1965	Las Vegas, Nevada, Parkdale BC	Lake Mead
1990	Las Vegas, Nevada, Pioneer BC	Southern NV
1968	Las Vegas, Nevada, *Primera Hispana*	Southern NV
1956.05.06	Las Vegas, Nevada, Redrock (Charleston)	Lake Mead
1985	Las Vegas, Nevada, *Segundo Bautista*	Southern NV

Date	City, State, and Church Name	Association
1989	Las Vegas, Nevada, Southwest BC	Southern NV
1988	Las Vegas, Nevada, Spanish Trails BM	Southern NV
1983.03.23	Las Vegas, Nevada, Spring Valley BC	Southern NV
1958.04.13	Las Vegas, Nevada, Sunrise BC	Lake Mead
1985.09.08	Las Vegas, Nevada, Sunnyside BC	Southern NV
1990	Las Vegas, Nevada, The Lakes BM	Southern NV
1970	Las Vegas, Nevada, Tropicana (Koinonia)	Lake Mead
1965.04.04	Las Vegas, Nevada, Twin Lakes BC	Lake Mead
1989	Las Vegas, Nevada, University BC	Southern NV
1983	Las Vegas, Nevada, West Craig Road BC	Southern NV
1967	Las Vegas, Nevada, West Oakey BC	Lake Mead
1985	Laughlin, Nevada, BM	Southern NV
1972.10.00	Lemmon Valley, Nevada, Fellowship BC	Nevada
1956	Lovelock, Nevada, FBC	Nevada
1987	Manhattan, Nevada, BM	Lahontan
1986.06.22	Mason Valley, Nevada, FBC	Spooner
1981	McDermitt, Nevada, BC	Northeast
1976.07.04	Meyers, California, Tahoe Paradise BC	Nevada
- - - -	Middle Gate, Nevada, BM	Lahontan
1996	Montello, Nevada, BM	Northeast
1996	Mountain City, Nevada, FBC	Northeast
1979	Mina, Nevada, Baptist Chapel	Northern NV
1972.10.00	Minden-Gardnerville, Nevada, FBC	Nevada
1989	Minden, Nevada, Sierra View BC	Sierra
1976.07.04	Myers, California, Tahoe Paradise BC	Nevada
1988	No. Las Vegas, Nevada, Frontier Comm. BC	Southern NV
1990	No. Las Vegas, Nevada, *Israel Bautista*	Southern NV
1957.09.29	No. Las Vegas, Nevada, Calvary BC	Lake Mead
1965	No. Las Vegas, Nevada, FSBC	Lake Mead
1960	North Tahoe, California, FBC	Nevada
1986.09.00	Overton, Nevada, Lake Mead BC	Southern NV
1989	Owyhee, Nevada, Indian BC	Lahontan

Date	City, State, and Church Name	Association
1979.09.30	Pahrump, Nevada, FSBC	Southern NV
1996	Paradise Estates, Nevada, BC	Northeast
1980	Paradise Valley, Nevada, BC	Southern NV
1974.09.22	Pioche, Nevada, Berean BC	Lake Mead
1980	Rachel, Nevada, BM	Southern NV
1959	Reece-Antelope, Nevada, BC	Nevada
- - - -	Reno, Nevada, Donner Springs BC	Sierra
1979.07.01	Reno, Nevada, Granite Hills BC	Northern NV
1954	Reno, Nevada, Highland Terrace (FSBC)	Feather Riv
1986	Reno, Nevada, Reno Park BM	Sierra
1967.10.13	Reno, Nevada, Second BC	Nevada
1974	Reno, Nevada, South Reno BC	Nevada
1981	Reno, Nevada, Steamboat BC	Sierra
1983	Round Mtn, Nevada, Smokey Valley BC	Northeast
- - - -	Rye Patch, Nevada, BM	Lahontan
- - - -	Ryndon, Nevada, BM	Northeast
1984.10.07	Schurz, Nevada, Walker River BC	Spooner
1961.10.18	Searchlight, Nevada, BM	Lake Mead
1981.10.00	Silver Springs, Nevada, Lakeview BC	Lahontan
- - - -	So. Lake Tahoe, California, *Christo Viene*	Sierra
1955	So. Lake Tahoe, Calif., Lakeshore (FBC)	Feather Riv
1989	Sparks, Nevada, Neighborhood BM	Sierra
1955	Sparks, Nevada, Temple BC	Feather Riv
1986	Spring Creek, Nevada, BC	Northeast
1994	Stead, Nevada, Cold Springs BM	Sierra
1977	Stead, Nevada, Granite Hills BC	Sierra
1986	Stillwater, Nevada, Indian BM	Lahontan
1958	Sun Valley, Nevada, FBC	Nevada
1987	Tahoe Paradise, California, FBC	Sierra
1976	Tahoe Paradise, California, Filipino BM	Sierra
1981	Tonopah, Nevada, Fish Lake BM	Lahontan
1965	Tonopah, Nevada, FBC	Nevada

Date	City, State, and Church Name	Association
- - - -	Tonopah, Nevada, Silverlake BM	Lahontan
1983	Tonopah, Nevada, Silver Peak	Lahontan
1977	Topaz Ranch, Nevada, FBC	Nevada
1963	Truckee, California, FBC	Nevada
1986	Valmy, Nevada, BM	Northeast
1979	Victoria-Currie, Nevada, BM	Northern NV
1965	Walker, California, FBC	Nevada
1978.06.30	Walker Lake, Nevada, BC	Northern NV
1970	Wells, Nevada, FBC	Nevada
- - - -	Wells, Nevada, Spanish BM	Northeast
1965	Wendover, Utah, FBC	Nevada
1989	West Wendover, Utah, FBC	Northeast
1981	Whitehorse, Oregon, BM	Northeast
1978	Wildhorse, Nevada, BM	Northeast
1955	Winnemucca, Nevada, FBC	Feather Riv
1984.06.00	Winnemucca, Nevada, Grass Valley BC	Northeast NV
1954.09.00	Yerington, Nevada, FBC	Feather Riv
1986	Yomba, Nevada, Indian BC	Lahontan

UTAH

Date	City, State, and Church Name	Association
1946.03.27	Artesia, Colorado, FBC	Grand Canyon
1959.12.10	Beaver, Utah, BM	Salt Lake
1957	Blanding, Utah, FBC	San Juan
1960.11.20	Bountiful, Utah, FSBC	Golden Spike
1988	Brigham City, Utah, *Capilla Bautista*	Golden Spike
1958.03.23	Brigham City, Utah, FBC	Salt Lake
1951.07.15	Casper, Wyoming, FSBC	Utah
1960.01.26	Cedar City, Utah, FBC	Salt Lake
1988	Centerville, Utah, BM	Rainbow Cyn
1951.04.01	Clearfield, Utah, FBC (Mountain View)	Utah
1985	Clearfield, Utah, Korean BC	Golden Spike

E. W. Hunke Jr.

Date	City, State, and Church Name	Association
1964.09.06	Cottonwood, Utah, BM	Salt Lake
1982	Delta, Utah, FSBC	Salt Lake
1951.08.19	Denver, Colorado, Temple BC	Utah
1950.09.01	Dragerton, Utah, Carbon Miss BC	Utah
1975	East Carbon, Utah, FBC	Utah
1960.06.17	Evanston, Wyoming, Hillcrest BC	Golden Spike
1985	Fillmore, Utah, Fillmore BC	Rainbow Cyn
1970	Ft. Duschesne, Utah, FBC	Utah
1959.09.13	Glendale, Utah, FBC	Salt Lake
1960.03.03	Granger (West Valley), Utah, FBC	Salt Lake
1959.03.19	Grantsville, Utah, FBC	Salt Lake
1985	Green River, Utah, FBC	Gideon
1988	Gunnison, Utah, Gunnison Valley BC	Rainbow Cyn
1953.05.28	Gusher, Utah, BC	Utah
1976	Heber City, Utah, Heber Valley BC	Salt Lake
1984	Huntington, Utah, Mountain View BC	Utah
1985	Hurricane, Utah, FSBC	Color Country
1979	Kanab, Utah, Victory BC	Rainbow Cyn
1977	Kaysville, Utah, Wasatch BC	Salt Lake
1956.09.30	Kearns, Utah, FBC	Salt Lake
- - - -	Kearns, Utah, Vietnamese BC	Salt Lake
1966	Layton, Utah, Bi-Lingual BC	Golden Spike
1959.09.06	Layton, Utah, FSBC (Layton Hills)	Golden Spike
1955.05.02	Logan, Utah, FBC	Utah
1978.02.00	Logan, Utah, Maranatha BC	Golden Spike
1974.08.25	Midvale, Utah, FBC	Salt Lake
1982	Midvale, Utah, *Mision Capilla Betel*	Salt Lake
1961.07.01	Milford, Utah, BM	Salt Lake
1955.01.28	Moab, Utah, FBC	Utah
1962.09.23	Montezuma Creek, Utah, Calvary BC	Gideon
1956.09.00	Monticello, Utah, FBC	San Juan
1982	Mt. Pleasant, Utah, FSBC	Rainbow Cyn

Date	City, State, and Church Name	Association
1976	Murray, Utah, Korean BM	Salt Lake
1989	Nephi, Utah, Nephi BC	Rainbow Cyn
1958.06.12	Ogden, Utah, Ben Lomond (Emmanuel) BC	Salt Lake
1981	Ogden, Utah, Bilingual BC	Golden Spike
1954.01.08	Ogden, Utah, Calvary BC	Utah
1971.09.21	Ogden, Utah, Second BC (Emmanuel)	Golden Spike
1964.11.08	Ogden, Utah, Valley View BC	Golden Spike
1963.01.00	Orangeville, Utah, BM	Utah
1964.08.02	Orem, Utah, BM	Salt Lake
1985	Panguitch, Utah, New Beginnings BC	Rainbow Cyn
1982	Park City, Utah, BM	Salt Lake
1981	Payson, Utah, FBC	Salt Lake
1957.10.06	Pleasant Grove, Utah, FBC	Salt Lake
1952.08.07	Price, Utah, FBC	Utah
1948.08.23	Provo, Utah, FBC	Grand Canyon
1957	Rangely, Colorado, FBC	Utah
1973.01.21	Richfield, Utah, FBC	Rainbow Cyn
1944.07.02	Roosevelt, Utah, BC	Grand Canyon
1952.12.11	Roy, Utah, FBC	Utah
1982	Salt Lake City, Utah, Cambodian BM	Salt Lake
1963.06.23	Salt Lake City, Utah, Central BC	Salt Lake
1988	Salt Lake City, Utah, Central Indian	Salt Lake
1976	Salt Lake City, Utah, Chinese BM	Salt Lake
1979	Salt Lake City, Utah, *El Sembrador* BM	Salt Lake
1957.02.12	Salt Lake City, Utah, Highland BC	Salt Lake
1962.04.00	Salt Lake City, Utah, Holladay BC	Salt Lake
1980	Salt Lake City, Utah, Japanese BC	Salt Lake
1983	Salt Lake City, Utah, Korean BM	Salt Lake
1989	Salt Lake City, Utah, Metro Spanish	Salt Lake
1968	Salt Lake City, Utah, Milford BC	Salt Lake
1969.03.16	Salt Lake City, Utah, Millcreek BC	Salt Lake
1922	Salt Lake City, Utah, New Pilgrim BC	Salt Lake

E. W. Hunke Jr.

Date	City, State, and Church Name	Association
1950.11.12	Salt Lake City, Utah, Rose Park (FSBC)	Utah
1968.03.10	Salt Lake City, Utah, Shiloh BC	Salt Lake
1964.10.25	Salt Lake City, Utah, Southeast BC	Salt Lake
1967.09.17	Salt Lake City, Utah, University BC	Salt Lake
1974	Sandy, Utah, Alta Canyon	Salt Lake
- - - -	Sandy, Utah, Korean BC	Salt Lake
1981	Spanish Fork, Utah, BM	Salt Lake
1969.06.08	St. George, Utah, FSBC	Rainbow Cyn
1961.12.14	Sunset, Utah, BM	Golden Spike
1985	Taylorsville, Utah, Bible Fellowship	Salt Lake
1952.07.11	Tooele, Utah, FBC	Utah
1985	Torrey, Utah, Wayne County BC (FBC)	Rainbow Cyn
1962.12.09	Tremonton, Utah, Bear River Valley BC	Golden Spike
1946.11.22	Vernal, Utah, FBC	Grand Canyon
1984	Wellington, Utah, FBC	Utah
1965	Wendover, Utah, FBC	Nevada
- - - -	Wendover, Utah, Spanish BC	Salt Lake
1966.11.13	West Jordan, Utah, FBC	Salt Lake
1963.06.30	White City, Utah, BM	Salt Lake
1953.05.28	White Rocks, Utah, Indian BM	Utah

APPENDIX C

CHRONOLOGICAL LIST OF MISSIONARIES

Idaho-Nevada-Utah

Beginning Date	Missionary and Wife	Convention	Place
The Decade of the 1940s			
1945.02.01.AZ	Allen B. and Laura Barnes	AZ	Utah
1945.08.23.AZ	Herbert and Hattie Spraker	AZ	Utah
1945.12.01.AZ	T. T. Reynolds	AZ	Utah
1947.00.00.CA	Edward Walter Moon	CA	Nevada
1948.03.02.AZ	Fred M. and Leona DeBerry Sr.	AZ	Utah
1948.03.02.AZ	Vester E. and Frances Wolber	AZ	Utah
1948.06.01.AZ	Troy E. and Katherine Brooks	AZ	Nevada
1949.03.01.CA	Leonard B. and Edrie Sigle	CA	Nevada
The Decade of the 1950s			
1950.01.01.WA	Gilbert and Sigrid Skaar	OR/WA	Idaho
1950.01.15.UT	Ira I. and Gracie Marks	AZ	UT-ID-NV
1952.03.01.WA	Lewis S. and Lucille Steed	OR/WA	Idaho
1955.00.00.ID	W. C. and Fannie B. Carpenter	OR/WA	Idaho
1955.11.01.NV	W. P. Brian	CA	Nevada
1956.01.01.ID	J. Kelly and Edna Simmons	AZ	Idaho
1957.03.01.ID	Barron E. Honeycutt	AZ	Idaho
1958.05.01.WA	Joe Theo and Elli Howard	OR/WA	Idaho
1958.11.01.AZ	Jack K. and Margaret Maben	AZ	Nevada

355

Beginning Date	Missionary and Wife	Convention	Place
1959.01.01.ID	Roy J. and Dorothy Ferguson	AZ	Idaho
1959.01.01.ID	J. Edwin and Mattie Byers	OR/WA	Idaho

The Decade of the 1960s

1960.01.01.UT	K. Medford and Dorothy Hutson	UT/ID	Utah
1960.01.01.NV	Foy O. and Lela Fay King	CA	Nevada
1960.03.01.AZ	W. A (Bill) and Emily Barker	AZ	Nevada
1962.03.06.UT	Charles Albert Ray	AZ	Utah
1962.05.01.NV	Don L. and Patsy Loving	AZ	Nevada
1964.04.15.NV	F. Milton and Mary Lee Gage	AZ	Nevada
1968.01.01.WA	Howard H. and Lawanda Ramsey	OR/WA	Idaho
1969.04.01.UT	Miles Mayo and Celia Brown	UT/ID	Utah
1969.09.01.NV	Robert A. and Sara Wells	CA	Nevada

The Decade of the 1970s

1970.01.01.NV	F. Leroy and Claudine Smith	AZ	Nevada
1971.01.01.NV	LaVern and Elva Inzer	CA	Nevada
1972.03.07.NV	M. E. and Juanita McGlamery	AZ	Nevada
1972.06.01.WA	W. K. (Bill) and Alice Peters	OR/WA	Idaho
1972.09.01.UT	Richard L. and Ruby Ashworth	UT/ID	Utah
1976.06.01.UT	Earl V. and Peggy Jackson	UT/ID	UT-ID
1978.08.01.WA	Donald K. and Barbara Laing	OR/WA	Idaho

The Decade of the 1980s

1980.03.01.NV	Tom L. and Thelma Bacon	NV	Nevada
1980.08.20.ID	Lloyd and Marjorie Garrison	OR/WA	Idaho
1981.02.01.ID	Arlie L. and Ella McDaniel	OR/WA	Idaho
1981.08.01.NV	David F. and Linda Meacham	NV	Nevada
1983.06.01.NV	Neal J. and Martha Eva Myers	NV	Nevada
1984.06.00.ID	Louis and Betty Denster Jr.	UT/ID	Idaho
1985.03.01.UT	Kenneth and Barbara Chadwick	UT/ID	Utah
1985.06.15.NV	Norman L. and Pauline Lewis	NV	Nevada
1988.00.00.WA	M. T. Tom and Brenda Vance	OR/WA	Idaho
1988.03.15.ID	James A. and Patsy Myers	UT/ID	Idaho
1989.08.15.NV	Mitchell W. and Sandra Bryant	NV	Nevada

APPENDIX D

COMBINED LIST OF ASSOCIATIONS AND MISSIONARIES

** Represents interim service or service
prior to constitution of the association*

IDAHO   **PAGE**

Boise Valley Baptist Association
Extinct (ID) 1957–1985

1957–1958	Barron E. Honeycutt	117
1959–1984	Roy Johnson Ferguson	130
1984–1985	Louis E. Demster Jr.	297

Eastern Idaho Baptist Association
Extant (ID) 1957–____

1957–1958	Barron E. Honeycutt	117
1959–1975	Roy Johnson Ferguson	130
1976–1997	Earl Vernon Jackson	232

Inland Empire Baptist Association
Extant (WA-ID) 1954–____

1949–1950	* Clifford Ervin Boyle	71
1950–1952	* Gilbert O. Skaar	73
1952–1958	Lewis S. Steed	83
1958–1967	Joe Theo Howard	125

1968–1971	Howard H. Ramsey	187
1972–1977	William Kenneth Peters	211
1978–1987	Donald Kersey Laing	251
1988–1994	Marion Tom Vance	323

Lewis-Clark Baptist Association
Extant (ID) 1959–____

1955–1959	William C. Carpenter	104
1959–1972	James Edwin Byers	131
1972–1977	William Kenneth Peters	211
1978–1980	William C. Carpenter	104
1980–1991	Arlie L. McDaniel	274

Magic Valley Baptist Association
Extant (ID) 1957–____

1957–1958	Barron E. Honeycutt	117
1959–1984	Roy Johnson Ferguson	130
1984–1991	Louis E. Demster Jr.	297

Silver Lakes Baptist Association
Extant (ID) 1988–____

1987–1988	Louis E. Demster Jr.	297
1988–____	James Arthur Myers	305

Treasure Valley Baptist Association
Extant (ID) 1985–____

1985–1991	Louis E. Demster Jr.	297

Twin Buttes Baptist Association
Extinct (ID) 1953–1957

1950–1955	Ira I. Marks	75
1956–1956	J. Kelly Simmons	111
1957–1957	Barron E. Honeycutt	117

Whispering Pines Baptist Association
Extant (ID) 1972–____

1972–1984	Roy Johnson Ferguson	130
1984–1988	Louis E. Demster Jr.	297
1988–____	James Arthur Myers	305

NEVADA

Lahontan Baptist Association
Extant (NV) 1979–____

1979–1980	* Charles Lloyd McKay	115
1980–1985	Tom Lee Bacon	266
1985–1989	Norman Lee Lewis	306
1989–____	Mitchell W. Bryant	332

Lake Mead Baptist Association
Extinct (NV) 1955–1977

1948–1958	Troy E. Brooks	66
1958–1959	Jack Knox Maben	128
1960–1961	Willie Allen Barker	142
1962–1963	Donald Lee Loving	154
1964–1969	F. Milton Gage	166
1970–1971	Francis Leroy Smith	199
1972–1977	M. E. McGlamery	210

Nevada Baptist Association
Extinct (NV) 1955–1977

1948–1949	* Edward W. Moon	57
1949–1954	* Leonard B. Sigle	68
1955–1959	* W. P. Brian	109
1955–1969	Leonard B. Sigle	68
1969–1977	Robert August Wells	193

Northeast Baptist Association
Extant (NV) 1979–____

1979–1980	* Charles Lloyd McKay	115
1980–1992	Tom Lee Bacon	266

Northern Nevada Baptist Association
Extinct (NV) 1977–1982

1977–1982	Robert August Wells	193

Sierra Baptist Association
Extant (NV) 1986–____

1986–1990	Neal Joe Myers	291

Southern Nevada Baptist Association
Extant (NV) 1977–____

1977–1980	M. E. McGlamery	210
1981–1992	David F. Meacham	277

Spooner Baptist Association
Extinct (NV) 1979–1986

1979–1982	Robert August Wells	193
1983–1986	Neal Joe Myers	291

Truckee River Baptist Association
Extinct (NV) 1982–1986

1979–1982	Robert August Wells	193
1983–1986	Neal Joe Myers	291

UTAH

Color Country Baptist Association
Extant (UT) 1985–____

1985–1990	Richard Lee Ashworth	213

Gideon Baptist Association
Extant (UT) 1959–____

1958–1961	Ira I. Marks	75
1962–1967	Charles Albert Ray	153
1967–1972	K. Medford Hutson	139
1972–1991	Richard Lee Ashworth	213

Golden Spike Baptist Association
Extant (UT) 1958–____

1958–1961	Ira I. Marks	75
1962–1969	Charles Albert Ray	153

1969–1976	Myles Mayo Brown	191
1976–1997	Earl Vernon Jackson	232

Mid-State Baptist Association
Extinct (UT) 1968–1969

1968–1969	K. Medford Hutson	139

Rainbow Canyon Baptist Association
Extant (UT) 1967–____

1967–1972	K. Medford Hutson	139
1972–1987	Richard Lee Ashworth	213
1987–1996	Alvin Ken Chadwick	303

Salt Lake Baptist Association
Extant (UT) 1955–____

1950–1961	Ira I. Marks	75
1962–1969	Charles Albert Ray	153
1969–1984	Myles Mayo Brown	191
1985–1996	Alvin Ken Chadwick	303

Utah Baptist Association
Extant (UT) 1950–____

1950–1961	Ira I. Marks	75
1962–1969	Charles Albert Ray	153
1969–1972	Myles Mayo Brown	191
1972–1990	Richard Lee Ashworth	213

SELECTED BIBLIOGRAPHY

Baptist Beacon. Phoenix: Arizona Southern Baptist Convention, selected issues. A weekly religious newspaper.

California Southern Baptist. Fresno: California Southern Baptist Convention, selected issues. A weekly religious newspaper.

Hullum, Everett, Jr. *1979 Home Mission Teaching Guide*. Memphis: Brotherhood Commission, SBC, 1978.

Hunke, Edmund William Jr. *Southern Baptist Jubilee in the West*. Atlanta: Home Mission Board, SBC, 1996. A research project of 258 associations and 433 missionaries (1940–1989), 4 volumes.

Hunke, Naomi Ruth. *Remember the Wonders: A Fifty-Year History of Grand Canyon Baptist Association*. Franklin, Tennessee: Providence House Publishers, 1996.

Ledbetter, Don. "History of Nevada Southern Baptists." Reno: an unpublished thesis, 1992.

Morgan, Dale L. *Jedediah Smith and the Opening of the West*. Lincoln: University of Nebraska Press, 1953.

Murphy, Nicy. *The 30th Child of Southern Baptists*. Rapid City: Northern Plains Baptist Convention, 1978.

Nevada Baptist Forerunner. Las Vegas: Nevada Baptist Fellowship, selected issues. A mimeographed newsletter published by the Nevada Baptist Fellowship president.

Northwest Baptist Witness. Portland: Northwest Baptist Convention, selected issues. A weekly religious newspaper.

Owen, Roy W. "Church Planting in the Twentieth Century." Atlanta: an unpublished story of Southern Baptist church planting.

Rocky Mountain Baptist. Denver: Colorado Baptist General Convention, selected issues. A Baptist state newspaper.

Salisbury, Albert and Jane. *Here Rolled the Covered Wagons* (Third Revised Edition). New York: Bonanza Books, 1948.

Southern Baptist Convention Annual. Nashville: Southern Baptist Convention, selected issues. A report of the annual meeting of the convention.

The Nevada Baptist. Reno: Nevada Baptist Convention, selected issues. A monthly religious newspaper.

Utah-Idaho Southern Baptist Witness. Sandy, Utah: Utah-Idaho Southern Baptist Convention, selected issues. A monthly religious newspaper.

ABOUT THE AUTHOR

The photographs below of the writer and his wife were taken in 1946, the year they were married and began their fifty-two years of mission service together. After three years in military service, the writer wanted a picture of himself out of uniform. Naomi had this picture taken on her graduation from high school in 1946.

Bill Hunke.

Naomi Hunke.

Edmund William (Bill) Hunke Jr. volunteered for service in both the U.S. Air Force and Army when eighteen years of age. Military journeys during World War II led him to salvation in Jesus Christ, to an Oklahoma transplant in California who became his companion and wife, and to the missionary challenge of the West.

He was born at Taylor, Texas, on September 22, 1924, to E. W. and Clare Lucille (Holding) Hunke Sr. He had three sisters and two brothers. He graduated from Waco, Texas, public schools, Pacific Bible Institute (Th.B.), Fresno State University (B.A.), Golden Gate Baptist Theological Seminary (B.D.), and Arizona State University (Ed.D.). He studied history at Georgia State University.

Hunke traveled west from Madison, Wisconsin, on a troop train. His corps of Army Engineers joined with the Ninety-Sixth Infantry Division at Camp White in Medford, Oregon, in February 1944. His military technical training led the Army to transfer him to the Air Force at Hammer Field at Fresno, Hawthorne, Van Nuys, and Burbank, California. After Hunke was saved on a P-38 flight line at Van Nuys, California, through the personal witnessing of Clifford E. Clark, the first Home Mission Board state evangelist in California, B. N. Lummus baptized him in the cold, melted snow waters of the San Joaquin River. He attended a West Los Angeles SBC storefront mission in Sawtelle near U.C.L.A. and met Naomi Ruth Savage at the Fresno Fountain of Youth Center in December 1945.

Hunke surrendered to preach in an Air Force chapel and was ordained by Madera, California, FSBC. He began his ministry in a sixteen-by-thirty-two-foot tent at Clovis, California. Robert W. Lackey, the retired SBGCC executive secretary, served as his associational missionary. He pastored at Clovis and Pittsburg, California, and Vernal, Utah, and served as missionary to the Gila Valley, Yuma, Estrella, San Carlos, and Mt. Graham Baptist associations in Arizona. The BGCA employed him as associate executive/state mission director, and interim *Baptist Beacon* editor from 1954–1966. He served as Alaska Baptist Convention executive director, led evangelism, and edited the *Alaska Baptist Messenger* from 1966–1971. The HMB employed him as the western regional coordinator from 1966–1987. After his retirement in 1987, Hunke served as Grand Canyon Baptist association missionary for six years (1987–1992) and as the Canadian Southern Baptist Seminary president for seven months. The Hunkes moved to Sedona, Arizona, in 1987.

Naomi Ruth Savage was born on May 14, 1929, at Wilson, Oklahoma, to Dixon Boza and Roxie Rebecca (Roberts) Savage. Her brother Kenneth became a Baptist pastor. On June 22, 1943, the Savages arrived in Fresno on a train from Oklahoma. That evening they attended Fresno First Southern Baptist Church in a basement because the church had no property. They became charter members of Bethel Baptist Mission the next Sunday. Naomi graduated from the Fresno Roosevelt High School, Pacific Bible College (B.A.) in 1950, Grand Canyon College (B.S.) in 1960, and Arizona State University (M.A.) in 1963. She attended Golden Gate Baptist Theological Seminary and Yavapai College. She taught English literature at the Grand Canyon and Alaska Methodist universities, University of Alaska, Anchorage, and DeKalb College, Georgia, for twenty-seven years. She married Bill Hunke August 29, 1946, at Fresno, and they had three children: Dixie Lynn, Jonathan David, and Jimmy Paul. They are the grandparents of five grandsons: Kenny, Tommy, Billy, Brian, and Daniel Joseph.

Naomi Hunke wrote extensively for the BSSB and WMU/SBC. She contributed articles for *Open Windows* and published four books: *In This Land, God's Warhorse, Volunteer Mission Opportunities for Senior Adults*, and *Remember the Wonders*.

The Hunkes enjoyed a long and fruitful ministry in the Intermountain West. They lived at Vernal, Utah (1953–1954), to lead FBC. When Hunke served as BGCA executive associate/state mission director (1956–1966), he directed the HMB mission program in the Intermountain West. As the HMB western mission coordinator (1971–1987), he worked for seventeen years with Utah, Idaho, and Nevada, and their sponsoring Arizona, California, and Northwest Baptist state conventions. He and his wife, Naomi, who now live in Sedona, Arizona, have served in SBC mission work in the West for fifty-two years.

ABOUT THE ARTIST

Edna Christine (Sroggin) Maxson, who did the paintings for the cover of this book, was born December 26, 1912, in Starkville, Mississippi. She began painting in her mid-fifties as a hobby.

Edna trusted the Lord Jesus Christ as her personal Savior at age thirteen at a little country Baptist church about four miles out of Crawford, Mississippi. She earned a B.S. degree from the University of Arkansas, Monticello, and taught elementary school in Arkansas for twelve years. For eighteen years, she was an elementary teacher and librarian in Palm Beach County, Florida.

Russell James Maxson won her heart and married her at McGehee, Arkansas, on January 29, 1932. They had two sons: Edwin, a lieutenant colonel in the U.S. Air Force, and Robert, a university president. Edwin suffered an untimely death when his plane went down in the rugged mountains north of Sedona, Arizona. Robert (Bobby) served as president of the University of Nevada at Las Vegas for ten years and is now president of the University of California at Long Beach. Edna's husband, Russell, died on March 2, 1990, and was buried in the Sedona cemetery.

Edna graciously consented to paint the four lovely scenes that grace the cover of this book. She is familiar with the Southern Baptist witness in the Intermountain West—her son lived in Las Vegas for ten years; Darwin and Anita Welsh, who led Utah-Idaho Baptists for twenty-five years, lived next door to her for three years; and Lavoid and Geneva Robertson, who are featured in the pages of this book, are her friends.

Edna Maxson and Naomi Hunke are prayer partners. They meet each week in the Village of Oak Creek, Arizona, to pray for the needs of missions, their friends, and the multitudes of other prayer concerns which are shared with them.